IEIR MARRIAGE ALLIANCES

NIO GONDI I

NE DE GONDI II
(du Perron)
m.
E PIERRE-VIVE

Four other sons;
eight daughters

RRE
hop of
s, cardinal
Gondi),
3–1616

CHARLES
(seigneur de
la Tour),
d. 1574
m.
HÉLÈNE
BON

Two other sons
(François, and
Jean abbé de
Saint-Hilaire de
Carcassonne);
three
daughters

| HIPPOLYTE m. *LÉONOR DE LA MADE- LEINE* (marquis de Ragny) | JEAN- FRANÇOIS (archbishop of Paris), 1584–1654 | CLAUDE- MAR- GUERITE m. *FLORIMOND* (marquis de Maignelais) | FRANÇOISE m. *LANCELOT* (sieur de Vassé) | Three other daughters (Louise, Madeleine and Gabrielle) |

S

| ANNE DE LA MADELEINE m. *FRANÇOIS DE BONNE DE CRÉQUY* (duc de Lesdiguières), d. 1677, whose son by a previous marriage was | ANNE DE MAIGNELAIS, d. 1641 m. (1) *COMTE DE CANDALE* (2) *MARQUIS DE SCHOMBERG* | RENÉ DE VASSY (seigneur d'Esguilly) | MAR- GUERITE m. *CHARLES* (marquis de Sévigné) |

NICOLAS IV
DE NEUF-
VILLE
(maréchal-duc
de Villeroy,
governor of
Louis XIV),
1597–1655
m.
*MADE-
LEINE DE
CRÉQUY*
(sister of
François duc
de
Lesdiguières)

MARGUERITE
m.
*LOUIS DE
COSSÉ* (duc
de Brissac),
d. 1661

HENRI
(marquis de
Sévigné)
m.
*MARIE DE
RABUTIN-
CHANTAL*,
1626–96

R- *FRANÇOIS
m. EMMANUEL
E DE BONNE
DE CRÉQUY*
(duc de
Lesdiguières,
maréchal de
Camp),
1645–81

HENRI-
ALBERT DE
COSSÉ
(duc de
Brissac),
1645–98
m.
*MARIE-
GABRI-
ELLE-
LOUISE DE
SAINT
SIMON*

FRANÇOISE
m.
*FRANÇOIS
DE
GRIGNAN*

PAULINE

MARIE-MAR-
GUERITE DE
COSSÉ-
BRISSAC

FRANÇOIS
DE NEUF-

This biography of Cardinal de Retz is the first to appear in English for many years. The author has drawn a colorful and fascinating portrait of one of the most extraordinary political cardinals of seventeenth-century France.

Born Jean François Paul de Gondi, third son of a prosperous Brittany family, Cardinal de Retz was destined for a career in the Church, although the conflicts of his personality showed early—he was a brilliant theology student at the Sorbonne, a duelist, a rake, and the author of a pamphlet on the hero as revolutionary.

In 1643, Anne of Austria appointed him Archbishop of Paris, and five years later he was actively involved in the uprising against the unscrupulous Mazarin, the successor of Richelieu. De Retz was able to harness the discordant forces of aristocratic faction, plebeian discontent, ecclesiastical privilege, and legal constitutionalism, yet the subtlety of his machinations eventually led to his failure and disgrace. He was arrested and imprisoned at Vincennes and Nantes, but escaped two years later.

It was not until 1662—ten years after his arrest—that Louis XIV received him back into favor. He devoted the last ten years of his life to the writing of his *Memoirs*—his last endeavor to cross the moral frontiers of his time—and these brought him lasting posthumous fame.

Professor Salmon's brilliant study vividly brings to life the complex and exciting personality of Cardinal de Retz, a man seeking his own identity through action, and the times, a turbulent era seething with political intrigue and unrest.

Cardinal de Retz

THE ANATOMY OF A CONSPIRATOR

J. H. M. SALMON is Professor of History at Bryn Mawr College, Pennsylvania. He is a graduate of Cambridge University and Victoria University (Wellington) and has held teaching posts in both Australia and New Zealand.

His principal field of research is the political theory of early modern French history, together with the social history and literature of the period. Among his previous books are *The French Religious Wars in English Political Thought* and *The French Wars of Religion*.

By the same author

THE FRENCH WARS OF RELIGION

THE FRENCH RELIGIOUS WARS IN ENGLISH
POLITICAL THOUGHT

Cardinal de Retz

THE ANATOMY OF
A CONSPIRATOR

J. H. M. SALMON

THE MACMILLAN COMPANY

Library of Congress Catalog Card Number: 73-77973

First American edition 1970
First published in Great Britain in 1969 by
Weidenfeld and Nicolson
The Macmillan Company

Printed in Great Britain

Contents

Preface

So many documents concerning the life of cardinal de Retz have been collected that the biographer is almost embarrassed by the wealth of objective fact he must set against the enigmatic evidence of the cardinal's own memoirs. The standard edition of Retz's works, in which most of these papers have been published as supporting material, is the ten-volume version which appeared in the late nineteenth century in the *Grands Ecrivains de la France* series. One of the editors, Régis de Chantelauze, spent twenty years searching the French archives for those sources, and his successor, Claude Cochon, discovered a further one hundred and seventy letters in Italian archives, which he published in a supplementary volume in 1920. In common with other biographers, such as Pierre-Georges Lorris, and recent editors of the memoirs, such as Maurice Allem, I am deeply indebted to the industry and scholarship of Chantelauze and his colleagues.

I should like to express my thanks to Roland Mousnier of the Sorbonne and Jean Hytier of Columbia University for their advice and encouragement; to A.J.Krailsheimer, J.T.Letts and D.A. Watts for the insights I have gained from their recent work on Retz; to Julien Mantout of Commercy for his comments on the cardinal's life there; to Bernard Barbiche for his help in the Archives Nationales; to Judi Bullerwell for her supplementary research in the Bibliothèque Nationale; to Coral Lansbury for her criticism; and to Mary Gordon for her assistance in the preparation of the typescript.

ONE

A question of identity

Personal identity is something more than the sum of a man's actions, his conscious memories and his self-acknowledged ideals. It involves what he contemplates doing as much as what he does, what he has forgotten as much as what he remembers, what he feels as much as what he thinks. Its historical reconstruction is more difficult than its contemporary analysis. It entails the retrospective study of the subconscious, and it is confronted with the problem of fixing identity within the flux of time. Cardinal de Retz was himself perplexed by these issues before ever they descended to his biographer. He was aware of the discontinuity of experience, and preoccupied with the search for his own identity in the past as well as in the present. He was anxious to explore what he might have been as well as what he had become, and he was also concerned to shape the reputation he left behind him. When he came to write his memoirs in the declining years of his adventurous life, he set out to recreate the experience of his youth and middle-age, to investigate alternative possibilities, to rediscover his past self, to reconcile it with the present, and to convey his own image of it to posterity.

It is not surprising that the image of Retz received by later generations should contain a variety of contradictory facets. His memoirs were not to be published until 1717, thirty-eight years after their author's death, and in the interval his enigmatic personality haunted the imagination of a society whose ethos seemed in many ways antithetical to his own. When the cardinal died in 1679 the splendour of Louis XIV was at its height. The king had inherited his throne in 1643 at the age of five. In the years of his boyhood his minister, cardinal Mazarin, had preserved the authority of the monarchy against the Fronde, the rebellion in which Retz had played so equivocal a part. Mazarin had discerned in Retz his principal enemy, and had taught his royal charge to regard him as personifying all the elements that troubled the security of the crown. After Mazarin's death in 1661 Louis had systematically crushed the forces which Retz had utilised in the Fronde – the wilful dissidence of the nobility, the spirit of independence within the church, the constitutional restraints asserted by the supreme court of the parlement and the turbulence of the common people. Within eighteen years the king had erected a vast and bureaucratic despotism upon the foundations laid by Mazarin and by Mazarin's greater predecessor, cardinal Richelieu. His bourgeois ministers and their provincial agents, the intendants, had superseded the political and administrative functions of both aristocrat and holder of venal office. The high nobility had been reduced to the role of subservient courtiers. The royal campaign to impose uniformity of religious belief had entered its most active phase. The parlement had become the compliant instrument of the king's sovereignty. The interminable cycle of peasant and plebeian revolt had been broken.

This was the age of conformity, and in his last years even Retz, whose turbulent career seemed to typify the proud and aristocratic individualism of the past, had striven to conform. When his endeavours to serve the king by a series of diplomatic missions to Rome had failed to evoke favour or forgiveness, he had appeared to conform to the will of another master by renouncing the world and seeking spiritual salvation. The debate about the sincerity of Retz's conversion, and about many other aspects of his personality, continued to intrigue polite society after his death. Bishop Bossuet was perhaps the leading apologist of the spirit which Louis xiv had imprinted on the age. His description of the late cardinal in a sermon which he preached in 1686 after the death of the chancellor, Michel le Tellier, revealed the spell which Retz still cast upon the court:

This man, so faithful to his friends and so redoubtable to the state, was of so high a character that no one could esteem him, fear him, love or hate him by halves. He was the firm genius whom we have seen overturning the world to acquire a rank which, in the end, he wished to resign as a thing too dearly bought. He had the courage to admit this in the highest place in Christianity, and he knew it was not sufficient to satisfy his ultimate ambition. He came to realize the enormity of his fault and the emptiness of human greatness. Yet in the years when he wished to acquire what one day he would contemn, he shook the state by his secret and powerful devices; and, after all the factions were beaten down, he seemed at the last to stand alone, and alone to threaten the victorious favourite with his sad and intrepid glance.[1]*

Here was a posthumous view of Retz that was neither unjust nor unsympathetic. Yet the hand of the king was so heavy that Bossuet dared not even mention the cardinal's name.

As the power and grandeur of Louis xiv increased in the second half of his reign so, too, did the frustration of his nobility and the suffering of his peasantry. A series of exhausting wars drained the resources of his kingdom. Religious persecution undermined the spirituality of the church, and the overriding claims of the state involved the crown in an ignoble conflict with Rome. Louis xiv lived on to see his splendour tarnished and his heirs, one by one, predecease him. When at last he died in 1715, his great-grandson inherited his throne in circumstances similar to those of his own boyhood accession. His subjects greeted his death with a joyous delirium. As the regency of his nephew, Philip of Orléans, was inaugurated, a wave of frenetic relief enveloped the capital. Old memories were awakened, and the attitudes and ideals of a previous age now suddenly assumed an immediate relevance.

By this time there were few surviving links with the cardinal. His niece, the duchesse de Lesdiguières, died in 1716, the last direct representative of his family, the Gondi. Her son, Jean-François-Paul de Bonne de Créquy, who bore the forenames of the cardinal, had died as the last duc de Lesdiguières in 1704. Although the duchess had for long tried to maintain the ostentatious traditions of her family, its decline was symbolised by the decay of the hôtel de Lesdiguières, where Retz had lain in his last hours upon earth. Its magnificent exterior, guarded by the two moors employed by the duchess, had masked its empty rooms and deserted corridors.[2] Now it passed into other hands and another link with the past seemed to have snapped. But within a few months of the death of the duchess the memoirs of her notorious uncle appeared in print for the first time. They seemed to herald the birth of a new Fronde.

The regent had made a bargain with the parlement to restore to

* See the list of notes at the end of this book.

that august body its right of remonstrance and in return to have it
dispossess the legitimised sons of the late king by madame de
Montespan of the share in the regency bequeathed them by their
father. The parlement began to test its new found strength against
the government, while the elder of the royal bastards, the duc du
Maine, was spurred on by his wife, the grand-daughter of the
great Condé, the general of the Fronde, to recover his rightful
position. The regent's attempt to appoint the traditional nobility
to the administrative councils, which had replaced the authority
of his uncle's secretaries of state, merely produced friction and
inefficiency. Religious pressures induced him to consider the
revival of the Papal bull *Unigenitus*, which Louis XIV had obtained
in his last years in a vain endeavour to repress the heterodox
Catholic tradition of the Jansenists. The Spanish ambassador,
Cellamare, assisted the duchesse du Maine to organise a network
of intrigue which was to be uncovered a year later. The maréchal-
duc de Villeroy, who was governor of the boy king as his father
had been governor of the young Louis XIV, sought to use his
office to defy the regent. He had married into the tradition of the
Fronde, for his wife was the daughter of the duc de Brissac, one
of Retz's fellow conspirators, and of Marguerite de Gondi, the
cardinal's cousin. Through his mother, a member of the house of
Lesdiguières, he had a further connection with the Gondi. A
swarm of minor noblemen were grouped by family association or
political interest into one or other of the factions which challenged
the regent, and all stood ready to re-enact the roles of such
frondeurs as cardinal de Retz and his vainglorious colleague, the
duc de Beaufort.

These were the circumstances described by the duc de Saint-
Simon, the chronicler of the courts of both Louis XIV and the
regency:

The memoirs of cardinal de Retz and of Joly [his secretary] were
then very much in fashion and everyone was bursting to read them.
The conversations which the maréchal de Villeroy had about the
memoirs quite turned his head, and made him want to be a new duc
de Beaufort, the chief of the Fronde, king of the markets and of Paris,
and supporter of the parlement.[3]

The regent was sufficiently alarmed by the effect of Retz's memoirs to consult the marquis d'Argenson, the controller of the police forces in the capital. D'Argenson was familiar with all the legends about the cardinal because his family was connected by marriage with that of Louis Lefèvre de Caumartin, Retz's most trusted confidant. In later years d'Argenson's son, the celebrated minister and memorialist of the court of Louis xv, recorded how his father had argued that the frankness with which Retz had described the imprudence of his actions should discourage others from imitating them. But the memoirs of the cardinal continued to make such an impact that at the time of the Cellamare conspiracy the regent again summoned the elder d'Argenson, and sought to neutralise them by the publication of the tendentious and pejorative memoirs of Retz's secretary, Guy Joly.[4] The project was accomplished with difficulty because Caumartin's son, who held Joly's manuscript, opposed the revelation of an account derogatory of his father's friend and patron.

As it turned out neither Retz nor any other ghost from the past could change the pattern imprinted by Louis xiv upon the history of France. The conspiracies against the regency collapsed, and in their aftermath the regent abandoned his reformist plans and returned to the internal policies of his predecessor. The secretaries of state were restored, and the aristocratic councils dissolved. The parlement was exiled and obliged to come to terms, and the bull *Unigenitus* was affirmed by the government. When Louis xv received the full authority of the crown from the hands of Philip of Orléans, he found himself bound by an inflexible system which no one but its creator could operate successfully. Social and political needs changed, but the structure of government was incapable of adaptation. Amid mounting fiscal disorder and the intransigent defence of privilege by parlement and aristocracy, the monarchy drifted towards a revolution far more intense than the crisis of the Fronde. Meanwhile Retz and his memoirs became fossilised in recorded history, and ceased to influence its course.

Thus by the middle of the eighteenth century the career of cardinal de Retz could be seen with a certain detachment. It was at this point that the complexity of his character became simplified in a variety of contradictory images. Voltaire accepted much in Retz's memoirs at its face value:

This singular man was the first bishop in France to start a civil war without using religion as its pretext. He described himself in his memoirs, written with an air of grandeur, an impetuosity of genius and a variability, which all reflected his own conduct. He was a man who, in the midst of debauchery and while still suffering from the infamous consequences his habits entailed, preached to the people and made them idolise him for it. He breathed faction and conspiracy; at the age of twenty-three he was the soul of a plot against the life of Richelieu; he was the author of the barricades; he thrust the parlement into cabals and the people into seditions. His extreme vanity drove him to undertake rash and imprudent crimes so that they would be talked about. It was this same vanity that made him repeat so many times: 'I am from a Florentine house as distinguished as that of the greatest princes.' And this from a man whose ancestors had been merchants, like so many of his compatriots!

In a later passage Voltaire went on to sketch the remainder of the cardinal's life:

As imprudent as he was audacious, he was arrested in the Louvre, and moved from prison to prison until he escaped to live for long the life of a wanderer. He ended this kind of existence in a place of retreat where he acquired the virtues that his great courage had never been able to realise amid the vacillations of his earlier career.

All this served Voltaire only to point a moral. He compared Retz with his adversary, Mazarin:

Anyone who reads the letters of cardinal Mazarin and the memoirs of cardinal de Retz will clearly see that Retz was the superior genius: yet Mazarin was all-powerful, and Retz was entirely defeated. To become a powerful minister a man may often require no more than a mediocre mind, common sense and good fortune: but to become a good minister a man must have the love of the public welfare as his dominating passion.[5]

In Voltaire's time the cardinal's memoirs had secured a posthumous literary revenge for his enemy's material triumph during his lifetime. An English contemporary, Lord Chesterfield, regarded them as the quintessence of worldly wisdom, and commended them to his natural son:

I hardly know any book so necessary for a young man to read and remember. You will find there how great business is really carried on, very differently from what people, who have never been concerned in it, imagine. You will there see what courts and courtiers really are, and observe that they are neither so good as they should be, nor so bad as they are thought by most people.[6]

In so far as there were perennial truths about the nature of power – and the so-called age of enlightenment was fond of generalisations of this kind – the experience distilled by Retz in his memoirs was regarded in the mid-eighteenth century as a shrewdly realistic appraisal of the way men reconcile self-interest with public morality. Chesterfield extracted sixty-seven such maxims from the memoirs, and translated them with annotations for the benefit of his son.[7] Hume observed in one of his essays that Retz had understood how irrational emotion could spread like an infection throughout a large political assembly, until they became 'mere mob, swayed in their debates by the least motive'.[8]

Some contemporaries preferred to recall the notoriety of the cardinal's private life, and the scandalous candour with which he had chosen to reveal his rake's progress. Others delighted in the rivalry of Retz and La Rochefoucauld, whose lives and subsequent literary reputations had run almost precisely in parallel. They had been at first uneasy allies, and later fierce opponents, in both politics and love. In their posthumous literary guise they both appeared to some as *moralistes*, that is to say, commentators on the psychological aspects of human behaviour. Chesterfield could set the maxims he had extracted from Retz's memoirs beside the more polished and more deeply cynical epigrams of the master of the *genre*. Each had composed a damaging portrait of the other which contained all the persuasive lucidity of a half-truth embellished with wit.[9] La Rochefoucauld had also written his memoirs, although in the eighteenth century they were known only through imperfect editions to which other hands had contributed. It was Voltaire's criterion for the reliability of historical evidence that, if ever the memoirs of the two agreed, their testimony would be accepted as unquestioned truth.[10]

Retz's political attitudes, his adventures and his amours came to be categorised with a variety of epithets, but his identity remained a mystery. Voltaire called him 'imprudent and audacious'. Chesterfield said he was 'a strange, but by no means uncommon, mixture of high and low, good and bad'. The penitent sinner represented by Bossuet stood in contrast to the ostentatious hypocrite, who, as La Rochefoucauld and his friends believed, had gained celebrity by displaying his defects in a flattering light. The turbulent intriguer depicted by the regency was offset by the urbane commentator recommended by Chesterfield and read attentively by Gibbon and Hume. The memoirs multiplied the contradictions. It was not merely that their author had rearranged certain facts in his conscious or unconscious endeavour to justify and rationalise the motives for his past actions. Had this been their primary purpose, their candour would have been false and the image they presented more consistent. It was Retz's own quest for identity in his memoirs that obscured his inner self from the eyes of his readers. His search led him to present a multiplicity of past selves, and the imperfections of his method confused the development of personality by mingling mature reflection with the imaginative recovery of the past. Lacking the personal immediacy of the author's experience, his readers selected whatever facet of his character best fitted their own preoccupations, and trimmed the others to suit the portrait they presented.

The key to the enigma of Retz is his own awareness of the problem of fixing identity in the flux of time. The discontinuous nature of his life, the abrupt changes of direction, the alternation of failure and success, the recurring leaps from elation to despair, the succeeding moods of indolence and enthusiasm, came at length to create both insecurity and curiosity, and stimulated him to embark upon his search. The man who wrote the memoirs was not the same man whose ambitions exploited the intrigues of the Fronde to his own advantage: nor was the frondeur the same individual who displayed such youthful zest to savour the first experiences of manhood. The personality of Retz changed and developed with each succeeding phase of his life. His conscious identity was a mixture of memories and ideals: his real self was the sum of personal and inherited experience buried in the subconscious. The discontinuity of his life induced him to search for the *moi passé* he felt he had lost, and, in the process, his conscious recollections superimposed the attitudes of the present upon the sensations of the past.

TWO

Tradition and environment

The aristocratic code which Retz absorbed in his youth was the product of the preceding century. The class into which the Gondi had been assimilated lost its roots and traditions and replaced them with all the frustrations and malaise known to the cardinal's generation. During the first half of the sixteenth century the nobility of France had served in the Italian wars against the Hapsburg emperor Charles V: in the second half they had fought each other in the so-called wars of religion. The Italian wars had loosened their ties with their lands and given them a taste for extravagant Renaissance luxuries. At the same time the influx of precious metals from the New World had set in motion the processes of economic inflation. Those whose incomes depended on fixed rents from land suffered in the price rise.

The trend was accentuated in the wars of religion, when the rhythm of rural life was interrupted, and many ancient lines were terminated either in battle or in bankruptcy. The circumstances in which first the Huguenots and then the Catholic League rose in armed revolt against the crown produced an aristocratic disillusionment of which Montaigne was the spokesman. Old loyalties disappeared as long-established families lost their roots in the land amid conditions of economic degeneration. In the concluding phases of the wars vast peasant risings defied the local nobility as fiercely as they did the foreign mercenary armies who despoiled their land. Representatives of the middle classes entered the nobility in increasing numbers, and the nobility of the sword saw themselves dispossessed of their role in government by the new nobility of the gown, who bought their judicial and administrative offices and secured the right to transmit them to their heirs. Although the newcomers defended aristocratic privileges with even greater determination than the *noblesse de race*, the feudal structure of society had lost its military and political justification. The monarchy under the sons of Henry II failed to provide it with leadership or to affirm its ideals. Even the first Bourbon king, Henry IV, who put an end to the League and rallied national sentiment with his war against Spain, could find no real solution to aristocratic disorder. He bought over the leaders of the League, and his attempts to restore economic prosperity in the peaceful years of his reign were continually threatened by aristocratic conspiracies.

While many noble houses wasted their strength in the turbulent anarchy of the time, royal favour, and an eye for the main chance, hastened the ascent of many Italians in sixteenth-century France. It seemed as if they were ready to repay two generations of French invasions with their own conquest of French taste and French finance. Princes from Savoy and Mantua became dukes of Nemours and Nevers. Adventurers such as the Strozzi made French fortunes in diplomacy and war. Bankers such as Sardini and Zametti profited from speculation in government loans. Scholars such as Jacopo Corbinelli became tutors to French princes. Clerics such as the Bonzi, who provided several generations of bishops to the diocese of Béziers, shared the spoils of the Gallican church. The Gondi were merely one among several such families, but their origins were more obscure than most, and their ascent more remarkable than any.

While Retz shared all the attitudes of the high aristocracy of France, he remained sensitive about his ancestry. His habit of boasting about the ancient and honourable lineage of his family in Florence was remarked by his travelling companion, Tallemant des Réaux, when they visited the city and called upon a distant Gondi cousin in 1638.[1] Seventeen years later, when he was attending the conclave which elected pope Alexander VII, Retz was stung by a reference to his family's humble origins by a Medici cardinal, and publicly declared that the Gondi had held noble rank in Florence four centuries before the Medici had been heard of.[2] This assertion was based upon the research of the genealogist, Pierre d'Hozier, whom Retz had commissioned to answer the libels against his family issued during the Fronde. D'Hozier published a nineteen-page summary of his researches into the ancestry of the Gondi in 1652. He announced on the first page that he was refuting 'certain calumnies', such as 'that all those of the name of Gondi who have come to France have been people of no account, whose name was not even known in Italy'. He identified in Retz's ancestry 128 quarters of nobility and discovered a certain 'Fort de Gondi, son of Belliqueux, who was a senator in Florence in 1176'. He quoted a Florentine poet, Ugolinus Verinus, who in 1490 had written that the Gondi were 'one of the most ancient and illustrious houses in the republic'.[3] D'Hozier, who was to die in 1660, continued his research and by 1655 had prepared over two hundred manuscript pages. He cited a Florentine genealogy of 1578, asserted that the Gondi were a branch of the 'house of Philippi ennobled by Charlemagne', and found 512 quarters of nobility for Antoine de Gondi. 'I should dare to boast', he wrote, 'that there are few crowned heads and sovereign princes in Europe who can trace their nobility so far back with such veracity.'[4]

D'Hozier's work was based on suspect sources. In his last years Retz turned to a friend and distant cousin, the philosopher Jean Corbinelli, who was a descendant of that Jacopo Corbinelli who had established himself at the court of France at the same time as the Gondi. Corbinelli prepared a new genealogy which was to be published in 1705 and dedicated to the cardinal's niece, the duchesse de Lesdiguières.[5] Its claims were by no means as extravagant as those of d'Hozier. It provided an accurate account of the ramifications of the Gondi in the preceding three centuries, and identified, in the middle of the thirteenth century, a certain Gondo de' Gondi, who was the first to use the hereditary surname and who signed a treaty of alliance between Florence and Genoa in 1251. Reputable historians and genealogists in the eighteenth century accepted the findings of Corbinelli.[6] Until the end of his life Retz probably continued to hope, if he could no longer believe with certainty, that his family was of much greater antiquity. Contrary to the opinions of its detractors, the Gondi family was an old and reputable Florentine house, though certainly not 'one of the most ancient and illustrious'.

It was more difficult to preserve aristocratic appearances concerning the early career of the Gondi in France. It owed more to the kennel than to chivalry, for it began with the sale of some lapdogs to Catherine de Médicis by Retz's great grandmother.

Antoine de Gondi settled in Lyon early in the sixteenth century, and became administrator of the revenues of the abbey of La Chassagne and of part of the income of the municipality. In 1516 he married Marie de Pierrevive, the daughter of a local tax-farmer.[7] She brought him more than new wealth and lands, for she possessed as sure an instinct for gain and as fierce a desire to rise in the world as he. It was an age when the paths to fortune lay open to the calculating as well as to the adventurous, and she proved herself both shrewd and ambitious. Five years after the marriage they bought a seigneurie, and Antoine de Gondi became the sieur du Perron. For many years opportunity eluded them, and then the king's new daughter-in-law passed through Lyon and took a fancy to the little dogs which madame du Perron bred. Catherine de Médicis took not only the dogs but also their former owner to attend to their needs. The death of the elder son of Francis I made her husband heir to the throne and raised the size and status of her entourage.

It was not surprising that Catherine should welcome Italians into her service, for despite the illustrious role of her family in Florentine history she was slighted at the French court as 'the banker's daughter'. Moreover, she saw her position usurped by her husband's elderly mistress, Diane de Poitiers. For ten years she bore no children to perpetuate the royal line and provide for her own security. It was said that she took a particular fancy to madame du Perron because the latter provided an effective recipe for pregnancy.[8] Certainly something put an end to her barren condition. From 1543 to 1556 she endured a succession of confinements, bearing three sons who were to reign in succession as Francis II, Charles IX and Henry III, and a fourth who was to die as duke of Alençon and Anjou, and three daughters who were to be queen of Spain, duchess of Lorraine and queen of Navarre. In 1547 Catherine de Médicis became queen of France with the accession of Henry II. The duties of madame du Perron were extended from the care of the royal dogs to the care of the royal children. Her position was later recognised by her appointment as *comise de l'intendance des bâtiments des Tuileries*, but while she served the queen she had also to serve Diane de Poitiers, who exercised a galling superintendence over the nursery. Her eldest son Albert, the grandfather of our cardinal, was summoned from his apprenticeship in business in the money market of Lyon to act as the companion and favourite of future kings.

Albert, who lived on until 1602, was by far the most celebrated of the second generation of the Gondi in France. He was the real founder of the family's fortunes, and all his relatives and descendants shared a particle of his glory. Albert de Gondi rose from rank to rank until he became a marshal of France and acted for a time as constable, the supreme military dignity. He served in scores of engagements and, as a commander, never lost a battle. As a diplomat he represented the throne in several embassies to Italy, and his imposing presence was remarked in England, Poland and the Rhineland principalities. As a courtier he was suave and agreeable. He was the boyhood companion of Charles ix, who acquired from him his singular gift for blasphemy. It was the marshal who aided the Medici queen mother to induce the king to sanction the massacre of his Protestant friend, admiral Coligny, and his Huguenot following on St Bartholomew's day, 1572. He served princes rather than causes, though for him there was one cause of paramount importance, his own self-interest.

The success of the marshal encouraged his less fortunate contemporaries to attribute every vice to him. Pierre de Brantôme, who in the sixteenth century fulfilled the role of purveyor of court gossip as Tallemant des Réaux was to do in the seventeenth, wrote that he was subtle and corrupt, 'a great liar and dissimulator'. He added that the marshal's grandfather was a miller, living near Florence, who had lived for a time in France in the fifteenth century. He described the marshal's father as a bankrupt in Lyon and his mother as a procuress.[9] In 1565 Albert de Gondi married Claude-Catherine de Clermont, the wealthy widow of baron de Annebaut and the daughter of Brantôme's aunt, madame de Dampierre. The latter did her best to prevent her daughter's second marriage, and when she was obliged to submit to the will of the queen mother she assumed the role of the wicked fairy and substituted her curse for her blessing.[10] Albert's bride brought him the barony of Retz, near Machecoul in the low-lying country south of the mouth of the Loire. The barony became a county and then, in 1581, a duchy, when Henry iii elevated Albert to the pinnacle of the social order as *duc-et-pair*.[11] In 1574, the year after his appointment as marshal of France, his annual income was thought to exceed 100,000 livres. His wealth increased during the remaining twenty-eight years of his life and included the marquis-ate of Belle-Ile and the county of Joigny, which passed to cardinal de Retz's father. Albert possessed a vast palace in the faubourg Saint-Honoré, and favoured among his country estates the château of Noisy-le-Roi near Villepreux.[12]

If cardinal de Retz owed his high estimate of his family's status to the worldy success of his grandfather, the marshal, he was in-debted to his paternal grandmother for his literary and linguistic gifts. Claude-Catherine de Clermont, who died in 1603, the year after her husband, was for over thirty years the hostess of one of the first and most celebrated of the literary salons. She read fluently in Latin, Greek and Italian, and was extolled by the poets of the Pléiade and their successors. Jean Antoine de Baif and Amadis Jamyn wrote verse in her honour, and Pontus de Tyard and Scévole de Sainte-Marthe dedicated their works to her. In 1573 and 1574 she kept an album into which she copied some of these tributes, together with poems of her own composition, including an imitation of Ariosto's *Orlando furioso*. The scholar and antiquary Etienne Pasquier mentioned her salon in 1591 in a letter to a friend. He described the throng of cavaliers, wits and poets who attended her, and listed topics of conversation ranging from the nature of love to current politics.[13]

Only two of the other six children of Antoine de Gondi and Marie de Pierrevive achieved any significance through their own talents. Pierre de Gondi established a family interest in the Gallican church, and, more specifically, in the diocese of Paris, which Retz was later to inherit. Although Pierre was made cardinal de Gondi in 1587, he preferred to serve the crown rather than Rome when the pope supported the rebellion of the Catholic League. He was accused of being an agitator among heretics and threatened with excommunication,[14] but his political judgment was vindicated by the triumph of Henry IV. Despite his notorious pluralism, by the time of his death in 1616 he bore a reputation for sanctity in the church and sagacity in the state. His younger brother, Charles de la Tour, made a brief and brilliant career as grand master of the wardrobe to Charles IX, until he died suddenly and mysteriously in 1574. Some ascribed his demise to the king's interest in his second wife, the celebrated beauty Hélène Bon: others whispered that his favour had excited the jealousy of his brother the marshal.[15]

The success of Antoine de Gondi and his family at the French court had encouraged an elder brother, Jérôme de Gondi, to send his sons to France on a similar mission. They, too, were advanced in the favour of Catherine de Médicis, and a grandson, also called Jérôme, enjoyed the confidence of her sons as did no other member of the Gondi save the marshal. He made his mark as an ambassador and received many material rewards – among them the château of Saint-Cloud where Henry III, the last Valois king, was assassinated by a fanatic of the League in 1589, and the hôtel de Gondi in Paris. This branch of the family accepted French naturalisation but retained close links with Florence. After the death of the second Jérôme in 1604, its representatives played no significant role in French affairs.

Retz's grandfather, his great uncles and their cousins displayed a ruthless opportunism that enabled them to accumulate wealth and honour and to ally themselves with several ancient French houses. His father, his uncles and his aunts tended to share the attitudes of the French aristocracy. They took their wealth and status for granted, and displayed an aptitude either for pleasure or for piety. Of the numerous children of the marshal and Catherine de Clermont, the eldest, Charles de Gondi, marquis de Belle-Ile, was cut down by the garrison of Mont-Saint-Michel in 1596 when he tried to execute a commission from Mercoeur, one of the chiefs of the League, to take command of the place. His widow, the sister of the influential duc de Longueville, joined the Feuillantines of Toulouse. She became the reforming abbess of Fontevrault, and founded the rigorous order of the Daughters of Calvary. Her son, Henri, succeeded to the title of duc de Retz on his grandfather's death. Henri married Jeanne de Scépeaux de Beaupréau, who had first been betrothed to the illustrious house of Montmorency, and based his reputation upon the duel he fought on her behalf. Montmorency had slightingly referred to him as the duc du Reste – the duke of the Leftovers – and the two had engaged in a desperate encounter. When honour had been satisfied without too great an effusion of blood the combatants had lunch together at the hôtel de Montmorency and subsequently dined at the hôtel de Retz. Tallemant de Réaux's account of the affair might have been

less romantic had he remembered that the marriage of the duc de
Retz took place in 1610 and the duel did not occur until five years
later.[16]

Henri, the second son of the marshal, was born in the year of the
massacre of Saint Bartholomew's night. He kept the see of Paris
within the family by becoming bishop on the resignation of his
uncle, cardinal de Gondi. In 1618 he was elevated to the sacred
college, taking the title of cardinal de Retz. He was a generous
benefactor of the Sorbonne, and the memory of his contributions
was to assist the academic career of the second cardinal de Retz,
his nephew. Cardinal Richelieu, who regarded all the Gondi with
contempt and aversion, observed that he had no letters and little
enough resolution. Nevertheless, he was respected as a political
as well as an ecclesiastical figurehead and served as president of the
royal council. At his death this honour went to cardinal de la
Rochefoucauld, the godfather and fourth cousin of our cardinal
de Retz's rival, and Richelieu in due course was to elbow him
aside in his advance to power. The first cardinal de Retz accompanied the court in Louis XIII's campaign of 1621 and 1622 against
the Huguenots in Gascony, and died of dysentery during the siege
of Montpellier. Unlike the other Gondi who served the church,
the anecdotes recorded of his life were generally to his credit.
After the surrender of Clairac in 1621 he bought a young Protestant girl from the soldiery and provided her with enough money to
enter a convent in Toulouse.[17] For his brother and successor to
the diocese of Paris, Jean-François de Gondi, such a story would
have implied motives very different from the cardinal's charitable
intent.

This generation of the Gondi family tended to run to extremes –
even those who seemed undistinguished made a virtue of their
mediocrity and embellished it with eccentric behaviour. Jean-
François was the only one of his uncles whom our cardinal de
Retz knew intimately, and he had cause enough to regret the
connection. His timidity was a standing joke among his retinue,
but he managed to combine it with a laxity of morals and a jealous
suspicion of his intellectual superiors, especially of his nephew.
Soon after his succession to the bishopric of Paris, the see was
removed from its dependency on the archdiocese of Sens and
Jean-François became its first archbishop. With his troop of musi-

cians and the splendour of his establishments at Noisy-le-Roi and Saint-Cloud his extravagance became notorious. He neglected his clerical duties to indulge his taste for gallantry and his liaisons were so various and conducted with such a want of discretion that he scandalised a society which could be tolerant of such matters, even among princes of the church. But this aspect of his life was less embarrassing to his nephew than his incapacity to perform the simplest clerical functions. His lack of latinity was the butt of the lackeys of Paris, and his ignorance of theology was revealed in his attempt to restrain the serious discussion of such topics in the more philosophically inclined of the salons.[18] The second cardinal de Retz recorded in his memoirs the opinion that his uncle's troubles were due 'more to the baseness of his inclinations than to the disorder of his habits'. He said that he found him at once the feeblest and the most conceited of men. It was Retz's misfortunes to begin his ecclesiastical career as his uncle's coadjutor.

Retz was more fortunate in his paternal aunts than in his uncles. The pious Claude-Marguerite de Gondi married the marquis de Maignelais and possessed the ear of the reforming movement within the church. Her husband's loyalty to the League had been suspected by its leaders, and he had been assassinated in 1591, the third year of their marriage. Françoise de Gondi married the sieur de Vassé, and her son, René de Vassé seigneur d'Esguilly, was a court gallant and an associate of the young Retz. Her daughter, Marguerite de Vassé, married the marquis de Sévigné and it was Retz who officiated at the marriage of their son, Henri de Sévigné, with Marie de Rabutin-Chantal, his celebrated correspondent and supporter in the darkness of his later years. Another aunt, Hippolyte de Gondi, married the marquis de Ragny, and it was their daughter, Retz's friend during the Fronde, who married into the ducal house of Lesdiguières and first allied it with the Gondi. Retz had three other paternal aunts, whom he never knew. One of them made a tragic marriage during the last phase of the wars of religion, and the others took the veil.

The single-minded worldliness of the marshal's generation of the family was lacking in their children. Retz's uncles, Henri the cardinal and Jean-François the archbishop, were ineffective political and clerical figureheads, while his aunts tended to display a strong sense of religious vocation. The Gondi tradition which Retz inherited contained a strange mixture of determination and weakness, piety and loose-living. While the pressures in his own immediate family circle were distinctly austere, his father's early career had alternated between the sword and the cloister. Philippe-Emmanuel, comte de Joigny, the third son of the marshal, was shy and introspective as a boy, but the early death of his eldest brother, Belle-Ile, and the careers of Henri and Jean-François in the church, obliged him to put aside his religious aspirations and follow in the military traditions of his father. In 1598, the year when Henry IV gave peace to his kingdom, Philippe-Emmanuel was appointed general of the galleys and the king's lieutenant-general in the Levant. He was then at the age of seventeen, and he forced himself with considerable success to adopt the conventions appropriate to his post. But he still thought longingly of the priesthood and offered a show of resistance in 1604 before accepting the marriage arranged for him with Françoise-Marguerite de Silly, the daughter of the comte de la Rochepot. Rochepot held the seigneurie of Commercy in Lorraine, which had been transferred to him by his wife and was to serve cardinal de Retz as a place of refuge in his last years. The count's brother, the comte de la Rocheguyon, died in 1627 during the siege of the Huguenot fortress of La Rochelle. He left no direct heirs and it was said that he would have left all his property to Retz if he had been able to find a notary to draw up his will.[19]

The angular Françoise de Silly was as pious as her husband, and together they fostered the career of Saint Vincent de Paul and devoted their energies to charitable works. Retz's mother had a sister, Madeleine de Silly, who married the comte du Fargis. In her scandalous amours and her inspired gift for political intrigue, madame du Fargis provided a feminine counterpart of Retz's own early career. Madame de Rambouillet, whose Parisian salon continued the tradition of the salon of the maréchale de Retz, remarked that the character of the future cardinal would have been much easier to understand if Madeleine, and not Françoise, de Silly had been his mother.[20] The observation was based on an intimate acquaintance, for the comte du Fargis was madame de Rambouillet's first cousin. However, madame du Fargis would hardly have suited the comte de Joigny.

In his endeavour to keep up appearances Philippe-Emmanuel frequented the worldly society of such military gallants as Guise, Chevreuse, Termes, Bassompierre and Créquy, the heir to the Lesdiguières title. Their dinners were renowned for their raillery, and Retz's father contrived to enter into the spirit of their proceedings. This eventually involved him in a duel. Tallemant des Réaux maliciously reported that Philippe-Emmanuel had arranged a mass to invoke divine support for his sword. More probable was the story that Vincent de Paul implored him not to confront his adversary, and that he agreed to leave the matter of vengeance to God.[21] The duc de Guise, who was the son of that hero of the League murdered by Henry III, developed a passion for naval warfare, and questioned the capacity of the general of the galleys. In 1622, when they were serving together in the fleet off La Rochelle, Guise even accused him of cowardice in the face of the enemy.[22] But, for all his thoughts of the priesthood, Philippe-Emmanuel was imbued with the sense of his family's honour, and at times he was capable of exhibiting a certain bravura. In 1625, when the governor of Toulon failed to salute his galleys, he threatened to take the port by assault. His early career was marked by a singular ambivalence, and, if court pleasures and the excitement of the battlefield occasionally distracted his melancholy, his pious wife continued to remind him that such pursuits endangered his salvation. It was Françoise de Silly who persuaded him to see mère Marguerite d'Acarie of the Holy Sacrament, a barefoot Carmelite reputed to have the gift of prophecy. In the course of this visit Philippe-Emmanuel first met cardinal Bérulle, the founder of the Oratorian order and the leader of that revival of piety affecting both church and court. In 1662 Retz signed a deposition recalling his father's remarks about this incident and attesting the holiness of mère d'Acarie.[23] Two years after the death of his wife in 1625, the general of the galleys entered the Oratory, and was known thereafter as père de Gondi. He continued, nevertheless, to take an interest in the affairs of his family.

While Philippe-Emmanuel vacillated between the world and the church he paid slight attention to the upbringing of his three sons. Pierre, the eldest, was an ill-formed boy who in later life made awkward jokes against his own ugliness. Despite his slowness of mind he was not without courage, and was wounded when

accompanying his father in an attack on La Rochelle. Henri, eight
years younger, seemed to possess grace, intelligence and ambition,
and his blond colouring distinguished him in appearance from the
dark hair and sallow complexion of his brothers. Jean-François-
Paul, the future cardinal, was younger again by three years. He
seemed to combine the physical characteristics of Pierre and the
intellectual traits of Henri. Jean-François-Paul was born in the
family home of Montmirail near Joigny in September 1613. When
he was composing his memoirs nearly sixty years later he tried to
recollect suitably miraculous portents and recorded that at the
time of his birth a 'monstrous sturgeon' was taken in the stream
that ran past the château. At about this time the general of the
galleys obtained the services of monsieur Vincent as a tutor to his
sons. But the tutor was far too involved in the prosecution of
madame de Joigny's good works to attend to the education of the
children. Then in 1617 the saint suddenly left the Gondi household
on a mission to evangelise the peasantry. Later Philippe-Emmanuel provided Saint Vincent with the post of almoner to the galleys,
which enabled him to work among the galley-slaves of Marseille
and to launch his Congregation of the Mission. There was no
opportunity for Vincent de Paul to influence the early development of the man whose career in the church seemed an unholy
travesty of the saint's ideals.

    Pierre de Gondi was expected to inherit his father's worldly
honours in the tradition of his grandfather, and there were hopes
that he might acquire the duchy of Retz, since his cousin, Henri
duc de Retz, had two daughters but no sons. Though the second
brother was accorded the title of marquis des Isles d'Or, he was
regarded as the heir to the family's material interests in the
church, and for this reason was granted the revenues of two
Breton abbeys, Busay and Quimperlé. In 1622 the twelve-year-old
marquis caught his foot in the stirrup as he fell from his horse, and
was kicked to death. The abbeys, together with the prospect of
high preferment, passed to Jean-François-Paul. Three years later
the household disintegrated when the pious Françoise de Silly
died. The future cardinal was packed off to a Jesuit college, and
Philippe-Emmanuel was able at last to indulge his taste for asceticism and religious contemplation. There was something of his
father's ambivalence in the young Retz, but he inherited no trace of

his piety. Nor did his mother's strict regimen make any impact upon him save one of revulsion. He accepted the high status and destiny of his family impressed upon him by his parents, but in every other respect he seemed far closer to the tastes and attitudes of his paternal grandparents.

The children of the marshal had been born into the anarchy of the religious wars. They had known its most destructive phases in adolescence, and reached maturity in the age when Henry IV reasserted the authority of the crown. The generation of the Fronde – of Retz, La Rochefoucauld, the great Condé and his sister, madame de Longueville – was born into another period of disorder – that which intervened between the assassination of Henry IV in 1610 and the advent of cardinal Richelieu to power in 1624. The political licence practised by the nobility during their economic decline in the religious wars had been barely restrained in the peaceful years of Henry IV, and reappeared during the minority of his son and successor, Louis XIII. In the year when Retz began his formal education a new power began to curb the indiscipline of the class to which he belonged. Cardinal Richelieu was himself a member of that rural nobility who sought to restore their shrinking fortunes by banditry, warfare and advancement at court. Richelieu won his way to supreme office by flattery, dissimulation and the ruthless pursuit of self-interest. He courted the favour of Henry IV's widow, Marie de Médicis, and first attained office for a few months before the collapse of her regency in 1617.

Richelieu's family background, his boyhood experience, and his long and devious climb to power gave him direct experience of the problem that faced him as first minister, and his acute intelligence enabled him to understand it and seek its resolution. He was determined to strengthen the monarchy by humbling the pride of the great. In Richelieu the high aristocracy, with which the third and fourth generations of the Gondi family in France were identified in every way, was confronted with a ruthless and disciplined power. He represented the sovereign forces of order that opposed the anarchic trends from the wars of religion. Seven major conspiracies had challenged the government in the twenty-six years between the end of the religious wars and the advent of Richelieu: an equal number of plots were directed against the cardinal's régime during the eighteen years of his rule. Nor was the disaffection limited to the great. The provincial nobility, from which the families of the high aristocracy drew their clientèle, were frequently associated with the peasant risings that proliferated during Richelieu's tenure of office. The cardinal contained these problems, but he could not solve them. He might dismantle the fortresses of the nobility, execute the leaders of rebellion and diminish aristocratic control of provincial government. But, so long as the king's mother, Marie de Médicis, and his brother, Gaston d'Orléans, provided a focus for noble discontents, he could not prevent the recrudescence of aristocratic sedition. And, though he might make increasing use of the intendants to undermine the local authority of the nobility of both sword and gown, he could not reform a social system which allowed the leaders of provincial society to turn peasant *jacqueries* to their own advantage. Nor could Richelieu fully succeed in utilising the support of the middle-classes against the aristocracy. For this the personal authority of the king was necessary, and the cardinal merely acted in his name. His policy towards the aristocracy was, then, one of repression, not of reform. The tensions of this conflict shaped the ethos of the aristocratic society in which Retz grew to manhood.

There were three contending bases of morality amid the stresses of Richelieu's régime: the reinvigorated doctrines of the church, the secular realism of the philosophical libertines and the heroic illusions of the great.[24] The last was the paramount influence in Retz's early intellectual development; the second dominated his attitudes in the middle period of his life; and the first was to exert an influence in his last years. He expressed his particular individuality in each mode, affirmed his personal attitude through the wilful force of his ambition, and, in the end, provided the confused synthesis of past and present revealed in his memoirs. Virtue had several meanings, and in their retrospective quest for personal identity the memoirs retraced their author's exploration of its frontiers.

To the nobility the church had long represented a source of wealth and patronage. Its higher benefices were virtually their exclusive preserve, and its policies had been guided by their material preoccupations. During the wars of religion the period of the League had seen the revival of Catholic religious enthusiasm, which engendered schismatic divergencies on the one hand and its sceptical antidote on the other. The Catholic reformation seeped into France in the aftermath of the League. One of its principal agents, the Jesuit order, had been associated with the ultramontane doctrines of the League, and was critically regarded by the nationalist forces of Gallicanism. New orders were introduced and the spirituality of the old orders was regained. Bérulle founded the Oratory to improve the education of the priesthood, and the seminary of Saint-Sulpice pursued similar ends. He was the centre of the party of the *dévots*, patronised by Marie de Médicis. A section of the nobility, whose minds, like that of père de Gondi, responded to spiritual needs, supported these objectives, and some of them formed a kind of secret society, the order of the Holy Sacrament. Bérulle was also responsible for the importation of the Spanish mysticism of Saint Theresa of Avila. The Capuchin friar, père Joseph, who was the principal agent of Richelieu's foreign policy, was no stranger to the search for mystic communion with the Deity, and in the abbé de Saint-Cyran, who was the spiritual director of the Jansenist house of Port-Royal, mysticism seemed curiously at odds with the general trend of Jansenist theology.

Virtue, as the Jansenists understood it, was confined to the elect of God, and never to be found in affairs of this world. The Arnauld family, who populated Port-Royal-des-Champs and its sister establishment in Paris, stressed the depravity of human nature and encouraged asceticism. They developed an Augustinian view of grace, and fiercely opposed the doctrines of free will expounded by the Jesuit followers of Molina, who extended the capacity of man to cooperate with his maker in the attainment of salvation. They took as their text the *Augustinus*, a commentary upon Saint Augustine by Jansenius published posthumously in 1640. Although the Jansenists drew most of their support from the ranks of the *parlementaires* and magistrates of other administrative courts, they also attracted recruits among Retz's friends in the traditional aristocracy. Richelieu imprisoned Saint-Cyran, and commissioned the sceptic, La Mothe le Vayer, to answer the Jansenist assertion that virtue was inconceivable without Christian revelation. It was the younger Antoine Arnauld, the most prolific of Jansenist polemicists, who responded to La Mothe's treatise, *The Virtue of the Pagans*.

Virtue was, indeed, depreciated and redefined by another doctrine which could be equally dangerous to a rationally-conceived morality. The scepticism of such so-called libertines as La Mothe doubted both the evidence of the senses and the conclusions of reason. The policies of Richelieu suggested that the criterion of virtue was success. His statecraft displayed a shrewd realism in which the morality of the state superseded the dictates of the individual Christian conscience. Gabriel Naudé, later to serve as Mazarin's propagandist, scorned moral and theoretical abstractions in politics and justified Richelieu's reason of state in his *Political Considerations on Coups d'État*.[25] In the salons patronised by the fashionable aristocracy the future frondeurs were sometimes exposed to a disillusioned realism and a pragmatic view of social convention. But the strands in this intellectual web could be strangely interlaced. At one extreme the philosopher Descartes could begin from universal doubt and conclude by affirming a rationalist system of mathematical truth: at another an equally celebrated mathematician and contemporary, Pascal, could use the sceptical ideas in Montaigne's *Apology for Raymond Sebonde* to undermine confidence in human reason and oblige his reader to accept the dogma of Port-Royal. Pascal also employed the vein of stoicism, contained in Montaigne but revealed more explicitly in *Of Wisdom*, the popular work of his disciple, du Charron. It was an attitude developed in direct response to the anarchy of the religious wars. When Pascal was composing his apology for religion in the aftermath of the Fronde he chose the Stoic Epictetus as epitomising the futility of human self-confidence.[26] Seneca and Plutarch were even more widely read by the educated aristocracy in Richelieu's time. In an earlier age Montaigne had commended their outlook, and another of Retz's contemporaries, the sceptical Saint-Evremond, was to repeat his eulogy.[27]

The interplay of *virtù* and *fortuna* had fascinated Machiavelli. The idea that the will might use reason to hold the passions in check provided both a guide to action and a means of insurance against the buffets of adverse fortune. This was the doctrine exemplified in Plutarch's tales of the heroes of antiquity, which Retz was to read with avidity. The Stoic ideal contributed to the current vogue of the noble hero, which, far more than the views of the sceptics and the rationalists, dominated the ethos of the aristocracy in the early part of Retz's life. It provided a code of anarchic individualism which resisted the pressures of Richelieu's rule. Virtue was entirely self-centred. *Devoir* did not mean an obligation to others: it meant the duty of being worthy of oneself. Social convention imposed no restraint upon aristocratic individualism, and, despite the Stoic influence, the full indulgence of the passions was seen as an end in itself. The acquisition of *gloire* required unlimited ambition and unfailing audacity. The heroic will carried the noble soul to the fulfilment of its destiny. The early plays of Corneille revealed these attitudes with dramatic intensity. It has been said that the source of all Corneillian virtue was a profound horror of personal humiliation.[28]

To subsequent generations there was an unreality about the world created by Corneille, where ideas often seemed to dominate the characters who acted as their vehicle. The machinery of his plots was based upon conflicts between duty and inclination, reason and passion – conflicts which were initiated and resolved by the heroic exercise of the will. Corneille, more than any writer of his time, represented the mood of the high aristocracy in reaction against the discipline imposed by Richelieu. The great cardinal had *Le Cid* condemned not because it extolled the chivalry of Spain, with which France was at war, but because it expressed that anarchic individualism to which he was so implacably opposed. Corneille distinguished absolute monarchy, and, more particularly, its exercise by a first minister, as the enemy of the class whose passions he depicted. Towards the end of Richelieu's life and in the early years of his successor's régime, his plays were preoccupied with tyranny. *Cinna*, *Pompée* and *Héraclius* were studies of the tyrant. *Polyceute* and *Héraclius* contained scenes of both popular revolt and aristocratic resistance. If in *Rodogune*, *Théodore* and *Héraclius* he could admit that kings could be generous, their ministers were invariably tyrants. The generation of the Fronde was nurtured on Corneille. Retz quoted him in his memoirs when he tried to recreate the mood of the past, and his friend, the marquise de Sévigné, confessed 'I am intoxicated by Corneille. Everything must yield to his genius.'[29] For Corneille the hero had no purpose save self-realisation: his passions and his ambitions served no other end.

The romantic aspect of the heroic ideal blended on a less sublime plane with the traditions of chivalry and with the elegant,

B

resourceful cavalier presented in Castiglione's *Courtier*. The fairy
tale adventures of d'Urfé's romantic novel *Astrée* were mingled
with abstract discussion of the psychology of love favoured in the
salons. It was customary to follow the hero of romance through a
bewildering succession of battles, love affairs and intrigues, and
these ingredients recurred in *Polexandre* by Retz's friend Gomberville, in mademoiselle de Scudéry's *Ibrahim*, and in the endless
volumes of La Calprenède's *Cassandre*, which all appeared in the
early 1640s. Sententious moralising at times obscured the romantic
hero, while the trend to elegant badinage in many *romans* reflected
the limitations of salon society. Inconstancy in love was a common
theme, and the marquis in *Ibrahim* was depicted as liberating
women from the fetters of convention and stressing the difference
between love and marriage. *Astrée*, from the previous generation,
was the most read of these novels, and Retz was to recall how its
scenes were re-enacted by some of the participants in the Fronde.

Beside these attitudes, polite convention required lip-service to
the concept of *honnêteté*, the quality of civility in the acceptable
man. The *honnête homme* should endeavour to set his equals and his
inferiors at their ease. One of the best known guides to polite
behaviour was Nicolas Faret's treatise, *The Honnête Homme, or the
Art of Making an Impression at Court*, which was thrice republished
in the last decade of Richelieu's régime. Faret was imitated by
other writers, who followed him in prescribing Christian virtue
as essential to *honnêteté*.[30] But Christian virtue was an ingredient of
less importance when the idea of the *honnête homme* became
assimilated to the heroic cult under the influence of the Spanish
writer Baltasar Gracián. Spanish fashions were then at their
height. Corneille was presenting his dramatisation of Spanish
chivalry in *Le Cid* and Scarron was plagiarising Spanish comedy.
Gracián's books were entitled *The Man of Discretion*, *The Politician*,
The Art of Prudence and *The Hero*. Spanish pride, reserve and
gravity became more highly regarded by the fashionable French
aristocracy than Italian elegance and courtesy. Gracián clothed the
concept of the hero with subtlety and artifice.[31] While the hero
must be of elevated birth, he must also possess a quick and
flexible mind (*destreza*) and the ability to sum up a situation behind
a mask of duplicity. 'A great stratagem (*treta*)', wrote Gracián, 'is
to display oneself to view but not to comprehension.' The first

rule of grandeur (*grandeza*) was to adopt subtle devices to give the appearance of possessing it. A variety of techniques was suggested to create this illusion. It was necessary to strike postures to display *señorió*, an aloof, mysterious ability to dominate the minds of others. Ambition and affection, pride and prudence, combined to produce the essential quality of *despejo*. When Amelot de la Houssaie, the nephew of one of Retz's friends, translated *The Hero* into French he used *je ne sais quoi* to convey the meaning of this indefinable attribute, and Retz himself used the same phrase in his memoirs. La Houssaie's translation was not published until later in the century, but at least one other French version had appeared before the Fronde.[32]

After the Fronde a revised version of the *honnête homme* was to displace the ideal of the hero, but, in the terms in which *honnêteté* came to be defined by the chevalier de Méré, it was shorn of Faret's Christian virtue and assumed human action to be rooted in self-interest. This was the age in which La Rochefoucauld declared that all apparent virtues were 'swallowed up in self-interest, as rivers in the sea'. Vices and virtues were never unmixed, but were mingled together as poison in medicine.[33] The worship of *amour-propre* proved a cynical substitute for the high-minded *générosité*, which La Rochefoucauld was to define as disguised ambition. But in the age of Richelieu, the cult of the hero predominated. Retz was to delineate his own version of *le généreux*. Its contemporary characteristic was a full and flamboyant affirmation of personal identity in an existentialist philosophy of action. Objective virtues were uncertain and subjective ones required individual discovery. This was the moral and intellectual environment which Retz knew in his youth. From it, as well as from the traditions of his family, he equipped himself for his own particular exploration of the frontiers of virtue.

The frontiers of virtue

At the death of his mother and the withdrawal of his father from the world, Retz, who was then twelve years old, attended the Collège de Clermont, the Jesuit school in Paris. In education the most remarkable successes of the Jesuits were often achieved with minds that showed little subsequent trace of their religious influence. The sceptical Saint-Evremond, who was precisely the same age as Retz, also had his schooling at the Collège de Clermont. The Jesuits taught Corneille, whose dramatic heroes scorned ordinary morality, and Descartes, whose philosophy threatened the scholastic basis of theology. Among the great figures of the church they educated the saintly François de Sales, the pious Bérulle and the eloquent Bossuet. They also educated Retz's future enemy, the supple-minded secularist, cardinal Mazarin. Perhaps the diversity of their results was due to the broad humanism of their curriculum, and to the flexibility of mind they encouraged in philosophical studies.

The Jesuit père René Rapin was himself educated at Clermont and taught classical literature there for a period of nine years. He attended the college a few years after Retz had left it, and referred in his memoirs to Retz's experiences there and to the reactions of his teachers. Rapin attributed the dislike and suspicion, with which the Company of Jesus was regarded, to the self-interest of its detractors and to the envy inspired by its success. However, he thought Retz's aversion for the Jesuits was based upon the treatment he received at Clermont: 'It was generally believed, and not without reason, that some secret incident had occurred which gave him cause for offence against them. Some spread the rumour that their lack of special consideration for him during his early studies at the college was one of his first reasons for discontentment against the fathers.'[1] Rapin, of course, was a biased witness. The general prejudice against the Jesuits was the result of their association with the extremist doctrines of the League, including the practice of regicide, during the last phase of the religious wars, when the Collège de Clermont had been closed down. Rapin was critical of Retz because of his own link with Mazarin, whose nephew, Alphonse Mancini, he had tutored until the boy's death in 1658. He tried to demonstrate that Retz had an early sympathy with Port-Royal as a result of a particular hatred he had conceived for the Jesuits. In fact Retz's later associations with the Jansenists were entirely opportunist, and any rancour he seemed to display against the Society of Jesus was the reverse aspect of this alliance.

Retz's unhappiness in his first years at school is easy to explain. The renewal of Jesuit activities in Paris after the religious wars owed much to the favour and patronage of the Gondi, and it might have been assumed that the young abbé would have enjoyed special privileges. He himself expected them: indeed, his arrogant, imperious nature demanded them. They were not accorded. He was obliged to conform with the established rules, and punished severely when he rebelled. His clumsy physique and his attitude of superiority attracted the persecution of his schoolfellows, and he looked for the discipline of the fathers to be directed against his tormentors, and not against himself. He soon started to entitle himself the abbé de Retz rather than the abbé de Busay, because his companions called him by the opprobrious nickname of *Buse* (simpleton).[2] His pride responded with violent outbreaks and wild escapades, and the Jesuits applied new and sterner curbs. Despite these difficulties Retz set out to learn all he could from his tutors. His natural intelligence and his desire to surpass his fellows won him as much praise from his masters as his wayward behaviour earned their disapproval. He learnt Latin, Greek, German, Spanish and Hebrew, and spoke the language of his ancestors fluently.

In July 1631, after six years at the Collège de Clermont, he presented a Latin thesis for his *baccalauréat* which he entitled *Conclusions drawn from general philosophy* and tactfully dedicated to his uncle, the archbishop. The arguments contained in these formal exercises carry little conviction for the modern mind: yet, beneath the scholastic categories he was obliged to accept, a strong and

logical intellect revealed itself. The thesis was divided into eight
short sections, with titles such as 'Of Natural Philosophy', 'Of
Moral Philosophy', 'Of the Natural Body in General', 'Of the
Animate Body', 'Of Natural Theology'. It was concerned with
classifying logical associations between what were then regarded
as branches of philosophy. It developed inbuilt tautologies and
made play with theological distinctions between actual and
potential, substance and accident. Sometimes it added a personal
twist, such as this parenthetical reference to prudence:

There are three particular parts of moral discipline – which is the
same thing as prudence – namely, the political, the economic and the
religious, and in terms of logic the three are associated by way of formal
opposition. Its intrinsic end is the rectitude of human activity: its
extrinsic end is the beatitude which consists essentially of the single
intuitive act of the mind of the highest being, which is accompanied by
impeccability and love.[3]

The abbé resumed his studies in 1633. Although he had by no
means resigned himself to a career in the church, he had resolved
to master all the theological intricacies of the profession. Retz
entered the Sorbonne, the theological faculty of the University of
Paris, and applied himself so well that he passed from grade to
grade with outstanding success and completed the final examina-
tions for his master's *licence* in December 1637. While he displayed
his mastery of the techniques of academic disputation, he was far
from scrupulous in the observance of its ethical standards. When
he was defending his master's thesis in open assembly in the
Sorbonne, he was challenged for omitting a relevant passage from
the proceedings of a church council. His first response was to deny
that the passage existed. Then, when his interlocutor found the
reference in the library, he asserted that it was missing from the
copy he had consulted. He was mistaken, but his bravado carried
the day.[4] Although he was later to dedicate his doctoral thesis to
the saints so that he would not be beholden to any worldly
authority, his academic achievements did not pass unnoticed by
secular powers outside the faculty.

According to his own account, he had earlier received an invitation to call upon cardinal Richelieu, but had rejected it high-
handedly by feigning to be ill and visiting the country for the sake

of his health. At the beginning of 1638 he chose again to defy the
omnipotent first minister. Richelieu had a distant cousin, Henri de
la Mothe-Houdancourt, who was Retz's rival for the first place on
the list of graduates. He was the brother of the marshal of the
same name, and later had a distinguished career in the church as
bishop of Rennes and archbishop of Auch. When Retz heard that
Richelieu was pressing his rival's claim with the professors of the
Sorbonne, he had a message conveyed to the cardinal, offering to
yield his probable place at the top of the list. His action was a
carefully contrived insult, not an act of submission. Richelieu
haughtily rejected the offer, indicating that his favourite possessed
merit enough to triumph without his support. Retz could rely
upon the Sorbonne's memory of the benefactions of his uncle,
the first cardinal de Retz. He exploited every possible factor in his
favour and obtained the prize by a majority of eighty-four members of the faculty. Richelieu was angered by the successful defiance of so young a member of a family he despised. He had already
described him as overbold after hearing reports of a sermon he
had preached at a Carmelite convent in the presence of the queen
and her ladies. Now he designated the young abbé 'ce petit
audacieux' and remarked that his appearance seemed to fit him for
the gallows.[5] So strong was his pique that he halted the construction of the new chapel he had ordered for the Sorbonne.[6]

Had Retz's appearance better suited the part he chose for
himself he might have played it worse. He had a large head and a
squat body on bent and spindly legs. His complexion was unusu-
ally dark, his lips thick and his nose bulbous en pied de marmite.
His eyesight was so bad that Tallemant told apocryphal stories
about it, such as the occasion on which he and his equally myopic
cousin, d'Esguilly, spent fifteen minutes silently looking for each
other in a small enclosed courtyard.[7] He was so clumsy with his
hands that he could scarcely button his doublet or buckle on his
spurs, and his writing spun drunkenly over the page as if it were
in three dimensions instead of two. He said in his memoirs:
'Madame de Carignan told the queen one day that I was very ugly:
it was perhaps the only time in her life that she didn't lie.' But
he redeemed his ugliness by the pride with which he bore himself.
His expression was alert and his face mobile. He could be bold
and sad, frivolous and bored, in an instant. He talked more than

he listened, but everything that he said was suffused with wit and
intelligence. It was not surprising that many ladies of the court
and subsequent frondeuses succumbed to his charm.

There had been no tenderness in Retz's upbringing. His stern
and pious mother had died when he was young. He hardly knew
the remote father who had left the profession of arms for the
Oratory. As an adolescent Retz was obliged to be entirely self-
reliant, closing his mind to sentimentality or affection. He had
none of his father's sense of vocation for the church, and much
of his grandfather's ruthless determination to succeed in the
world. The prospect of a clerical career appalled him, but his
ambition drove him to surpass his fellow students. While he
persevered in his theological studies, he was no less assiduous in
the pursuit of the sensual pleasure and physical excitement that
went to the making of the *honnête homme*. He had been tonsured at
the age of ten, but this meant little, and he affected a white collet
at his neck and refused to wear the soutane. At fourteen he had
been appointed a canon of Notre-Dame, a measure which did
not require his ordination. Until he had been ordained he could
live in both worlds and join the throng of gallant abbés whose
only ecclesiastical interest was in the continued receipt of the
revenues of their benefice. He flung himself ardently into the life
of the Parisian aristocracy with its ceaseless procession of amours,
affairs of honour and political intrigues. There was no sign of
prudent restraint in any of these activities. No moral consideration
curtailed his zest to explore sensation and measure his mental and
physical dexterity against his rivals. He acted upon impulse, for in
action he was affirming his own heroic identity.

When he was recalling this early phase in his memoirs, he
wrote down all the details with the same frank insouciance in
which he had wilfully defied the authority of Richelieu, or faced
an adversary's sword in the Bois de Vincennes, or stolen the
virtue of his latest mistress:

It would take a volume to set out all the ways in which our love-
making was embroidered. One of the simplest was when I had to swear
to let this beauty keep a handkerchief over her eyes when the light was
too strong in the room. Since it covered no more than her face it did
not prevent me from appraising her other qualities, which, without
any exaggeration, surpassed those of the Medici Venus which I had

only just seen in Rome. I had brought back a copy of the statue, and this inanimate marvel from the century of Alexander had to yield place to the living.

This passage in the memoirs is incomplete because it occurs at that point in the manuscript where an unknown hand has ripped out many of the pages. But enough remains to reconstruct the pattern of Retz's amours.

In one of the passages of rationalisation that interrupt the sense of immediacy in the memoirs, Retz argued that he had deliberately pursued his rake's progress in order to convince his father that he was unsuited to a career in the church – that he was, as he put it 'the least ecclesiastical soul that ever was in the universe'. If he had really intended to convey this impression he would have discontinued the studies at the Sorbonne, where he was so successful. Yet there was one occasion when an assault on the temple of Venus was designed for this motive. A constant struggle was waged among the families of the great for precedence, and particular importance was attached to the status of *duc-et-pair*. The La Rochefoucauld family, whose ancestry was more ancient than that of any other with this rank, finally acquired it in 1622, although a quarrel between Richelieu and the father of the author of the *Maximes*, prevented its registration for fifteen years and involved a dispute as to precedence with the ducal houses of Retz and Saint-Simon. There was no obvious heir to the ducal title of marshal de Retz. Henri de Retz, the grandson of the marshal and son of Belle-Ile, had the better claim, but Pierre de Retz, the brother of the future cardinal, also sought the title. Henri had two daughters, Catherine and Marguerite. In 1633 it was agreed that Pierre should marry Catherine, that both he and Henri would bear the ducal title, and that the inheritance should pass to Pierre and his heirs after Henri's death.[8] It was at this time that the abbé de Retz fixed his attention on the dowry of the second daughter, Marguerite, which included the substantial inheritance of Beaupréau in Anjou, acquired through Henri's wife, Jeanne de Scépeaux.

At the age of twenty Retz accompanied his father on a visit to the ducal branch of the family and met Marguerite de Gondi. He recalled in his memoirs how he admired her complexion, her eyes and her mouth, and how he was prepared to overlook a slight curvature in her spine in the light of the eighty thousand livres of rent representing the income from the duchy of Beaupréau. He noted that mademoiselle de Beaupréau responded favourably to his approaches, although 'her air was somewhat severe'. One of her attendants had a brother in Retz's abbey of Busay, near Machecoul. Retz used this contact to bribe the attendant to help him win her mistress's affection. He discovered that Marguerite hated her sister as much as he himself hated his brother, and for the same reason – that the elder child was the father's favourite. Feeling secure of his prospects, Retz resolved to elope with her to Holland, and raised money for the purpose by alienating a large part of his income from Busay in a secret negotiation with a merchant from Nantes. But the plot was revealed when the tender regards passing between the abbé and mademoiselle de Beaupréau were observed in a mirror by a fellow guest at a dinner party near Machecoul. He informed Catherine de Gondi, now the duchesse de Retz, and she hastened to warn Philippe-Emmanuel. Retz's father was a man of tact as well as piety. He removed his son without upbraiding him for his duplicity, and merely shook the abbé's heavy purse at him to indicate that all was discovered. Retz did not abandon his project immediately, for he consulted his cousin d'Esguilly and borrowed money for a new attempt. A gap in the memoirs conceals the explanation of the second failure. Marguerite de Gondi was to marry the duc de Brissac, but this did not prevent her from becoming Retz's mistress. She contracted venereal disease from her husband and passed it on to her lover.

Inconstancy in love was fashionable in a society where marriage was arranged in terms of family alliances and property contracts. Feminine virtue was not common, and where it existed Retz regarded it as a challenge to his ingenuity. He agreed with La Rochefoucauld that prudery was a kind of cosmetic with which women enhanced their beauty. Retz passed from one liaison to the next, and sometimes maintained them concurrently, as much from curiosity as from passion. He had 'gallantry on the brain', as Tallemant des Réaux put it. He had little regard for the feelings of his mistresses, and his arrogance and caprice made mutual love impossible. Only two of these relationships had any stability, his liaisons with madame de Pommereuil and mademoiselle de Chevreuse. He enjoyed the conspiratorial aspects of his affairs.

After he became a bishop it was his practice to emerge at night in disguise from the cloisters of Notre-Dame and to take a borrowed carriage to visit madame de Pommereuil, whence he would return four or five hours later. The double intrigue of deceiving one mistress for another amused him even more, but he felt no bitterness when he was himself the object of deception.

Many of Retz's affairs were connected with his family circle. The maréchale de la Meilleraye, whose charms were not matched by her intelligence, and who at one stage even believed that Richelieu was pursuing her, was the sister of the duc de Brissac, and hence the sister-in-law of Marguerite de Gondi. Retz admitted to the abbé de Choisy that she was his greatest passion. She may have been the lady with the handkerchief. The duc de Saint-Simon, whose father was a member of the same circle, remarked in his memoirs that Retz for once lost his self-composure and embarked on what Saint-Simon called an 'incredibly stupid' scheme to have her marriage annulled so that he could wed her himself.[9] She broke off the affair when she left him in favour of one of the officers in her husband's command as grand master of the artillery.

Anne de Rohan, princesse de Guémenée, was seven years older than Retz, and vacillated between notorious love affairs and the religious seclusion of the Jansenists. In the years of Retz's adolescence she was a frequent visitor to his family home, where she joined Retz and d'Esguilly in such literary guessing games as the identification of characters and situations from *Astrée*. Retz's affair with her was punctuated by a series of violent scenes provoked by her jealousy. Whereas madame de la Meilleraye left him for her artillery officer, madame de Guémenée abandoned him when the pious Arnauld d'Andilly persuaded her to join his relatives at Port-Royal. Retz also pursued his cousin, the duchesse de Lesdiguières, the daughter of the marquis de Ragny, but she was conducting a feud with another cousin, Anne de Maignelais, the daughter of the most pious of Retz's aunts. Retz was often in trouble with the latter cousin, who possessed a sharp tongue and looks to match, and the duchesse de Lesdiguières took a malicious pleasure in contriving to make them dance together at her parties.[10]

Retz gained even greater notoriety for his affairs outside the circle of his cousins and their friends. We may dismiss Tallemant's stories of how he drove off six armed men sent by an indignant

husband, and then continued with his love-making; and how he
went to Germany to rescue a rich Catholic heiress from the
Protestant relatives who persecuted her, and fought a duel on her
behalf with another suitor named Weimar. But there is no doubt
about his association with the passionate madame de Pommereuil,
whose lovers were so numerous that they created a constant
problem for the hostesses of Parisian society. Madame la présidente's promiscuity was the outcome of an unfortunate marriage,
forced upon her by her father, with the president of the high court
of the *grand conseil*. She had been foolish enough to want to marry
the man she loved and, after her marriage with the president, she
expected her lover to rescue her from her predicament. When he
failed to do so, she refused to accept the convention of keeping up
marital appearances. The complexity and unconcealed nature of
her love affairs were possibly less scandalous than her assault
upon the legal dignity of her husband. When monsieur de Pommereuil brought a number of archers to claim his part of the
household furniture, she led a body of armed men to resist them,
arming herself for the occasion with a halberd.[11] This formidable
lady remained a loyal friend to Retz in the years of his disgrace.
Some of his other affairs were even less reputable. Though he
smeared Richelieu by claiming that he had an association with
Marion de l'Orme, whom he called a prostitute, he himself shared
a courtesan named Le Noble with the swaggering comte d'Harcourt. It was with d'Harcourt that he fought one of his first duels.
When still at the Collège de Clermont he had approached madame
du Châtelet, d'Harcourt's mistress. She had laughed at his youthful
effrontery, and in his pique he had called out the count.

Retz was far less successful as a duellist than he was as a lover,
but this, too, was part of the role he chose, and he was determined
to provide a distinguished performance. His clumsiness in martial
pursuits was legendary. Speculating on what would have become
of him had his mother's uncle, the comte de la Rocheguyon, succeeded in bequeathing his property and tradition to the abbé,
Tallemant recalled with incredulity how Retz had told him he
would cut a dash if an opportunity for a military career presented
itself to him. Not the least of the dangers he incurred in his
sword-play was the risk of prosecution by the authorities. Unlike
his predecessors, Richelieu was resolved to enforce the edicts

against duelling, not so much because it annually decimated the nobility but rather because the ban upon it was a means of establishing his own authority over them. Thus he refused to reprieve Montmorency-Bouteville, a member of one of the most illustrious houses in France, when he flagrantly defied the law on the subject. Retz took pains to conceal the combat with d'Harcourt, and, though the story became known, he was not arrested. The duel was not one in which he acquired much merit. After receiving a light wound in the stomach he was pinned to the ground and then released by his opponent. He fought another duel at this time with sword and pistol against the nephew of marshal Bassompierre in the Bois de Vincennes. On this occasion he wounded his adversary before being disarmed. His best known encounter was with the abbé François de Choiseul, later marquis de Praslin. The cause of the quarrel was quite inconsequential, but both parties, as well as their seconds, were severely wounded. Although in this instance Retz deliberately publicised the affair, there was apparently no official reaction.

Retz's escapades alarmed his family, and they were still more concerned by his defiance of Richelieu over the place list at the Sorbonne. In March 1638 they insisted that he leave Paris and embark on a grand tour of Italy. He chose Tallemant des Réaux as his travelling companion, together with the latter's two brothers, Tallemant de Lussac and François Tallemant, and several other gentlemen. They descended the Rhône to Avignon, passed through Aix-en-Provence and embarked at Marseille for Livorno. They lingered for some time in Florence, where Retz was received by the Tuscan grand duke, Marie de Médicis' cousin, Ferdinando II. They were entertained by Retz's distant cousin, Giovanni Battisto de' Gondi, who had been educated in France and had served as the Tuscan envoy in Paris before returning to Florence in 1636 to become a secretary of state. Retz was delighted to inspect the Gondi portraits in his host's house, and in order to give visible effect to his boasts about his family's prestige he so indulged his taste for extravagant clothes that his finery provoked the laughter of the dowager grand duchess.

From Florence the party moved to Venice, where they remained until the end of the summer. Tallemant later described their reception by the French ambassador, and the deliberate offence

which Retz gave to a yet more distinguished French resident, the
comte de Laval, by ignoring an invitation to visit him. Tallemant
stated his astonishment at the abbé's disregard for his usual pleasures, observing that if he conducted any amorous liaisons he
employed such discretion that they were unknown to him. In his
own memoirs, however, Retz recalled his pursuit of a noble
Venetian signora, and said that the ambassador had become so
alarmed for his safety as a result of this affair that he hurried him
off to Rome. There Retz was read a lecture on deportment by
another French ambassador, marshal d'Estrées, who spoke in
terms of the only argument that was meaningful to the abbé, his
self-interest. Although he had not made a final decision to seek
preferment in the church, he realised that it would not be to his
advantage if his reputation for gallantry were borne out by his
activities in the holy city. He adopted a modest attire, eschewed
debauchery, and attended learned debates at a Dominican theological college. But he offset this by the extravagant display of
his escort and his successful defiance of the Imperial German
ambassador in a matter of precedence. After three months in
Rome Retz was so short of money that he was obliged to return
to Paris.[12]

Although Retz's journey to Italy was intended to withdraw
him from Richelieu's notice, it led to a contretemps which confirmed the cardinal's disfavour. Richelieu's relations with pope
Urban VIII, Maffeo Barberini, were often near breaking point,
and it followed that Retz, when in Rome, should seek an intro-
duction to the household of the pope's nephew, cardinal Francesco
Barberini. When Retz entered Italy he brought with him a parcel of
books, including the sentence pronounced by the Academy against
Le Cid. The books were sent by Retz's friend, the poet Chapelain,
to the erudite sceptic Jean-Jacques Bouchard, who was Francesco
Barberini's secretary. Retz despatched the parcel from Venice and
when he reached Rome he checked their receipt by Bouchard.
This was probably the occasion when Retz discovered Agostino
Mascardi's history of the coup d'état attempted in 1547 by the
Fieschi against the ruling Genoese dynasty of Doria. Mascardi was
highly esteemed as an historian, and in 1636 Mazarin, who was
then the papal nuncio in Paris, imported copies of another of his
works to sell on the local market.[13] Bouchard had made a French

translation of Mascardi's book on the Fieschi plot. Although the enmity of the Barberini for Richelieu made him cautious, Bouchard had heard that Richelieu was interested in the work, and as early as 1636 had begun to make tentative enquiries as to whether the great cardinal would accept its dedication. The suggestion was understandable. Mascardi's book, which first appeared in 1629, depicted the affair as a violent and irresponsible plot against a prosperous and stable government. Adopting the style of Fontenay-Saint-Geneviève, Bouchard eventually published his manuscript in 1639, with a dedication asserting that Richelieu had commissioned it. In the same year Retz completed a very different version of his own.[14]

Gianluigi de' Fieschi, count of Lavagna, had devised a wild and bloodthirsty scheme to destroy Andrea Doria and his adopted son, Jannetin, only to die ignominiously at the very moment when the coup seemed likely to achieve his aims. His younger brother, Scipio de' Fieschi, who had escaped to France after the conspiracy, had been an associate of Retz's grandfather, the marshal. Scipio had established himself at the court of Henry II with his wife, the daughter of Roberto Strozzi and Madeleine de Médicis. He had become chevalier d'honneur to Catherine de Médicis, and the interests of the Gondi, the Strozzi and the Fieschi had advanced in common under her protection. The comte de Fiesque, who was Retz's fellow conspirator in the Fronde, was descended from the chevalier. However, Retz was not interested in the family connection. While he used the facts presented by Mascardi's version of the plot, he substituted his own conclusions for those of the historian he plagiarised. He represented the Doria as tyrants and Fieschi as seeking glory in a noble cause. His indictment of the Doria régime was a thinly-disguised attack upon Richelieu, and a justification of those who conspired against him. When Retz put into the mouth of one of the conspirators the accusation that Doria had 'crushed the heart of all the nobilty of Genoa by instilling a shameful fear or engaging them through servile self-interest', he was expressing the resentment felt by the French nobility against Richelieu.

In his memoirs Retz claimed he had composed his history when he was eighteen, that is to say, within a year of the presentation of his bachelor's thesis in July 1631.[15] His memory, prompted perhaps by the desire to impress the reader with his precociousness, betrayed him. The book was not published for many years, and, when it was, its text had been substantially altered. In 1639 Retz was fully aware of the danger of allowing his manuscript to circulate, but he showed it to the poet, Chapelain, and passed it to Pierre de Lozières, a companion in his pleasures. Lozières lent it to another friend, the poet François de Boisrobert, who enjoyed the favour of Richelieu. The ready wit of Boisrobert, abbé de Châtillon-sur-Seine, was constantly involving him in scrapes at court, but his capacity to flatter the great enabled him to emerge unscathed from one predicament after another. It was he who produced a burlesque version of Corneille's *Le Cid*, when the play aroused Richelieu's jealousy and anger.[16] Boisrobert saw an opportunity to gain further credit for himself with Retz's version of the Fieschi conspiracy, and promptly showed it to the cardinal. Richelieu denounced the work of two friends of Philippe-Emmanuel de Gondi, remarking: 'Here is a dangerous mind at work!' One of them, Henri de Senneterre, a minister in Richelieu's government, called on père de Gondi the same evening to warn him of the cardinal's view of his son. But Retz, if his memoirs are to be believed, was not in the least put out. He continued to play some part in the personal feud which his mistress, madame de Guémenée, was conducting against the first minister.

Retz's *Conspiracy of Fieschi* deserved its reputation as the catechism of a revolutionary. It also showed how the heroic ideal dominated his early attitudes. Not only did Retz ascribe to Fieschi all the attributes of *le généreux* but he identified himself with his hero. Fieschi was twenty-two. He sprang from a noble and wealthy family. He was 'endowed with one of the finest and most elevated minds in the world, ambitious, bold and enterprising'. He had a 'passionate love for glory', and the tyranny of his enemies prevented him from following his natural inclination. Disinterested, high-minded and a man of action, Fieschi was given all the virtues which Retz admired.

The story was one which lent itself to the display of Retz's literary talents. The manner in which Fieschi was persuaded to lead the plot, the thrill of intrigue, the physical perils of the actual coup and its ironic dénouement, contained all the elements for a dramatic presentation. Retz's characterisation revealed the particular influence of Plutarch. The closest classical model was Sallust's history of Catiline's conspiracy, and there was a curious parallel between the irregular political and private lives of both authors. Retz, like Saint-Evremond, who was later to be fascinated by Catiline, knew his Sallust intimately. He did not imitate the dry terseness of Sallust's style, but he used the same dramatic effects, and he drew an analogy between Fieschi's role and Catiline's.

In justifying Fieschi Retz generalised about the nature of tyranny: 'It was the extraordinary elevation of the house of Doria that provoked this great movement. It gives a memorable example for all states that they should never suffer a person so eminent in their government that his authority provokes the desire to destroy him and provides the pretext for undertaking his destruction.' The personalities and policies of the Doria aggravated the process. Retz endowed Jannetin Doria with the obverse aspects of Fieschi's qualities. He was 'vain, high-handed and insolent', and his jealousy and self-interest led him to suppress all rival talent. Andrea Doria, the admiral, had shown his duplicity in abandoning his alliance with the French and in reshaping the Genoese constitution to perpetuate his family's monopoly of power. There was a general discontent at the shift of authority from popular to aristocratic control, and a particular resentment within the nobility against the tyranny of the Doria.

Mascardi had presented a completely antithetical interpretation. Fieschi was moved by a base self-interest. He had been corrupted by reading the lives of Nero and Catiline, and by the study of Machiavelli's *Prince*: 'From the reading of these books little by little his mind became obsessed with cruelty, perfidy and the love of his own interest, above every consideration of accepted law, whether human or divine'. The benevolent rule of the Doria in Genoa had allowed the nobility to live in an honest repose. The insolence of Jannetin's behaviour had, it was true, antagonised a section of the nobles, but this did not excuse the dissimulation of Gianluigi Fieschi in cultivating his friendship to allay suspicion while secretly planning his murder. The plot rested upon nothing but selfish ambitions, and, had it succeeded, anarchy would have been its consequence.[17]

In his anxiety to represent Fieschi as the master of his own destiny, Retz entirely omitted the passages in which Mascardi had described the bad influence exerted upon him by his mother, Maria della Rovere. He did not omit Fieschi's pretence of friendship for the younger Doria and respect for the admiral, but he condensed Mascardi's account of this aspect and minimised its conclusion. Where Mascardi had put into the mouth of Fieschi a brief mention that Jannetin was planning his murder, Retz denied that Fieschi had invented the story in self-justification, and expanded the account of the instructions for Fieschi's murder. He insisted that the conspirator was moved by a sense of honour and a generous ambition, ridiculing claims that he loved fortune more than glory. Where Mascardi had had Fieschi conclude an oration with a threat to the lives of those of his associates who would not follow him, Retz ended the speech with the words: 'Let us conserve the liberty of our country and make it known today throughout all the land that there are still good men in this republic who know how to deal with tyrants.' He mentioned briefly the killing of Jannetin in the course of the rising, but left out the details where Mascardi had praised his honour and courage. Mascardi had implied that the conspirators had met their deserts when, after the drowning of Fieschi, the coup had failed and the plotters had been executed or banished. Retz, on the other hand, stressed the cruelty of Andrea Doria and the pusillanimity of the Genoese senate in his description of the way in which Doria, returning after the coup, had insisted upon the breaking of the amnesty granted by the senate to Fieschi's accomplices.

While Retz was describing the pattern of the revolutionary hero in the *Conspiracy of Fieschi,* he was himself involved in a plot to destroy Richelieu. His life of gallantry necessarily entailed a simultaneous apprenticeship in political intrigue. Conspiracy went hand in hand with the duels and love affairs he conducted. In this respect the *romans* of the time were not far removed from reality. After all, it was not surprising that the intrigues of love should interlace with schemes for assassination and revolt when ladies such as madame de Chevreuse and madame du Fargis were at the centre of the web. The threads of their plots extended through Richelieu's régime from its earliest years. Retz learnt much from them both. The first became his partner in the Fronde: the second was his aunt.

Retz's aunt, Madeleine de Silly, had had two scandals to her name when she was still single and was sent in disgrace to the seclusion of the Gondi home at Montmirail, where Retz, as a small child, presumably met his wicked aunt. The pious company of the general of the galleys and his wife soon bored her. For purposes of expediency rather than conviction she decided to take the veil. She inveigled her way back to Paris by transferring to the Carmelite order, and played her part so well that she won the approval of cardinal Bérulle, the director of the Carmelites. All the nuns affirmed that she was a saint, but they soon had cause to revise their opinion. When her father died, Madeleine de Silly inherited sufficient property to enable her to leave the order and marry Charles d'Angennes, comte du Fargis. In 1620 she accompanied him to Spain when he was appointed ambassador. After her return in 1624 she was appointed a lady of honour to the queen, and resumed her old scandalous way of life, renewing an earlier liaison with the comte de Cramail.

These were the years when the archpriestess of intriguers, madame de Chevreuse, used her position as confidante of the queen to begin her varied conspiracies to topple Richelieu from power. She was the elder sister of the prince de Guémenée, whose wife became Retz's mistress. The cardinal's most influential enemies were the king's mother, Marie de Médicis, his queen, Anne of Austria, and his brother, Gaston duc d'Orléans, and it was Richelieu's constant purpose to divide their interests. Madame de Chevreuse sought their combination, and played a leading role in one plot after another. In 1626 she used her gallant but hare-brained lover, the comte de Chalais, as the front-man in a conspiracy to enable Gaston to evade a distasteful marriage by the overthrow of the cardinal. Gaston hastily inculpated his accomplices when the facts were discovered. Chalais paid for his devotion with his life, while madame de Chevreuse retired to exile in Lorraine. There she attracted the admiration of its ruler, duke Charles IV, and encouraged him to launch an alliance with England and Savoy against Richelieu. Meanwhile madame du Fargis slipped into her shoes at the French court.

Although Anne of Austria was a Spanish Hapsburg, and deeply resented Richelieu's Protestant alliances and anti-Spanish policies, she had kept aloof from the political intrigues of the queen mother and her younger son. The cardinal hoped to use madame du Fargis to isolate Anne of Austria from Marie de Médicis, but in fact she achieved a rapprochement between the two queens. She became the close ally of both Marie de Médicis and Marillac, the keeper of the seals and critic of Richelieu's warlike policy. Like madame de Chevreuse, she dragged her lovers in her wake, notably Cramail and the king's valet, Béringhen. Early in November 1630 madame du Fargis held secret conferences with the queen mother and Marillac at her former Carmelite convent in the rue Saint-Jacques.[18] As a result of these meetings Marie de Médicis denounced Richelieu to his royal master, and for a time the three confederates appeared to have triumphed. But, after this 'Day of Dupes', Louis XIII recalled Richelieu and arrested both the keeper of the seals and his brother, marshal Marillac, who commanded the French armies in Italy. Marie de Médicis managed to protect madame du Fargis while the latter prepared a new network of conspiracy round the queen mother's doctor, François Vautier.[19] This, too, was discovered, and madame du Fargis escaped to Lorraine. In November 1631 she was tried *in absentia* and condemned to death. Béringhen was exiled, while the punishment of Cramail, for whom Richelieu had a high regard, took the form of a stay in the Bastille and the publication of his love letters to madame du Fargis.[20] Both the queen mother and Gaston eventually fled to the Low Countries, where madame du Fargis joined their émigré court at Brussels. For a time Richelieu's enemies reposed their hopes in the revolt of the duc de Montmorency in Languedoc, but Montmorency was defeated and executed at Castelnaudary in September 1632.

Madame de Chevreuse was behind the next conspiracy, which resulted in the arrest of her agent, the marquis de Châteauneuf in February 1633. Châteauneuf, who was later to play an important role in the manoeuvres of the Fronde, had been appointed by Richelieu to succeed Marillac as keeper of the seals. His correspondence with the duchesse de Chevreuse, which was seized at the time of his arrest, revealed that he had been inspired to hope for yet higher office by plotting against his benefactor. Despite the continuation of her activities, madame de Chevreuse was allowed to remain at Tours. Although Gaston was forgiven and returned to France in 1634, madame du Fargis remained at Brussels and

acted as a link between Anne of Austria, Charles of Lorraine and
the Spanish. From 1635 France was openly at war with Spain, but
this did not prevent further plotting on the part of Gaston and
private negotiation with the enemy on the part of the comte de
Soissons, prince of the Blood and commander of a French army
on the Netherlands frontier.

In August 1637 the apartments of Anne of Austria were
searched, and her agent, La Porte, arrested. She was interrogated
by Châteauneuf's successor, Pierre Séguier, and finally induced
to confess to Richelieu. Some thirty letters were discovered between madame du Fargis and the queen, together with another
half dozen in Spanish which madame du Fargis had passed between Anne of Austria and the marquis de Mirabel, formerly the
Spanish ambassador in Paris and now in Brussels.[21] Madame de
Chevreuse was implicated too, and in September she rode from
Tours to Poitou in disguise to seek the help of the gallant La
Rochefoucauld.[22] He was then an inveterate supporter of chival-
rous causes, and his indignation at the queen's position had led
him to retire from court. He had earlier conceived the extravagant
design of rescuing the queen together with her attendant, mademoiselle d'Hautefort, who, though she was the king's favourite,
had also attracted his own attentions. His recollection of the
enterprise in his memoirs conveys the atmosphere in which the
perils of conspiracy were spiced by affairs of the heart:

> I was at an age when one likes to do colourful and spectacular things,
> and I could find nothing more to this effect than the project of carrying
> off the queen from the king her husband and from the cardinal de
> Richelieu, who was jealous of her, and at the same time removing
> mademoiselle d'Hautefort from the king, who was in love with her.[23]

If he had failed in this plan, he did succeed in arranging the escape
of madame de Chevreuse to Spain, whence she travelled to
England to conspire with Marie de Médicis and other exiles.
Late in 1640 she moved to Flanders to participate in a new plot
headed by Soissons. Madame du Fargis had died in Brussels in
1639.

Retz's wicked aunt had set the fashion, and his own love affairs
were eventually to involve him in the thread of these conspiracies.
He explained in his memoirs how Richelieu held the princesse de

Guémenée responsible for the queen's antipathy towards him. While the princess was involved in one of madame du Fargis's plots to place evidence in the hands of the queen mother with which she could compromise the cardinal, Richelieu was trying to secure certain letters composed by madame de Guémenée, which had been found on the person of the rebellious duc de Montmorency after his capture at the battle of Castelnaudary. Marshal de la Meilleraye, whose wife was also the subject of Retz's passionate attachment, had himself fallen in love with the princess and sought to turn his knowledge of the whereabouts of the letters to mean advantage. Retz found himself identified with madame de Guémenée's interests, incurring the hatred of Richelieu and the anger of the marshal, who was a first cousin of the cardinal. The princess felt obliged to retire to the country, and a gap in the memoirs prevents our knowing Retz's account of the sequel.

Before long Retz entered deeper waters. The comte du Fargis had returned to France when Gaston was granted an amnesty in 1634, but after a few months Richelieu found it safer to seclude him in the Bastille. However, his son enjoyed his liberty as a member of Gaston's retinue. Charles d'Angennes du Fargis, marquis de la Boissière, and known to Retz as La Rochepot in view of his mother's inheritance, was the same age as his cousin, the abbé. At his death in battle in 1640 he was to leave Retz all his possessions, including the seigneurie of Commercy. In the summer and autumn of 1636 La Rochepot associated Retz with a group of professional conspirators. Two of these, the comte de Montrésor and his cousin the marquis de Saint-Ibal, were distantly related to Retz through his grandmother, Catherine de Clermont. Another, Charles de Varicarville, also known as Valliquierville, possessed a considerable reputation as a neo-Pythagorean philosopher.[24] La Rochepot, together with the poet Alexandre de Campion and his brother, the memorialist Henri, were members of the entourage of the comte de Soissons, while the others served Gaston d'Orléans. The two groups worked upon Soissons and Gaston to sanction the assassination of Richelieu. Their first plot involved the killing of Richelieu in the Tuileries when he was baptising Gaston's daughter, the 'Grande Mademoiselle', who was to play a celebrated role in the Fronde. Gaston was to signify his approval of the act, and the conspirators, having posted relays along the route, were to retire to Sedan until the king recognised the value of the service they had done him. The plan was frustrated by the illness of the cardinal, and the conspirators temporarily dispersed.

In his memoirs Retz mistakenly dated the Tuileries plot in the early months of 1637, whereas Mademoiselle was baptised there in July of the previous year. The other memorialists of the time provide no corroborative testimony for this affair, but Montrésor and others recalled the details of the next attempt, three months later. This plan required Montrésor and Saint-Ibal to strike down Richelieu when he attended a council of war at Amiens to plan the recapture of Corbie from the Spanish. Gaston and Soissons would have been present, with an escort of five hundred gentlemen, to sanction the killing. Gaston, however, refused to give the signal, and the leaders, fearing treachery, withdrew to places of refuge.[25] Retz's brother, who was on the periphery of the group, fled to Belle-Ile. Richelieu heard of the participation of the Gondi in the plot and exiled père de Gondi.

Retz placed the Amiens plot, in which he was at most a very distant accomplice, before the Tuileries attempt. Though his memory of the events was confused, his recollection of their aftermath was clear enough. Soissons had resigned his command and withdrawn to the security of Sedan, a semi-independent principality in the possession of a fellow plotter, the duc de Bouillon. Soissons began once more to recruit the support of dissident families, and where necessary he was prepared to offer bribes to win their support. Assuming an air of piety, he wrote to père de Gondi, indicating that he had realised the sin of receiving the revenues from his ecclesiastical benefices, and offering to bestow them on the abbé de Retz. Retz remarked in the memoirs that this suggestion revived his interest in a career in the church. He returned with zest to his studies and restricted his pleasures to his dalliance with madame de Guémenée. He claimed that the assassination would have been 'one of the greatest and most famous events of our century', and called it a 'crime which appeared to me consecrated by great examples and justified and made honourable by great peril'. He made other comments in the memoirs which were the result of his mature attitudes: 'There is quite frequently foolishness in conspiracy, but there is nothing like it as a means to make men wise after the event, at least for a time.' 'It would have overwhelmed us with glory, had it succeeded,' he added. This contrasted with the contemporary attitudes he expressed in the *Conspiracy of Fieschi*, where his enthusiasm was for the heroic enterprise in itself, and success was not a primary criterion. Nor, in his old age, did Retz offer the same unqualified approval for the morality of the plot: 'Ancient Rome would have esteemed it, but it is not for this that I esteem ancient Rome.'

Early in 1638, when Retz was defying Richelieu to win first place among the graduates of the Sorbonne, he renewed his links with the plotters. As he put it, 'a declaration of monsieur le comte drew us from our dens and we awoke to the sound of trumpets'. Soissons was under constant pressure from the Spanish, as well as from Montrésor and Saint-Ibal, to revoke the promise of loyalty he had given the king. In March 1638 his agent in Paris, Alexandre de Campion, brought Retz a letter saying that he was being accused by his friends of weakness and cowardice. Campion asked how he should reply, and Retz wrote across the draft he had prepared: 'As for me, I accuse them of stupidity.' The same day he left on his journey to Italy. The advice was endorsed by Varicarville and apparently the count accepted it, for two years elapsed before the trumpets actually sounded. Late in 1640 Retz was summoned to Sedan and asked for his views upon the disaffection of Paris. Despite his youth he played a considerable part in the deliberations of the plotters. He felt bound to say that Richelieu was hated and Soissons loved in the capital, but he joined Varicarville in urging caution. It was true, he argued, that a prince of the Blood was justified in engaging in civil war when his honour was impugned, but the glory of such an undertaking depended upon its outcome. The cardinal was in ill health in any case, and the occasion did not seem favourable for lighting a fire they might not be able to control. However, the more violent counsels of Bouillon and Saint-Ibal prevailed, and Retz returned to Paris equipped with money and letters to build up a following which might seize vital points in the city when the rising was proclaimed.

While the abbé was at Sedan, monsieur le comte changed his mind five times in two days, and this irresolution caused Retz to reflect in his memoirs on his favourite theme, the qualities needed in a '*chef de parti*'. Soissons, he said, had as much valour as any man, but he lacked audacity of mind:

The first is ordinary, and even vulgar; the second is even rarer than one might think: yet it is even more needed than the other in great enterprises, and is there any enterprise in the world greater than the direction of a faction? By comparison the command of an army offers fewer opportunities, and, while the government of a state offers more, there is far less scope for skill and subtlety. Finally, I am persuaded that more great qualities are needed to form a faction leader [*chef de parti*] than to make an effective ruler of the whole world; and that, in the hierarchy of qualities that make up such a man, resolution marches side by side with judgment – I mean with heroic judgment, whose principal function it is to distinguish the extraordinary from the impossible.

Retz believed that Soissons completely lacked both judgment and resolution. He was too susceptible to unjustified doubts and suspicions, and this was a fatal flaw in a *chef de parti*, who should suppress even legitimate doubts of the success of his enterprise.

But Retz was committed to a considerable part in the conspiracy, regardless of his misgivings about his leader. He decided to form the nucleus of his revolutionary group from the political prisoners in the Bastille. They included the gay old maréchal Bassompierre and the reckless maréchal de Vitry, who, long ago, had assassinated the queen mother's favourite, Concini, in Louis XIII's personal coup d'état. With them was du Coudray-Montpensier and both the husband and the lover of Retz's notorious aunt, the comte du Fargis and the comte de Cramail. La Rochefoucauld, who spent a week in the Bastille following Richelieu's suspicions about his role in the escape of madame de Chevreuse, mentioned these inmates among others in his memoirs and said that there were 'an infinite number of people of all ranks and sexes, miserable and tormented by their long and cruel imprisonment. The sight of so many pitiable objects increased the hatred I already possessed for the administration of the cardinal de Richelieu.'[26] But La Rochefoucauld was exaggerating. They were quite a convivial group, although, as might be expected, not without tensions. Anne of Austria's servant, La Porte, and Marie de Médicis' doctor, Vautier, were also confined there, and La Porte remarked how Vautier spent his time alternately studying astronomy and wandering along the battlements echoing the words of David: 'How long, O Lord, how long?' Vautier, it seems, also

annoyed Bassompierre, for the latter recorded in his journal that
his personal habits were unpleasant and that he conspired with the
servants against him.

The life of the prisoners was remarkably free and easy. They
were allowed visitors, and Retz assumed that he might, as a
relative, visit du Fargis without arousing suspicion. Retz preferred, however, to make his initial approach to the elderly
Cramail, for whose judgment and discretion he had the greatest
respect. Cramail was descended from the celebrated general of the
Italian and civil wars, Blaise de Montluc, but his own interests
were intellectual and literary. He was the author of several light
comedies, and he had been daring enough to appoint as tutor to
one of his nephews the free-thinking Italian philosopher, Vanini,
who was subsequently burnt for his radical opinions. He was also
an experienced conspirator and he had good reason to hate Richelieu – not only because of his involvement with madame du Fargis
but also because the cardinal had mocked one of his books. Retz
secretly agreed with Richelieu about the quality of Cramail's
writing, but he knew he had selected the right man for his purpose.
Cramail successfully won over his fellow prisoners and drafted a
plan of action.

At Cramail's suggestion Retz began to recruit certain officers of
the Parisian militia, who were also legal officials and bore a grudge
against Richelieu's high-handed attitude to their profession. He
devised a means of distributing the large sum of money provided
by Soissons among the lower classes. He informed his pious aunt,
madame de Maignelais, that a dying friend had passed it to him
with a request that it be given to the non-mendicant poor. As he
did not know how to begin such a task, and he knew his aunt's
reputation for almsgiving, he wondered if she would assume the
responsibility. Madame de Maignelais was delighted. She insisted
that her nephew accompany her through the poorer quarters of
the city to seek out the worthiest recipients, and she made it clear
to them that they owed their gratitude to the abbé de Retz. Retz
recounted this trick in his memoirs with boyish exuberance. He
also added some thoughts on the technique of exciting the support
of the masses. He believed that those who were most useful in
popular disturbances were neither the substantial bourgeois, who
sided with authority from fear of pillage, nor the beggars and the

unemployed, who could not be relied on, but rather the poorer artisans and labourers, 'who are sufficiently troubled in their private affairs to desire alterations in public affairs'. This was a policy he was to employ in the Fronde. He had no thought for the welfare of the common people and considered them simply as an instrument in his 'glorious' enterprise. The hypocrisy of his alms-giving was extended by the pretence of piety, by which he hoped to increase his popular reputation. He began to attend the Tuesday meetings of Vincent de Paul's Congregation of the Mission at Saint-Lazare, founded under the protection of Retz's parents.

While the affairs of the conspirators prospered in Paris, uncertainties again emerged at Sedan. Varicarville warned Retz that Soissons was considering new offers of reconciliation. Retz attended four days of debate at Bouillon's stronghold, and when the issue was once more resolved in favour of the rising he was careful not to reveal the irresolution of the leader to his accomplices in Paris. He made a final trip to Sedan when all was ready, and on his way back to the capital inspected a Spanish mercenary contingent which was to cooperate with Soissons. Vitry drew up the orders of the day. To Retz's astonishment his fellow conspirators were confident of winning the support of the garrison of their prison. The Bastille and the Arsenal were to be seized, and the leaders were to march through the streets with drums beating to the call of '*Vive le Roi and Monsieur le Comte*'. Retz was to lead two companies of suborned militia to hold the Pont Neuf and assist Vitry in an attack on the Palais de Justice. But the conspirators were cautious enough to delay the execution of their plan until they had news of the success of Soissons. In the second week of July 1641 they heard that Soissons had defeated the royal army at Marfée near Sedan, but had himself perished in the engagement. The accidental and the unforeseen had again frustrated all Retz's hopes. Fieschi's enterprise had been ruined when at the moment of success he had slipped on a gang-plank and drowned in the mud. Soissons' undertaking ended in farce, when, as his troops were winning the day, he carelessly opened his visor with the muzzle of his pistol, and blew out his brains. Retz was to call him 'the last of the heroes'.[27]

The conspirators in Paris went to ground and, fortunately for Retz, no word of their plot leaked out to Richelieu's spies. This

was not the last of the intrigues against the cardinal. Shortly before
his death in December 1642, a conspiracy by the king's young
favourite, Cinq-Mars, was unmasked. Varricarville, Montrésor and
another plotter with whom Retz was later to be associated, the
vicomte de Fontrailles, fled to England. But Retz had no part in
this affair. For the moment at least he had resolved to reconcile
himself to the career his father intended for him in the church.

FOUR

The coadjutor

Individual identity is threatened on the one hand by conformity to external patterns, and on the other by discontinuity of personal experience. The ability to choose and to act as an individual is limited by the problem of reconciling discordant decisions within the framework of coherent personality. Retz's early life displayed a singular ambivalence. He could accept the archetypal images of the *honnête homme* and the *généreux* because, within the ethos of his class, these ideals demanded self-affirmation. He respected the prestige of his family, but he was sensitive to the disparity of attitude between one Gondi generation and the next. His grandfather had acquired worldly glory by the unvarying pursuit of self-interest. His father had been torn between the obligation to continue the marshal's tradition and the desire to turn away from the world and conform to the moral values of the church. Retz, in his turn, was expected by his father to enter the church, while his temperament and worldly ambition inclined him to the path of his grandfather. Hence, on the one hand, he had lived the life of libertine, duellist and conspirator, and, on the other, he had conscientiously pursued his theological studies. His attitude to life could be called existentialist in that he acted upon impulse and gave free rein to his passions, seeking to affirm himself in action. But the indulgence of his appetites did not solve the problem of his career. When rational decision could no longer be postponed, he resolved to effect a compromise. As he grew to maturity he recognised the contradictory promptings of his rational mind and his senses. He contrived to train the one and indulge the other. He decided outwardly to accept the moral disciplines which in his bachelor's thesis he had so boldly labelled 'prudence'. He sought to achieve worldly *gloire* by a career in the church, while inwardly rejecting the spiritual values it professed. Thus he made the choice which redefined the canons of hypocrisy.

When Retz later rationalised his conduct in his memoirs he habitually tried to show that his early attempts to choose his own path had been frustrated by some fortuitous event and not by his own lack of will or foresight. His scheme to elope with Marguerite de Gondi had been ruined by a chance regard in a mirror. His role as conspirator had failed through the unexpected illness of Richelieu or the accidental death of Soissons. At the same time he had to struggle to preserve his freedom of action against the combination of circumstances that drove him in a particular direction. But there were times when he confessed his own weakness. In his account of his part in the last conspiracy of Soissons he wrote:

I hated my profession in the church more than ever: I had been thrown into it at first by the obstinacy of those near to me; destiny had held me there by all the chains of pleasure and duty. I felt myself tied in a situation whence I could no longer see a clear way of escape. Twenty-five [actually twenty-six] years of my life had passed and it was easy to believe that I was too old to start carrying a musket; and what troubled me even more was the thought that there had been moments when, by attaching myself too strongly to my pleasures, I had myself tightened the chains by which fortune seemingly wanted to bind me, despite myself, to the church.

At the death of Soissons, Retz admitted, 'The archbishopric of Paris began to flatter my ambition.' Everything seemed to conspire to persuade him to accept his fate. Madame de Guémenée had finally heeded the exhortations of Arnauld d'Andilly and had left the Place Royale for Port-Royal, while at the Arsenal the maréchale de la Meilleraye had succumbed to her captain of guards. 'If God had taken the Place Royale from me [Retz wrote], the devil had refused to leave me the Arsenal. . . . That is the kind of thing that makes one become a saint.'

Retz did not try to become a saint but he endeavoured to regularise his life in order to cultivate the respect of the clergy, particularly those canons and curés of the diocese whose good opinions might be useful to him. He did not pretend the extreme piety of the *dévots*, but he esteemed them, he said, because piety meant something to them which he himself felt unable to counterfeit. He continued his studies at the Sorbonne, where he was to graduate as a doctor of theology in October 1643. He gathered round him writers and poets such as Ménage, Chapelain, Sarasin and Scarron, some of whom were later to be permanently attached to his retinue. He pretended that these were all men of learning and piety, that his dwelling had become 'something very close to an academy', but in fact these were often his drinking companions, whose libertine conversation he enjoyed. He could not live without gallantry, so he decided he would pay his attentions to madame de Pommereuil alone. He described her as young and coquettish in a way that suited him, and her popularity allowed him to hide his own liaison under the others which she conducted. Although he did not, perhaps, regulate his irregularities as well as he thought, he felt he was making an impression upon the *dévots*, and recalled that they echoed at this time the opinion that monsieur Vincent had given of him – that he was lacking somewhat in piety but that he was not too far estranged from the kingdom of God.

An opportunity soon arose for Retz to improve upon his new reputation. He frequented the salon of a cousin of Tallemant des Réaux, a Huguenot widow named Marie d'Harambure, whose combination of intellectual pretension and moral prudery made Retz apply to her the epithet *précieuse*. There he engaged in a series of debates with a minister from the Protestant temple at Charenton, Jean Mestrezat. Retz claimed in his memoirs that the maréchal de la Force and the Huguenot vicomte de Turenne, brother to the duc de Bouillon, added *éclat* to these gatherings – although other sources suggest that neither was in Paris at this time.[1] The abbé's eloquence, according to his own account, was such that he converted a Protestant onlooker from Poitou, while Turenne, on hearing a courteous exchange on the nature of the authority of the pope, reputedly said that nothing should prevent Retz from becoming a cardinal. Retz also impressed the duchesse de Vendôme, the wife of Henry IV's illegitimate son, César de Vendôme, whose opposition to Richelieu might have cost him his head were it not for his royal blood and the irresolution which limited his effectiveness as a conspirator. Madame de Vendôme took a motherly interest in the abbé, and from this came two important events in his life – an affair with her daughter and the protection of her spiritual director, the bishop of Lisieux. Philippe Cospeau, the septuagenarian bishop, believed that Retz was seriously preparing himself for the church and coached him in the art of preaching, by which he had himself become celebrated. 'His

disinterestedness', Retz wrote, 'was beyond that of the Anchor-
ites.' Moreover, his reputation for holiness and his ignorance of
political motives made him generally respected at court, particularly with Richelieu, whom he had once instructed in theology.
Three times a week Retz visited the bishop, with whom he discussed the epistles of Saint Paul and the possibility of converting
Turenne.

The bishop of Lisieux lived in the hôtel de Vendôme and while
Retz was receiving professional guidance from him he was also
pursuing mademoiselle de Vendôme. Retz remarked that he did
not regard her as a great beauty and that he found her far from
intelligent, although 'her stupidity had not developed very far
at that time'. She was of serious disposition, with an appealing
languor in her movements, and she concealed her faults by a not-
unbecoming air of hauteur. Unfortunately Retz had a rival in the
comte de Brion, who in order that he might accompany Turenne
to the hôtel de Vendôme had persuaded him to pretend an interest
in the bishop's religious discourse. Brion was himself extremely
pious, and had twice entered the Capuchin order, only to withdraw again. Retz contemptuously called his conduct 'a perpetual
salmagundi of devotion and sin'. The meetings, ostensibly to
convert Turenne, usually ended in walks round the garden while
the good-natured old bishop remained blind to the tensions and
motives among his pupils. Once it was suggested that they should
go in a party to the house of Retz's uncle, the archbishop, at
Saint-Cloud, where the bishop hoped to see a performance by his
favourite playwright, Corneille. The players arrived late, and
afterwards the younger people amused themselves with music and
dancing until dawn, when they all entered their carriage to return
to Paris. On the way they encountered some strange and diabolic
shapes moving through the mist. Turenne and Retz boldly went
to investigate, whereas Brion was as paralysed with fear as were the
ladies, and could do no more than fall upon his knees. The phantoms turned out to be a group of monks, but mademoiselle de
Vendôme was so disgusted with Brion, and so delighted with
Retz's conduct, that the abbé henceforth enjoyed her affections.
Retz made some humorous play with his puzzlement at the
general consternation (caused by his short-sightedness) but in
relating the anecdote he clearly wanted his reader to appreciate

his own courage. After this incident he went often to visit the bishop and read Saint Paul. The affair lasted until the marriage of mademoiselle de Vendôme with the gallant duc de Nemours about a year later, when Retz returned to her the portrait, the letters and the lock of hair she had given him.

It is clear that, if the abbé was determined to follow his profession, he had merely modified his old habits, and his worldly inclinations were as strong as ever. The scorn with which he regarded his ineffective and dissolute uncle, and the disrepute into which the see of Paris had fallen under the government of Jean-François de Gondi as archbishop, contributed to Retz's doubt about the wisdom of a final commitment. It may be, as he said, that he brought himself in 1641 to regard the archbishop's chair as a means of fulfilling some of his ambition, and that he set himself to win as much support for this aim as he could: yet he was not prepared to take holy orders until he could be sure of the succession. There had been some talk of nominating père de Gondi in 1637, but Retz's father, having accepted Richelieu's command to resign the naval post for which neither temperament nor inclination had fitted him, was determined to force Richelieu to agree to his son's elevation in the church.

The cardinal was no more likely to sanction the promotion of the abbé de Retz than he was to hand back the conquests of his generals to the Spanish. His aversion to the Gondi family was strengthened by their adherence to the pro-Spanish party of the *dévots* and their suspected implication in the plots against his régime. He had already made known his personal opinion of the abbé as a result of reading his *Conspiracy of Fieschi*. The acclaim which Retz received in the pulpits of Paris for the oratorical skill he had acquired from the bishop of Lisieux did nothing to modify Richelieu's attitude. Moreover, he had no need of political reasons to refuse the importuning of Philippe-Emmanuel and his friends. Retz's wayward moral conduct was already notorious, and it was difficult for the good bishop of Lisieux to prove that his protégé had reformed. In his memoirs Retz provided other reasons for Richelieu's obduracy. He had made a *mot* about the cardinal's faults being merely the cause or the effect of his good qualities, and the story was soon repeated. Further, he had made a special journey to visit président Barillon, who was imprisoned for

c

encouraging the constitutional remonstrances of the parlement, to warn him that he was being falsely accused of implication in a supposed plot led by the duc de Vendôme.[2] Richelieu replied to the pleading of the bishop of Lisieux that the abbé appeared to be the friend of all his enemies.

When the great cardinal died at the end of the year Retz was one of many who felt that a shadow had been lifted from their lives. Yet in later years Retz showed respect, mixed with a trace of envy, for the achievement of the first minister. He wrote that Richelieu had conceived two designs 'as vast as those of the Caesars and Alexanders' – to crush the Huguenots (a project where Retz also attributed the initiative to his uncle, the first cardinal de Retz) and to attack the Spanish and Austrian Hapsburgs. He had 'completed the first, and at his death he had made great progress with the second'. Retz might also have added the third great aim which Richelieu defined in his *Testament Politique*, 'to humble the pride of the great'. It was this that made him the arch enemy of all that Retz stood for, and it was here that he had failed, as Retz himself was to demonstrate.

Since Louis XIII kept Richelieu's ministers in power there was little outward change in the régime, but Retz hoped that the efforts of his friends on his behalf would now be successful. The king was particularly gracious to him, praised his studies and his sermons, and even conversed with him in a tone of raillery. Retz explained in the memoirs that the king had taken a liking to him because of two stories about him: the first that in his youth a valet who acted as his procurer bought a young girl for him whom Retz treated with respect and passed on to his aunt, madame de Maignelais, so that she might enter a convent; the second that Retz had been engaged in an affray with a captain of light-horse who tried to commandeer his mount, and that when the captain had slipped and lost his sword the abbé had refused to take advantage of his opponent. Both these stories were probably apocryphal. Retz had the habit of using his imagination to elaborate some small incident until it became an engaging personal anecdote, and, like many raconteurs, became unable to distinguish fact from fiction after frequent re-telling of the story.

New obstacles arose which negated the king's favour. The archbishop resented the ambition and ability of his nephew. As the abbé expressed it, 'my uncle was extremely small-minded, and in consequence he was both jealous and difficult'. But Retz was already popular among the lower clergy and the pressure of both the chapter and the remainder of the Gondi and their friends obliged the archbishop to withdraw his opposition. Unfortunately the promoters made the mistake of publicising his consent, and three ministers and former protégés of Richelieu (Mazarin, Chavigny and Sublet des Noyers) persuaded the king of the impropriety of the proposal. When the maréchal de Schomberg, son-in-law to madame de Maignelais, formally asked Louis XIII to recommend the appointment of the abbé as coadjutor-bishop of Paris, he was told that the abbé was too young for such responsibility. Des Noyers then intrigued to exclude him altogether from the succession to the archbishopric. Retz remarked that des Noyers was not merely a *dévot* but also a secret Jesuit, and that he designed to exchange his secretaryship of state for the archbishop's chair. Des Noyers had indeed attempted to enter the Jesuit order. He had built the Jesuits a chapel and he expressed the wish to be buried within it. He used the king's Jesuit confessor to persuade Louis XIII to offer Retz the diocese of Agde in Languedoc. The abbé was now in difficulties. It was not easy to refuse the mitre, yet his devotion, as he put it, 'did not carry me as far as Languedoc'. Using the reason for the previous refusal, he told the king that he was too young to do without experienced advice, and in Agde he would be too isolated. The explanation was accepted with good grace. Des Noyers lost his place to Chavigny when he foolishly suggested to the king that he should nominate Anne of Austria to act as regent after his death. Louis was always mindful of Richelieu's warnings against the queen, and he preferred the idea of a regency council containing cardinal Mazarin, chancellor Séguier, Chavigny and others. Nevertheless, when he died in May 1643 the parlement gladly overthrew his arrangements and gave Anne of Austria supreme authority during the minority of her five-year-old son, Louis XIV. All Richelieu's enemies flocked to court, and new prospects of advancement were opened to Retz.

Five days after the death of the king, the young duc d'Enghien crushed the Spanish infantry at the battle of Rocroi. The victory marked the advance of the objectives defined in Richelieu's lifetime, and there could be no repetition of the early events of the regency of Marie de Médicis, when the queen mother had reversed the anti-Hapsburg policies of Henry IV. But there was some similarity in the way in which those whose support was necessary for the regent exacted favours for themselves in return. 'The felicity of particular individuals [wrote Retz] seemed fully assured by the general public happiness.' The shadow of the tyrant was finally dispelled by the death of his master: 'All exiles were recalled; all the prisoners were set at liberty; all the criminals were exonerated; all those who had lost their offices had them restored; every favour was available; no request was refused.'

It was not quite so simple as Retz pretended. Several contenders for power were waiting in the wings. Gaston thought for a moment of asserting a claim to the regency, but accepted the office of lieutenant-general of the kingdom instead, just as Henry IV's father had done at the institution of Catherine de Médicis before the wars of religion. The timid prince de Condé, the cousin of the late Soissons and the father of Enghien, became chief of the council. La Rochefoucauld had procured Enghien's support for the queen, and he also persuaded her to recall her former confidante, the notorious but unchanging madame de Chevreuse. Anne of Austria had hesitated about this decision, for she remained committed to some of Richelieu's policies, and, in particular, she favoured the man he had recommended to Louis XIII, cardinal Mazarin. Madame de Chevreuse and others, such as Beaufort, the son of the duc de Vendôme, were by no means satisfied with either the direction of the government or their own share of the spoils. It seemed inexplicable to them that the man who had nourished the king's distrust of the queen in the immediate aftermath of the great cardinal's death should be appointed by Anne of Austria to succeed him. But it was to Mazarin's advantage that he had no faction or following on which to rely. He brought all the charms of his brilliant mind to bear upon the queen's mediocre intelligence, and it may be that she accepted the assurances of the English envoy, Lord Montagu, that Mazarin had in reality opposed his predecessor. Mazarin did not, however, appear to have any permanent claim to office. The queen considered the bishop of Beauvais, whom Retz described as 'a mitred fool', and even approached père de Gondi, who refused to quit his cloister.

Madame de Maignelais, the bishop of Lisieux and Vincent de

Paul besieged the regent to grant Retz the coadjutorship: yet the
queen demurred until Retz's father could be induced to visit the
court and personally beg the favour. He came at last, and the royal
request on the abbé's behalf was sent to Rome a month after the
death of the king. Retz hurriedly explored his credit with his
friends in order to pay for the canonical bulls, and eventually
managed to borrow 16,000 crowns from Lozières, the man who
had so carelessly lent the manuscript of the *Conspiracy of Fieschi* to
Boisrobert. The bulls were slow to arrive and Retz wrote anxiously
to cardinal Barberini in Rome, who had given him hospitality
during his visit in 1638.[3] The papal authorisation reached Paris
at the end of October 1643, and on All Saints' Day the coadjutor-
elect preached a triumphant sermon to the court in the church of
Saint-Jean-en-Grève. It was a theatrical appearance and he chose
theatrical imagery to describe his elevation in his memoirs:

> It seems to me that up to this point in my life I had been down in
> the pit, right in the middle of the orchestra, playing without serious
> purpose among the violins: I am now to mount upon the stage where
> you will see me perform in scenes which may not be worthy of you,
> but which are a little less unworthy of your attention than that which
> has gone before.

Before his ordination Retz went into retreat for six days at
Saint-Lazare. He thought less about the meaning of his religion
than he did of how it could serve his ambition. 'The great secret
of those who take up an office [he was to write] is at the beginning
to seize the imagination of men by some act which touches the
intimacy of their own lives.' He reflected again upon the debase-
ment of the diocese under his uncle's jurisdiction. It was not so
much the immorality of the archbishop's private life that he condemned as the scandalous dereliction of his formal religious duties.
He himself could accept neither the mysterious power nor the
simple charity of the Christian message, but he did not ignore their
existence for others. He could not deny himself the indulgence of
his senses, and yet he knew that to mix sin with piety invited
ridicule. He resolved, then, to separate his religious role from his
private life more thoroughly than he had ever done before. He
would continue his amorous liaison with madame de Pommereuil. At the same time he would meticulously perform his

duties in a church in which he held no personal commitment. He could thus succeed in his profession and use his success for worldly purposes. He would save the souls of others while condemning his own to perdition. This was the frame of mind in which he decided 'to do evil by design, which is without comparison the most criminal thing before God, but which is doubtless the wisest thing in the eyes of the world. ... It was in this holy disposition that I left Saint-Lazare.'

While Retz was awaiting his canonical bulls, the unnatural harmony between the various interests at the regent's court disintegrated. Anne of Austria had seemed to many an unloved, lonely, persecuted figure, but, as her new coadjutor-bishop shrewdly observed, 'she was adored much more for her disgraces than she was for her merit'. She had yet to show capacity to govern, and her popularity began to wane soon after the initial distribution of favours and rewards. The principal agent of discontent was madame de Chevreuse, abetted by her henchman Châteauneuf, the former keeper of the seals, and the impetuous duc de Beaufort. Retz said of his future collaborator in the Fronde that 'his fund of common sense was considerably less than average', and La Rochefoucauld remarked that 'he possessed a certain boldness and style, but his actions were contrived and lacked sincerity: his mind was ponderous and uncouth'.[4] Vain, handsome, and fond of posturing, Beaufort imprudently intervened in a quarrel between two great ladies of the court, madame de Montbazon and madame de Longueville. The former was the second wife of Hercule de Rohan and thus the stepmother of madame de Chevreuse, though considerably younger than she. Her robust attractions had drawn many lovers, including the abbé de Rancé, who was later to reform the Trappist monks, and the comte de Soissons, who had abandoned her when he found his intermediary, the chevalier de Senneterre, had exceeded his instructions.[5] Madame de Motteville, the queen's servant and companion, remarked the extravagance of her dress and described her on one occasion as covered with pearls and a large scarlet feather; but she was obliged to confess that even when madame de Montbazon had passed the age of forty she remained one of the great beauties of the court.[6] Retz wrote of her that he 'had never seen anyone who preserved in vice so little respect for virtue' – a remark that recalls La

Rochefoucauld's maxim: 'Hypocrisy is a homage which vice renders to virtue.' Although she was currently pursued by Beaufort, she had for long been the mistress of the duc de Longueville. Longueville had left her to marry Anne-Geneviève de Bourbon, daughter of the prince de Condé. Added to the jealous resentment felt by madame de Montbazon for her successful rival was the spite of Beaufort, whom madame de Longueville had earlier rejected. In her own way madame de Longueville was quite as attractive as her opponent, and if she lacked the latter's venom she far exceeded her in intelligence, finding a deserved place among the wits of the hôtel de Rambouillet. La Rochefoucauld had not yet fallen in love with her blue eyes, for which he was to declare himself ready to rebel not merely against kings but against the gods themselves.

Madame de Montbazon managed to procure two compromising letters which she claimed had passed between her rival and the comte de Coligny. The house of Condé demanded that madame de Montbazon's gossip be silenced, and the queen called for a retraction. According to her lady of honour, madame de Motteville, she sat up all night with Mazarin, the princesse de Condé and madame de Chevreuse drafting a suitable formula. But madame de Montbazon, stumbling over the words of the retraction pinned to the back of her fan, convinced no one, and further manifested her defiance by appearing at a function which the queen had forbidden her to attend.[7] Orders were then issued to expel her from the court, and Beaufort immediately rushed to her defence.

By openly declaring against madame de Longueville, Beaufort chose to defy Condé, and the latter promptly moved into alliance with Gaston. Under the direction of madame de Chevreuse, Beaufort then conspired with his faction, the *Importants*, against the government. The cabal included the comte de Fiesque, the vicomte de Fontrailles, the comte de Beaupuy, a particular friend of the new coadjutor, and many of his associates in the plots of Soissons against Richelieu. Retz said in his memoirs that, although his friends were members of the inner circle of the *Importants*, and although he was invited by Montrésor and Beaupuy to join them, he was sufficiently grateful to the regent for his elevation to refuse to be compromised. He was also very prudent. Beaufort hoped to control the government and, with the sympathy of the *dévots*, to reverse its foreign policy. To achieve this aim it was necessary to eliminate Mazarin. Both Retz and La Rochefoucauld denied in their memoirs that the conspirators went so far as to plan Mazarin's assassination, but such was in fact their intent. Early in September 1643 Beaufort was arrested and imprisoned in the château of Vincennes. His followers fled in terror, while madame de Chevreuse was sent for a second term of exile to Tours.

The memoirs of the coadjutor described the sobering effect of Beaufort's arrest upon the careless gaiety which had prevailed since the death of Louis XIII; but he dismissed the affair as trivial and Beaufort as a man of straw. Gaston and Condé had also been contemptuous of Beaufort's faction, and it was they who had slightingly labelled the group the *Importants*. Yet the repercussions of the affair were far from trivial, and, while its setting appeared more like a salon intrigue than a coup d'état, the entanglement of political and amorous alliances was at once a re-enaction of the conspiracies of the previous generation and a foretaste of the Fronde. Continuity was certainly provided by madame de Chevreuse, who in 1645 escaped to Saint-Malo and set sail in a small boat. She was picked up by an English vessel under the control of the rebellious Long Parliament and reluctantly given a passport to the Spanish Netherlands. There she renewed her old intrigues until the opportunity came for her to return to Paris in 1649 to participate in the Fronde. In the meantime the defeat of the *Importants* facilitated the triumph of cardinal Mazarin.

Giulio Mazarini had those same subtle qualities of mind that Retz possessed, but he did not share the coadjutor's weaknesses. Where Retz was wayward and excitable, Mazarin was patient and steadfast. Where the one would sacrifice his long-term objectives to win acclaim by a moment of self-dramatisation, the other could be self-effacing and deferential in trivialities so that he might ultimately bend his opponents to his will. Both men were so devious in their policies and so adept at concealing their motives and opinions from their associates that their enemies saw them as the embodiment of that Italianate influence which the French often affected to despise. In this respect the first minister was at a far greater disadvantage than the coadjutor. He was not of so mean an origin as the pamphleteers of the Fronde asserted, but his family had no French connections whatever. He was born in 1602, the son of the chief steward of Filippo Colonna, the grand constable of Spanish Naples. His youth was marked by a propensity for gambling that marred his education at the Jesuit College in Rome and the University of Alcalá in Spain. He became a captain of infantry in the papal army, and transferred to the pontificate's diplomatic service by acting as secretary to cardinal Antonio Barberini, the brother of Urban VIII. In 1630 he negotiated with Richelieu at Lyon, and captivated the cardinal by his judgment and his charm. Later in the same year he proclaimed a papal truce at Casale, by riding, with plumed hat and crucifix held on high, between the opposing French and Spanish armies. After acting as nuncio in Paris in the years 1634–6 he served as Richelieu's agent in a Rome increasingly dominated by Spanish influence. When father Joseph died in 1638, Richelieu began to consider the possibility of giving Mazarin comparable responsibility. Mazarin left Rome for the last time in 1639 and settled permanently in France, although there is no evidence for the general belief that he was naturalised. Two years later he became a cardinal as a mark of his advancement in the confidence of his patron. His career was that of a condottiere of diplomacy. His astonishing success provoked both the emulation and envy of the new coadjutor.

Mazarin had used Beaufort's conspiracy to reconcile the factions of Gaston and Condé with each other and with the court. Indeed he let it be known that it was they who had obliged the regent to arrest Beaufort. The affair had enabled the cardinal to establish himself permanently as the regent's principal minister, and thenceforth as understanding developed between them which was sealed by the ties of their mutual affection. It had also reaffirmed Richelieu's foreign policy and preserved his internal emphasis upon a strong central government. Retz himself admitted these consequences, but his own analysis was written with an eye to his self-justification. He regarded the emergence of Mazarin as the result of the folly of the *Importants* and the indolence of the princes. Mazarin was seen as his principal enemy, but an enemy for whom, unlike Richelieu, he refused to admit respect. Retz emphasised his loyalty during the intrigue, and bent his subsequent narrative to show how he had been driven into a justifiable opposition by the wilful mismanagement of the régime.

On 22 January 1644 the coadjutor received the additional but
honorary title of archbishop of Corinth 'with special reference to
infidels and heretics' (*in partibus infidelium et haereticorum*), and he
was enthroned with all attendant pomp on the last day of the
month. He had resolved to begin his ministry by catching the
popular imagination, and, apart from his sermons, his first essay
was the reform of the clergy within the diocese. An opportunity
presented itself when the archbishop left Paris in March for two
months. Retz established a series of tribunals and proceeded to
examine the clergy to determine their competence. He classed
them in three categories: those who performed their duties satis-
factorily, those who did not but possessed the capacity to do so,
and those who were neither effective nor capable of improvement.
The coadjutor proposed to provide appropriate training for those
who needed it, but his reform had not progressed far when Jean-
François de Gondi was summoned to return and to order his
nephew to abandon his scheme. Retz swallowed his anger and
obeyed. He was determined to make a contrite and courteous
impression until he was properly established.

The other side of his activities continued as usual, but he
adhered to his decision to avoid promiscuity. Among his duties
was the requirement to inspect certain convents in the area. He
noted that some of the inmates were young and flirtatious but he
sternly resisted temptation. 'This conduct [he wrote] gave a
marvellous lustre to my chastity. I believe the lessons I received
every night from madame de Pommereuil greatly fortified it for
the following day's inspections.' These 'lessons', he explained,
could not be entirely concealed, because madame de Pommereuil
insisted upon publicising her more illustrious liaisons.

The archbishop's jealousy for his nephew grew in proportion
to the reputation Retz established for the strict performance of his
duties among the clergy, for the charities which he dispensed
ostentatiously among the poor and for the eloquence and learning
with which he graced the pulpit. Tallemant told the story that on
one occasion the archbishop fell on descending from his carriage,
and was supported by Gilles Ménage, a member of Retz's suite.
As soon as he recognised to whom he was indebted, he drew back
in indignation, saying that he refused to lean on one of his
nephew's creatures.[8] Retz turned this unconcealed resentment to

his own advantage, stressing his own good intentions and turning the chapter against his uncle.

It was at this point that Retz began to court popularity with Port-Royal and its adherents. His father had been a friend of Saint-Cyran, and had protested when the spiritual director of Port-Royal had been arrested on Richelieu's instructions. His uncle, the archbishop, had never been one to allow connections of this kind to impair his relations with the secular power. In the years before Jansenist theological issues had begun to trouble the Arnauld establishment at Port-Royal, archbishop Gondi had been ready to extend his protection. When mère Angélique Arnauld and her family had moved to Paris in 1626, conflict had arisen with the Cistercians, whose general had threatened to forbid the austerities practised by the nuns. Mère Angélique had asked for new direction, and the archbishop had welcomed a bull from Urban VIII transferring Port-Royal to his jurisdiction. But after Saint-Cyran's arrest Gondi tried to put pressure on the Jansenist *solitaires* to leave Paris for Port-Royal-des-Champs. When Urban VIII issued a bull against Jansenius' *Augustinus* in 1643, archbishop Gondi hastened to accept it, only to find that he had misjudged the reaction of his colleagues in the Sorbonne, who in January of the following year refused to receive it.[9] These vacillations angered those among the lower clergy of the diocese who had Jansenist leanings, and Retz won such firm supporters among them as du Hamel, the curé of Saint-Merry. Jansenism had a certain influence at court, and in any case the regency was anxious to avoid an appeal to Rome which would have provoked Gallican sentiment in the parlement and the Sorbonne. Anne of Austria told the princesse de Guémenée that the government had no wish to harry Port-Royal if the aggressive attacks of Antoine Arnauld upon the Jesuits could be muted.[10]

There was no hint of heterodox opinions in the coadjutor's sermons. His preaching brought him the immediate acclaim in his profession that he desired. His first sermons were delivered in the years 1635 and 1636, when their audacity, but not their theology, had angered Richelieu. The rhetorical flourishes which he had learnt from the bishop of Lisieux now enabled him to engage the attention of all that was fashionable, and much, even, that was pious, in Parisian society. His contemporaries were quick to attest his fame. In a letter addressed to Retz in December 1644, Guez de Balzac declared: 'You treat divine matters with all the force and all the dignity of which human eloquence is capable.' In his *Christian Socrates* Balzac compared his oratory with Saint Chrysostom's.[11] A number of Retz's sermons have survived in the notes and reconstructions left by his contemporaries. One, which was preached to the Ash Wednesday text 'remember, man, that thou art dust and unto dust shalt thou return', stressed human frailty and repeated Montaigne's adage 'know thyself'.[12] Its theme was the stoicism of Seneca, suggesting that Retz was moving away from the heroic attitudes of the *Conspiracy of Fieschi* towards reasoned action and the control of the passions. But it would be rash to attribute sincerity to the opinions professed in the sermons. Some of them were frankly political, as were one delivered on the eve of the erection of the first barricades in the Fronde and another preached during the siege of Paris in January 1649. Others again were instances of direct and calculated hypocrisy.

It was an audacious piece of cynicism to preach on this very topic. In his sermon on hypocrisy Retz eloquently declaimed against the sin he was himself committing with every word he pronounced. He spoke of avarice, lust and worldly ambition, declaring: 'These are powerful attractions to a feeble soul, and the hypocrite who makes use of piety to arrive at these ends may add perhaps some colour to his sin. Yet it must surely be a grave threat to society when a man uses such means merely to satisfy his vanity and parade himself in the sight of others.' He elaborated the various forms hypocrisy might take, and calculated their effect upon the hypocrite:

> The corruption passes from his conscious will to permeate his entire mind. He comes to believe that he may traffic in piety, that he may bend to his own interest things which reason would normally forbid, that he may sell what he ought to buy at the cost of life itself. ... And, to speak frankly, there is nothing to compare with the anxiety of a man who always hides his true self behind a mask, who is obliged always to be on guard lest he be found out, and whose conscience is in a continual state of revolt.[13]

The coadjutor's conscience seemed very much under control. In November 1646 he chose to preach in honour of Carlo

Borromeo, the sixteenth-century archbishop of Milan, who, having repented for the dissipations of his early life, earned beatitude through his contribution to the reformed Catholic church in the immediate aftermath of the Council of Trent. In describing the saint, Retz sought to present the public image he was trying to create to himself, and at the same time he sought to answer those who discerned the true motives for his supposed works of piety:

He sold his property, founded hospitals, instituted colleges, built seminaries, nourished all the poor. They imputed criminal motives to his charities. They wanted to think that his benevolence and his alms-giving were baits distributed to win the friendship of the people. The author of his life tells us that some took this malice to strange excess. They suspected him of reviving the ambitious thoughts of the former archbishops of the house of Visconti: they even accused him of having secret intelligences with certain princes of Italy to seize the government of the state of Milan.[14]

The coadjutor expatiated upon the saint's virtue amid lies and persecution, and declaimed how, as if to confute 'the wickedness of these black and dastardly minds who customarily find evil in good', God had sent the plague to Milan so that his ministry to the afflicted could disprove such evil. This theme in Retz's mouth was indeed 'evil by design', for he deliberately had chosen to commit the crimes alleged against Borromeo, and by identifying himself with the saint he compounded his offence.

Not everyone praised the coadjutor's performance in the pulpit. Pierre de Montmaur, professor of Greek at the Collège Royal, was particularly critical, and his censure was vigorously refuted by Retz's literary protégés. The abbé Gilles Ménage, who was one of the first to defend his patron, had already been engaged in controversy with Montmaur over the accuracy of his Greek quotations, and had been supported by Scarron and Sarasin.[15] While Retz's literary friends defended his sermons in public, they probably accorded them a very different reception in the intimacy of their own circle. Ménage was renowned for his raillery; Scarron's irreverent comedy The Hypocrites might well have been a burlesque version of the sermon on hypocrisy; and Sarasin became notorious for his imitations of the preaching styles of the various religious orders, especially the Cordeliers and the Capuchins.[16] While the coadjutor was occupied in building a public reputation for piety, his private relaxation was spent with the sceptical friends whom he described as his 'academy'.

It was the practice for literary talent to seek the patronage of the great, and those among the high aristocracy who sought to set the fashion vied with each other in attracting the most eminent men of letters. Enghien, the conqueror of Rocroi, who became prince de Condé on the death of his father in 1646, was the idol of the hôtel de Rambouillet. He and his following spent each summer on the frontier and each winter in the salons of Paris or the voluptuous seclusion of his palace at Chantilly. The young Condé seemed to personify the hero of the *romans*. Madeleine de Scudéry admired him as much as she detested Retz, and La Calprenède designed Oroondate, the hero of the twelve volumes of *Cassandre*, to idealise the prince, his patron. Condé himself admired Gomberville's *Polexandre*, a heroic romance in which queen Alcidiane despatched her knight to punish the various kings who had the temerity to propose to her. The amoral tone of *Polexandre* was more to the taste of the real Condé than the idealised heroes of the genre. The tone of his circle was openly blasphemous, and he set a personal example of brutal sensuality in his relations with women. The circle of Gaston of Orléans, where rakes such as Brissac and Fontrailles set the moral tone, was even franker in its debauchery.[17] The cult of the hero rapidly deteriorated into scepticism and moral anarchy. Every courtier of fashion and repute maintained his literary client. The libertine comte d'Harcourt protected the poet Saint-Amant. Another duellist, Charles-Léon, comte de Fiesque, who was obliged to leave Rome because of his notoriety, was the patron of Segrais, the friend of Ménage and Scarron. The comtesse de Fiesque was the companion of Gaston's daughter, la Grande Mademoiselle, and aided her in establishing her own literary salon.

The coadjutor's 'academy' outshone all those of his rivals, and its libertine atmosphere was assured by its membership of poets rather than of writers of fabulous romance. Its leading member, Jean Chapelain, was acknowledged, with Guez de Balzac, as the leader of the republic of letters. His reputation was derived from his conversation rather than his writing. He was an original member of the French Academy, established by Richelieu, and composed its censure of *Le Cid*. He had been working for more than twelve years on his vast and formless epic on Joan of Arc, *La Pucelle*, when the coadjutor installed his literary circle in his house behind Notre-Dame. Chapelain and Gomberville dined with Retz on the eve of the barricades in August 1648. Gomberville had also accepted Retz's patronage, and in 1646 dedicated his *Dialogue on the Reading of the Old Romances* to the coadjutor.

Two permanent members of the private academy of Notre-Dame were Gilles Ménage and Jean-François Sarasin, who lived in Retz's house and enjoyed a considerable pension from him. In one aspect the abbé Ménage was a distinguished philologist who published a work on the origins of the French language, edited a collection of classical satires and translated the survey of Greek philosophy by Diogenes Laertius. In another, he was the composer of dozens of amorous lyrics addressed to the ladies of the court and salons under such soubriquets as Iole (madame de Sévigné) and Florida (madame de Montbazon). He sang his poems in the gardens of the Gondi country houses, and, while he might praise his patron's sermons, he clearly preferred Retz's ministry to other gods, and addressed him in verse as 'the adorable Gondi, mighty priest of the great Pan'.[18] His epigrams were very much in demand in the salons, and these together with his anecdotes, which provide valuable insights into the tone of Retz's household, were eventually published as *Menagiana* in 1693, the year after his death. His wit was accompanied by a fiery temper. Chapelain was obliged on one occasion to reconcile him with his master after a violent quarrel. In 1652, after nine years with the coadjutor, he was to leave Retz's service as a result of a drunken brawl in which his associates tried to throw him into a tub – but they had mistaken their Diogenes.[19]

Sarasin had been the protégé of Chavigny, and had accompanied the minister on a mission to Italy. Mazarin provided him with 4,000 livres for the expenses of the journey, but he decamped with the money and spent it on a lady.[20] Sarasin lived with the coadjutor in the years 1644–8 and subsequently became secretary to Condé's brother, the prince de Conti. He passed his time writing pastoral poems in imitation of Virgil's *Eclogues*, composing light satires, and touting clerical favours behind Retz's back. Like his friend Scarron, he was to become a vigorous writer of *Mazarinades* during the Fronde. Scarron, however, was to write on behalf of the coadjutor, not against him. In the early years of his coadjutorship Retz had a particular liking for Scarron's burlesques. He called regularly at his house, and would sit on the end of his bed discussing the gossip of the day. Another future pamphleteer of the Fronde, and an intimate friend of Scarron and Sarasin, was Jacques Marigny, whose honorific title disguised the fact that as Jacques Carpentier he was the son of an iron merchant from Nevers. His particular skill lay in the composition of parodies and scurrilous songs.

Other poets in Retz's circle were La Lane, d'Alibray, and Adrien de Valois. The abbé d'Aubignac wrote anti-feminist satires directed against mademoiselle de Scudéry and the *précieuses*. The poet and *libertin*, Marc-Antoine de Saint-Amant, had had the younger duc de Retz as his protector as well as the comte d'Harcourt. Like Chapelain, Saint-Amant was an original member of the French Academy, and he, too, strove to sustain his reputation as an *académicien* by composing a remarkably tedious epic, *Moses Rescued*. The critic Furetière suggested that *Moses Drowned* would be an apter title. Voiture, a more reputable poet, looked more to Condé and the hôtel de Rambouillet than to the coadjutor. Nevertheless, he had contacts with Retz dating from the latter's visit to Rome and from his association with Gaston's court of conspirators in Flanders. Tallemant recorded his colourful procession of loves and duels in the *Historiettes*. He also recalled an incident concerning Voiture which reveals the character of the coadjutor's entourage. The poet had taken a vow to eschew gambling and went to visit Retz to obtain a dispensation. While waiting in the anteroom he encountered the marquis de Laigues, who assumed Voiture was joking and persuaded him on the spot to play him at dice. Voiture went away three hundred pistoles the poorer and without his dispensation.[21]

The libertine attitudes current in Retz's household were often brittle and superficial. Gomberville later drifted into sympathy with Port-Royal and wrote *La Jeune Alcidiane*, designed to counteract the damage to public morals caused by *Polexandre*. Sarasin was later to repudiate indecency and to inveigh against blasphemy. If the coadjutor kept among his retainers the grotesque priest Dulot, who was notorious for his foul tongue, he also employed a worthy theologian, Dr. Paris, who helped him with his professional studies. There was in general a curious vacillation between sin and devotion. Remarkable variations could appear in the same family. In 1644 Retz officiated at the marriage of Marie de Rabutin-Chantal, the granddaughter of a saint, and Henri, marquis de Sévigné. The latter lived according to the fashion by pursuing Ninon de L'Enclos, the most celebrated courtesan of the century, and in 1651 died, again in the fashion, in the course of a duel. Yet his uncle, the chevalier Renaud de Sévigné, was from time to time a recluse at Port-Royal, and in the interim a frondeur and partisan of the coadjutor. The pious Arnauld d'Andilly, who condemned the libertine morals, the duelling, and the blasphemy of the aristocracy, lived side by side at court with the most accomplished sinners of the age.

The contrast between the public and private faces of the coadjutor, however, cannot simply be explained by the general coexistence of two standards of morality. As he said in his memoirs, Retz made his choice in a deliberate and calculated fashion. His decision, and the manner in which he fulfilled it, stultified the impulsive, heroic element in his early life. He was in every way as ambitious as before, and the development of court and clerical intrigue was to set his ambition in opposition to the rule of Mazarin. Yet in the course of this struggle Retz was to be guided not by the precepts he had depicted in Fieschi but by a shrewd and cynical realism.

Mazarin was more secure than any of his enemies imagined. He held the queen's confidence because he had also captured her heart. Few secrets were better kept than the love between Anne of Austria and her first minister, and only the expressions of fervent affection in their ciphered correspondence revealed their relationship to posterity. Retz at first strove to enter this charmed circle. Once a week he attended mass with the regent, and afterwards dined with Mazarin. The cardinal, he remarked in his memoirs, treated him with friendship and showed appreciation of the coadjutor's refusal to join his friend's cabal among the *Importants*. This situation did not long endure, for Mazarin came to regard Retz as an unscrupulous and ambitious troublemaker. The antagonism between the two developed gradually in the first four years of the regency – the period when the deteriorating political situation presaged the revolt in which the coadjutor sought to replace the cardinal.

The temptation to join those who intrigued actively against the cardinal-minister was nearly as strong as the fear of being compromised by the mistakes of those who were fools rather than knaves. The folly of the *Importants* was infectious, and it was not long before a successor to the imprisoned Beaufort announced himself. The coadjutor had never had much time for the duc de Guise, the son of the duke who had questioned the conduct of Retz's father before La Rochelle. Like Condé, Guise found that the reputation of his ancestors was a burden rather than an advantage. He had tried to hold a daily *levée* as if he were a prince of the Blood, and Retz, when once accorded the honour of holding the duke's shirt, had contemptuously dropped it in the ashes of the hearth.[22] He had married and abandoned the comtesse de Bossu in Flanders, and her return to court to reclaim her erring husband caused considerable embarrassment. Guise placed himself at the head of the malcontents by declaring his love for madame de Montbazon, and attacking the reputation of madame de Longueville. Gaston himself was induced to support him because his wife was Guise's cousin. The Condé family consequently moved closer to the government. Enghien persuaded the comte de Coligny, the supposed correspondent of madame de Longueville, to challenge Guise to a duel. The latter proved a better swordsman than he was a politician: their encounter in December 1643 resulted in the wounding and subsequent death of Coligny. Apart from Guise, the opposition found a focus in Beaufort's father, the duc de Vendôme. Retz had twice visited the latter's château of Anet during his pursuit of mademoiselle de Vendôme. The duke gave out that Mazarin planned to have him murdered, but when this story threatened to rebound to his discredit he fled to Italy to join the coadjutor's friend Beaupuy.[23]

These continuing intrigues proceeded against a background of court festivities in the winter of 1643–4. The pleasures and gallantries of the season were recorded in the verse of Voiture and Sarasin, while Corneille busied himself with the production of *Le Menteur* and *Polyceute*. In the provinces a new series of peasant revolts defied the authority of the central power. For many months the famished armies of the *croquants* moved at will through

Rouergue, Poitou and Saintonge. Soon after their dispersal the towns of Languedoc began to experience a succession of mob riots. Popular sedition was generally provoked by the endeavours of the tax-collectors to provide for French armies fighting in Flanders, Germany and Catalonia. During the summer of 1644 Gaston and Enghien achieved a series of victories in the north east, but French arms failed before the fortress of Lérida in Catalonia. The strains imposed by the war against the Hapsburgs, and the growing sympathy of local authorities with the disobedience of the masses, were to create the conditions for the revolt in which Retz was ultimately to participate. In the meantime he found a political role within his chosen profession.

The assembly of the Gallican church met periodically with the ostensible object of voting the *don gratuit*, the 'voluntary' contribution it made to the national finances. It had become in fact a kind of national religious council to review the administration of the French Catholic church. It dealt with appeals and abuses as well as financial matters, and the representatives of each province submitted a *cahier* or list of grievances. Like the high court of the parlement, it could issue remonstrances against the government's ecclesiastical administration, but these could be abrogated by decrees of the royal council. Retz represented his diocese in the long-drawn-out session from May 1645 to July 1646. The temper of the clergy at this meeting was very different from their attitude in the preceding assembly at Mantes in 1641. There the imperious fiat of cardinal Richelieu had dominated the proceedings, and six bishops who had ventured to criticise his policy had been expelled from Mantes and banished to their diocese. The assembly of 1645 displayed a tougher spirit of independence. It was resolved that the six bishops should receive special invitations to attend the meetings as observers. When the coadjutor was asked to open the debate upon the matter he made the most of the opportunity to act as the spokesman of the general discontent against the invasion of clerical immunities. His views established his popularity within the meeting, and he was personally charged with conveying an invitation to the bishop of Toulon, one of the six disgraced prelates. Thereby he incurred the angry resentment of the regent and her minister. Summoned to the presence of the queen, Retz found her lying on a bed in the small grey-coloured room to which she retired in moments of stress. She spoke, Retz recalled, in 'the bitter voice that was natural to her' of the coadjutor's disrespect for the memory of the late king. Retz's explanations were waved aside, and he was told to refer them to Mazarin. The cardinal was even less sympathetic, for he peremptorily demanded the retraction of Retz's speech in the assembly. Retz returned later with the bishop of Arles to repeat his explanations, and pretended to conclude that Mazarin was too much of a man of the world to understand the clerical viewpoint.

Retz's representation of the first of his clashes with Mazarin reveals the artistry with which he played his selected role. It was the coadjutor who had tactfully to defend the legitimate interests of the church, and the cardinal who had so aggressively denied them. Five months later he again assumed the pose of the injured party in a second brush with the minister. In October 1645 king Wladyslaw VII of Poland sent three ambassadors to Paris to arrange his marriage with Marie-Louise de Gonzague, the daughter of that duc de Nevers whom Richelieu had installed as ruler of Mantua. The Polish bishop of Varmia desired to celebrate the match in Notre-Dame, and Retz was sent a royal command to make the cathedral available. He claimed that the bishops and archbishops of Paris could only cede their right to officiate in Notre-Dame to cardinals of royal blood. His uncle, he asserted, had been blamed for allowing cardinal de la Rochefoucauld to marry Charles I of England with the king's aunt, Henrietta Maria, in the cathedral twenty years earlier. The coadjutor quickly secured the support of the dean and canons, and visited the court at Fontainebleau 'personally to clarify this misunderstanding'. Mazarin met him with angry words and sent him to see the queen. She, too, was incensed, but Retz persuaded her to grant an interview with the chapter. Next day he presented the dean and sixteen deputies to Anne of Austria, only to be referred once more to the cardinal. When Mazarin publicly rebuked Retz for his insolence, the coadjutor affected to believe that he was joking. 'To whom do you think you are speaking,' replied Mazarin, 'I shall teach you how to behave.' Although he was choking with rage, Retz regained his status in the eyes of his subordinates by inquiring whether Mazarin believed he was the cardinal de Lorraine addressing the suffragan bishop of Metz – referring to a celebrated member of the house of Guise who was remembered both for his pluralism and his discourteous treatment of those who carried out the duties which he himself neglected.

After this scene Retz was dining with his supporters when he received a message suggesting a change of attitude on the part of the regent. He and the deputies found first the queen, and then Mazarin himself, transformed with airs of sweetness and grace. The minister explained that he had intended the Italian word *insolito* (extraordinary) and not the French *insolent*. Although the deputation returned to Paris with unexpected courtesies ringing in their ears, within a few days Retz received a letter from his uncle, the archbishop, instructing him to comply with the bishop of Varmia's request. Irritated by Mazarin's deceit, the coadjutor organised the chapter to continue their opposition. He informed mademoiselle de Nevers that unless the Polish bishop personally requested his consent to the ceremony in the cathedral, he would declare the marriage void. Fearing a diplomatic incident, the court gave way and transferred the wedding to the chapel of the Palais-Royal. Retz had won a victory, but the affair had intensified Mazarin's distrust and enmity. Each man had measured the other's strength, and each prepared for future conflicts.

Clerical tensions were invariably complicated by court intrigues. Gaston's retinue included the capable abbé de la Rivière, whose hopes of eventually succeeding Mazarin were tempered with a caution proper to a statesman of vision. Gaston was again in touch with his group of professional conspirators, especially the exiled Fontrailles. He began to attract new recruits to his schemes, such as the Savoyard duc de Nemours, who was as unstable as his captive brother-in-law, the duc de Beaufort. Even madame de Montbazon, allowed to return to court after her period of exile, was associated with these clandestine discussions. A popular preacher, Charles Hersent, who had once been a critic of Richelieu, took it into his head to advance the conspirators' cause at Rome. Although Urban VIII had been favourably disposed towards Mazarin, his successor was not. In November 1645, two months after the election of Innocent X, Hersent journeyed to the holy city to put before the new pope certain suggestions about ending the war against the Hapsburgs. Mazarin had begun negotiations at Münster in the previous year, but, since they had proved abortive, it was easy enough to represent the cardinal-minister as the principal opponent of peace. Innocent lent his approval to the overthrowing of Mazarin so that Gaston might dominate the regency and La Rivière might be declared first minister. Such a régime, the pope considered, might succeed in ending the war with Spain. Hersent returned to Paris to reveal these plans to La Rivière, but the latter promptly denounced him, and Mazarin had him arrested.

At this time Mazarin had taken under his protection the nephew and the brother of the previous pope, who were persecuted by Innocent. Francesco and Antonio Barberini had also been courted by the coadjutor, and their arrival in Paris could have eased the bitterness between Retz and the cardinal. Moreover, the coadjutor still kept aloof from the various factions which sought Mazarin's downfall. Léon le Bouthillier, comte de Chavigny, was for a time more dangerous to the first minister than the great aristocratic families. He moved with subtlety within the councils of the regency to destroy confidence in the cardinal. His father, Claude le Bouthillier, had been Richelieu's last superintendent of the finances, and the new régime had dismissed him within a few weeks of its institution as a gesture of appeasement to its critics. As a minister in his own right, Chavigny had kept his place by disasociating himself from his father. This had brought him into contact with the forces opposing Mazarin, whose rise he claimed to have assisted in Richelieu's last years. Late in 1645 rumours began to circulate that some of his friends among the *Importants* might be recalled to offset the growing influence of Condé. The rumours proved baseless, and in January of the following year Chavigny was sent in temporary exile to the provinces. Retz was not personally implicated, but his own assertive pride soon afterwards exacerbated the enmity between the Condé and Orléans factions, and revived the cardinal's active hostility towards himself.

In Notre-Dame the coadjutor occupied a place immediately below the chair of his uncle, the archbishop. When Gaston made known his intention of attending a particular service, one of the officers of the guard placed his emblem in Retz's seat. Such an apparently trivial matter of protocol could cause violent repercussions. Smarting under the offence to his *amour-propre*, the coadjutor immediately enlisted the support of the chapter. When he believed that he had roused sufficient indignation among his supporters, he called on the king's uncle to acquaint him with his rights under pretext of offering his submission. At first Gaston good-humouredly insisted that Retz should have his rightful place, but he later revoked this concession when the court ridiculed him for his weakness. As the coadjutor refused to yield, the government intervened. Anne of Austria instructed him to submit publicly in his next sermon, and Mazarin reinforced her demand with a display of mingled suavity and firmness. Retz was for once worsted in the ensuing argument. He quoted the occasion when Saint Ambrose had barred the cathedral of Milan against the emperor Theodosius, and the cardinal remarked wryly that if one wished to cite the precedent of a saint one should endeavour to conduct one's own life according to his example. Retz could only respond that he felt obliged to follow Saint Ambrose's advice in the hope that he might obtain the grace to imitate him in all matters. Angry words followed, and the coadjutor departed in no very saintly mood. He chose to believe that he was in danger of being kidnapped by Gaston's bravoes, and enlisted sixty or more gentlemen to defend his dwelling. This audacity delighted Condé's son, Enghien, who lent his military reputation to Retz's cause. A rift between Gaston and Enghien just before they were due to resume their joint campaign against the Spanish in Flanders caused consternation within the government. The elder Condé, his fear outweighing his desire to score points off Gaston, obeyed the queen's injunction to counsel moderation to the coadjutor. Picking his way through the ranks of Retz's makeshift army he confronted him with a mixture of imprecations, threats and caresses. But, if we are to believe the account in the memoirs, Condé was himself persuaded to see the advantage of discomfiting his rival, and ended by joining his son in Retz's defence. The court gave way, and Retz was publicly reconciled with Gaston.

Gaston rejoined the army in Flanders, which continued its run of successes, capturing Courtrai in June 1646 and Mardyke in August. Nothing that had happened during his last visit to the court had given the nominal commander-in-chief any added incentive to support Mazarin. While his officers won his victories, Gaston conspired against the cardinal in the hope of arranging a truce with his country's enemies. Scurrilous attacks on the first

minister began to circulate in the army and there were rumours of
a military plot to assassinate him. The situation was not unlike
that when Soissons had launched his coup, but Retz had no intention of repeating his earlier mistake. When Gaston rejoined the
court in September to find Mazarin in an unassailable position, he
turned his spleen against Condé. The latter was only too glad to
accept an order of exile to his estates. He died three months later,
regretted only by those who saw in Enghien a much greater threat
to their own security. However, the new prince de Condé removed
his arrogant presence to Catalonia, where Retz's fellow-gallant and
duelling-opponent, Harcourt, had suffered a new reverse before
the fortress of Lérida. The war continued in 1647 with indifferent
success. Condé was no more successful in aiding the rebellion of
the Catalans than his predecessors had been, and Mazarin was rash
enough to appoint his own brother as the king's viceroy in
Catalonia. Naples also exploded in revolt against the Spanish, and
the fire-eating duc de Guise was despatched to command the
French forces supporting the new republic.

Although Mazarin conducted both the strategy of the war and
the inconclusive, and therefore equally strategic, peace negotiations with a skill little inferior to that of Richelieu, his popularity
did not increase. When Condé was obliged to lift the siege of
Lérida in June 1647, a spate of satires appeared against the first
minister as well as the field commander. Retz came under some
suspicion when his protégé, Sarasin, was recognised as the author
of one of these pieces and imprisoned in the Bastille. At the same
time his former academic rival, bishop La Mothe-Houdancourt,
and the comte de Fiesque, Retz's friend who bore the name of his
revolutionary paragon, were exiled for similar activities. Mazarin
provoked further criticism by the advancement of his family. His
brother, the archbishop of Aix and viceroy of Catalonia, was
named to the sacred college of cardinals under a dispensation from
the rule banning two brothers from holding such rank. The death
of Michel Mazarin in 1648 cut short reproaches of nepotism in
this direction, but the favours Mazarin distributed to his nephew,
Paul Mancini, and to his nieces, Anne-Marie Martinozzi, and
Laura and Olympe Mancini, who had arrived in France in the
summer of 1647, excited the scorn of his detractors. The cardinal
was to use these 'Mazarinettes' to divide his enemies by a series

of political marriages. In the meantime he made use of the respect
shown him by the abbé de la Rivière to damp the enthusiasms of
Gaston's hot-headed entourage. His policy was to balance the
influence of Gaston with the prestige of Condé.

None of these manoeuvres directly involved the coadjutor.
Without overt association with the malcontents Retz continued
to cultivate his following in the church and to promote his own
popularity among the Parisian lower classes. He even found it
politic to seek the favour of the government in the concluding
sessions of the assembly of the clergy.[24] When he advised his colleagues to accept the government's estimate of the *don gratuit,*
Mazarin invited him to dinner with every appearance of amica-
bility. Another issue in the assembly revealed the hollowness of
this rapprochement. Before dispersing, the clerical deputies commissioned the coadjutor to negotiate the restitution of the bishop
of Léon, who had been suspended from his revenues and his
office by Richelieu. Although Mazarin had undertaken to give
satisfaction, Retz found that the minister was evading his promises
by skilful procrastination. In his memoirs Retz explained how his
own popularity in Paris earned the distrust of the government,
and prevented him from winning the queen's personal favour.
'One is more often duped by suspicion than by confidence,' he
commented. The less secure he felt against Mazarin's machinations, the more he indulged in his own schemes to ensure his
future. None of these compromised him by any fresh taint of
conspiracy. His outward relations with Mazarin were formally
correct, and he could approach the cardinal to demand satisfaction
when the comte de Roquelaure insulted his cousin, madame de
Lesdiguières. But his breach with the first minister was clear from
the three occasions when formal politeness dissolved into acri-
mony. The early proceedings of the assembly of the church, the
affair of the Polish marriage, and the dispute over precedence with
Gaston, had revealed an hostility that was deeper than mistrust.
Retz could afford to await his opportunity. Apart from court
factions and intrigues, new forces of opposition were gathering
against his enemy.

FIVE

The barricades

The war to which Richelieu had committed France exacerbated the unsolved social problems also inherited by his successor. The burden of direct taxation fell upon the masses, and especially upon the peasantry. Poor harvests and marauding armies combined with the weight of the general poll tax, the *taille*, to produce popular insurrections which flared sporadically from province to province with no coordination and little leadership. Since the local seigneur was dependent upon the dues he received from his peasantry, and the government's taxes restricted their ability to contribute to his upkeep, it was not uncommon for the nobility to sympathise with popular rebellion against the central power. To meet the problem of provincial anarchy Richelieu had extended the practice of appointing intendants, officials with wide administrative powers who acted as the direct agents of the royal council. The authority of the intendants was resented by a host of local officials, many of whom bought their offices and paid a tax for the privilege of transmitting them as property to their heirs. The holders of these venal offices often bought noble land, identified themselves with local interests and moved into the lower ranks of the aristocracy. The leading judges and officials of the provincial courts or parlements formed a solid phalanx of constitutional resistance to the central power. Their social aspirations were inherently conservative, but they were none the less hostile to Richelieu's autocratic innovations. Thus the declarations of the parlements against the fiscality and its agents often served to support the popular risings, which usually began with the murder of a particular fiscal emissary of the central government. The risings of the *croquants* in the early months of the regency were typical of disturbances which had continued for nearly a generation. The Fronde itself would be incomprehensible without this background. Mazarin and his predecessor had never previously been confronted with a national insurrection because there was no one focus for discontent. In 1648 the parlement of Paris was to provide this focus.[1]

Retz himself was one of the few to sense the strength and suspect the motives of popular discontent. His demagogy was directed entirely to selfish ends. For similar reasons he was also to associate himself with the aspirations of the parlement. In May 1643 the judges had regained their constitutional privileges suppressed by Richelieu in return for their part in the installation of Anne of Austria as regent. Ever since this bargain they had maintained a steady pressure against Mazarin and the council. They claimed the right to register the edicts of the council before they became effective in law and the right to remonstrate against measures which they held to be inconsistent with custom. The fiscal edicts of the new régime came under their disapproving scrutiny. While the judges of the senior bench, the grand'chambre, remained politically conservative in most matters, and the next chambers those of requêtes, generally followed their lead, their juniors on the preparatory bench of the enquêtes tended to adopt radical attitudes. The enquêtes were especially critical of the ingenious devices which sprang from the brain of Mazarin's principal economic adviser, a Lyon financier of Italian origin named Particelli d'Emery.

The first of Emery's innovations was a tax upon dwellings outside the walls of the old city of Paris – the so-called édit du toisé. Led by Retz's friend, président Barillon of the enquêtes and his colleague, président Gayant, the parlement engaged in a bitter struggle with the council to have the tax revoked. Before it was suspended, rioting mobs had burst into the Palais de Justice and threatened to burn down Emery's own house. The controller-general then substituted the taxe des aisés, levied as a compulsory purchase of government stock upon the wealthy bourgeoisie in the capital. The financiers rebelled against this proposal, and, though Omer Talon, the advocate-general in the parlement, denounced them, the regency was obliged to surrender. Reimposition of the toisé caused widespread distress, and Talon described in his memoirs how the wives of the poor entered the grand'chambre and begged piteously for relief.[2] In March 1645 a radical group from the enquêtes attempted to force the senior bench to protest.

Several of their number were exiled by order of the regent, and président Barillon was imprisoned.

Six months later the government tried new measures, creating fresh offices for sale and levying taxes upon certain trades. The parlement was forced to register Emery's edicts by the procedure of the *lit de justice*, whereby the boy king appeared to command their obedience. Murmurs of backstage opposition among the judges encouraged popular resistance. The duc de Montbazon, whose duties as governor of Paris occasionally induced him to abandon his addiction to wine and his complaisant interest in his wife's infidelities, led a deputation of the representatives of the city guilds to plead before Mazarin. Merchants and shopkeepers closed their premises and sent their wives to follow the queen through the streets when she returned from a service in Notre-Dame to the Palais-Royal. Both Barillon and Gayant died before the year was out, but there were others ready to inherit their radical leadership. The financial situation deteriorated further in 1646. Revenues were anticipated by as much as eighteen months, and interest on government stock was unpaid. In the following year a new expedient, the *tarif*, levied duties on food entering Paris, and resulted in a wrangle between the courts and further resistance to the government.

The lower-class elements who criticised Emery's taxes had once seen the parlement as the agent of the crown. When the parlement resisted Mazarin and his minister the populace could begin to regard it as a bastion against tyranny. The magistrates campaigned bitterly against the financiers and the intendants, and the more radical among them were ready to welcome popular support. It was not easy to control the forces of plebeian discontent. On 7 January 1648, when the parlement had accepted expedients for the sale of new offices and a forced loan in return for the abolition of the *tarif*, a crowd of some eight hundred artisans and shopkeepers staged a demonstration against royal taxes. On the following day the mob invaded the Palais de Justice and shouted abuse at Emery's son, Thoré, who held the office of president in the third chamber of the *enquêtes*. On 9 January the boldness of the demonstrators increased, and they threatened Mathieu Molé, the first président of the parlement. Molé, whose inflexibility and courage were proverbial, responded with the promise of a newly-erected

gallows. His colleagues supported him by ordering the arrest of
the leaders of the demonstration, but the warrant could not be
executed. Although the Palais de Justice was no longer in danger
when royal guards were sent to protect its deliberations, the popular unrest continued. Armed bourgeois roamed the streets on the
night of the 10th, and next day two hundred women pursued the
queen from Notre-Dame, screaming for redress with none of
the humility evidenced in the similar demonstration of 1645.
Musket shots were heard in the night and looting was reported.
Amid the tolling of alarm bells the regiments of guards were
placed on the alert and the mayor of Paris, the *prévôt des marchands*,
told the court that the city was on the brink of rebellion.[3]

In the first four years of his office as coadjutor to his uncle, Retz
had consolidated his own position in contradistinction to the
archbishop's authority. He had built up a following among the
clergy of the diocese and exploited their Jansenist sympathies in
his own cause. His most ostentatious gesture in this regard had
been his appearance at Port-Royal in Paris to bless mère Angélique
Arnauld when, on 13 May 1648, she left her sister, mère Agnès,
in charge and led a section of the nuns back to Port-Royal-des-
Champs.[4] The coadjutor knew of the spread of Jansenist opinion
among the magistracy, and here, too, he had carefully acquired
supporters. The lower clergy had represented him in the pulpit
as the protector of the poor, and his own almsgiving had created a
popular response among those who had launched the January
riots. He had gained a reputation among the higher clergy as a
defender of clerical interests against the predatory hand of the
state. Within the aristocracy he had retained his associates among
those who had plotted against Richelieu, but he had refused to be
compromised by their early intrigues against the regency. In these
same four years a mutual antagonism had developed between
Retz and Mazarin. The coadjutor had not forgotten the role he
had elaborated in his *Conspiracy of Fieschi* of the arch-conspirator
and *chef de parti*. If the idealism of the *généreux* had been modified
by the realism he shared with many of his *libertin* literary friends,
the driving force of ambition had in no way diminished. In the
refractory mood of the parlement and the rebellious passions of
the mob, the coadjutor discerned the means to overthrow Mazarin
and seek his own advancement.

In his memoirs Retz provided a general analysis of the causes of the crisis remarkable for its lucidity and insight. He discerned clearly that the main challenge to the regency came not from the aristocracy but from the conservative magistrates of the Paris parlement, who were always the first to denounce disobedience in others. To explain this paradox he elaborated his view of the constitution. It was an appealing argument to conservative minds, for it demonstrated that the forces of revolt aimed at the restoration of something sound and venerable and the destruction of something new and alien. Theories that cloak revolution in conservatism by reference to practices supposedly sanctified by history are apt to take an unhistorical turn. To prove from history that there has existed some immutable spirit of the constitution is to mock the processes of historical change. The common lawyers who opposed the pretensions of the Stuarts in England were guilty of this contradiction, and so, too, were the magistrates of the parlement. But Retz was at once both more subtle and more realistic than this.

He rejected the religious doctrine of rule by divine right and the juristic one of absolute and undivided sovereignty. The practice of registering treaties and verifying royal edicts through the parlement appeared to him as surviving traces of what had once been a limited monarchy. He admitted that the French crown was not limited by any written laws, as he held the English and Aragonese crowns had been limited. Instead, the French monarchy was tempered by certain received customs which had been preserved at first by the representative estates-general and then by the parlement. In this way a balance had existed between what he called the licence of kings and the *libertinage* of the people. Retz did not claim that this balance had been so clearly defined that it could never have been misinterpreted, nor that it formally expressed a perfect solution to the problem of reconciling authority with freedom. He preferred to argue that those who had been prudent had discerned its advantages for both the rulers and the ruled. Wise kings had made the parlements custodians of their ordinances, because it was better for parlements, rather than kings, to shoulder responsibility for unpopular measures. It was a matter of common sense that an effective ruler must depend both upon the law and the force to execute it. Armed force without the moderating influence of law became despotism which degenerated into anarchy: laws without arms were no laws at all. Retz looked back to jurists who had defended the laws in earlier times and claimed that they had 'dispersed more factions by their good and holy maxims than all the gold of England and Spain had ever been able to arouse'. Their doctrines were the same as those for which his friend, président Barillon, had been imprisoned by Richelieu and Mazarin.

The balance had not, however, been absolute. There had been kings such as Louis IX and Henry IV who had observed the law, but there had been others, such as Louis XI, who, because they believed themselves cleverer than their ancestors, or because, simply, they were evil-minded men, had seen customary practices as obstacles to their own caprice. They had tried to increase their authority by changing the law, and the consequence had been that they had immediately weakened it. Sometimes the rulers were well intentioned but the avarice of their favourites had unduly extended royal authority. This had been so for the half-century preceding the wars of religion. At other times neither the king nor his favourite had understood the traditional balance. Richelieu's predecessors, Concini and Luynes, had been as ignorant of the nature of the authority they represented as had been Louis XIII himself.

In this way Retz could justify the role of the parlement in terms of both good sense and historical precedent, but he neither developed elaborate philosophical arguments on the one hand nor needed to distort history overmuch on the other. Moreover, his general view of the constitution was combined with a particular view of the policies of Richelieu and Mazarin, for it was the intention of this part of his memoirs to justify not only the Fronde but also his own part in it. Retz expressed his admiration for Richelieu, although he conspired against him. He admired the great cardinal's perspicacity and firmness, but he detested all that he stood for. Richelieu had studied all conscious and unconscious endeavours to subvert the balance of the constitution over the preceding two centuries, disguised them in the maxims of *raison d'état*, and applied them to the advance of despotism in his own interest. He had formed 'in the most legitimate of monarchies the most scandalous and dangerous tyranny which, perhaps, has ever

enslaved a state'. At the same time he was skilful enough to
maintain an appearance of good faith and, while he thought only
of France in terms of his own life-span, he convinced others that
he planned for the future. Thus 'his qualities, and the semblance
of those he lacked, easily enough maintained the respect which
separates mistrust from hatred, and which, in a state which no
longer has laws, at least for a time provides some substitute.'

Where Richelieu had provided a just cause for resistance, Mazarin provided its opportunity. The great cardinal had designated
the Italian as his successor rather after the fashion in which
Augustus had named Tiberius. Mazarin, Retz contended, had
followed Richelieu along the same narrow path, but failed to
notice the precipices which Richelieu had avoided along the route.
Fear governed him rather than prudence. When he did foresee
disaster, he was afraid to take resolute measures. All his subtlety
was negated by his craven personality, and such qualities of mind
as he did possess merely made him appear ridiculous in adversity.
He was naturally corrupt, and the malpractices of his principal
lieutenant, Emery, brought his régime into general disrepute.
Unlike Richelieu, he failed to provide himself with supporters
within the groups that opposed him. He openly mocked religious
observances, whereas his predecessor had had 'enough religion
for this life'. He ignored the plight of the provinces, despoiled
by the intendants, and even when discontents in Paris gave a focus
for revolt he failed to see the need for a general remedy. Retz saw
Mazarin as a poltroon unworthy to sit in the place of his predecessor, who, though a tyrant, had earned the respect of his
enemies:

> On the steps of the throne, whence the harsh and redoubtable
> Richelieu had blasted, rather than governed, the king's subjects, one
> saw a soft, benign successor who desired to achieve no particular pur-
> pose, who was in despair that his rank as a cardinal did not allow him
> sufficiently to abase himself before everyone, who drove through the
> streets with two little lackeys sitting behind him in his carriage.

It was, therefore, an act of providence that such a successor should
inherit Richelieu's policies and create the conditions for their
reversal.

Retz concluded his general explanation by introducing another element – the popular masses. He had argued that the traditional laws which had exercised a mediating influence between prince and people had been destroyed, and that French society, like the Swiss peasants who revolted against Austria and the Dutch who rose against Philip II of Spain, had reached a state of discontent which seemed unendurable because it appeared to be permanent. It so happened that the very body which gave the lead against Mazarin happened to be that which was most devoted to the preservation of order. But the parlement could not act in secrecy. It searched for legal justifications for resistance in an age when a whole generation had become accustomed to the methods of tyranny. The ancient laws had become unfamiliar, and the parlement, in trying to resurrect them, publicised their intent among the masses. But the very virtue of the laws was the mystery that ought to surround them. When the parlement became the idol of the people, the endeavour to restore legality evoked the passions of the mob and transformed the learned exercises of the lawyers into vulgar riot. This is the meaning of the well-known passage with which Retz ended his analysis:

The people entered into the sanctuary. They lifted the veil that should always shroud all that can be said and all that can be believed about the respective rights of peoples and of kings – rights which are never so well reconciled as when they remain unspoken. What happened in the hall of the Palais de Justice was a profanation of these mysteries.

The account Retz gave in his memoirs of the events of the Fronde was the most successful part of his endeavour to recreate the moods and experiences of the past. He gave no hint of any insincerity of attitude in his defence of contemporary constitutionalism. He did not hesitate to reveal his scorn for the political incapacity of the magistrates who represented these ideals, but he did not attack the ideals themselves. He often claimed in his memoirs to be acting in the public interest rather than in pursuit of his own ambition, but this was as much the reflection of his contemporary self-delusion as it was the consequence of a later desire to justify himself to posterity. While he analysed the actions and motives of others with objectivity, he was often less detached about himself in the memoirs because he was trying to recover the immediacy of his past experience. His first years as coadjutor

D

had been marked by an increasing prudence and an awareness of
the need for realism and foresight in political intrigue. Nevertheless, he could subscribe to the constitutionalist viewpoint with a
measure of conviction, because, in the first place, he did not believe
that others, who accepted it, allowed it to determine all their
actions, and because, in the second place, he was not accepting a
group of defined ideals but a mystery – the arcana of the ancient
laws. The very vagueness of his attitude gave a flexibility to his
actions at that time, and in later years it did not restrict the realism
of his general assessment of the Fronde. The memoirs reflect the
mood in which he had accommodated himself to the political
climate of 1648.

The magistrates began to assume the role of a constitutional
opposition on the very day that Molé's life was menaced by the
mob. Emery's next device was a proposal to create twelve new
masters of requests – officials who arranged the business of the
council and possessed the right to sit in the parlement. This
appeared as a threat to the magistracy in general, for the creation of
new venal offices diminished the perquisites of existing office
holders and depreciated the value of office on what was already a
saturated market.[5] When the existing masters of requests suggested
that it was illegal for the regent to create offices during a royal
minority, the note of constitutional resistance had been sounded.
The government reacted with a *lit de justice* to force the registration
of this and other measures. Omer Talon, who was himself a royal
official in the parlement, gave an eloquent description of popular
suffering under the weight of taxation, and responded to the royal
command with the words: 'You, Sire, are our sovereign lord.
Your Majesty's power comes from on high and no account of it
need be rendered save to God; but it is important for your glory
that we should be free men and not slaves.'[6] Some were prepared
to go further, for on 18 January the parlement took the unprecedented step of re-examining the edicts it had been compelled to
register. A month later the magistrates were proposing not merely
that they should remonstrate, but that they should insist the edicts
be modified.

The agitation continued in the parlement and its sister courts in
Paris and the provinces throughout the spring. In an ill-conceived
attempt to divide his enemies, Mazarin proposed to suspend the

salaries of the officials of the *grand conseil*, the *cour des aides* and the *chambre des comptes*, while promising the renewal of the annual tax or *paulette* paid by the magistrates of the parlement in return for hereditary rights in their offices. This manoeuvre had effects antithetical to those which the first minister had intended. The three courts threatened by Mazarin appealed to the parlement, on the 13 May the latter issued a decree of union, authorising a conference of delegates from all the sovereign courts. The government suspended the *paulette*, arrested some of the delegates and, with the cooperation of Molé, succeeded for a time in postponing the joint session. However, the younger and more radical judges of the *enquêtes* defied the first president, and on 15 June the parlement declared that the union should be executed, only to see the declaration quashed by the council. In an act which the coadjutor described as 'the most base and ridiculous conceivable' the government tried to seize the register containing the decree of execution, and the crowd demonstrated in support of the parlement. Where the magistracy had once been the object of suspicion, it was now idolised by the lower-class elements in Paris. Retz, who was well aware of the mutability of popular emotions, was to remember how the parlement had earlier been cowed by the mob. Meanwhile Gaston of Orléans intervened between the parties to suggest that the *paulette* be granted and the delegates allowed to assemble, provided they restricted their discussion to the domestic interests of the sovereign courts. The parlement again rejected the moderate counsels of Molé, and insisted upon the debating of public affairs.

Towards the end of June the government effected another *volte-face*. Emery was dismissed, and the ban was lifted on the assembly of the delegates of the sovereign courts in the Chambre Saint-Louis. This inaugurated a constitutional revolution. Although a few cautious spirits, especially Molé and président de Mesmes, counselled moderation, their voices were drowned in the clamour of the radical group in the *enquêtes*. These were the men through whom Retz endeavoured to align the parlement with the other elements in the Fronde. They included the abbé Pierre Longueil, whom Retz singled out as the most treacherous and self-interested of the agitators. Longueil was counsellor-clerk in the *grand'chambre* and was subsequently to be bought over by Mazarin.

He possessed great influence over the honest and simple-minded
Broussel, who stood high in the popular estimation for his long
and outspoken opposition to the fiscal policy of the crown, and
who, in the eyes of the coadjutor, had 'more reputation for integrity than for ability'. Associated with these two was Pierre
Viole, president of the fourth chamber of the *enquêtes*, a man who
preferred his pleasures to his profession and was notorious for the
indelicacy of his love affairs. Viole was an intimate friend of
Mazarin's enemy and former patron, Chavigny. Also in the cabal
were présidents Charton and Blancmesnil, while other leading
spokesmen for the opposition were présidents Novion and Le
Coigneux. Retz expressed contempt for their abilities as conspirators. With their legal habits of thought, they seemed to
him to exhibit 'an air of pedantry and chicanery', and to lack the
insight and flexibility necessary for political success, as he understood it.

Though they were indifferent plotters, the radicals inspired the
assembly in the Chambre Saint-Louis to launch an entire reformation of the state. If the ancient laws, which were so much venerated
and yet so difficult to define, remained elusive, the assembly could
at least attack the visible instruments of the alleged tyranny of the
cardinals. Within ten days they enumerated twenty-seven articles
reforming the administration of justice and finance. These required
the suppression of the intendants and the tax-farmers, the abolition
of *lettres de cachet* (whereby arrests could be made without charges
and prisoners held without trial), the reduction of direct taxation
and the removal of certain dues such as the *tarif*. They demanded
the prior consent of the parlement for the establishment of new
taxes and new offices. They would have submitted the monarchy
to the control of a body far less representative of society than the
English parliament, and given the parlement at least as much
authority as its very different namesake had possessed before the
revolution against the Stuart crown.

Mazarin's policy of fostering divisions among the magistrates
proved to be a lamentable failure. When he tried to win the support
of certain members of the *grand conseil* and the *cour des aides* he
invited ridicule, and he received it, not merely among the magistrates but in all circles of Parisian society. As the queen's confidante and lady of honour, madame de Motteville, put it: 'At a

time of revolution such gentle words merely increased distrust for the minister, and produced much mockery of his conduct, which was sometimes too imperious and then all of a sudden became too humble for words. Such stories spread as far as the bedside receptions of the ladies. . . .'[7] The actual proposals of the Chambre Saint-Louis were a greater challenge to the regency than the determination of the delegates to execute the decree of union in defiance of the government. The queen herself exhibited that particular kind of obstinacy which is born of weakness and limited understanding. She was determined to preserve the powers of the crown intact, and, when Mazarin's devious subtleties persuaded her to grant concessions, her change of front was generally accompanied by sulkiness and petulance. Negotiations with the delegates by Gaston, Mazarin and the chancellor, Séguier, produced no weakening in the demands of the magistrates. Mazarin announced that reform could be achieved only by royal declaration, and arranged a *lit de justice* to dissolve the Chambre Saint-Louis.

The royal session on 31 July accepted many of the reforming articles and modified or omitted others. The intendants were abolished, the *taille* reduced, the new office cancelled and the *paulette* guaranteed. Even these concessions failed to mollify the reforming zeal of the parlement. The royal declaration was declared insufficient and a committee established to report on those recommendations ignored by the government. The provincial parlements showed signs of adopting a common front. At Rouen the magistrates refused to register one of the edicts derived from the royal declaration. At Aix-en-Provence the parlement disobeyed a government order affecting the dates of its sessions, and sent delegates to a neighbouring town to expel a group of newly-appointed royal officials. On 21 August the Paris parlement resumed its discussions of the missing articles, and Mazarin began to consider a new show of force.

There was, of course, a third element, besides the opposition of the parlement and the stirrings of popular revolt, which Mazarin had cause to fear, the aristocracy. The queen forbade the discussion of the political crisis within the court, but no one took such a ban seriously and the kaleidoscope of love, faction and intrigue continued to revolve. The irresolute Gaston of Orléans had been actively cooperating with the regent and had taken a major part in the negotiations with the parlement. While he busied himself with matters of such importance he seemed more anxious to work for the preservation of his royal nephew's inheritance than to indulge in the subversive intrigues to which he was so habituated. But his greed for tangible rewards was as insatiable as ever, and he was known to covet the governorship of Languedoc. The duc de Beaufort had escaped from confinement at Vincennes in June and was brooding upon rebellious schemes within the protecting walls of the Vendôme fortress of Anet. Although Condé was campaigning in Flanders against the Spanish, his faction at court pressed his claims, as a prince of Bourbon blood, for such rewards as the admiralcy and the control of parts of Lorraine and Franche-Comté. La Rochefoucauld sought the governorship of Le Havre, and the duc de Longueville had shown signs of disloyalty from the seat of his provincial government at Rouen. Bouillon demanded the return of the principality of Sedan, which Richelieu had confiscated after his plots against the previous régime. His brother Turenne, whose military reputation was second only to that of Condé, commanded the French army on the Rhine.

Retz might himself be numbered among those members of the great nobility whose greed and ambition could no longer be appeased by a bankrupt government. He sensed, if he did not precisely foresee, the role he might play in aligning the three centres of opposition to Mazarin. During the spring and early summer he had distributed vast sums of money to his clientèle among the Parisian lower classes, and, Mazarin, alarmed by reports of these activities, had told him in the queen's presence that he was a wolf rather than a shepherd to his flock. Retz had watched the steady advance of the challenge which the radical group in the parlement presented to the first minister, and, although he claimed in his memoirs that it was a sudden inspiration 'to put into practice those speculations which had preoccupied me from my youth', it was apparent that those elements of the mob to which he had been distributing his largesse rapturously supported the proceedings of the Chambre Saint-Louis.

On 22 August news reached Paris that Condé had won a great victory at Lens. A day later Chavigny met the coadjutor in the hôtel de Lesdiguières, and warned him that Mazarin planned to use the occasion to strike against the opposition. On the 25th Retz preached a panegyric to Louis IX before the court.[8] He warned his audience by declaiming against blasphemy, reminding them how Saint Louis had pierced the tongues of blasphemers who were far less culpable than those who sat before him. Then he turned to hector the king on the need to exterminate the Huguenots, as the Albigensians had been hunted down in Saint Louis' boyhood:

It is not without cause that God confided to you the sword of his justice. His cause must be avenged and the crimes committed against His divine majesty must be punished. Clemency is the virtue of kings, and without it the most legitimate princes in no way differ from tyrants. Yet it loses its lustre and merit when it is employed to drag from the hands of justice these black and infamous criminals who have directly attacked their creator.

Having created his mood, Retz audaciously reproached the government for trying arbitrarily to tax the property of the church. His defence of the immunity of the church was the clerical counterpart of the parlement's defence of private property against arbitrary taxation. Retz illustrated his point from the career of Thomas Becket, and it must have seemed to his audience that the coadjutor was offering himself in the role of the murdered English archbishop. After so much moral passion and rhetoric, Retz went back to his house to dine in the gay company of Gomberville and Chapelain.

On the following day the parlement obeyed the queen's orders to attend a ceremonial *Te Deum* at Notre-Dame to mark Condé's victory. Mazarin had stationed troops along the approaches to the cathedral with the intention of arresting the most troublesome magistrates at the conclusion of the service. The queen paused at the doors to give the appropriate orders to Comminges, a lieutenant of the guards. The act was observed, and the magistrates, who were already suspicious of the troops, hurriedly dispersed. The guards succeeded in arresting one of them, président Blancmesnil of the *enquêtes*. Comminges was then despatched to the house of Broussel, the most outspoken of the government's critics. Broussel was ill in bed, and while he was being hustled into a carriage his family gave the alarm. At once an angry crowd blocked the street and overturned the carriage. A regiment of guards then cleared the way, requisitioned another vehicle, and escorted the prisoner to Saint-Germain. Broussel was a popular figure. As the news of his arrest spread through the city, the streets were filled with people, shops were shut and chains and barricades placed across the road. Paris took on the atmosphere of mass emotion it had assumed in the popular riots of the League in May 1588, when the barricades had enclosed Henry III in the Louvre and isolated the troops in the suburbs.

The coadjutor hurried out into the middle of the commotion, still dressed in the robes he had worn for the *Te Deum*. As he passed the Pont Neuf he saw marshal de la Meilleraye and a small body of guards being stoned by the mob that had surrounded them. The marshal was a personal friend, though this had not prevented Retz from seducing his wife. Raising his hand to bless the crowd, the coadjutor made his way to La Meilleraye and escorted him to the Palais-Royal, while the rioters followed behind, calling for the release of Broussel. At the palace Retz found the queen with Mazarin, Gaston, Longueville, La Rivière and a group of courtiers. La Meilleraye stressed the serious nature of the rising and pleaded for authority to use force against the mob. Others played down the affair, and one courtier tried to amuse the queen by parodying the manner in which Broussel's nurse had called for help against Comminges. But the queen was enraged that anyone should even talk of a rising against the royal authority.

Retz described the scene vividly in his memoirs, recalling his impression that nearly everyone was acting a part. Mazarin was hypocritically praising Retz's concern for the people, the city and the government, while the coadjutor was assuming innocence. Longueville put on a mask of melancholy to hide his joy at the beginning of a revolution from which he hoped to profit. Gaston was pretending an intense urgency, while actually admiring the charms of one of the queen's ladies. Each adopted his pose until the arrival of chancellor Séguier, when Mazarin asked Guitaut, a captain of the guards, for his advice. Guitaut believed that Broussel should be surrendered, whether dead or alive it did not matter. Retz suggested that violence against Broussel would not be prudent, and that his release would certainly calm the tumult outside. The regent flushed with anger and turned on Retz, saying: 'I follow you, monsieur le coadjuteur, you want me to set Broussel at liberty. I would rather throttle him with my own hands.' As she spoke she lifted her hands as if she could willingly strangle Retz in similar fashion. Mazarin was at once whispering in her ear, advising her to moderate her fury. At that moment one of the city magistrates entered, pallid with fear, and described the menaces and manhandling he had received in trying to reach the palace. His terror proved contagious and those who had ridiculed the affair were no longer in doubt of its gravity. It was agreed that Broussel should be released, and Mazarin asked the coadjutor to carry the news to the people. Retz saw the trap that was laid for him, for if the promise were dishonoured he would lose his credit with the crowd. He could hardly refuse, however, and so he walked back into the streets with La Meilleraye, bestowing benisons in all directions as he went. He was careful to tell the crowd that the queen assured him that Broussel would be freed if the riot were ended. In this way he took no personal responsibility.

These endeavours to restore public order were not assisted by the clumsiness of the marshal, who called out at the top of his voice: 'Long live the King! Freedom for Broussel!' The intention behind the words was not made clearer by the fact that La Meilleraye waved his sword as he shouted and was followed at a little distance by a troop of light horse. In an instant the crowd became menacing and weapons were exposed. The soldiers advanced. La Meilleraye pistolled a man flourishing a sabre. Armed men began to arrive on all sides. Retz pressed through the mob to place himself between the marshal and a group of armed bourgeois. La Meilleraye seized the opportunity to restrain his men from opening fire, and it seemed momentarily as if further violence would be avoided. But a number of the rioters charged the soldiers, and amid shots and blows the coadjutor was felled by a stone beneath the ear. He was lifted by an apothecary's boy who levelled a musket at his head. According to his own account, Retz saved his life by the quick use of his wits. The boy hesitated when Retz told him his father would be distressed to see him in such circumstances, thinking that his victim knew his family. A moment later he recognised Retz from his robes and cried out: 'Long live the coadjutor!' The cry was taken up on all sides, and Retz and the marshal began to withdraw towards the Palais-Royal:

Now everyone was following me, and it was just as well, for this swarming mass of refuse was armed to the teeth. I flattered them, I caressed them, I insulted them, I threatened them, and at last I convinced them. They put away their weapons, which was the saving of Paris, because, if they had still been carrying them as the night drew on, the city would most certainly have been sacked.

Thirty thousand or more disarmed men followed him back to the palace. Retz expected gratitude from the queen, or so he alleged. Yet, despite La Meilleraye's expostulations, she received him quizzically and dismissed him with mockery instead of praise. As he returned to his house the crowd pressed about him, requiring an explanation of affairs inside the palace. He mounted the roof of a carriage with the aim, as he put it, of quietening the throng about him. Then, as it was nearly time for their supper, the crowd let him pass, still bleeding from his wound. He was soon pressed to act by those professional plotters, Montrésor and Laigues, who told him that the court regarded him as an agitator who had incited the populace to riot. They added to these reports stories of the way in which the court wits were elaborating his misadventures earlier in the day. Retz maintained in his memoirs that despite such malignity on the part of the court, he would have stood firm in his duty to the queen, had not another of Soissons' former confederates, the seigneur d'Argenteuil, arrived with a report that the government intended to send the parlement to Montargis and to exile the coadjutor to Quimper in Brittany.

Retz withdrew from his companions for fifteen minutes and reflected upon his past designs, upon the role of a *chef de parti* as he had admired it in Plutarch, upon his career in the church, and upon the way in which a concatenation of accidents had suddenly opened to him an opportunity greater than that which many of his heroes had had offered to them. The vices of an archbishop, he reflected, could become the virtues of a faction leader. He took the decision to 'abandon my destiny to all the fluctuations of glory'.

Midnight sounded as he returned to the room where Montrésor and Laigues were waiting. He told them that he was less concerned with justifying himself against the slanders of the court than with protecting the public from oppression. By midday on the morrow, he announced, he would be master of Paris. He at once summoned his principal agent within the militia, a certain Miron who was an official in the *chambre des comptes* and also a colonel of the citizen guard in the district of Saint-German-l'Auxerrois. Miron promised to arrange the beating of drums and the general call to arms in the morning. As they were conferring, a spy came in to report details of the government's military plans, and the plotters immediately re-arranged their dispositions to frustrate the movements of the royal troops.

Such, at least, was Retz's version of the first day of the barricades. According to his secretary, Guy Joly, who was then a magistrate of the local city court, or *châtelet*, the coadjutor was far less heroic and disinterested. In Joly's account Retz tried to dissociate himself from the royal troops, and was accidentally stoned while confessing a dying criminal shot down by La Meilleraye. His benedictions were designed to provoke rather than appease the mob, and he was so exhausted by the street fighting that he had to be supported to his house by Argenteuil and the poet Marigny. He had been planning the affair for some time and was in touch with Noirmoutier, Saint-Ibal and Varicarville as well as Laigues and Montrésor.[9] But Retz in his memoirs adjudged things quite differently. His motives were honourable and his loyalty firm, even though he was misjudged and slandered by the court he had tried to serve. He had been calm and resourceful in a bewildering succession of tense and dangerous circumstances. He had indulged in no intrigue to provoke the revolutionary situation. This had arisen gradually and spontaneously in response to the oppression of the régime and the foolish vacillations of Mazarin. Chance had obliged him to follow the road he had once traced out for Fieschi. This would be more convincing had he not admitted his link with the cabal in the parlement of Longueil, Viole, Broussel, Charton and Blancmesnil, and his careful cultivation of a popular party. The fact is that Retz had been playing one part, while providing secretly for another and postponing the decision to exchange roles as long as possible.

After a few hours of sleep the coadjutor was awoken at 6 a.m. by a messenger from Miron. Parties of armed citizens were already at their appointed posts and reconnaissance revealed that the guards had been unable to occupy the strategic points selected by the government. Everywhere the city answered the call to arms.

Everywhere Retz seemed to have his agents. In the rue Saint-Jacques, where Martineau, a judge in the *requêtes* and captain of the quarter, was too drunk to perform his duties, his wife sounded the alarm and posted the militia. Madame de Martineau was the sister of Retz's mistress, madame de Pommereuil, and apparently possessed the same martial qualities.[10] Memories of the popular risings in the time of the League were still alive. The duc de Brissac, married to that cousin with whom Retz had once tried to elope, accompanied the coadjutor on a tour of inspection, and pointed out a standard with a representation on it of 'Saint' Jacques Clément, the assassin of Henry III. Retz estimated twelve hundred barricades to have been erected within two hours, each strengthened with barrels of earth and ordure and crowned with cobble stones ready for use as missiles. Even young children were observed carrying poignards. Two companies of Swiss guards had advanced on the Port de Nesle, where they were attacked by Argenteuil, at the head of a contingent of revolutionaries, and driven back with casualties. Séguier, the chancellor, had been intercepted on his way to the parlement with a royal order to suspend proceedings, and had taken refuge in the hôtel de Luynes, which was promptly pillaged by the mob. He saved his life by hiding in a cupboard, whence he was ultimately rescued by La Meilleraye with four companies of guards. After this all movement by troops or representatives of the court became impossible. While anxious consultations were carried on in the Palais-Royal, the populace waited grimly behind their barricades. Retz had fulfilled his promise.

The parlement had assembled very early in the morning. It debated the policy to be adopted while the crowd outside chanted for the return of Broussel. A decree was passed against Comminges, and a deputation of sixty magistrates set off in their robes to intercede at the Palais-Royal. The barricades were opened as they approached and cries of acclamation were mingled with shouts for the downfall of Mazarin. The deputation found the queen transported with fury. 'You will answer for this to me,' she told them, 'you, your wives and your children.' Then she retired into her grey room, slamming the door in their faces. Molé and Mesmes pleaded with Gaston for a further audience, and eventually a third of the delegates were ushered into the inner room. The

regent again withdrew, refusing to hear them. Mazarin promised
to release the prisoners if the parlement undertook to cease their
intervention in public affairs. The judges resolved to return to
deliberate this offer, but when they emerged from the palace without an order for Broussel's release the mood of the crowd changed
dramatically. They managed to pass through two barricades, but
at the third Molé found a halberd thrust against his stomach and
an offer to face death or to go back and recover either Broussel or
Mazarin and Séguier as hostages. A large part of the deputation
tucked up their gowns and fled, but Molé, as ever, stood his
ground and maintained his dignity. He led back the remainder to
the Palais-Royal, and found the queen still inflexible. At last, with
Gaston and a group of princesses begging her on their knees to
relent, she adopted Mazarin's advice. Copies of the order for the
release of the prisoners were prepared so that the magistrates could
report to their masters that this time their mission had been
achieved.

The coadjutor had meanwhile been receiving approaches from
malcontents within the court. He used Argenteuil, Laigues and
Renaud de Sévigné as his intermediaries with dissident members
of the aristocracy. Longueville was reported to have seen him,
although Retz did not mention it in his memoirs.[11] The queen's
personal treasurer brought a request that he should use his
influence with the people to moderate their violence. Retz replied
that his efforts to serve the queen had cost him his credit with the
crowd. With the cries of 'Long live the coadjutor' ringing in his
ears, the messenger could hardly find this convincing. Retz was in
no position to control affairs once the queen had surrendered
Broussel to the parlement. As soon as the news spread, the barricades began to be dismantled and the shops reopened. On 28
August there were few surviving signs of the events of the two
preceding days, and Retz, knowing that he would never be forgiven for forcing the hand of the government, prepared himself
for the next round of the contest.

SIX

Civil war

Retz scarcely needed the warnings of the princesse de Guémenée to know that the court regarded him as the author of the barricades. He listened with 'somewhat less sincerity than respect' to the queen's explanation that it was the pernicious advice of Chavigny, and not the counsel of Mazarin, that had persuaded her to attempt her coup. When he obeyed her injunction to 'console the poor cardinal', he was as sceptical of Mazarin's effusive gestures of goodwill as the first minister doubtless was of Retz's own assurances. No solution to the constitutional deadlock appeared in sight. The radical group among the magistrates resolved to exact the queen's acceptance of the outstanding articles of the Chambre Saint-Louis. The queen was determined to withdraw the government from the pressures of the Parisian lower classes and to preserve the rights of the crown, especially that of issuing *lettres de cachet*. A fortnight after the barricades Mazarin and the king left Paris for Richelieu's former house at Rueil. The queen lingered to bid farewell to the civic dignitaries and to visit her nuns at Val-de-Grâce. Upon her arrival at Rueil she began to reveal her hand by exiling the minister Châteauneuf and locking up Chavigny in the fortress of Vincennes, where he was supposed to be governor. Both men were Mazarin's rivals and were known to have links with the dissidents. The court then moved to the greater security of Saint-Germain and began to concentrate troops near the capital. Meanwhile Condé returned from his frontier campaign and both sides strove to secure his allegiance.

The parlement had obliged the regent to agree to the postponement of its normal vacation so that it might debate the *tarif*, the *taille*, and Mazarin's manipulation of the interest rates on government bonds guaranteed by the hôtel de Ville. On 22 September 1648 the radical magistrates, strengthened by popular agitation against the absence of the king from Paris, began to debate public security. Président Viole asked whether the capital was about to be besieged and suggested the re-enaction of a 1617 decree against the Italian favourite of Marie de Médicis, Concini, preventing the appointment of foreigners as ministers. Molé stood firm against so challenging a measure, but he could not prevent a declaration requiring the reasons for the 'arbitrary and tyrannical imprisonment' of Châteauneuf and Chavigny. When a delegation arrived at the court bearing this document, together with a demand for the return of the king, Anne of Austria refused to reconsider her action against the ministers, and pretended that the Palais-Royal was still infected with the smallpox which her second son had recently contracted there. The royal council then quashed the declaration of the parlement and ordered it to confine its attention to the *tarif*. The magistrates chose to ignore these instructions, and again referred to the edict of 1617. Everything seemed now to depend upon the attitude of Condé.

In the portraits which prefaced his account of the opening of the civil war in the memoirs, Retz showed more sympathy for Condé than he did for any of his other opponents in the Fronde. He regarded the victor of Rocroi and Lens as the military genius of his age, and compared him with Caesar and Alexander. Retz found it difficult to identify that flaw in Condé's character which prevented him from attaining complete supremacy in either government or faction. He praised the quality of his mind as well as of his heart, but concluded that his narrow upbringing had limited his political talents. The truth was that Condé was too arrogant to appreciate any merit save his own. His dash and intrepidity on the battlefield was ill-suited to the subtle manoeuvres in which both Retz and Mazarin delighted. He thrust his impatient presence into the political counsels of the regency as if he were leading a cavalry charge, and then rapidly became bored with the endless negotiations between the court and the parlement. His self-interest was expressed in terms of the status to which he had been born as a prince of the Bourbon blood, and his thirst for glory was accompanied by none of the cynical appreciation of the interests of others manifested by the coadjutor. His underlying weakness, as the duchesse de Nemours described it, was that he cared more about gaining victories than he did about winning hearts.

Retz saw that Condé would willingly displace Mazarin. He recorded in his memoirs the prince's contemptuous opinion of the first minister as a 'Sicilian scoundrel' ('*gredin de Sicile*'). Yet Condé wavered uneasily between the conflicting advice of his friends. The new duc de Châtillon, who was in touch with the coadjutor, counselled him to join the frondeurs, whereas the comte de Gramont besought him to offer his sword to the regent. Retz felt he possessed Condé's sympathy because of the latter's support in his dispute over precedence with Gaston of Orléans. Moreover, he had offered to help Condé in a scheme to make the prince's brother, Conti, a cardinal. This scheme was very much in Retz's own interest since a rival contender for a place in the sacred college was Gaston's henchman, La Rivière, for whom Retz displayed his distaste as 'the lowest and most selfseeking mind of the age'. Condé twice accepted the coadjutor's invitation to dine with him and other frondeurs at Broussel's. Retz claimed that the prince gave him assurances of support and agreed to his suggestion gradually to replace Mazarin in the queen's counsels, while at first pretending to accept the cardinal's views. Guy Joly, on the other hand, recorded Condé's subsequent denial that he had ever given such promises. Indeed Retz himself admitted that, while Condé was prepared to decry Mazarin and to call the magistrates 'those devils in square bonnets', he responded to the least hint of sedition with the proud words: 'I am named Louis de Bourbon and it is not my wish to unsettle the throne.'

The coadjutor feared that his friends in the parlement might move too quickly, and, further, that popular agitation might force them to defy the court before Condé was committed to his cause. He could see a danger that the prince might turn impetuously to the queen as soon as the royal authority was directly impugned. Condé revealed to Retz his discovery that his fellow frondeur, the duc de Noirmoutier, was in secret correspondence with Mazarin. Noirmoutier, whom the coadjutor already distrusted, had been responsible for the administration of the French army in Flanders, and had resigned his post after a bitter quarrel with the prince. There was sufficient common ground for Condé to agree that he would dissuade the government from ordering an immediate attack upon the capital. Already the comte d'Erlach, who had inherited Bernard of Saxe-Weimar's mercenary army which was employed by Richelieu, had crossed the Somme with four thousand Germans. The parlement began to issue orders to prepare to withstand a siege, and the *prévôt des marchands* was instructed to marshal the militia and to lay in supplies of food. Condé did in fact point out to the regent that so small a force would be swallowed up in the streets of Paris. Mazarin himself was anxious to avoid civil conflict at a time when his negotiations to end the European war in Germany seemed on the brink of success.

It was Anne of Austria who was determined to use force rather than surrender any more of the royal prerogative: but the cumulative caution of Mazarin, Gaston and Condé began to have its effect. She allowed Séguier to discuss with Molé the possibility of restricting the use of *lettres de cachet* for a limited period, and she even agreed in early October to the abolition of arbitrary imprisonment if the parlement would renounce its newly acquired authority in financial matters. The parlement responded by voting large reductions in both direct and indirect taxation. On 22 October she accepted Mazarin's advice that concessions exacted under pressure might subsequently be withdrawn, and with tears of frustration signed a document admitting all the articles drawn up by the Chambre Saint-Louis. The parlement registered the declaration two days later in the belief that it had secured a total victory. The treaty of Westphalia, ending the Thirty Years' War, was signed at Münster and Osnabrück at the same time; Chavigny and Châteauneuf were allowed to return; and the court resumed residence in Paris at the end of the month.

It seemed as if a second confrontation had been narrowly averted, but to Retz the situation was still one he hoped to exploit. Mazarin had been endeavouring to buy his good will, or else to neutralise his influence. Marshal de la Meilleraye, who had replaced Emery as superintendent of the finances, approached him with a gift of forty thousand crowns as a mark of the crown's appreciation for his services on the day of the barricades. This the coadjutor refused with a 'sincerity proportionate to that of the offer'. Another temptation came with the suggestion that Retz might combine his clerical status with the governorship of Paris. The eighty-year-old duc de Montbazon was ready to resign this post for a consideration, although it was also necessary to buy out the

claims of his son, the prince de Guémenée. With his links with
Montbazon's daughter, madame de Chevreuse, and his more
intimate liaison with the princesse de Guémenée, Retz might
already assume a rather irregular association with the family.
The governorship would have complemented the very different
kind of authority he already possessed in the city. He reproached
himself in the memoirs for even considering so dangerous a proposal. As soon as Mazarin felt he could discredit the coadjutor by
disclosing his worldly ambitions, he broke off the negotiations.[1]

The royal declaration included arrangements for the payment of
the troops, and Mazarin chose to bend these provisions to the
financial advantage of his friends. In December, when the mutin-
ous and still-unpaid soldiery began to pillage the outer suburbs,
the parlement started to investigate alleged infractions of the
declaration. Gaston of Orléans had been showing a greater
sympathy for the magistrates, which became more pronounced as
Condé advanced himself in the queen's favour. However, La
Rivière was induced to recover Gaston's cooperation for the court
by pointing out the foolishness of allowing the prince to monopo-
lise the regent's confidence. At the end of the month both the
king's uncle and Condé took their places in the parlement in an
endeavour to mediate between the court and the magistrates.
Matters took a very different turn when Condé suddenly lost
patience with the government's critics and made a threatening
gesture against président Viole. The prince withdrew in anger
amid the murmurs of Viole's friends in the *enquêtes*. Condé's
reputation among the radicals vanished in an instant, and he, for
his part, was now resolved to make the parlement pay for its
indiscipline. Alarmed at his growing dependence on Condé,
Mazarin was now obliged to revert to the queen's preferred policy
of force.

Like his fellow frondeurs among the aristocracy, Retz was fully
prepared to provoke civil war. He and his associates now welcomed the name frondeur, which had originally been applied to
the gangs of young criminals who used slings (*frondes*) as weapons
of offence in their brushes with the Paris watch. As the leaders of
resistance to Spain in the Netherlands had gloried in the name
'beggars' given them by the Spanish regent, so the frondeurs took
pride in what had once been a term of opprobrium. Retz had

continued to intrigue with his coterie of aristocratic dissidents while alternately stimulating and restraining his friends in the parlement. Since the situation was far from being within his control, and since his plans were by no means as precise as either he or his enemies subsequently pretended, he had allowed affairs to drift in the expectation that a more favourable opportunity for action would present itself. He had held back the magistrates in the hope that he would win over Condé, but this policy had proved an entire failure. On the one hand it had nearly resulted in an accommodation between the parlement and the court, and on the other it had resulted in a breach between the parlement and Condé. His house, like that of the magistrate Longueil, was the centre of perpetual discussions between the plotters, as his secretary, Guy Joly, recalled in his memoirs.[2] Retz saw that the weeks following the royal declaration were critical to his enterprise. Now, when the tension in the capital had intensified and the continuing resistance of the parlements of Bordeaux and Aix-en-Provence maintained the possibility of general revolution,[3] he made one last attempt to win over the arrogant and impetuous Condé.

The arguments which Retz employed with Condé were worthy of the high estimate he formed of himself as the master of conspiracy and intrigue. The prince's anger against the parlement had turned to contempt, and he told Retz that he scorned the prospect of becoming 'general of an army of madmen'. The coadjutor interpreted this opinion to suit his own purposes. The parlement, he argued, was really more concerned than anyone with the maintenance of the royal authority, and it was not aware of the consequences of its present attitude. It ought to stand between the power of the crown and the obedience of the people: instead, it had given a lead to popular discontents and revealed the mysteries of government to the vulgar gaze. Every monarchy had its own mystique. That of France consisted of 'a kind of sacred and religious silence' which hid the right of the individual to dispense with royal authority on occasions when obedience would not actually be in the crown's best interest. The popular movement aroused by the parlement could not now be arrested, and it was associated with provincial disobedience. Condé alone was in a position to check the growing anarchy. The queen was dominated by Mazarin, and Gaston by La Rivière. If the prince were to join them he would be hated as they were hated. But if he were to join the parlement he would become its master. He would not have to contend with any challenge to his leadership such as that which his ancestors had sustained from the Calvinist burghers and pastors, who had disputed the authority of the first princes of Condé within the Huguenot party during the wars of religion. He could control the parlement with the severe methods that Mayenne, the leader of the Catholic League, had employed in the same period. And the national movement which he might lead would be far more effective than that of the League, because he was of royal blood, whereas the leaders of the League, the Guise family, had been regarded as foreigners in alliance with Spain. La Rivière was a craven soul: Mazarin was feeble and universally execrated. In fact the role which Condé might play was not only a great one: it was also singularly easy to execute.

None of these arguments had much effect. It was the fault of heroes, Retz reflected, that they did not think deeply enough before they acted. Condé rejected the part in which the coadjutor had cast him – that of restorer of the public welfare – and declared his preference for the role of preserver of the royal authority. He sacrificed an opportunity to achieve a success far more resounding than that of the Guises because, in Retz's opinion, he lacked the vision to comprehend it. Indeed he attempted to drag Retz along the path he had chosen. He vowed to discipline the parlement on behalf of the king, and, if need be, to starve the capital into sub-mission. As Condé saw it, the coadjutor was foolish to compromise himself with men as variable and untrustworthy as the magistrates. He would be wiser if he allowed the prince to reconcile him with the court. It was now Retz's turn to reject advice. He was, he said, coadjutor to the people of Paris, and he would serve them as his conscience directed.

No sooner had Condé refused the part proposed for him than Retz began to search for a new leading actor for his drama. He found, at first, another entrepreneur – madame de Longueville, sister to Condé and Conti and mistress to La Rochefoucauld. His interest in her was not confined to politics. Despite the ravages of smallpox her beauty was still remarkable, and her charms were enhanced by the quality of her intelligence. The coadjutor wished to instal her in his affections between the princesse de Guémenée and madame de Pommereuil, but this proved impossible. As he put it, 'the benefice was not vacant, but neither was it occupied: La Rochefoucauld was in possession, but he was in Poitou'. Retz pretended that he valued his friendship with the duc de Longueville sufficiently to place it before both pleasure and politics. Longueville had already been in touch with the coadjutor during the barricades. His wife was estranged from the queen, and pleaded her advanced pregnancy as an excuse for not attending the court. While she bitterly opposed the prince, her relationship with her younger brother, Conti, was quite otherwise. Conti so admired and pursued his sister that several contemporaries suspected an unnatural liaison between them. Retz, however, denied this in his memoirs, pointing out that Conti's attentions had not varied even during the height of her passion for the unfortunate Coligny, whose gallantry had cost him his life in the aftermath of the affair of the *Importants*. Conti had never been a party to his elder brother's schemes to make him a cardinal. He had some sense of religious vocation, but he feared that such a step would deprive him of his patrimony to Condé's advantage.

Retz went through his list of malcontents with madame de Longueville to see whom they might promote as faction leaders. The duc de Longueville, who in the coadjutor's view never quite possessed the ability to achieve the grand designs he formulated, was to be reserved for the second act. Marshal de la Mothe-Houdancourt had been rewarded for his failure in the Catalan campaign with a short imprisonment, and was now ready to lend his sword to any group opposing Mazarin. But the marshal's lion-hearted courage was not matched by his good sense, and the demerits that made him a second-class captain rendered him impossible as a political leader. The duc d'Elbeuf of the house of Guise and Lorraine was also rejected. Retz described him as possessing thrust and initiative but inclined to substitute an unnecessary artfulness where straightforward judgment would suffice. Beaufort, who was still sheltering in Anet, was equally fond of posturing, but he did not come into consideration at this stage. La Rochefoucauld could be relied on to follow his mistress into the Fronde, although Retz already had strong prejudices against him which he could not, of course, mention to his accomplice. He felt that La Rochefoucauld had been compromised by making a private peace with the court at the expense of the *Importants*. For that matter Retz did not entirely trust madame de Longueville, for he recorded his opinion that passion obliged her to put politics in second place – that she was too much of an adventuress to become the heroine of a great party. La Rochefoucauld's memoirs expressed this view with a little more gallantry. It was her weakness, they stated, to accept the opinions of those who adored her to the point where she forgot her own.[4]

The conspirators expected that the duc de Bouillon would play a large part in the opening scenes of their production. Retz remarked that they were concerned about 'his probity being more problematical than his talent'. Yet in another place in the memoirs Retz praised his acute political judgment and said that it was wrong to impugn his good faith. He was capable, he said, of doing all the great things which he never in fact achieved. Bouillon's intrigues were abetted by his wife, one of the leading frondeuses, whom Retz could never quite make out. Madame de Bouillon was a great beauty, like her friend madame de Longueville, and the coadjutor, who was piqued by her habit of seeing through his designs and rebuffing his gallant advances, questioned her sincerity. Also connected with Bouillon was his stern and taciturn brother, Turenne, who commanded the army of the Rhine. Retz admitted in the portraits of the frondeurs prefacing his description of the first civil war that Turenne's character and motives were equally difficult to penetrate. He concluded that Turenne lacked political enterprise and was more suited to command an army than a faction. It was resolved that Conti should become the figurehead of the malcontents. To the coadjutor it was a good sign in such a *chef de parti* that his lieutenants were apt to forget to take account of his opinions. His only importance was that he was a prince of the Blood. He possessed no positive qualities, and differed from Gaston of Orléans only in that he substituted malice for the latter's feebleness. Conti was entirely at the disposal of his sister, and she agreed that at the appropriate time he, La Mothe-Houdancourt and Longueville should all declare themselves. Bouillon was prepared to commit himself to an undertaking with Retz alone, but not as yet to a joint declaration.

The whole account of these intrigues in Retz's memoirs repre-
sents the preparations for the civil war as a deliberate mise en
scène, a contrived piece of theatre. He described the way in which
Broussel, Longueil and Viole were taken into the confidence of the
frondeur nobility, and how they planned to commit the parlement
to the cause. He told of the comings and goings at the Gondi
estate at Noisy, where his brother, the duc de Retz, was in attendance and Conti and his sister pretended to take the waters. He
provided details of the manner in which he used the clergy of the
diocese to denounce the financial expedients of the government
and to foment hatred of Mazarin. But in fact the initiative was by
no means in the hands of the coadjutor and his friends. Before
dawn on the morning of 5 January 1649 the court stole out of
Paris and established itself at Saint-Germain. There were few
furnishings in the palace, because the queen had been anxious not
to give any prior warning of her intention. Yet, despite the discomfort, everyone was in high spirits at the prospect of decisive
action at last. Orders were given for Condé's troops to seize all
points of communication round the capital, and Turenne was sent
instructions to hold his army in readiness to march back from
Germany. Gaston had been given so many favours that he
appeared committed to the government, while Conti and other
leading malcontents within the court had been obliged to accompany the government to Saint-Germain.

Paris reacted to the escape of the court with both revolutionary
zeal and lively apprehension. The militia occupied some of the
city gates, while the parlement assembled in what Retz called 'a
tumult of consternation'. The government had left a letter for the
municipal authorities at the hôtel de Ville, explaining that the
king had had to flee because of 'the pernicious designs of certain
members of the parlement, who were in secret intelligence with
the enemies of the state'. The coadjutor had sound sources of
information within the hôtel de Ville. He was in close touch with
président Le Féron, the *prévôt des marchands*, who was also chair-
man of the second chamber of the *enquêtes* and a colonel in the
militia. The leading councillor, Fournier, who overshadowed
the mayor, was also committed to the frondeurs. On the assumption that one fear is likely to be dissipated by another and greater
fear, Retz arranged for the contents of the hôtel de Ville letter to

be disclosed to the parlement. This stimulated the magistrates into an act of public disobedience. They voted that the letter should be debated later, and in the meantime issued a call to arms and took measures for the security and provisioning of the city, as they had done in the preceding October.

Early on the following morning the coadjutor was wakened by a messenger from the queen who brought specific orders for him to attend the court at Saint-Germain. He decided to add colour to his excuses by feigning his forcible retention by the mob. His carriage was overturned by his own agents in the Marché-Neuf, and he was placed upon a table and carried back to his house amid the shouts and tears of his admirers from the markets. He wrote dutifully to both the regent and Condé that his attempt to escape had been foiled, but his explanation was received with scepticism.[5]

On 7 January the parlement received a royal *lettre de cachet* ordering its transference to Montargis. At the same time the *chambre des comptes* was ordered to Orléans, and the *grand conseil* to Mantes. The former body began to compose remonstrances, while the *grand conseil* endeavoured to obey, only to find the necessary passports refused by the municipality. In the parlement Molé was doing his utmost to prevent hostilities, but he was unwilling to surrender the independence of the judiciary by accepting the royal command. He managed to frustrate a move by the radical lobby to declare Mazarin exiled, and agreed to a proposal that the royal officers in the parlement should go to Saint-Germain to assure the queen of their obedience and also to ask for details of the charges implied in the hôtel de Ville letter. The queen had already told a delegation from the municipality that the court would return by one gate if the parlement left by another. She refused to receive any of the magistrates until they had obeyed her order to move to Montargis.

The receipt of this news encouraged Broussel, Longueil, Viole, Charton and their associates to press once more for a declaration against Mazarin. This time they carried the day, and Mazarin was denounced as 'author of the disorders and present trouble, disturber of the public peace, and enemy of king and state'. He was required to leave the court within twenty-four hours, and the kingdom within a week. Should he fail to obey, he might be legitimately attacked by any subject of the king.

On the afternoon of the same day (8 January) representatives from the four sovereign courts and the municipal government met the governor to concert common measures for the defence and administration of the city. The mayor was instructed to raise an army of four thousand horse and ten thousand foot, and taxes were voted for their maintenance. The heaviest burden was to be borne by those magistrates whose offices had been created by Richelieu. The coadjutor's friend, président Novion, made a voluntary contribution of 200,000 livres, and Retz himself raised a regiment at his own expense which soon became known as the regiment of Corinth, after the special title bestowed by the pope on its patron. At the same time such funds as were found in the royal treasury were seized, and orders given for the confiscation of property belonging to real or supposed supporters of Mazarin. Many who wished to remain aloof from the conflict hid their wealth in the churches, where it was often discovered and transferred to the revolutionary funds. Retz gave instructions for the collecting of all ecclesiastical silver in the churches so that it might be melted down to provide for the war. Among the many doggerel verses composed at the time, one such *triolet* was devoted to this incident:

> Monsieur our coadjutor
> Is selling his cross for a sling;
> What a fine and valiant pastor!
> He knows that David, once a frondeur,
> Became the world's greatest king;
> So monsieur our coadjutor
> Is selling his cross for a sling.[6]

During these days Retz was occupied with an endless series of meetings and discussions. He had resisted the call of Saint-Ibal to contact the Spanish army in the Netherlands. He hoped to control the parlement through his friends there and through the maintenance of popular agitation. But, while he had eventually succeeded in committing the magistrates as a body to armed defiance, he was alarmed at the failure of the high nobility to declare themselves. A few nobles had come forward who were as careless of their loyalties as were Retz's habitual group of aristocratic plotters – Noirmoutier, Laigues, Montrésor and Saint-Ibal. The marquis de la Boulaye was among the first to offer his sword,

and the duc de Brissac arrived with the frank avowal that he would
fight for whatever cause best favoured his own interest. But the
absence of Conti was a growing embarrassment. The coadjutor
could not announce that the cause was led by a prince of the Blood,
because the news would have caused Conti's immediate arrest at
Saint-Germain. Although La Rochefoucauld had been sent to the
court a few hours after its escape so that he might strengthen
Conti's resolution, it was feared that Condé would oblige both his
brother and Longueville to serve the regency. Noirmoutier reported that they were still firm in their support for the Fronde,
and this was confirmed by a letter received from La Rochefoucauld
by madame de Longueville. Yet a military leader was urgently
required, and neither La Mothe-Houdancourt nor Bouillon were
ready to declare themselves without Conti.

At this point all Retz's plans seemed to be disrupted by another
unforeseen event. Soon after the meeting of the representatives
at the hôtel de Ville the duc d'Elbeuf and his three sons arrived
in the city. Elbeuf had already told Brissac that he intended to
become generalissimo of the Fronde and that he would make a
better success of it than his cousin Mayenne had of the League.
But even if he had been a capable commander, Elbeuf was no
friend to the coadjutor and had no intention of fitting in with the
latter's plans. He had been the sworn enemy of Soissons, to
whose conspiracy Retz had formerly been a party, and, like
Soissons and Beaufort, he had been the lover of madame de
Montbazon. Elbeuf called on the coadjutor on his way to the
hôtel de Ville, and, although Retz tried to have Fournier delay
matters, the duke was in fact offered the command he sought. The
appointment was to be confirmed by the parlement on the following day. Retz at once instructed the clergy to spread the rumour
that Elbeuf was secretly in touch with La Rivière at Saint-
Germain.

The coadjutor could no longer delay the announcement of
Conti's support to his trusted associates in the parlement. The
night was spent concerting measures to defeat Elbeuf's claim to
the leadership. Then, at 2 a.m. Retz was informed that Conti and
Longueville had arrived from Saint-Germain and were awaiting
admission at the Porte Saint-Honoré. The coadjutor dressed
hurriedly and collected Broussel on his way to the city gate. But

Condé's brother was so much the object of suspicion to the bourgeois guard that dawn was breaking before the prince and his companion were allowed to pass the barrier. The party retired to their beds and while they slept Elbeuf appeared before the assembled magistrates. Molé seized the opportunity to divide the frondeurs and procured the parlement's endorsement of Elbeuf's command, despite the resistance of Retz's group. Later in the day the parlement reassembled to hear Conti. Retz conducted the prince to the Palais de Justice in his own carriage and noted that the crowd would not extend to his companion the acclamation they accorded their coadjutor. Elbeuf stage-managed his own arrival before the magistrates with a military escort, and assertively restated his claims to retain the command. Since Conti was as distrusted by the parlement as he was by the people, Retz saw that the time was inopportune to challenge Elbeuf, and withdrew with his own candidate, exchanging taunts with the duke as he went.

Longueville, La Mothe-Houdancourt and the coadjutor repaired later to the house of Bouillon, who was kept to his bed by gout. Their discussions resulted in a new plan of campaign against Elbeuf. Retz's agents in the militia and the suburbs reported a change in public opinion, as greater numbers were initiated into Retz's 'secret' concerning Elbeuf and La Rivière. A further libel was set on foot in the form of supposed collusion between Elbeuf and the commanders of Condé's troops. On 11 January, when the duke's credit with the masses had been sufficiently shaken, Retz had Conti and Longueville return to the parlement to play out the rest of the farce. Longueville entered at the appropriate time to announce that he was prepared to bring over Normandy to the cause of the parlement. Then the gouty Bouillon appeared, leaning on two gentlemen, and proclaimed that he would be content to serve the parlement under a prince such as Conti. Elbeuf, however, remained obdurate, so Retz set in motion the next part of his scheme.

Le Coigneux defeated Molé's attempt to adjourn the assembly, and while the debate continued the coadjutor escorted the wives of Longueville and Bouillon to the hôtel de Ville. The two duchesses appeared to their best advantage when they showed themselves with their infant children to the crowd gathered in the square. Their beauty and their neglected air excited cries of rapture

from the men and tears of tender affection from the women – or
so, at least, Retz described it in his memoirs. He added to the
general effect by distributing five hundred pistoles to the audience.
The ladies were to act as hostages for the good faith of their husbands, and to take up residence in the hôtel de Ville. Retz left
them there with Noirmoutier and Miron, and returned to the
Palais de Justice with the mob at his back. Elbeuf received a report
of these proceedings from one of his captains, and realised that the
day was lost. When président Bellièvre inquired, as he had been
instructed to do, why the crowd was shouting and the drums
beating, Retz replied that the people were angry at the failure of the
parlement to settle the disputed command. Conti was then elected
as the supreme military leader, while Elbeuf, Bouillon, Noirmoutier and La Mothe-Houdancourt were appointed lieutenant-
generals, to act in rotation.

The coadjutor's promotion of the unpersonable and incompetent Conti, and his general management of the discordant interests
of the bourgeois, the magistrates and the aristocratic frondeurs
within his party, suggested an entire cynicism. But it was the kind
of cynicism which, while exposing the realities underlying conventions, could playfully create new illusions of its own. These
were his greatest moments, for he was playing the part he had
designed for himself, the part to which he felt himself best suited.
To guide the self-interest of others in accord with his own self-
interest, and yet to convince them that they served their own ends
– this was the art at which Retz excelled. The theatrical imagery
he employed in his memoirs to recount these manipulations was a
just reflection of his own attitude of mind at the time. The tricks
and manoeuvres in which he delighted were the décor of his production. The element of uncertainty, the fear that some of the
actors might *ad lib* their lines or effect a dénouement unforeseen
in the script gave a sense of personal excitement to the venture.
The histrionic quality of it all had a twist towards the mock-
heroic. It was the virtue of the actors as well as of the producer to
live completely in the present, so that the pose of the moment
had no deeper or more permanent significance than the representation of a particular phase of *amour-propre*. Hence the sudden
translation into unreality and romance: hence the kind of gay
insouciance that led the actors to forget the darker aspects of the

war they were supposed to be conducting and to impersonate the characters of d'Urfé's idyllic *Astrée*. One of these moments occurred on the evening of the day when Retz had mounted his farce in the parlement:

Noirmoutier, who had just been made a lieutenant-general, left Paris with five hundred cavaliers to throw back the advance elements of the troops we chose to say belonged to Mazarin, who were discharging their pistols in the outer suburbs. When he returned to the hôtel de Ville with Matha, Laigues and La Boulaye, all of them still wearing their cuirasses, they entered madame de Longueville's room, which was full of ladies. This mingling of blue scarves, of ladies, cuirasses, violins playing inside the room and trumpets sounding in the square outside, made a spectacle to be found more often in romances than elsewhere. Noirmoutier, who was a great lover of *Astrée*, said to me: 'I am beginning to believe that we are beseiged in Marcilly [the capital of the mythical Gaulish kingdom in *Astrée*]'. 'You are right', I replied, 'madame de Longueville is as beautiful as Galathée [the nymph who was the daughter of the princess Amasis]: but Marcillac [La Rochefoucauld] is not such an *honnête homme* as Lindamor [the knight who served Galathée].'

A similar attitude prevailed during the attack on the royal garrison in the Bastille two days later. Elbeuf had been given command of this operation as a sop to his pride, but he derived little glory from it. The women placed their chairs in the gardens of the Arsenal to watch the assault. The royal commander allowed five or six cannon shots to be fired at the fortress in order to satisfy honour, and then promptly surrendered. To please the lower classes Broussel's son was installed as the new governor of the place.

At about the same time the duc de Beaufort decided that the Fronde had made sufficient progress for him to put in an appearance. Retz was sceptical of the real worth of his new ally. He had 'the intention rather than the conception' of political greatness, but while 'he had learnt no more sense during his imprisonment, he derived an increased reputation from it'. Although Conti was the figurehead, Retz needed a more military figure, and in this respect Beaufort was 'the wraith' he required. Neither La Mothe-Houdancourt, who was the agent of Longueville, nor Bouillon, who kept his own counsel, suited Retz half so well in this capacity.

Longueville had withdrawn to Normandy, and new recruits from the aristocracy, such as the marquis de Vitry, the duc de Luynes (the son of madame de Chevreuse by her first marriage), and the duc de Chevreuse, lacked Beaufort's popularity. Retz described the character of his new associate in terms similar to those he used for Elbeuf, who was Beaufort's uncle by marriage.[7] But, while Beaufort was equally self-opinionated, his vanity was of the more manageable kind. He was still as naïve as he had shown himself to be in the affair of the *Importants*. Yet he bore the mystique and something of the charm and familiarity of his grandfather, Henry IV. He was the idol of the fish-wives of the markets, and enjoyed nothing more than caracoling on his fine white horse with his blond hair flying in the wind. Beaufort took his place, a little resentfully, as one of the lieutenant-generals, and, while Retz knew that any confidence he gave him was likely to pass swiftly to the ears of madame de Montbazon, he used him to direct the popular emotions of the Fronde.

The court and the Fronde each had some twelve thousand troops at their disposal for the campaign in the environs of the capital, but, whereas the royal forces composed of veterans seasoned in both battle and pillage, the bourgeois militia at the disposal of the frondeurs lacked discipline and training in open warfare. The regiments of horse raised in Paris were committed to action even before they had acquired the basic techniques of organisation and manoeuvre. There were so many coachmen and servants within their ranks that the marquis de la Boulaye, commanding the cavalry, was named 'General Carriage-Way'. The coadjutor's regiment under the command of Renaud de Sévigné went into action on 28 January, three weeks after its formation, and one of its squadrons sustained a charge by a force six times its size. The squadron was decimated and its commander left for dead in a ditch, while the supporting squadrons galloped off the field in terror.[8] Retz omitted to mention the disaster in his memoirs, and he also said nothing of the term used by the wits of the Fronde to describe the encounter – 'First Corinthians'.

Longueville led the revolt in Normandy, where, with the assistance of Fontrailles, Fiesque and Varicarville, he tried to concentrate his forces in Rouen. His lack of success was satirised in a pamphlet attributed to Saint-Evremond. Fontrailles and Fiesque, who dominated Longueville's counsels, were depicted as embarrassed by the succession of misfortunes that followed their advice. Varicarville was asserted to be too engrossed with his pose as an *esprit fort* to accept the commands offered him by Longueville. Saint-Evremond pretended that he was followed everywhere by a rabbi who explained to him the mysteries of the Old Testament, suggesting there was some method in Nebuchadnezzar's madness and that he should eat grass to clear his head. The coadjutor's brother, the duc de Retz, was expected in Rouen with a strong force from Brittany, but arrived, according to the satirist, with an escort consisting only of his page.[9]

It was Condé's strategy to blockade Paris and thereby to induce it to surrender through starvation and the dissensions among its defenders. His army was not large enough to attempt a siege, so he concentrated upon seizing the small towns that formed the city's supply points and maintaining patrols between them. The generals of the Fronde were too anxious to surpass each other in martial valour, and too neglectful of the limitations of the troops they commanded, to counter this policy systematically. Retz had little to do with their military dispositions. Bouillon was probably their most accomplished strategist and Noirmoutier their most successful field commander, but Bouillon was for the most part confined to his bed with gout, and Noirmoutier was frequently overruled by the recklessness of Elbeuf and Beaufort. Condé found that he could not occupy all the vital points along the Seine and also maintain an adequate field force. The generals of the Fronde attempted from time to time to reoccupy these points, and to lead sorties to cover the advance of food convoys to the city. In this way a kind of cat-and-mouse series of manoeuvres took place in which Condé, while trying to block the convoys, also hoped to lure the bourgeois militia into the open and commit them to a set battle with his superior troops. It was the misfortune of the Fronde that its commanders often failed to appreciate that theirs was the role of the mouse.

The government at Saint-Germain was restricted by the general dissidence of the provinces. Normandy and Poitou were entirely disaffected. The parlements of Guyenne and Provence continued to lead resistance to the respective royal governors, Epernon and Alais, while the parlements of Brittany and Languedoc followed the lead of Paris in issuing injunctions against Mazarin. Retz and his fellow frondeurs did little to unite these movements into a national revolt, although the Paris parlement despatched delegates to some of its sister courts. From time to time members of the provincial nobility led their personal following into the Fronde, while in Poitou and Normandy troops were raised on a provincial basis to support the rebellion. The provincial movements were often divided by the same suspicion between the social groups that composed them as existed within the Parisian Fronde. But, if there was no unity between the forces of revolt, the court had still to disperse its resources in the endeavour to maintain its authority. Even if the finances had been available, the general anarchy suggested caution in the raising of new forces which might defect *en masse*. Thus the government largely depended upon its mercenary troops, and had to balance their deployment in the civil war against the need to guard the frontier in the continuing conflict with Spain.

The first military ventures of the Fronde invited ridicule. A sortie was attempted on 21 January to bring in a grain convoy, but the convoy could not be found and most of the troops caught cold.[10] Three days later Beaufort and La Mothe-Houdancourt led a foray towards Corbeil. Conti, Retz and Brissac accompanied the force of some five thousand men to the city gates. Beaufort marched out in all his splendour to the cheering of the crowd and the benedictions of the coadjutor. He returned next day, his troops having declined to face the enemy, with nothing more to show for his expedition than a few captured cattle. Meanwhile Condé had been occupying Saint-Cloud and Saint-Denis, and investing Lagny and Brie-Comte-Robert. The defeat of the 'Corinthians' followed, and then, at last, Beaufort gained a minor success. He created a diversion with three hundred cavalry while Noirmoutier brought through a food train from Etampes. During his absence the rumour spread that he had been captured, and a mob of armed bourgeois, including a large number of women, assembled with the vague intention of rescuing him.[11] At his return candles were lit in every window and the crowd acclaimed his deliverance with a joy approaching delirium.

There followed, on 8 February, the one major battle of the war, when the generals rejected Bouillon's advice to withdraw their garrison from Charenton. Condé trapped the garrison, and his victorious veterans slaughtered their prisoners and threw the bodies into the Seine.[12] This disaster closed the last route open for supplies. There were accusations of treachery against the generals, especially against Elbeuf, who was obliged to explain to the parlement his failure to relieve the place. He argued that he had only five thousand men against Condé's eight thousand and had thought it imprudent to give battle. In fact the armed militia who assembled in their companies at the news of the battle were reputed to number twenty thousand, with at their head 'the coadjutor riding his horse with grey accoutrements and armed with two pistols'.[13] Two days later Beaufort recovered some prestige by capturing Villejuif and admitting another convoy. Noirmoutier and La Mothe-Houdancourt completed similar covering actions in the ensuing two weeks, although La Rochefoucauld, who on 19 February led seven squadrons to hold off an intercepting force at Brie-Comte-Robert, sustained a dangerous wound. The son of the gallant 'Lindamor' by his 'Galathée' had been born three weeks before, and had been named Paris in tribute to the hôtel de Ville. In later years he was to be known as the comte de Saint-Paul. Retz, who was already accusing La Rochefoucauld of turning Conti and his sister against him, was pleased at the temporary elimination of his rival. The coadjutor at this time was fully occupied with his intrigues to hold the Fronde together and preserve his own position within it.

As Retz observed, the daily debates and eternal quibbles of the parlement were not the most effective means of conducting a revolution. The majority of the magistrates would have sued for peace at the first opportunity, and it was the coadjutor's principal task to keep them under pressure. He was in constant touch with the radicals from the *enquêtes*. On the occasions when these agents seemed to offend the susceptibilities of their fellows, he had to consider whether he should use the mob to cow the Palais de Justice, or whether he should have the generals effect some kind of coup de main. But he knew that once the passions of the lower classes had been aroused they might well escape his control, and he was equally aware that the frondeur aristocracy was too divided to supersede the seeming legality of the sovereign courts. He encouraged Marigny and other writers to produce a constant

E

stream of pamphlets denouncing Mazarin and justifying the constitutional rights of the parlement. At no stage did the writers of the *Mazarinades* challenge the monarchy: they did not advocate rebellion but merely the overthrow of a régime which had illegally extended its powers. The clergy were an effective means of spreading these views among the masses, and on 25 January the coadjutor himself preached an eloquent sermon to sustain the enthusiasms of the beleaguered city. Yet propaganda was not in itself enough. It was necessary to obtain a more direct control of the proceedings of the parlement. On 18 January Retz secured a permanent seat in the assembly, on the grounds that the absence of his uncle, the archbishop, made representation of the diocese imperative. On the same day a meeting took place at Bouillon's house of the frondeur nobles. The names of Beaufort, Bouillon, La Mothe-Houdancourt, Noirmoutier, Vitry, Brissac, La Rochefoucauld and others were appended to a document swearing that no peace would be made until the declared objectives of the Fronde had been achieved. Although Molé refused to treat seriously Retz's demand that this should be registered by the parlement, the magistrates were made to realise that they were no longer in command of the movement.

Retz claimed in his memoirs that the blockade produced few visible effects upon the life of the capital. In fact the arrival of the food convoys prevented a repetition of the sufferings of the Paris of the League during its siege by Henry IV in the wars of religion. But as the blockade continued, dangerous pressures became evident in the city. Winter rains swelled the Seine to flood proportions. The cost of food rose alarmingly, and when prices were fixed a black market soon became established. Enthusiasm to pay the taxes voted by the parlement declined noticeably, and an air of defeatism followed Condé's victory at Charenton. The seizure of the property of suspected *mazarins* occupied the passions of the mob for a time, and the persecution of food-hoarders and supposed spies was intensified as reports came in of the pillage and atrocities committed by Erlach's Germans in the outlying towns. Talon in his memoirs observed that the commercial life of the city was paralysed by the blockade, and that the merchants feared ruin if the king did not speedily return.[14] While the fury of the poor against Mazarin increased with each new hardship the war

imposed upon them, the desire for peace grew among the politic-
ally-uncommitted and the well-to-do.

Suggestions for the opening of peace negotiations from
neutralist magistrates within the parlement were speedily reported
to Saint-Germain. The government was itself ready to negotiate
under the financial pressures of the conflict. Moreover, Mazarin
knew that, as the war into which Condé had forced him continued,
the prince was extending his authority over the regency. On 12
February, as the parlement was debating the case of the chevalier
de la Valette, caught distributing royalist literature on the previous
day, the arrival of a herald from Saint-German was announced.
The parlement agreed that, before receiving the herald, it should
consult the generals. The respite allowed the coadjutor to prepare
measures to frustrate the peace party. A herald, he reasoned, could
only be sent to enemies or equals. By despatching the herald
Mazarin was trying to trap the parlement into regarding itself as
the queen's equal, and hence to discredit it. Broussel pleaded this
rather specious argument to his colleagues with tears in his eyes,
and, although Molé, Mesmes and others saw through Retz's
subterfuge, it carried the day. Conti and the authorities of the
hôtel de Ville, to whom the herald had also been commissioned,
answered in similar terms. The herald returned unheard to Saint-
Germain, and the parlement resolved to send a delegation to the
regent to explain the reasons for its action. As Guy Joly pointed
out, the coadjutor had congratulated himself on his success too
soon.[15] The delegation in itself offered the opportunity for which
the peace party had been waiting. A week later Omer Talon
reported to the magistrates that the queen had received their
representatives with grace and good will.

While the movement for peace was gathering strength, Retz
was racing against time to find a new means of prolonging the
conflict and of committing the waverers to an act which the
government could only regard as treason. He was now determined
to come to an understanding with the Spanish forces in Flanders.
His justification of this step in his memoirs was singularly uncon-
vincing, for while he argued that he was unwillingly forced into
the Spanish camp by Bouillon, he also admitted the expediency of
the measure with a bravado that mocked his supposed scruples.
On the very day that the advocate-general described the queen's

benevolent attitude to the delegation, Conti told the parlement that
an envoy from archduke Leopold, the governor of the Spanish
Netherlands, was awaiting audience. In fact the announcement was
the fruit of secret negotiations and intrigues conducted by Retz
since the beginning of the month.

Saint-Ibal had been pressing the coadjutor for some time to
establish contact with the Spanish general, Fuensaldagne. He had
finally lost patience with Retz's tentative refusals, and gone off to
Brussels to join madame de Chevreuse. Then Retz changed his
mind. He approached Bouillon and they agreed to use Elbeuf,
who had spent many years of exile in Brussels, to further the
negotiations. In the meantime a letter was sent through Montrésor
to Saint-Ibal, and Fuensaldagne responded cautiously by sending a
Bernardine monk, disguised as a cavalier, to Elbeuf. Not without
reason the Spanish commander distrusted the frondeurs both
individually and as a group, and his agent was despatched merely
to reconnoitre the situation. At this point Retz discovered that
Bouillon, with his eye on the recovery of the independent principality of Sedan, had committed himself to Spain more completely
than Retz had supposed, and that madame de Bouillon had for
long been corresponding with the Netherlands. Fuensaldagne's
secret agent spent two days at the Bouillon household before
making himself known to Elbeuf. 'Madame de Bouillon', Retz
wrote, 'never indulged in any acts, or rather words, of flirtation
without her husband's knowledge, and on this occasion she
omitted nothing that might make her the most charmingly persuasive person on this earth – even though her beauty made this
unnecessary – to induce me to sign an agreement without further
hesitation.' But the coadjutor knew that he was fencing with a
mind as subtle and devious as his own. He and Bouillon agreed
to recognise and respect each other's personal interests. Retz
refused to sign Bouillon's private treaty with Spain, and the
Spanish were to be told that there was an advantage in having the
coadjutor secretly in accord with their plans but appearing not to
be implicated at all. The immediate problem was to persuade the
parlement to accept an envoy from an enemy state when it had
just refused to accept one from its own sovereign.

Elbeuf, of course, knew nothing of these prior discussions and
assumed that Fuensaldagne had selected him as the effective leader

of the Fronde. With deliberate *éclat* he announced the arrival of the Spanish agent at a dinner for the leaders of the Fronde. Since Fuensaldagne had never intended his bizarre messenger to act as an ambassador, plans were laid to forge credentials from the archduke and have the disguised monk present them to the parlement. In the assembly on 19 February président de Mesmes bitterly criticised Conti's proposal to receive the Spanish envoy. The radicals from the *enquêtes* responded with a personal attack on Mesmes and Molé for supposed dealings with a suspect financier, and amid the subsequent uproar the bogus envoy was allowed to present his false credentials. His message, as it had been contrived at Elbeuf's dinner table, was a clever mixture of half-truths. Spain, it was asserted, had a sincere desire for peace, and recognised that the parlement alone had the right to ratify a treaty. The Spanish army on the frontier would therefore cooperate with the Fronde in the hope of securing conditions where a stable peace could be negotiated. In Retz's account of the sequel to this speech the farcical element in the proceedings was again accentuated. He had himself to rebut allegations by Mesmes of collusion with the national enemy, while Le Coigneux, one of the leading plotters at Elbeuf's, frustrated Molé's demand for the original letter from the archduke. Le Coigneux told his colleagues that they had become arbiters of the fate of Europe, and the magistrates felt sufficiently flattered to receive the envoy at his face value, and to consider sending a deputation to report the matter to Saint-Germain.

This extraordinary scene followed the favourable reaction shown to Talon's report of the queen's reception of his delegation. It took place at the very time when La Rochefoucauld was being heavily defeated at Brie-Comte-Robert and Noirmoutier was leading a vital food train into the city. The nice balance in which the affairs of the Fronde rested was reflected in the long discussion which the coadjutor had with the Bouillons in the evening of the same day. The time seemed to have come for the Fronde to supersede the authority of the parlement. Although the peace party had received a temporary set-back, it could revive its strength if the government twisted the incident of the Spanish envoy to its own advantage. The report which Molé might give the queen of this affair could be used to justify negotiations, and to divide and discredit the aristocratic frondeurs. Retz drew an elaborate historical parallel with the problems experienced by the League. He recalled how the revolutionary element among the Parisian lower classes had been used at that time to purge the parlement of its royalist sympathisers, and also how Mayenne had had in turn to purge those who had terrorised the magistrates. It might be argued that the time had come for Beaufort and himself to use the mob against Molé, Mesmes and their supporters, but Retz believed that it would be prudent merely to threaten such action, because he could not foresee where a popular riot would lead. The coadjutor tried to shake the addiction of his accomplices to the Spanish cause with a further elaboration of his parallel. He pointed out that Mayenne had seen the dangers of too great a dependence upon Spain, and yet in the end had been powerless to prevent the Spanish alliance from splitting his party.

This analysis of the issues facing the Fronde was far more acute than Retz's proposed solution to these problems. His knowledge of the history of the League sharpened his insight into the politics of his own time, but it also suggested that the obstacles which had been insuperable to Mayenne could defeat the leadership of the Fronde. Indeed, Retz defined the issues with so much subtlety that he found himself incapable of proposing any decisive remedy. The explanation of his failure as a man of action was contained in this predicament. Bouillon would not go as far as Elbeuf, who wanted to lock up the whole parlement in the Bastille, or as Longueil, who advocated an immediate purge of the mass of his colleagues. Instead, he felt inclined to allow the parlement to negotiate with the regency to the point where it was entirely discredited in the eyes of the lower classes and a coup could be effected at the hôtel de Ville. But Bouillon possessed a secret which gave greater cause for optimism, and he chose the opportunity to impart it to Retz. It concerned the intended declaration of his brother, Turenne, and his army of the Rhine, to throw in their lot with the Fronde.

As the coadjutor had feared, the delegation led by Molé and Mesmes to Saint-Germain on 24 February was used by Mazarin as a means of initiating discussions to end the war. Three days later Molé told the parlement that the queen was ready to negotiate, and called for consultations with the generals. A restive crowd gathered outside the Palais de Justice shouting for the delegation to be thrown into the Seine. The distrust of the leading frondeurs for each other became more evident at the next meeting at Bouillon's house. Although Conti had sent a formal invitation to the Netherlands to discuss the use of Spanish troops, Retz suspected that he was being directed by the wounded La Rochefoucauld, and was secretly in favour of negotiation. Noirmoutier, who was tired of seeing Beaufort receive the laurels for his military successes, was resolved to become the Fronde's representative to Brussels, although Laigues, intending to conquer the heart of the imperishable madame de Chevreuse, had already installed himself there. Elbeuf was anxious to provoke the Paris mob against the magistrates, and took steps to play the demagogue on his own account. Bouillon, unable to risk a premature announcement of the adherence of Turenne, hoped for a more positive move from Fuensaldagne. His wife intrigued with all her might to force the frondeurs to become unequivocal masters of Paris. She suspected the coadjutor's loyalty to the party, and catching him alone one evening, obliged him to prick his finger and write in his own blood an undertaking not to betray her husband. Bouillon, who was well aware that the coadjutor's blood was scarcely as binding as a holy relic, destroyed the document with some amusement. His wife's fears were not unjustified, for Retz, like most of his associates, was preparing a line of retreat in the event of a peace with the court. He did not want to declare himself for Spain until Turenne's troops had marched to the relief of Paris. To compromise himself by open alliance with Spain at this juncture would, in the event of peace, mean his permanent exile and the end of his career in the church.

On 28 February the parlement moved a step closer to peace by naming a negotiating committee. Rumours of this move spread rapidly through the city and an angry crowd barred the egress of the magistrates and denounced any peace proposal that included the survival of Mazarin. Retz maintained in his memoirs that he was entirely innocent of complicity in the riot, and described how he and Beaufort quietened the mob to allow Molé and Mesmes to leave the Palais de Justice without danger. Another account, however, declared his intervention to be an unwilling one, and suggested that in any case the demonstration did not reach serious proportions.[16] An unexpected delay in the peace discussions occurred when Condé and Gaston refused to honour an undertaking to allow food convoys to enter Paris during the negotiations. It was not until 4 March that the delegations conferred at Rueil, half-way between Saint-Germain and the capital. Bouillon persuaded the frondeur nobility to boycott the deliberations, hoping that the support of Turenne and Spain would shortly redress the balance, and enable him to dispense with the parlement altogether. As the talks started, the generals moved the bulk of their army to Villejuif in expectation of seizing the military initiative.

The discussions at Rueil were so complex and drawn out that the coadjutor had hopes of their failure. The news that Mazarin was himself participating in the negotiations stirred the parlement to declare that it would refuse to receive its representatives if they had been contaminated by contact with the first minister. Gaston and Molé overcame this problem by agreeing to meetings between a subcommittee from each delegation. On the day of the protest against Mazarin (5 March) don Francisco Pizarro, an officially accredited envoy from the archduke, arrived in Paris with full powers to negotiate an alliance with the Fronde. But the imminent prospect of peace, and the thought of the personal spoils to be derived from it, induced some of the frondeurs to abandon their previous enthusiasm for Spanish support. Retz believed that Elbeuf was ready to receive money from both sides, and that Beaufort and his mistress, madame de Montbazon, had already accepted Spanish gold. Longueville was thought to be negotiating privately with Saint-Germain, while Conti and La Rochefoucauld, having allegedly failed in similar negotiations, were now at the opposite extreme and fervently in favour of the Spanish alliance. To Retz the probable defection of the parlement made an arrangement with Spain more necessary than ever, and he took a major part in the discussions with Pizarro and his embassy. Once again he faltered before a critical decision. He maintained his opinion that the mob should not be used against the parlement, argued that the treaty with Spain must limit the sphere in which Spanish troops should operate, and, amid so many conflicting lines of possible action, resigned himself to the view that every frondeur 'should do his own duty and hope for a favourable outcome'.

While the conference at Rueil argued whether the parlement

should make some gesture to obey the royal command to go to Montargis, whether certain restrictions should apply to the parlement's freedom of assembly and debate, and how literally the declaration of 22 October should be interpreted, Bouillon strove to conclude the Spanish alliance, and his brother made the final preparations for his defection. Then, just as the queen offered new compromises which promised agreement, Turenne declared himself. On 7 March the royal council branded him a traitor, and on the following day the parlement in Paris proclaimed the council's order invalid. News arrived from Normandy that Longueville was leading a new army to Paris, and from Anjou and Poitou came reports that the duc de la Trémoille, who had been joined by La Boulaye, was ready to march to the aid of the Fronde. The hopes of the frondeurs suddenly revived, and Molé was told to break off negotiations. But the queen offered new concessions, and on 12 March Molé signed a preliminary peace agreement.

Everything hinged upon the attitude taken by the parlement to the report on the Rueil agreement which Molé presented on 13 March. The prince de Conti expressed some surprise at the signature of an agreement without his being consulted. Retz placed his hopes in président Le Coigneux, although the latter habitually so overacted his part that the coadjutor referred to him as maître Gonin, a celebrated comic actor of the time. Le Coigneux demanded that the deputies should return to Rueil so that the interests of the generals could be taken into account. But before the proceedings were far advanced the crowd chose once more to intervene. So loud were the threats and cries outside the Palais de Justice that a sergeant was sent to investigate. He returned with the news that the mob were shouting for Beaufort. The idol of the Parisian markets quietened them, but only for a moment, and when président Novion tried to placate them he made no impression whatever. One of their leaders, an unknown attorney called du Boisle, insisted that any document signed by Mazarin must be burnt by the public executioner, and the chorus behind him chanted: 'No peace, no Mazarin!' The first president maintained his habitual calm in circumstances where the crowd seemed likely to invade the Palais de Justice and threaten his own life. The coadjutor, whom Molé held jointly responsible with Beaufort for staging the demonstration, went out to remonstrate with his supporters, as he had done during the less threatening riot of 28 February. Once again his presence seemed to calm the mob, sufficiently at least for the parlement to leave in solemn procession, with Retz escorting Molé, and Beaufort walking beside president de Mesmes. The clamour continued as the magistrates passed, but, though some voices were heard shouting '*République!*' the line of the procession remained unbroken.[17]

Events now began to move so quickly that Retz found it difficult to accommodate the stand he took at the council table of the Fronde on one day to the altered political balance of the next. On 16 March the parlement accepted Le Coigneux's suggestion and sent back its deputies to reconsider the terms of peace. That evening the news arrived that Turenne's adherence had become worthless. Mazarin, as alert as ever to the intrigues of his enemies, had borrowed a vast sum from Condé and commissioned Erlach to buy over Turenne's army. Erlach had been entirely successful, and Turenne, deprived of his troops, had been obliged to escape to Holland. Soon after the arrival of this disastrous report, Retz deciphered a despatch from Laigues and Noirmoutier advising that the Spanish army had begun to advance. With the people in arms, the parlement moving towards peace, and Turenne's force no longer available to preserve the independence of the frondeurs from their Spanish allies, the coadjutor groped frantically for a new rationale for action. He refused the Spanish gold of the Bouillons, and resisted Beaufort's desire to expel the parlement, establish a revolutionary government at the hôtel de Ville, and admit a Spanish garrison to the capital. Fuensaldagne, he believed, would list the coadjutor as the first of the frondeurs to be eliminated if he were to occupy Paris. The generals were divided, and the uncontrolled ascendancy of the lower classes might destroy the very structure of the state. Yet he was anxious, before all else, to retain his popularity with the masses. He feared that his rescue of Molé and his resistance to a proposal that Mazarin's library should be sold, would be misinterpreted. He felt that he could confide in no one, and decided to consult his father, who was still in religious seclusion. Even as he set out on this mission, a new policy formed in his mind. He would secretly promote peace while appearing to oppose it, and his outward action would preserve his position as the potential leader of a faction he might revive when opportunity offered.

Over the ensuing two weeks the frondeur nobility gradually adjusted their ground. They informed the Spanish envoys that they were powerless to prevent the continuance of the negotiations, and declared publicly that they were obliged to press their own individual peace terms as a guarantee against the possibility of Mazarin remaining in power. After this the attempts of their representatives to insist upon the dismissal of the cardinal were certain of failure. Their own popularity in Paris was undermined by the exposure of their selfish demands. The government, still fearful of the spectre of Spanish intervention, granted an amnesty and a further crop of concessions, and on 1 April 1649 the parlement duly registered the treaty of Rueil. The frondeurs flocked to the court, where their cold reception by the queen was balanced by the effusiveness of her first minister. Retz was not among them. He had managed to have his name omitted from the list of the great mentioned in the amnesty, and, with his popular image preserved among the lower classes, he pretended to confine himself to his religious duties. On the day of the verification of the peace he performed the ceremony of the holy oils at Notre-Dame. Afterwards he walked through the streets, attempting, so he said, to reconcile an angry populace to the terms of the treaty. He was late taking his place in the *grand'chambre* of the parlement, and, when he offered his excuses, Molé made an audible aside: 'He has a talent for mixing gunpowder with his oils.' But, for a time at least, the coadjutor's powder train of revolution had been quenched.

SEVEN

Changing partners

During the first civil war Retz's schemes and intrigues had been directed towards reconciling the divergent interests of the various elements in the Fronde and maintaining their hostility to the court. He had been less the heroic *chef de parti* than the theatrical director of a farce in which the actors kept assuming roles for which they had not originally been cast. But up to a point, at least, he had coordinated the production, and his memoirs could reflect his pride in his achievement. In so far as he had failed, his failure had been due to an excess of subtlety rather than a lack of enterprise. He had understood the complexity of the shifting situation so well that he had been quite unable to act at the decisive moment. Amid the conflicting motives of his confederates he had seen a disadvantage to counterweight the desirability of each particular course of action. And so, in the end, he had remained one step behind the march of events, and had had eventually to adjust himself to the peace, and preserve what he could of his ambitions.

Two years separated the peace of Rueil from the next major civil war. They were years in which the factions executed a double pirouette and exchange of partners. There was a significant change of tone in that section of his memoirs which Retz devoted to this period. The special pleading for the constitutional aims of the Fronde disappeared, and the bravado with which other conventional attitudes had been disdained was muted. At the same time Retz displayed greater anxiety to justify his personal conduct and was no less reticent in praising his own subtlety in political manoeuvre. He continually represented himself as betrayed and misrepresented by his opponents in a way that was oddly inconsistent with his own delight in deceiving others. He was in fact excusing his own decline as a political force. He described at length the motives that led him to seek promotion to a cardinalate, for within the ambivalent course of his career political disappointment was inevitably succeeded by renewed ambitions in his alternate vocation.

Behind the justificatory note in Retz's personal account of his life in the next two years it is possible to detect his continued trend towards the cynical acceptance of self-interest as the criterion of all conduct. The general climate of opinion shifted in the same direction. Heroic and romantic elements became less important. The re-enactment of *Astrée* seemed inappropriate to the perpetual round of sordid intrigue and unashamed deceit. The republic of letters had been scattered by the onset of war. Descartes had composed his treatise on the passions for Retz's friend, the princess Palatine, and sought sanctuary at the court of Christina of Sweden, where he died in the following year. His parting theme – that the mind must hold passion in check – sounded a warning to polite society. There was an exodus of the men of letters from the salons. Scarron and Segrais considered emigration to America. Descartes' scientific opponent, Gassendi, retired to Provence. Saumaise, the critic of the regicidal Milton, and Naudé, the defender of Machiavelli, were later to follow the road to Stockholm. The coadjutor's own literary circle was severely reduced. Sarasin defected to the party of the princes and sustained their cause with his pen. The writers who had entertained the great with the poetry of love and adventure now earned their living with political satire and propaganda.

During April 1649 the queen received her rebellious aristocracy at Saint-Germain, with the notable exception of the coadjutor. Early in May the court moved to Compiègne, and soon afterwards the government began to test the strength of the frondeur control of the capital. A group of young swordsmen in the queen's service established themselves in Paris and began systematically to bait Beaufort and his retinue. Their leaders were Candale, the son of the duc d'Epernon, and the gallant Jarzé, who had been sent to Anjou at the end of the war to disarm the marquis de la Boulaye. Their provocations became extreme. They jeered at the exploits of the frondeurs in the war, and Beaufort and the coadjutor's brother were obliged to choose a new path for their promenade to avoid more direct humiliation. The court gallants dined frequently at a restaurant in the Tuileries owned by Renard, a valet of the bishop of Beauvais, who had been given leave to construct the place in the royal gardens in reward for his daily preparation of the queen's flowers. These supper parties were generally observed by passing crowds, and Beaufort chose one such occasion to respond in kind. Accompanied by the younger duc de Retz, Brissac, La Mothe-Houdancourt and some fifty others, Beaufort strode into Renard's on the evening of 18 June and demanded whether the party had any violins they might borrow for their entertainment. When Jarzé answered that none were available, Beaufort seized the table cloth and deposited its contents in the laps of the revellers.

The story of this exploit was read by all Paris in the mock-heroic terms of the broadsheet *Mazarin's Dance, performed at the supper party of some of that faction at monsieur Renard's, when monsieur de Beaufort gave the Ball*:

> Monsieur de Beaufort, this tutelary demon of Paris, this father of the people, incorruptible in face of temptation, invincible in danger and generous in victory, this prince, who deprived the miscreants of state of their honour by supplying Paris with bread, has just sustained the honour of the city by removing from the said miscreants not only their bread but a little more besides.[1]

The coadjutor, who asserted that the court blamed him for organising the affair, gave an equally colourful account of it in his memoirs. According to Retz, Beaufort denounced Jarzé and beat him with the flat of his sword, while his companions broke the instruments of the attendant musicians and inverted bowls of soup on the heads of some of the guests. It was certainly true that swords were drawn, and that Candale tried to lead an attack on Beaufort. The affair of *la nappe renversée* continued to cause bitterness until a formula for the reconciliation of Beaufort and Candale was accepted a month later.

The mood of the frondeurs was quite as irresponsible as that of the courtiers. Their public debauchery caused Retz considerable embarrassment. He presumably did not object at the time (though he did in his memoirs later) to their singing of sacrilegious and scurrilous songs, which were frequently a part of the entertainment of his domestic entourage, but when Brissac, Vitry, Matha and Fontrailles drew their swords and made a mock attack upon a crucifix in a public procession, he might justifiably claim that the

revels of his friends had compromised his position. In another
incident the same group attacked two royal lackeys in the street,
and openly insulted the queen and Mazarin. Anne of Austria
ordered both Molé and the chancellor to proceed against them, but
no action was taken.[2]

It was just at this time that Retz began an open liaison with the
lady who was to become known as la coadjutrice. The perennial
madame de Chevreuse had secretly returned to Paris a few weeks
after the peace, and the coadjutor set siege to her daughter's heart.
He first met her at a baptism when 'she dressed, as one did in
Brussels on such occasions, with every jewel she possessed, and
she had many fine pieces. She was lovely. I was angry with madame
la princesse de Guémenée, who as early as the second day of the
blockade of Paris, had left me and gone off to Anjou in terror.'
Madame de Motteville concurred with the coadjutor's estimate of
the beauty of mademoiselle de Chevreuse, although the praise was
qualified by the remark that she was too thin and her complexion
was too sallow.[3] Retz had no illusions about her intellect. He
observed that she was so stupid as to be ridiculous. She was an
intense and passionate creature, but she concentrated her affection
upon one person at a time. Retz developed the association by
planning with the daughter to provide a new lover for the mother,
who had grown tired of Laigues in Brussels. When the queen
seemed determined to enforce the ban on her former confidante,
the coadjutor invoked the aid of Molé, and threatened to provoke
a new crisis by declaring the use of *lettres de cachet* against madame
de Chevreuse an infringement of the peace terms. Molé was
obliged to agree, although Retz's statement that the first president
sympathised with his real motives seems improbable. The coadjutor made use of his link with madame de Rhodes, a friend of
mademoiselle de Chevreuse and an illegitimate daughter of Louis
de Lorraine, cardinalde Guise. He soon destroyed the girl's
esteem for her fiancé, the duke of Brunswick, and, as he put it: 'I
loved her, or, rather, I convinced myself that I did, for I did not
put an end to my association with madame de Pommereuil.' Nor,
for that matter, did he cease to see madame de Guémenée. The
latter bitterly resented his presence at the hôtel de Chevreuse, and
caused several violent scenes. On one occasion, Retz recorded, he
seized her by the throat and she attacked him with a candlestick.

But, if there was nothing monogamous about the coadjutor, mademoiselle de Chevreuse served him loyally, and the liaison lasted until a little before her death four years later. It involved certain political dangers, for in August the queen accepted madame de Chevreuse at court again, so that Mazarin could use her to manage the frondeurs.

In the summer of 1649 Retz began to see a chance of exploiting the rift between Condé and Mazarin. The prince was angry at his inability to dominate the government, and withdrew sulkily to his provincial seat in Burgundy. Mazarin, as La Rochefoucauld summed up the situation, found it impossible to achieve any stable relationship with one who was ruled more by caprice than self-interest. He planned to provide himself with allies to counter-balance Condé's influence, and courted the houses of Vendôme and Lorraine. The old duc de Vendôme had been living in exile in Florence after his discomfiture at the time of the *Importants*. He returned to France during the first Fronde, and, though he disavowed the rebellion of his son, Beaufort, he criticised the latter severely for not securing from it the spoils of the admiralcy, an honour which his house disputed with Condé. Mazarin pro-posed that Vendôme's other son, Mercoeur, should marry Laura Mancini, the cardinal's niece. It was a suggestion that Beaufort resented and Condé implacably opposed. Condé appeared again at Compiègne early in August, to be followed by madame de Chevreuse and then by Conti. Rumours spread that Condé was trying to oblige the court to go to Paris. Although the frondeurs generally resisted the move, the coadjutor resolved to gain per-sonal credit for the return of the king and to align the Fronde with Condé against the first minister. Retz consulted with président Bellièvre, Beaufort and madame de Montbazon, and set out alone for Compiègne.

The journey was not without its dangers. Fearing that he would appear to be seeking reconciliation with Mazarin, Retz protested vehemently before his departure that he would have no traffic with the cardinal and sought only to see the queen. Guy Joly asserted that Retz did have a secret interview with Mazarin, but madame de Motteville's narrative confirmed the coadjutor's own account that he refused to speak with his enemy.[4] He told the queen that he could not serve her so well if he compromised his reputation with the people by associating with Mazarin. His reputation was possibly safer than his person at Compiègne. He received warning of a plot to assassinate him as he mounted the stairs to the royal apartments. But he was neither killed nor arrested, and the queen received him well enough. Mazarin made his own arrangements for the return of the court. He distributed bribes in the capital, secured Beaufort's agreement, and neutralised the radical magistrate, Longueil, by promising the superintendency of finance to his brother, président de Maisons. The coadjutor went back to Paris to boast that it was he who had secured the king's return. On 18 August the court entered the capital without any sign of public hostility, and installed itself once more in the Palais-Royal. Retz called at the head of the clergy to pay his respects on the following day, and madame de Motteville noticed that he refused to look towards Mazarin, who was standing behind the queen's chair.[5] Nevertheless, he did visit the cardinal on 20 August, though he said nothing of it in his memoirs. The meeting appeared amicable, though neither man believed the other's profession of good will. Retz was now actively engaged in winning the support of the prince.

Condé possessed an infinite contempt for the Fronde, with its mixture of private interest and public hypocrisy, but even he was prepared to mask his disdain in order to discomfit Mazarin. The Fronde remained a powerful force in the capital. Retz and Beaufort still swayed popular emotions. Their pamphleteers continued to issue libels against the cardinal. Their bravoes challenged the swordsmen of the court and swaggered behind Beaufort and the coadjutor in the streets. The parlement remained hostile to Mazarin, and many of its members sympathised with their colleagues in Bordeaux in the continuing struggle against the royal governor, Epernon. The prince could count upon Bouillon, who was agitating for the return of Sedan, and a certain mutual respect existed between him and the coadjutor. Condé was critical of Epernon, although he would not condone the resistance of Bordeaux. He sought to isolate Mazarin by winning the sympathy of Gaston of Orléans, and he revived old animosities against the cardinal, such as that evidenced by the disgraced minister, Chavigny. The prince harassed Mazarin by his opposition to the Vendôme marriage proposals and by incessant demands for the surrender of a Norman fortress, Pont-de-l'Arche, to his brother-in-law the duc de Longueville.

Retz made the most of this situation. He went with Beaufort to the hôtel de Longueville and promised Condé his support. His protégé, Marigny, interrupted his stream of propaganda against Mazarin to compose a song in praise of the prince. Condé responded to these approaches. His pride might suffer in his association with the lesser frondeurs, but it could endure this more readily than the humiliation of Mazarin's refusal to accept his demands. On 10 September he turned ominously on the cardinal as they left the queen's apartments and remarked contemptuously: 'Adieu, Mars.' But Mazarin was used to insults. He appreciated that the alliance of Condé with the Fronde presented a coalition far more formidable than his own league with Vendôme and Elbeuf, especially since Gaston of Orléans was beginning to waver towards the prince. A week after the incident he gave way, abandoned the Vendôme marriage and conceded Pont-de-l'Arche to Longueville. Condé had already told Retz at a meeting at Noirmoutier's house that his opposition could never proceed as far as civil war. He accepted Mazarin's gesture in an act of seeming reconciliation, but he showed his independent attitude by dining with the frondeurs on the following day. By this time no one could rely upon Condé's support. The frondeurs criticised his reconciliation with Mazarin, and Retz found it difficult to conceal the resentment expressed by his faction.

Soon after the reconciliation, an affair of court precedence cut across the alignments of the nobility, and provided a new twist to the growing tension between the factions. Madame de Longueville sought honour for her lover, La Rochefoucauld, by claiming for his wife the right to use a footstool – the *tabouret* – in the queen's presence. To achieve this aim she sponsored another candidate, the comtesse de Fleix, for the privilege, upsetting established priorities among those ladies who already possessed the *tabouret*, and exciting the rivalries of their husbands. The marshals and dukes protested vigorously at the implied elevation of La Rochefoucauld, who was then still merely prince de Marcillac, and assemblies of the nobility began an impassioned debate on the subject at the hôtel de Chevreuse. Condé intervened to press for the grant of the *tabouret* to the comtesse de Fleix, and the house of

Rohan gathered its strength to deny the privilege. Mesdames de Chevreuse, de Rohan, de Montbazon and de Guémenée created a formidable coalition against Condé, and suppressed their personal differences in their common detestation of madame de Longueville. Madame de Montbazon openly declared that she would have La Rochefoucauld mutilated and make an unpleasant presentation to madame de Longueville upon a silver tray. Inevitably the imbroglio fascinated the coadjutor. It seemed designed for his talents in intrigue, especially since his rival La Rivière, who was actively seeking nomination for a cardinalate, was deeply involved in the Longueville cause. Retz intervened on the specious pretence of his formal relationship with madame de Guémenée (her paternal grandmother, Catherine de Silly, was the aunt of Retz's maternal grandfather). He persuaded Condé not to disturb the Rohan *tabouret*, if madame de Montbazon withdrew her statement. This by no means settled the affair, but it renewed hopes of an understanding between Condé and the Fronde.

These hopes were furthered by a fresh disagreement between Condé and Mazarin. The gallant Jarzé stood high in the graces of the first minister, and prudently concealed the attachment he had to the prince. He also believed that he was well regarded by the queen – so much so that he aspired to a conquest far beyond his station. He conspired with one of Anne of Austria's ladies of honour, and began to make extravagant declarations to the queen, which she for a time treated as a joke. One day Jarzé's announcement of his passion went too far, and Mazarin at once discerned the directing hand of Condé. The prince had actually had no part in the affair, but he made the mistake of publicly defending Jarzé. The queen mocked her would-be gallant, and exiled him from the court. Madame de Motteville commented that Mazarin's enemies were given proof of the affection between the queen and the cardinal, but only, she added, in the role of her minister.[6] Retz and his associates might conclude that Mazarin was still far from united with the faction of the princes – Condé, Conti, the Longuevilles, La Rochefoucauld and Bouillon.

The Fronde turned once more to the exploitation of the parlement. It had been agreed at the peace negotiations that there would be no further full assemblies of the chambers without royal permission. The radical group in the *enquêtes* could not bring pressure on the conservative Molé without such an assembly, and were continually in search of a suitable pretext. Affairs in Guyenne afforded one possibility, but the financial situation and the manipulation of the government bonds seemed more promising still. The Spanish war was still an intolerable strain upon the fiscal system. At the end of June 1649 an offensive had been launched to recover Cambrai. Mazarin had personally attended some of these operations, and had hoped to secure a stronger position from which to negotiate. But the offensive failed, the negotiations proved abortive, and the war continued. The intendants were no longer available to instil some efficiency into the taxatory system, and there was not enough revenue to support the ordinary processes of government, let alone the military campaigns. Omer Talon wrote at this time that no one paid taxes, and that officials were afraid to collect the *taille* and the *aides*. Despite the general situation, the magistrates pressed harder than ever for their full salaries, and the rentiers demanded payment of the interest on their investments. A few months later he observed that the tax-farmers had been ruined, and that the very persons who stirred up the rentiers to demand payment of arrears of interest also encouraged the provinces not to pay the taxes.[7] Mazarin sought a new superintendent of finance to devise measures to meet the crisis. The commissioners who carried out the work for marshal de la Meilleraye were equally as honest as he and nearly as incompetent. Promises had been made to président de Maisons, and Mazarin had suggested to Gaston the name of La Vieuville, a minister banished by Richelieu a generation earlier. But the man who alone possessed the confidence of the tax-farmers and the ability to attract their credit was the disgraced financier, Particelli d'Emery. He had been allowed by Mazarin to return secretly to Paris, and he had won the support of Condé and also of La Rivière, who spoke to Gaston in his favour. In November Emery was reappointed with the promise that the debts of the rentiers would be met. Among the frondeurs and the magistrates, however, the name of Emery was synonymous with corruption. An unexpected exception was Retz's histrionic colleague, président Le Coigneux, who had compromised his standing with the frondeurs by negotiating a profitable marriage between his daughter and Emery's son.

When it became clear that Emery would be unable to honour his promises to the rentiers, the coadjutor saw the opportunity to cause Mazarin new embarrassment. Although there were a number of wealthy rentiers, including many of the magistrates, the bulk of those holding stock guaranteed by the hôtel de Ville were what Retz described as 'people of the middling sort who are always the most redoubtable in revolutions'. Late in November 1649 large meetings of the bond-holders were convened in the city. The parlement followed the government's instructions to prohibit these assemblies, but the meetings continued, and one of them, composed of 'three thousand rentiers, all good bourgeois dressed in black', appointed a committee of twelve syndics to secure payment of the arrears of interest. Retz claimed the credit for organising the syndicate, through half a dozen agents he had placed in the crowd. His purpose, he explained disingenuously, was really to serve the state, for without his intervention the rentiers would have run riot. There were several magistrates among the syndics, who included both président Charton and the man who acted as Retz's secretary and wrote his own account of the affair, Guy Joly. Beaufort and the coadjutor received a deputation of the syndics and placed the association under their protection. Molé had the *grand'chambre* of the parlement declare it illegal, but the syndics collected five hundred signatures to a petition demanding that the parlement hear their case. Mazarin placed his own agents within the association, providing them with *brevets* of indemnity. The rentiers marched on the Palais de Justice on 4 December, and, though they were not admitted, they had the satisfaction of knowing that the *enquêtes* had criticised the legality of a ban that had not been imposed by the full assembly of the chambers. Retz described the failure of a detachment of archers to arrest one of the syndics soon afterwards, and Joly reported a conference at Molé's house between some of the syndics and the presidents of the chambers. Harsh words passed between Guy Joly and Molé's son, Champlâtreux. As the conference broke up fighting occurred and several shots were fired.

The coadjutor refused to accept responsibility for the extraordinary events that followed. Montrésor, he asserted, set the fuse. At a dinner attended by the frondeurs at the house of président Bellièvre he suggested that they should stage an attack upon one of the syndics, and thereby lead the parlement to suspect the government and order an enquiry in full assembly. Retz described in his memoirs how he had denounced this plan and had warned the plotters of the discredit it would bring upon them in the event of failure. But Beaufort, Brissac, Noirmoutier, Laigues and Bellièvre were enthusiastic, and all that the coadjutor could do was to quote a tag from Corneille's *Horace* expressing his disapproval.[8] Guy Joly was chosen as the supposed victim, and one of Noirmoutier's retinue was appointed to execute the mock attack. Joly's own memoirs gave a slightly different account.[9] The vital meeting was at the coadjutor's house and not Bellièvre's. Retz, he said, had proposed a popular riot in support of the syndics that would move the *enquêtes* to demand a full assembly. Noirmoutier suggested a simulated assault on Broussel or Beaufort (who was absent because no one could trust madame de Montbazon). Montrésor and Joly had already discussed something of this sort, and now proposed that Joly himself should provide the target for the assassin. The coadjutor's criticism was thus provoked less by his doubts of the plan than by his pique at having his own suggestion capped by a more daring and ingenious one.

Joly then stuffed his doublet with straw and fired a pistol at it to render his 'wound' convincing. He was in the habit of visiting président Charton, and it was outside Charton's house on 11 December that Noirmoutier's horseman galloped up to his carriage and discharged his pistol. Joly immediately scratched himself through the hole in his doublet and loudly sounded the alarm. He was carried into Charton's house and attended by surgeons who subsequently vouched for the authenticity of the wound. Charton, who commanded the militia in the quarter, promptly decked himself in his colonel's regalia and issued a call to arms. Attended by a troop of frondeurs and rentiers he made his way to the parlement, where the chambers were hastily assembled. Charton believed that it was he who had been intended as the victim, but his more sceptical colleagues would do no more than order a routine investigation.

It was now the turn of others to seek profit from the situation. According to Joly, the marquis de la Boulaye, an admirer of madame de Montbazon and an associate of the complaisant Beaufort, had planned a riot on his own account, and had warned

Beaufort to prepare to assume the leadership if it gathered sufficient momentum.[10] As soon as the rumour reached him of an attack on Charton, the marquis rode through the streets calling on the populace to follow him to the parlement. Only a handful of vagabonds responded, and he left the Palais de Justice disconsolately to urge Broussel and Retz to support him. After the coadjutor had threatened to have him thrown from the window of his residence, La Boulaye retired to plan a fresh piece of folly. Some contemporaries, Retz included, believed that La Boulaye had been receiving instructions from one of Mazarin's spies, a certain madame d'Ampus, and that Mazarin had countered Joly's plot with a bogus plot of his own, designed to discredit the frondeurs.[11] Others considered that La Boulaye had been acting in concert with Beaufort alone, and that he tried to cover the fiasco of his attempted riot by planning to assassinate Condé. If this were so, Mazarin certainly heard of the conspiracy and used it to convince Condé of the hatred of the frondeurs. When the prince appeared uncertain, the cardinal proposed that he send an empty carriage to the Pont-Neuf, where a number of armed men had reputedly assembled. Condé's carriage passed unscathed over the bridge, but the following vehicle was fired on, and a lackey wounded. Joly recorded La Boulaye's subsequent admission that he thought the death of Condé would please both Mazarin and madame de Montbazon. But whether Mazarin had contrived all or part of La Boulaye's wild and murderous doings – whether the shots on the Pont-Neuf were connected with La Boulaye or were merely the accidental result of the tension prevailing in the streets[12] – the cardinal succeeded in neatly turning the tables on his enemies. Nothing would persuade Condé that the frondeurs had not been seeking to destroy him, and he insisted that the investigation be aimed not at the government but at the coadjutor and his friends.

On 12 December the rumour spread that the Fronde had conspired to kidnap the king, murder Condé and invite the Spanish to occupy Paris. Realising their peril, Retz and Beaufort conferred with their supporters but decided against defensive measures. Although La Boulaye's activities perplexed the frondeurs, the coadjutor guessed that Beaufort was implicated in some way. Condé refused to grant Retz an interview, and although the prince did meet Beaufort, he showed that his fury against the frondeurs

had in no way abated. Madame de Montbazon was more frightened than anyone. Two of her current lovers, marshal d'Albret
and Vineuil, had warned her of the government's intentions, and
she was far more deeply compromised by La Boulaye than was
Beaufort. Beaufort had found her fear infectious and had arrived
at Retz's house at 5 a.m. to suggest immediate flight. Madame de
Montbazon later pressed the same advice upon the coadjutor, and
he countered by saying that, though his life was in danger, he
could not lose his honour. It was not his honour that detained
him, responded madame de Montbazon, but his unwillingness to
leave his 'nymphs'. She suggested that they should take with them
the 'innocent one' (mademoiselle de Chevreuse) and leave madame
de Guémenée behind. When Retz remained unpersuaded, she
tried a different tactic. She confessed that she had never seen him
as her friend because of his connections with mesdames de Chevreuse and de Guémenée, but she felt that they might overcome all
obstacles were they united. Why, she asked, did the coadjutor
amuse himself 'with an old woman who was more malicious than
the devil and a young woman of incalculable stupidity?' Beaufort,
she declared, loved her only for her mind and had never been
interested in physical passion. Retz recalled in his memoirs how,
since it was his 'natural disposition to yield on such occasions',
he nearly succumbed to madame de Montbazon's blandishments.
Yet he still refused to escape with her to Péronne, and this, he
remarked, 'proved the end of our love affair'.

The plight of the frondeurs seemed grave when on 13 December, the princes, together with Gaston, Vendôme, Mercoeur and
Elbeuf attended the parlement. The unity of the great proved less
convincing when Vendôme and Elbeuf chose the occasion to
quarrel about precedence.[13] They had come to press the government's demand that the investigation should proceed as though
it were concerned with an act of treason against the king and state.
On the following day the parlement heard a demand for satisfaction from Condé, and agreed to extend the scope of the inquiry.
Charges were laid against La Boulaye, who was hiding in the
hôtel de Vendôme. Over the ensuing five days the commissioners
gathered their evidence, most of it from the spies planted by
Mazarin among the rentiers. On the 19th accusations were prepared against Charton and Joly, but, although Retz, Beaufort and

Broussel had been named by the witnesses, no decision was yet taken to proceed against them. The frondeurs began to regain confidence as they saw that the evidence against them was tenuous, and that nothing connected La Boulaye's affair with their own conspiracy. On 20 December Retz and Beaufort took their places in the parlement, supported by Luynes, Brissac, La Mothe-Houdancourt and the younger duc de Retz.

It seemed for a time that the legal inquiry would reach no conclusion. Joly submitted a plea that his case be heard by a special tribunal. The judges of the *enquêtes* began to raise their voices in the *grand'chambre*, demanding that prior consideration be given to affairs in Bordeaux. Hours were consumed in debate upon the technicalities of whether Charton might be allowed to speak in open court. While the court party and the princes seemed to be losing the initiative, Retz relied upon the curés of Paris to excite the sympathy of their parishioners. He turned to his friend Louis Lefèvre de Caumartin, a judge in the parlement and a relative by marriage,[14] to guide him through the intricate maze of legal technicalities. Then, on 21 December, he received warning from his cousin, madame de Lesdiguières, that the government was resolved to lay charges against Beaufort, Broussel and himself. The leaders of the Fronde met at Longueil's, where they were pressed by their host to re-enact the day of barricades, and even to invest the Palais-Royal itself. Retz insisted, however, that the time was inopportune for a new gamble of this kind, and persuaded the meeting that they should attend the parlement and rely on their friends there to rebut the accusations.

This policy was assisted when the judges assembled in the *grand'chambre* on the following day, for Talon, the advocate-general, held that the prosecution was not only politically unwise but unlikely to succeed in any event. He refused to assist the solicitor-general in the conduct of the case. Talon saw that the three principals had much in their favour. Broussel's advanced years, his probity and his impartiality were all to his advantage. Beaufort was as popular as ever, relying upon the sympathy he had acquired for his years of imprisonment and the military reputation he had gained during the siege of Paris.[15] Retz could depend upon his position in the church. He could not, however, rely on the support of his friends among the magistrates. When he arrived in the great hall he found that he was snubbed as though he were already condemned. Perhaps he could count himself fortunate to be there at all. He was nearly excluded from his place by Mazarin's manoeuvre to have the archbishop assume his seat. The coadjutor had anticipated this move and spent the previous night with his brother and Brissac, trying to convince his uncle to support the family interest. Four months earlier there had been a family quarrel when the archbishop had suspended the Jansenist preacher, Singlin, for delivering a sermon on grace. Retz, his father and the Jansenist duc de Liancourt had vigorously intervened and obliged the archbishop to revoke the suspension.[16] Now Retz's uncle seemed bent on obeying his new orders from Mazarin, but at the last moment his natural timidity prevailed and he pretended to be sick with fever.

The novelty of having three such eminent members of the parlement facing charges of conspiracy to kidnap the king and murder Condé caused lengthy procedural wrangles. Some said they might offer their explanations and withdraw; others maintained that they had the right to be present throughout the deliberations. Broussel solved this problem simply by refusing to leave his seat, and Retz and Beaufort followed his example. They demanded, in their turn, that Molé, his son Champlâtreux and Condé should withdraw, as prejudiced parties. Molé managed temporarily to brush such accusations aside, while the prince, who had lost patience and was about to quit the court, was restrained by Gaston. The statements from the witnesses, for whom Retz generally seemed to find criminal records, paraded a certain amount of circumstantial or hearsay evidence. They claimed that it was commonly said at the meetings of the rentiers that Retz and Beaufort wanted Condé assassinated. They had seen La Boulaye at the houses of Broussel and the coadjutor. They had watched Charton issuing his call to arms, and had heard Joly say that both Condé and Molé must be destroyed. It was not a very convincing indictment, especially when one of the commissioners, who had taken the statements, defended the granting of pardons to the witnesses for their crimes by saying that without the *brevets* to this effect the king would never receive the information he needed.

Président de Mesmes had already described the whole affair as a new tumult of Amboise, recalling a Huguenot conspiracy to destroy the Guises and take the royal family into safe-custody nearly a century before. Retz made use of this when the opportunity came for him to speak. He said that men of quality apparently stood condemned by the lies of infamous scoundrels. The witnesses, he claimed, had been suborned by Mazarin, who sought vengeance against him because of his defence of public liberty.

Is it possible [Retz asked] that a grandson of Henry the Great, that a senator of the age and probity of monsieur de Broussel, that a coadjutor of Paris can be even suspected of seditious acts when nothing substantiates them save this hare-brained farrago from fifteen miserable fellows of the commonest kind? I am persuaded it would be shameful of me to speak further on the subject, and that, messieurs, is what I think of this modern conspiracy of Amboise.

The *enquêtes* received this address with acclamation, and the parlement as a whole returned to its procedural disputes. A sympathetic crowd had gathered outside and the frondeurs found it difficult to push through their enthusiastic supporters at the end of the day. But the case was far from decided. The court met again on 24 December and adjourned the hearing for five days.

On Christmas day the coadjutor stepped out of the role of attainted felon and back into the part of a prince of the church so that he might deliver a sermon in the church of Saint-Germain-l'Auxerrois beside the Louvre. He selected Christian charity as his theme, and expanded so eloquently on analogies with the supposed injustice of his own persecution that many of the ladies present wept – or so Retz described the scene in his memoirs. But the *éclat* of this sermon was spoilt by one embarrassing incident. During this period the coadjutor was suffering from venereal disease, which he had caught from that cousin with whom he had once tried to elope in his youth – Marguerite de Gondi, the duchesse de Brissac. She had been infected by her husband, Retz's fellow frondeur, and had begun a liaison with the coadjutor after a quarrel with Brissac. Retz's doctor was ill at the time, and a second doctor in whom he trusted was under a cloud for killing a man. The coadjutor knew no one to whom he might go to seek treatment, and imprudently consulted Noirmoutier. When mademoiselle de Chevreuse praised her lover's sermon, Noirmoutier indiscreetly observed that it was indeed remarkable in view of the

preacher's illness. He then proceeded to reveal the nature of this
affliction to his companion. It appears that Retz was soon forgiven
by madame la coadjutrice, and he for his part forgave Noirmoutier.
But he had no compunction in leaving all these unpleasant details
for posterity.

After this double piece of hypocrisy Retz resumed his defence
in the treason trial. He and Beaufort arrived at the Palais de
Justice on the day proceedings reopened with an escort of three
hundred cavaliers, as well as a large crowd of their lower-class
supporters. They tried to substantiate their allegations of prejudice
and corruption against Molé, and for several days it appeared as
though it were the venerable first president who was on trial. No
one appeared free from suspicion at this time. Anger flared easily,
and talk of treachery and assassination was in every mouth. Many
of the magistrates bore concealed weapons. Brissac persuaded
Retz to carry a poignard, and when Beaufort observed its handle
protruding from the episcopal robes he announced: 'Ah! Such
is the breviary of monsieur le coadjuteur.' Some steadying influence was needed in such an atmosphere. Oddly enough, it was
provided by Gaston of Orléans, who played a directing part in
the affairs of the parlement. Perhaps it was to be expected that one
so congenitally incapable of making up his mind in political
matters should take refuge in the search for legal precedent, and
derive comfort from the cloudy haze of quibbles and evasions in
which the men of the law delighted. The party of moderation
within the parlement felt in their turn that these strange proceedings assumed greater dignity and purpose from the presence of the
king's uncle. Indeed Gaston became so imbued with the customs
and thinking of the senior magistrates that he actually began to put
legal formality before political interest.

To Condé such attitudes were inexplicable and unpardonable.
As the evidence was read and re-read, as the accused continued to
protest their innocence, and as the lawyers pressed their interminable arguments about the conflicting rights of Molé and his
critics, the prince's patience rapidly evaporated. Finally he quarrelled with Gaston, who declared that he was tired of Condé's
wish to be master of all things, and sick of his quest for private
vengeance under cover of public justice. The princes ceased to
attend the trial, and Gaston himself did not return to the parlement

until 10 January 1650. Another two weeks passed before Beaufort, Broussel, Charton and Retz were formally exonerated, while Joly, who had arranged privately with Champlâtreux to drop his counter-accusations,[17] was not acquitted until 1 February, and La Boulaye was granted a pardon shortly afterwards. But in the meantime the political situation had been transformed by a dramatic and unexpected event. Mazarin had arrested Condé, Conti and Longueville.

The cardinal had not taken this step without a great deal of deliberation. He had finally concluded that the overbearing Condé and his faction of the princes would never rest content until they had full control of the regency. Had the prosecution of the frondeurs succeeded, a powerful counter-weight to the princes would have been eliminated. Moreover, Condé's angry contempt for the Fronde was exceeded by his resentment against the government. His understanding with Gaston had broken down, and it seemed likely that he would repeat the manoeuvres of the previous summer and contemplate a coalition with Retz and his party. In fact Chavigny and La Rochefoucauld had already begun negotiations on Condé's behalf with Noirmoutier and the duc de Retz.[18] Thus it became an urgent necessity for Mazarin to anticipate such a coalition by seeking a rapprochement with the faction whose prosecution he had so recently ordered. It was not difficult to obtain the queen's agreement for such a reversal of alliances. Condé had recently arranged the marriage of the duc de Richelieu and the daughter of the marquis de Vigean without the queen's permission, and had connived at their seizure of Le Havre. Her anger against the prince still smouldered with the humiliating memory of Jarzé's ardent declarations of love. Yet no negotiation could be more delicate than one which involved the frondeurs in secret cooperation with the government. The smallest error would warn Condé to take precautions, and might drive him to overbid the government's offers to the Fronde. For this complex and sensitive intrigue Mazarin selected his former enemy, madame de Chevreuse.

The first step taken by this most experienced of all conspirators was to arrange a secret audience for Retz with the queen. He went in disguise to the cloister of the church of Saint-Honoré, and at midnight he was conducted to a hidden oratory where the queen

was waiting. While the coadjutor assured her of his loyalty, Anne
of Austria vehemently expressed her dislike of Condé and her
anxiety that Retz should make peace with her 'poor cardinal'.
Mazarin joined the conversation after half an hour, and once
again there was a mockery of reconciliation, as the two embraced
each other with effusions of mutual friendship and an unspoken
understanding that each was acting solely in pursuit of his self-
interest. Mazarin indicated that the coadjutor should have the
nomination to the sacred college of cardinals reserved for La
Rivière, and Retz made it clear that, as Condé might not remain
in prison for ever, he needed appropriate guarantees for his
friends and himself. The coadjutor had a second secret meeting
with the queen and Mazarin, and held several discussions with the
minister Hugues de Lyonne. Noirmoutier and Laigues negotiated
with madame de Chevreuse and also attended the conference with
Lyonne. Beaufort had to be excluded from the secret at this stage,
because any indiscretion he committed before madame de Montbazon would most likely have reached the ears of her current lover,
Vineuil, who was attached to Condé. Gaston was brought into the
plot by madame de Chevreuse, for whom he still retained considerable affection. It was important that Gaston should conceal
matters from the untrustworthy La Rivière, who was also in
Condé's confidence. Governorships were promised to Vendôme,
Noirmoutier and Brissac. Laigues was to become a captain of
Gaston's guards, and the chevalier de Sévigné was to receive a
pension. The house of Vendôme was to obtain the admiralcy it
had for so long coveted.

Although all the preparations had been completed for the arrest
of the princes, Mazarin hesitated to give the final order. Retz
counted seventeen persons who were privy to the secret, and knew
that discretion was a mutable quality among them. He feared
that the plot would fail if the cardinal delayed much longer. The
tension among the frondeurs communicated itself to the other
factions. 'If a lackey had decided to draw a sword', Retz wrote,
'we should all have been killed in less than fifteen minutes.'
Laigues and Noirmoutier began to suspect that Mazarin was
playing them false, and that he had contrived a situation where
Condé's faction and the Fronde would exterminate each other.
Condé, however, discounted the rumours that reached his ears. If

Retz made any move to approach Gaston, he felt assured that La Rivière would inform him of it. According to Guy Joly, the prince actually discussed this possibility with Mazarin, and they laughed together at a report that Retz had been visiting the Palais-Royal disguised in a red cloak, a plumed hat and an array of weapons.[19] Condé, in fact, was completely duped. But Retz was less disposed to praise the deceptions practised by his new ally than he was to deplore his timidity and irresolution. Laigues began to threaten Lyonne, and the frondeurs suggested that, if Mazarin would not act, they expected Gaston to reveal the conspiracy in the parlement. At last the cardinal gave his orders. A bogus council meeting was called on 18 January and the officers of the guards arrested Condé, Conti and Longueville – the lion, the monkey and the fox, as Gaston named them.

The supporters of the princes were taken completely by surprise. One of them tried to appeal to the populace, but the Parisians remembered Condé as their oppressor in the recent war, and their only alarm was occasioned by a rumour that Beaufort, not the princes, had been arrested. The coadjutor and Beaufort went out into the streets to reassure the crowd, and as they passed, *feux de joie* were lit amid public rejoicing. The princes were held securely in the château of Vincennes. The queen sent a lame explanation of the affair to the parlement, which was on the point of absolving Retz and his friends from the supposed plots of Joly and La Boulaye. She said that the arrest was necessary for the security of the state, and added soon afterwards that it was the will of her government to observe the declaration of October 1648. Talon commented in his account of the matter that it was imprudent in any case for the regent to reveal the secrets of statecraft to the vulgar gaze, but, if she did attempt to justify her acts, she ought at least to give some indication of the nature of Condé's treason.[20]

With all the fury of a woman to whom being outwitted was far less tolerable than being betrayed, madame de Longueville withdrew to Normandy to raise the province in the cause of her husband and her brothers. Neither the nobility nor the parlement of Rouen responded. She retired to Dieppe and, when Mazarin had the king make a royal progress through the province in February, she fled to Holland and thence to join Turenne at Stenay. Her lover, La Rochefoucauld, gathered forces in Poitou, while Bouillon prepared to do the same in Limousin, and Condé's father-in-law, marshal Brézé, breathed defiance in Saumur. The parlement obligingly registered a royal edict that these supporters of the princes should appear in Paris within fifteen days or be declared traitors. In Burgundy there was some armed resistance to the replacement of Condé as governor by Vendôme, but this collapsed when the royal army besieged and occupied Bellegarde. Where violent means were unsuccessful, the faction of the princes tried emotional appeal. In April Condé's mother appeared at the Palais de Justice and embarrassed Retz and Beaufort by humiliating herself in their presence. At the end of May Condé's wife, together with Bouillon and La Rochefoucauld, entered Bordeaux, whence they continued to defy the government. Madame de Longueville and Turenne gathered a small army on the eastern frontier and entered into a close alliance with the Spanish forces in the Netherlands.

As soon as the reaction to the arrest of the princes was reduced to manageable proportions, the understanding between Mazarin and the coadjutor began to break down. In the first days of Condé's defeat the frondeurs had swaggered about the court as though they were now in control of the government. Madame de Chevreuse took to herself all the credit for the reconciliation of court and Fronde, and hoped to re-establish the ascendancy over Anne of Austria she had possessed in the time of Richelieu. But Mazarin had not the least intention of resigning power to either madame de Chevreuse or the frondeurs – nor did he intend to fulfil his promises to the Fronde where he could avoid them. With the faction of the princes virtually eliminated, he believed he had little to fear from Retz and his associates, who might always be brought to heel by the threat of releasing Condé. The coadjutor himself was most uneasy about the loss of personal popularity which association with Mazarin must entail. He found others superseding him in his own demagogic role. After Gaston's disenchantment with La Rivière, the king's uncle began to look towards Retz for advice, and Mazarin feared that Retz would control Gaston in his own interest. Retz professed that he would accept no responsibility for Gaston, for the latter's habitual irresolution and political vacillation made him an onerous and impossible charge.

There were times when Mazarin spoke of the possibility of

cementing their alliance with a marriage between his young nephew, Paul Mancini, and one of the daughters of the duc de Retz. For the most part, however, his attitude to the coadjutor was one of querulous suspicion. On his side, Retz pretended that he was constantly covering Mazarin's mistakes and apologising for his clumsiness, while being unjustly accused of deceiving him in return. Mazarin reproached him for not using his influence with the lower classes to prevent the sympathy excited by the appearance of the dowager princesse de Condé. Retz reproached the cardinal for delaying the amnesty promised to the rentiers and for not honouring his undertakings to pay the interest on the *rentes*. He declared his resentment of a statement by Mazarin's agent, Ondedei, that the coadjutor was conspiring with the rentiers to cause a new upheaval. Mazarin created trouble by intimating to Beaufort that Retz was responsible for leaving him in ignorance of the coup against the princes until the last possible moment, and the coadjutor had to appeal to président Bellièvre to allay Beaufort's suspicions. Retz harassed Mazarin by questioning the wisdom of the government's support for Epernon in Guyenne, and suggested that the opposition of the Bordeaux parlement would eventually evoke a response from the Parisian magistrates. Finally, he distrusted Mazarin's motives in reappointing Châteauneuf to his former charge of keeper of the seals, thereby forcing the retirement of the chancellor, Séguier. When Emery died in May 1650, président de Maisons had been given responsibility for the finances, and Retz suspected his loyalties and his probity. Châteauneuf's return seemed even more sinister, for he was a former lover of madame de Chevreuse and an admirer of madame de Rhodes. No trace remained of the sympathy for the Fronde he had shown before the first civil war. Though he was now seventy years old, and had suffered nearly ten years of imprisonment under Richelieu and seven years of exile after the affair of the *Importants*, the new keeper of the seals had lost none of his vigour. He was brusque and domineering in his manners and an enemy of moderation in his politics. It seemed to Retz that Mazarin was using him to exacerbate rather than to solve the problems of the *rentes* and of Guyenne. Above all, he appeared to have been commissioned to disrupt and discredit the Fronde.

Despite these signs of friction, the court left Paris on 4 July on a

F

long journey to pacify Guyenne. The Bordeaux parlement had allowed the entry of Bouillon and his party to the city on the understanding that the supporters of the princes undertook no overt action against the regency. The parlement there was generally sympathetic to Condé's cause, and responded to his wife's request for justice by sending a protest against the arrests to the central government. The conservative magistrates, however, were apprehensive that Bouillon might use the populace to force them into open resistance to the crown and alliance with Spain. Their leader, président de Gourgues, was asked to suggest to the government that the city's loyalty might be preserved by the dismissal of the governor, Epernon. Gaston and the moderate group within the Paris parlement supported this request, but Mazarin continued to back Epernon. In these circumstances the fears of the Bordeaux magistrates were soon realised. The popular party gained the ascendancy, and a campaign began between Epernon's forces and those of Bouillon. Such was the background to the government's expedition to Guyenne. Its strategic necessity appeared less urgent than the need to retain control of Paris. But perhaps Mazarin judged that Retz was sufficiently ensnared, both by the Chevreuse household and his hopes of a cardinal's hat, to respect their agreement. Perhaps he also reasoned that Châteauneuf could manoeuvre more successfully against the Fronde in his absence. In any event, he took leave of the coadjutor with professions of friendship, and left Châteauneuf and the minister Michel le Tellier to manage Gaston, the parlement and the Fronde.

Mazarin had not been gone two days when a deputation from the Bordeaux magistrates was received in the *grand'chambre*. With the respect that one strong will extends to another, Molé was inclined to sympathise with Condé. The arrest had outraged his sense of propriety, and confused his already-divided loyalties to crown and constitution. The first president was consequently inclined to allow the parlement to debate the case against Epernon, and to press for peace in Guyenne, although he was not prepared to see the radicals from the *enquêtes* take the lead in such issues. After several days of discussion the parlement commissioned président Bailleul to follow after the court and make known the desire of the magistrates for a just and speedy settlement of the war. Mazarin, however, was not in the mood to heed such opinions. During July marshal de la Meilleraye manoeuvred the royal army against Bouillon between the Dordogne and the Garonne, and in August began to press the siege of Bordeaux itself. Bouillon distinguished himself by his military strategy and La Rochefoucauld by his bravery, but little help arrived from Spain and a royal victory appeared likely. As the plight of Bordeaux increased, the local parlement pressed more strenuously for the intercession of its Parisian counterpart. Président de Gourgues himself arrived in the capital and was granted an audience by Gaston. Support for the princes was growing daily among the men of the law. Although Châteauneuf suggested an arbitrary ban on the full assembly of the parlement, Retz maintained that such an action would drive the lawyers over to Condé's cause in a body. While Châteauneuf accused the coadjutor of intriguing with the Bordeaux rebels, président Viole – once an ardent frondeur and now the most fervent of Condé's supporters – reproached him with subservience to Mazarin. Le Tellier seemed less reactionary than Châteauneuf but by no means as favourably inclined to the parlement as Gaston. When he looked back at the situation in later years, Retz concluded that Le Tellier had been instructed by Mazarin to encourage the keeper of the seals to quarrel with him.

Officers from the army of the princes had begun to infiltrate Paris at this time. According to Retz, a group of men led by an officer in the disguise of a mason tried to apprehend Gaston as he entered the Palais de Justice. Shots were fired and the guards of Gaston and Beaufort had to drive out Condé's supporters after a brisk encounter. The coadjutor's robe was ripped by a dagger in this affray. Joly related that Retz boasted of personally disarming his assailant, but he added that he doubted whether the coadjutor had been involved at all. The boast, he declared, was typical of Retz's self-vaunted martial and amorous exploits. A few weeks later Beaufort's carriage was set upon and one of his servants killed. The murderers were said to be merely a gang of footpads, and they were executed before Beaufort could press for their interrogation as possible agents of the princes.[21]

As Condé's partisans became more active in the capital, the Spanish army from the Netherlands linked up with Turenne's

forces and began a steady advance through Picardy and Champagne. The government began to fear that the princes might be
rescued from Vincennes, but the Fronde was anxious lest they
should be taken too far from Paris, where their imprisonment,
and possible release, would be more directly under Mazarin's
control. Mazarin was not yet ready to dispense with the Fronde,
so the princes were transferred to a new fortress at Marcoussis,
not far to the west of the capital. A week after this compromise
président Bailleul returned, having fulfilled his commission from
the parlement to press the regency to negotiate peace in Guyenne.
The queen, he reported, was in favour of peace, but the alliance
of the faction of the princes with the Spanish prevented it. It did
not seem to be an entire coincidence that within a few days – on
12 September – don Gabriel de Toledo, one of the Spanish envoys
who had negotiated with Retz during the siege of Paris, should
arrive in the capital as an emissary from the archduke. The
minister Abel Servien believed that Retz and Turenne had persuaded the archduke to treat with Gaston behind Mazarin's back,
and the cardinal appeared to accept this opinion. Three weeks
earlier a letter from the archduke to Gaston in his capacity as
lieutenant-general of the kingdom had suggested a conference,
and Gaston had used it to quieten the clamour of the peace party
in the parlement. Châteauneuf worked vigorously to prevent the
Spanish move, but Gaston was now speaking openly to the frondeurs of his bitterness against the cardinal. Le Tellier again adopted
an attitude of moderation. Everyone now assumed the lieutenant-
general to be dancing to the strings manipulated by the coadjutor,
and Le Tellier did not hesitate to confirm this opinion in his
correspondence with Mazarin.

Retz would not take the credit for so expert a piece of duplicity
in his memoirs. Instead, he vehemently denied it. While Mazarin
was accusing him of trying to steal the initiative in peace negotiations with both Bordeaux and Spain, he was, he said, busily
working in Mazarin's interest to prevent the growth of Condé's
party. Despite the follies of the government's policy in Guyenne,
he remained true to the cardinal's cause, acting with such sincerity
that one might have thought him to be 'cardinal Mazarin's own
nephew'. All this was very damaging to his public reputation. At
this very time placards were being posted in the streets of Paris

by Condé's agents warning the populace against 'false tribunes who had used the people for their own ends and were now in the service of Mazarin'. But Retz insisted that he had even defended the cardinal against Gaston's reproaches, while being accused of directing the latter's actions. He protested his innocence too loudly. In the middle of September he was already considering the adjustment of his party's position. He himself admitted that after Gaston's outbursts against Mazarin he went to the king's uncle and persuaded him that he should not only negotiate peace with Spain but should have the parlement ratify it before notifying the cardinal.

While Retz was making the first moves to detach himself from an alliance that was becoming unprofitable as well as embarrassing, he had a curious encounter with an envoy from Cromwell's republican government in England. The coadjutor always congratulated himself on his patriotism where the interests of foreign nations were concerned. He had proceeded warily when the Bouillons had involved him in their association with Fuensaldagne during the first civil war. His memoirs covered this involvement with transparent apologies about the need to end the conflict with Spain. When he received further approaches from the Spanish after the peace of Rueil, he claimed that he had earned their respect by protesting that he was too good a Frenchman to accept their gold. His account of his contact with revolutionary Protestantism was equally disingenuous. His relations with the exiled court of the Stuart monarchy had been more than harmonious. He spent much of his time with one of the most gallant soldiers who fought in the Stuart cause, the marquis of Montrose. Montrose, who came to France before the civil war and returned to Scotland in the spring of 1650, was likened by Retz to one of Plutarch's heroes. But Montrose and his fellow exiles were coldly treated at the French court. Although the queen of England was the king's aunt, she did not receive the support she had expected from Mazarin's government. Retz had visited her just before the flight of the court from Paris in January 1649. When he found that she was obliged to remain in bed because she could afford no fuel, he ordered supplies of firewood for her. She remained in Paris during the siege and, as Mazarin had not paid the pension allowed her for the preceding six months, he had the parlement vote a

subsidy for her household. The news of the execution of Charles I
reached Paris on 10 February 1649, and the only personal condo-
lences she received from the French court came from an envoy
sent by her brother, Gaston, whose real motive (or that of his
confidant, La Rivière) was actually to establish contact with La
Rochefoucauld. When Charles II arrived at the French court over
two years later, Retz was to borrow money to help the young king.
Indeed the Stuarts had cause to be far more grateful to the
coadjutor than to Mazarin.

The cardinal appreciated that Cromwell saw Spain as the
national enemy of England, and inevitably he considered the
possibility of a military alliance with the de facto government
across the Channel to relieve the Spanish pressure on the French
armies. But in the autumn of 1650 Cromwell sent an agent not to
Mazarin but to Retz. An Englishman named Fielding, whom Retz
had known in Rome, called on him late at night to introduce the
younger Sir Henry Vane. Vane was still serving Cromwell's
government, and had not yet discovered that his republican
sentiments could be outraged as well by a military dictator as by a
legitimate king. He flattered Retz by saying that Cromwell sought
his friendship as one who had established a reputation in defending
public liberty. The two evidently liked and respected each other,
but Retz was careful to say in his memoirs that, while he was
impressed by Vane's capacity, he was not seduced by his persuasive
charm. He gave an answer similar to that with which he had responded to the overtures of Fuensaldagne. He could not, he said,
do anything unbecoming a good Catholic and a good Frenchman.
Retz was obliged to be cautious. The court party tended to see
analogies between events in England and the actions of the parlement and the Fronde. The magistrates themselves were the first
to insist upon their loyalty to the crown, however much they
might wish to hedge it about with so-called 'fundamental' laws.
Despite the realism of Mazarin's foreign policy, the cardinal could
not afford to dispense with so useful a weapon against his internal
enemies. A note has been preserved in which he recorded a report
of a conversation between Retz and Ménage. Retz had reputedly
told his protégé that, if Beaufort wanted to be a French Fairfax,
he would be the French Cromwell.[22] In February 1651, when
Retz finally broke free from the cardinal's embrace, Mazarin

was to use this statement in a desperate endeavour to ruin the coadjutor.

Madame de Chevreuse became increasingly alarmed as the signs of a rift between Mazarin and Retz became more obvious in the autumn of 1650. Her chagrin at the idea of the dissolution of the coalition for which she thought herself responsible was exceeded only by her horror at the vision of the triumph of madame de Longueville reunited with the frondeurs and their ladies. Retz had been led to join Mazarin against the princes by hope of a reward that had not materialised. It seemed to madame de Chevreuse that he might be retained by the fulfilment of his ecclesiastical ambitions. She believed herself to be in Le Tellier's confidence, and she importuned the minister to tell Mazarin that the coadjutor had been misjudged, and must be mollified at once if the Fronde were not to declare for Condé. Le Tellier did actually write to the cardinal to this effect, but Mazarin would not be hurried into any indiscretion where Retz was concerned. He replied that the coadjutor was rather like a ship with too much canvas aloft: so long as he was not given much wind he would yaw idly about. Nevertheless, Mazarin had no cause for complacency. At the beginning of October he reversed his policy in Guyenne, dismissed Epernon, made peace with the Bordeaux parlement and pardoned Bouillon and La Rochefoucauld. Alarmed both at the Spanish advance in Champagne and Gaston's peace negotiations, he hurried to Fontainebleau with the court. There madame de Chevreuse, whose colourful past made her a bizarre advocate in such a cause, pleaded before him and the queen for Retz's cardinalate. Others, including Gaston, joined in the chorus, for Retz had been developing his own plan to secure his elevation.

Retz affected a certain diffidence about his promotion, though he never doubted the suitability of his qualifications. It was, he asserted, the reasoning of his friend Caumartin that persuaded him to press his candidature. Caumartin argued that the bogus assassination plots of December 1649 had not only unjustly damaged his reputation but incurred the inveterate enmity of Condé. And Mazarin was now as offended by the service he had rendered the queen as he had formerly been by Retz's service to the parlement. The coadjutor had to fear both the resentment of a prince and the jealousy of a first minister, and, though they might at present be divided, their reconciliation would spell his ruin. Only the dignity of a cardinal's hat would preserve him from such an eventuality. The logic of all this was probably Retz's long before it was Caumartin's, but the coadjutor pretended in his memoirs that he remained dubious about his friend's suggestions. 'There is a great distance, he wrote, between being persuaded of the wisdom of a course of action and being so convinced that one will set it in train against one's own inclination.' Then, with a flash of candour, Retz confessed to the outlook he had adopted in earlier crises: 'When one finds oneself in this midway position [*état mitoyen*], one takes the opportunities that offer without going in search of them.'

He found just such an opportunity in the politics of the papacy. Cardinal Panciroli, whom Mazarin had once served as a secretary and whom he had betrayed, was high in the favour of Pope Innocent x, and suggested that Retz might be made a cardinal to spite the French minister. Retz was sent a message from the Vatican in September 1650 indicating that the pope would welcome his nomination to the sacred college. But it was difficult for Retz to secure such a nomination from the government without Mazarin revoking it. Accordingly, he had Caumartin play on the fear of madame de Chevreuse that he might be reconciled with Condé, and he instructed président Bellièvre to convey to madame de Montbazon the impression that he was afraid the government would disown him. He himself worked upon the irresolute Gaston, and found to his surprise that the lieutenant-general was ready to endorse his candidature officially. Perhaps Gaston believed Caumartin's suggestion that, as a cardinal, Retz would help him preserve a balance between the complete triumph of Mazarin and a return to factious conflict. Retz explained the decision by saying that Gaston was like a person about to swim in cold water: he shut his eyes when he took the plunge. With so much support for Retz's advancement, it seemed for a moment as if Mazarin would give way. But Châteauneuf argued that the government should not yield to threats from the coadjutor and his friends. Soon afterwards Retz made the mistake of informing Le Tellier that if he could not be a cardinal he would be obliged to revert to the role of *chef de parti*. This indiscretion reinforced Châteauneuf's argument, and Mazarin now firmly opposed the nomination. He indicated to madame de Chevreuse that the best that could be done for her friend the coadjutor would be an offer of a few minor benefices and the payment of his debts. Smarting under the humiliation of refusal, Retz now determined to ally himself with the princes and thereby accomplish Mazarin's destruction. The circular dance was about to be completed. Retz was soon to stand again upon the place whence he had begun.

EIGHT

The war of the chamber pots

It was not Retz's habit to pursue any course of action without developing an alternative policy which he might adopt in the event of failure. He began to consider the possibility of an alliance between the Fronde and the princes almost as soon as he launched his campaign to make Mazarin honour his undertaking about the cardinalate. The scheme offered the advantage of being both an alternative should Mazarin refuse his nomination and an additional gambit should his candidature be recognised. There were, of course, considerable difficulties to overcome. Some of the frondeurs, especially Laigues and Noirmoutier, were still conducting a personal vendetta against Condé. The scheme could not succeed without involving Gaston at some point, but Gaston was possibly more afraid of the prince than anyone. It had also to include Beaufort, whose claim to the admiralcy divided him from Condé, and whose companion, madame de Montbazon, was still bitterly jealous of madame de Longueville. Madame de Chevreuse was dedicated to the preservation of the agreement between Retz and Mazarin. While she was endeavouring to make the cardinal support the coadjutor's claim in Rome, Mazarin was using her to control and also to disrupt the Fronde. Retz's own ties with her daughter provided a further problem, although, as it turned out, mademoiselle de Chevreuse was quite prepared to keep confidences from her mother. There remained the question of Condé's enmity for the Fronde – an argument used by Caumartin in advising the coadjutor to seek protection through promotion in the church. Retz, however, had always respected and admired the prince, and he had believed in the past that something of the respect, if not the admiration, had been reciprocated. Finally, there was the problem of secrecy common to all intrigues of this kind. Should Mazarin hear of the negotiations he might effect his own reconciliation with Condé, and utterly destroy not only Retz's plan but also his entire faction.

There was, at least, no problem about communicating with the princes. Conti's secretary, Montreuil, acted as their point of contact with the world outside Vincennes and Marcoussis, and madame de Longueville could be assumed to possess the authority to commit her brothers and her husband in any formal agreement. Moreover, there were several intermediaries ready to take the affair in hand. The subtle Caumartin was prepared to handle the most delicate contacts for the Fronde. The princes possessed a number of supporters within the corps of magistrates who were prepared to put the interests of their faction ahead of any attachment to the legal and constitutional principles of the parlement. These included président Viole, the *conseiller* Fouquet de Croissy, and Antoine de Corbeville, a junior member of the Arnauld family. Far more important than these as the *metteur en scène* for the princes was Anne de Gonzague de Clèves, daughter of the duke of Mantua and Nevers and sister of that queen of Poland whose marriage in Notre-Dame Retz had once opposed. Through her mother, the daughter of Mayenne, the leader of the League, she inherited a tradition of aristocratic intrigue. By virtue of her marriage to the elector palatine she was invariably known as madame la Palatine. Retz admired her enormously. He praised the way in which her love of gallantry never interfered with other personal commitments, and he regarded her political ability so highly that he compared her in this respect with Queen Elizabeth of England. Bossuet was to recall the 'unending fertility of her political expedients' and her ability 'to penetrate the secrets and attract the trust of all parties'.[1] She was a close friend of madame de Rhodes, who was also to play a prominent part in the intrigue. Madame de Rhodes, according to Guy Joly, entrusted her confidences to Caumartin. She was a lady of unusual tact, as evidenced by her ability to remain on good terms with madame de Longueville while being the confidante of the Chevreuse household. Her pursuit by the aged Châteauneuf afforded the conspirators the opportunity to mislead the court faction.

When the court returned to Fontainebleau from Bordeaux in mid-October 1650, Retz began to receive warnings of personal danger. Châteauneuf had in fact advocated the arrest of both

Beaufort and Retz,[2] but Mazarin had other plans. Madame de Rhodes convinced the keeper of the seals that she would hold the coadjutor through his attachment to her friend, mademoiselle de Chevreuse. The cardinal was not deceived so easily. He rightly suspected that madame de Chevreuse was beginning to lose her enthusiasm for the association of the Fronde and the government. He also perceived that Gaston was thoroughly discontented after his discussions at Fontainebleau, and that, though he had sanctioned the transfer of the princes to a new prison at Le Havre, he was beginning to approve of the movement within the parlement for their release. It was therefore Mazarin's intention to divide madame de Chevreuse from the king's uncle. He was astute enough to see, too, that instead of Retz being controlled by the daughter, it was the coadjutor who was actually controlling la coadjutrice. He tried to use the dashing good looks of the duc d'Aumale, the younger brother of the duc de Nemours, to seduce Retz's mistress. Retz frustrated this move by warning mademoiselle de Chevreuse, and Aumale then attempted to pay an assassin to eliminate him. According to the coadjutor, the assassin revealed the plan to his intended victim. But although Retz had countered these measures, he could not rely upon the loyalty of all his friends in the contest with Mazarin. The jealous madame de Guémenée was protesting against the scandals of his private life, regardless of her own contribution to this aspect of his reputation. She repeated stories about Retz's association with both madame and mademoiselle de Chevreuse, as well as with Marguerite de Gondi, the duchesse de Brissac. She even proposed to the queen an extraordinary scheme to lure the coadjutor into a greenhouse and turn the key upon him.

The plans of the conspirators remained concealed but their intentions were often suspected. Châteauneuf's ardour for madame de Rhodes had begun to cool, and he was no longer as easily deceived as the object of his desire assumed. His contact with madame de Rhodes led him to renew his association with the Chevreuse family, and mademoiselle de Chevreuse dropped into the habit of calling him 'Papa'. They all dined together with the coadjutor, and Retz recalled another of those occasions when everyone knew the other's real sentiments and acted a comedy in which they pretended to accept the attitudes they assumed,

Châteauneuf still had ambitions to replace Mazarin and, although he had opposed Retz and denied him his cardinalate, he would have been quite prepared to cooperate with the coadjutor against his patron.

Retz and Gaston had now agreed to work together for the liberty of the princes. Retz went disguised by night to visit madame la Palatine, while Caumartin kept in touch with Montreuil and with Condé's supporters in the parlement. The two factions were concealing the discussions from their less trustworthy members, and each was becoming increasingly apprehensive that the other would suddenly reveal matters to Mazarin and secure his support. The duc de Nemours, whose politics were the direct reverse of those of his brother, tried to put himself forward as the agent of the princes, but no one would trust him. Meanwhile, his wife succeeded in winning over madame de Montbazon, with Beaufort inevitably in train; but so notoriously indiscreet were this pair that their adherence provoked more fear than comfort to the conspirators. The Fronde agreed to mislead Mazarin by giving the impression that it distrusted the princes, and Condé's faction tried to confuse the government by pretending that it would prefer to secure the liberty of the princes through Gaston, Molé and the parlement. Perhaps these attitudes were the more convincing because they were not entirely feigned. Retz, for instance, suspected at times that Montreuil was a double agent employed by the cardinal. Mazarin added to the maze of distrust by encouraging marshal Gramont, and others sympathetic to the princes but not within the conspiracy, to think that they might free the princes of their own accord. His purpose in this was to prevent Gaston from joining the Fronde.

Amid so much uncertainty it was not surprising that the coadjutor should accept the proposal from the princess Palatine and her friend madame de Rhodes that a formal treaty should be drawn up. It was to be signed on behalf of the princes by madame de Longueville and was to consist of two parts. In the first, it would be agreed that one of Gaston's daughters should marry Condé's son: in the second, Condé would resign to Beaufort his pretensions to the admiralcy, the princes would agree not to oppose Retz's elevation to the sacred college, and mademoiselle de Chevreuse would marry Conti.[3] According to Joly, madame de

Montbazon was still so vindictive towards the Chevreuse family that Beaufort had to hide the proposals from her.[4] Neither the coadjutor nor his friends had the slightest qualms about the marriage of Conti and madame la coadjutrice. Personal attachments often provided new initiatives in politics, but political necessity overrode everything else, and nothing was as vital in a treaty as the guarantee of dynastic alliance.

At the beginning of December Mazarin joined the royal army in Champagne, where marshal du Plessis was manoeuvring against the Spanish in Rethel and against Turenne's winter quarters in Château-Porcien. His departure was the occasion of new agitation in the parlement, where proceedings had been restrained since the October announcement of peace in Guyenne. Demands were made for the freeing of the princes or, at least, for the hearing of charges against them. The queen denied these requests by declaring the matter to be one of royal prerogative, and when the magistrates returned to the attack she retired to bed and had Châteauneuf forbid further debate in full assembly. The Fronde could not participate in making these demands without revealing its new alignment. Gaston also appeared to defend the court, but his attitude was a subterfuge agreed by Retz and the princess Palatine. The parlement was about to issue new petitions criticising Mazarin and requiring the prisoners to be freed when, on 18 December, the news reached Paris that Mazarin (or, more accurately, du Plessis) had won a victory at Rethel. Many remembered the government's use of the victory of Lens just before the barricades of August 1648. The parlement relapsed into timidity, and the coadjutor noticed an air of depression about the people he passed in the streets of Paris.

It seemed to Retz that there was no longer any point in maintaining the pretence that he supported the government. Some positive lead had to be given to the opposition if it were not to lose its impetus. The coadjutor appeared in the parlement on 20 December and declared that, since the end of the war was now in sight, it was time to reveal the oppression suffered by the people and to call for the liberation of the princes. Retz had warned both his own followers and those of Condé of his intention, and after his speech a procession of carriages made its way to his residence, as the factions united to congratulate him. Ten days later the parlement sent the queen a new demand to free the princes. At the same time the magistrates besought Gaston to endorse their stand, but Gaston, gripped once more by the paralysis of indecision, replied evasively. Mazarin returned from Champagne on the following day, and under his direction the queen postponed her reply from one week to the next.

As the days passed and the government remained inactive rumours began to circulate that Mazarin intended to spirit the king away from Paris and re-enact the opening scenes of the first civil war. Parts of the secret treaty prepared by Retz and the princess Palatine were signed by the representatives of the two factions opposing the cardinal. Although the dependence of the various parties upon the king's uncle was mentioned in the text, the treaty in no way committed him, for the final version made no mention of the proposed marriage between his younger daughter and Condé's son. He was anxious, nonetheless, lest the secret should become known, and, inevitably it did reach the ears of Mazarin. La Rochefoucauld, to whom the idea of an alliance with the coadjutor was abhorrent, met the cardinal secretly on three or four occasions, and, according both to his own account and madame de Motteville's narrative, proposed an alliance between the court and the princes, whereby Mazarin should free Condé and thus isolate the Fronde.[5] But Mazarin would not risk reliance upon La Rochefoucauld.

The tide of general opinion was running strongly in Condé's favour. It was just at this time that Corneille produced *Nicomède* as a dramatic representation of the Fronde. The characters Arsinoe and Laodice seemed to depict madame de Longueville and madame de Chevreuse. The atmosphere of past events was evoked by scenes of mob riot and the siege of the royal palace. Nicomède, who had been unjustly imprisoned by his king, was the counterpart of Condé, whom Corneille wished to see reconciled with the crown. The words of Nicomède reflected the popular sentiment:

> Rebel? It is a word that I would never own.
> I come not here to sport before your hate the pose
> Of former captive, daring to reject his chains.
> I come as loyal subject, wishing to restore
> The peace which other interests wantonly disturb.[6]

For the Fronde, the princes and the parlement everything depended upon Gaston declaring himself. Gaston would do nothing, and Retz could not reveal to him that his real purpose was to restrain the government by force. 'One of the greatest embarrassments with princes', he wrote disconsolately, 'is that one is often obliged, out of consideration for their own interest, to give them advice without telling them its real purpose.' At the end of January Mazarin made an attempt to frighten Gaston into declaring for the court. He took him aside in the grey room of the queen's apartments and announced that in his opinion the parlement was trying to fulfil the rebellious role of the English Long Parliament, while Beaufort and Retz wanted to be its Fairfax and Cromwell. The opposition, he said, aimed at overthrowing the monarchy and establishing a republic.[7] The words were imprudent. Gaston vigorously denied the parallel, turned on his heel and abruptly left the cardinal. There was an opportunity for Mazarin to repair this error with the queen's reply to the remonstrance of the parlement concerning the princes. She still maintained that the matter was outside the jurisdiction of the parlement, but she was prepared to promise the liberation of the princes if certain conditions were fulfilled. These involved the surrender of Turenne and his army, the renunciation by madame de Longueville of her treaty with Spain, and the evacuation of her base at Stenay.

The parlement did not accept the queen's reply in the mood of conciliation with which it had been framed. Président Viole headed the opposition by denouncing it as an evasion designed to cover the flight of the court from Paris. Such views would not have persuaded the bulk of the magistrates unless Gaston had endorsed them, and Gaston chose to be absent. At this point the coadjutor intervened, more in the spirit of a gambler making a last throw than a director of an intrigue who had calculated the consequences of every move. He declared in the parlement that he was empowered to announce the lieutenant-general's adherence to the movement to secure the liberty of the princes. Retz had no such authority. Since Gaston could not make up his own mind, he had resolved to make the decision for him. But he could not be sure of Gaston's response, and he anxiously awaited his confirmation or denial. After hours of consultations with his entourage, Gaston called Retz to him, embraced him and announced that he

had instructed Le Tellier to tell the queen he stood by the coadjutor's words. He would refuse, he said, ever to attend the Palais-
Royal until Mazarin had been dismissed. Yet, even with this
subterfuge, Retz had not succeeded in fully conquering Gaston's
tremulous irresolution. He expected the lieutenant-general to
prevent the escape of the court, but Gaston would not even inform
the king's governor, marshal Villeroy, that he held him responsible
for the person of the king.

On 3 February Retz gave the parlement a highly-coloured
account of Mazarin's analogy with the Long Parliament, and the
magistrates forgot their inhibitions and clamoured for the trial or
banishment of the first minister. Gaston meanwhile refused the
queen's request to consult with her, either at the Palais-Royal or
at his own residence. On the following day he managed to find
sufficient courage to tell the parlement personally that he would
support the release of Condé and the dismissal of Mazarin. Soon
afterwards a *lettre de cachet* was presented requiring the immediate
attendance of a deputation before the queen. While Molé departed
with the senior magistrates, the others remained in the Palais de
Justice, ready to resume proceedings. The queen informed the
deputies that marshal Gramont had been sent to Le Havre to free
the princes, and would do so when certain conditions had been
met. Her main purpose, however, was to spring a trap for the
coadjutor carefully prepared by Mazarin and Châteauneuf.
Prompted by the queen, the keeper of the seals read an indictment
against Retz, signed by the four secretaries of state, denouncing
him as a factious troublemaker, who had given false advice to
Gaston and had boasted that he would relight the fires of civil war
because he had been refused nomination to the sacred college.[8]
Near midday the deputies returned to the Palais de Justice, when
Molé began to read the allegations against the coadjutor. The first
president was so anxious to frustrate Retz's intrigues that he did
not recognise the court's manoeuvre to distract attention from
Mazarin and the princes. Retz met the challenge judiciously. The
paper, he said, was a libel prepared by Mazarin, and was so infamous a document that it profaned the sacred name of the king.
The parlement should insist upon supervising the measures of the
government for Condé's release and Mazarin's exile. This speech
was generally applauded. Molé still hoped to reconcile Gaston

with the court and prevent his alliance with either the Fronde or Condé. He appealed to him as the one person who could save the state from disruption. As Gaston hesitated, Omer Talon went down on his knees to invoke the shades of Saint Louis and of Gaston's father, king Henry IV.[9] Retz alone sensed the ludicrous element in this piece of rhetoric, but he knew that, if Gaston accepted Molé's request to speak to the queen on behalf of the parlement, he might well weaken in the queen's presence. Once again he put words into Gaston's mouth, suggesting that he had already decided not to attend the palace until Mazarin had gone. Gaston grasped eagerly at this respite, and, following his refusal, the session was adjourned.

Next day the crisis was complicated by the meeting of an assembly of nobility in which several frondeurs participated, notably Fiesque and Montrésor. The assembly was ostensibly to defend aristocratic privileges, but the court assumed it presaged an attack on the Palais-Royal, and placed the royal guards on the alert. Retz had posted some of his own supporters nearby, and he continued to press Gaston to order the militia to close the city gates. For a time he entertained a scheme to have a certain captain of the palace guards arrest Mazarin, but he was not prepared to order this without Gaston's endorsement, and Gaston would still make no move which might provoke civil war. The most that the king's uncle would do was to authorise a number of armed patrols.

On 6 February the queen informed the parlement that it had no right to suggest the dismissal of her minister, and that she wished to guarantee the security of the state before Condé was liberated. The declaration concealed the fact that she had already yielded, for that very night Mazarin left the Palais-Royal and withdrew to Saint-Germain. Next morning the parlement resolved to thank the queen for giving the cardinal his *congé*, and inquired as to the steps taken to release the princes. Gaston insisted that he would not go to the palace to discuss how the release should be effected until he had an assurance that Mazarin would not return. The deadlock lasted for two more days, until the queen announced that Mazarin would leave France within a fortnight. The city remained tense, and the crisis did not end without a fresh alarm. A message had awoken Retz and sent him to Gaston in the early hours of the morning of 10 February. The message came from madame de Chevreuse, who had received news that the queen and the king were secretly rejoining the cardinal. When the coadjutor insisted upon immediate counter-measures, Gaston stubbornly refused to give orders to restrain the king, lest it involve him in conflict with Molé. Retz took matters into his own hands. He sent a message to Beaufort, and had mademoiselle de Chevreuse awake La Mothe-Houdancourt to gather a group of cavalry. Another agent was sent to rouse the militia and seize the city gates in the direction of the court's alleged escape route. Martineau, the colonel of the quarter near the Porte Saint-Honoré, was absent from his home, and his wife, the sister of madame de Pommereuil, went out into the streets to sound the alarm – precisely as she had done on the day of the barricades. One measure, at least, had been approved by Gaston. He had instructed a captain of guards to call at the Palais-Royal to dissuade the queen from her supposed flight. With the mob clamouring behind him, the captain was admitted to find the king asleep, and Anne of Austria in tears of humiliation. She denied that she had ever intended to take the king from Paris. Nevertheless, Beaufort and La Mothe-Houdancourt continued to patrol the streets for the rest of the night.

Retz knew that if moderate opinion within the parlement questioned the military measures taken against the crown, Gaston would be likely to disavow him. At dawn the frondeurs marched in a body to the Palais de Justice, escorted by a body of militia. The parlement had assembled before daybreak in the customary way, but Molé insisted upon transacting normal business while he awaited the reactions of Gaston. The latter delayed his entry until 9 a.m. in the hope of obtaining a preliminary indication of the magistrates' response. Once again the fate of the Fronde hung in the balance. But Gaston did not pass responsibility for the events of the previous night to the conspirators. Instead, he announced that he had arranged the details with Châteauneuf for the release of the prisoners at Le Havre. Though Molé murmured sadly that the Fronde had substituted the king's imprisonment for that of Condé, the parlement greeted the news with acclamation, and Gaston was sufficiently encouraged to pretend he had given authority for the guarding of the gates.

While the parlement continued to discuss the procedure for restoring the princes and their party, Mazarin journeyed to Le Havre, and on 13 February personally released Condé, Conti and Longueville. He had appreciated that the forces which Retz had combined against him were too strong to resist, but he still hoped that his mission to Le Havre might prevent the junction of Condé with the Fronde. In this he was mistaken. The princes gave him no thanks, and he retired towards the frontier. On the afternoon of 16 February Gaston, with Beaufort and Retz in his carriage, met the princes at Saint-Denis, and on the 17th he led them before the parlement amid the rejoicing of the same crowds who had previously acclaimed their imprisonment.

The cardinal retired slowly towards his place of exile at Brühl, near Cologne, and assuaged his bitterness by denouncing his enemies in his correspondence with the queen and his supposed allies at the court. At first these exchanges were irregular and, despite the ciphered interchange of endearments with the regent, his sense of frustration mounted.

Perhaps I am wrong, and I ask your pardon for it [he wrote] but I believe that, if I were in your place, I should already have opened a way for the Friend [himself] to return. . . . I should love the greatest enemy I have in the world with all my life and to the bottom of my heart if he could do anything to enable me to see Serafin [the queen] once more.[10]

By the time he offered these sentiments, in May, he had exchanged frustration for despair. A month earlier his letters had traced with relentless animosity, all the tergiversations of madame de Chevreuse, the coadjutor and the nobility of the Fronde. He respected the subtlety but not the morals of madame de Chevreuse, who, he said, had habitually been prepared to prostitute herself to gain a political advantage. He pointed out that Retz had changed sides six times in eighteen months. He had been loyal to the queen during the affair of the *Importants*, only to betray her at the barricades. He had seduced the party of the princes from their allegiance, Condé excepted, and had organised a party from the parlement, the hôtel de Ville and the Parisian populace to expel the king from Paris and resist the royal troops blockading the capital. He had sent Noirmoutier and Laigues to obtain the help of the

Spanish, and had had Bellièvre and the parlement sanction the sale of Mazarin's property while Molé was negotiating peace at Rueil. After the peace, when Condé and the cardinal had quarrelled, Retz had first joined forces with the prince and then persuaded the court to arrest him. While ostensibly cooperating with Mazarin, he had tried to turn Gaston against him, and had resurrected his faction in the parlement and the city. When Mazarin had returned to Paris after the victory of Rethel, Retz had intrigued with Condé's party to free the princes and expel the cardinal.[11] It was an accurate enough summary of the coadjutor's changes of front, but its fixed point of reference was Mazarin's self-interest. If Retz's own account of his motives were accepted as the basis of judgment, the politics of the cardinal, or for that matter of the princes, appeared equally variable.

Mazarin had hardly disappeared when the factions, and rival personalities within the factions, began a struggle to dominate the government. The posts within the ministry were the apparent rewards to be retained or secured, and existing and former ministers vied with each other for the possession of these offices. Châteauneuf and Chavigny, whose ambitions had comprised a minor theme throughout the whole period of the regency, began to assert their claims, while Le Tellier, Lyonne and Servien manoeuvred against each other. To Condé, whose disdain for bureaucrats was unchanging, this struggle for the ministry was an ignoble affair. He named it the war of the chamber pots. Yet it was not a matter he could afford to ignore. Behind the scramble for the supreme offices of state, a more profound contest was waged between Retz and himself, between the old Fronde and the new – a contest in which Gaston performed his accustomed role of political pendulum, swinging uneasily from one party to the other. As Mazarin saw the situation, the divisions and suspicions between those who wished to gain the queen's favour might enable her to revive her own authority and procure his return.[12] And this was precisely the policy Anne of Austria was to follow.

The queen, according to madame de Motteville, controlled her feelings at her public farewell to the man upon whom she had come to rely. It was at least two months before regular communications were established with Brühl, and perhaps it was her very isolation, and the intensity of the dangers surrounding her, that compelled her to think for herself and to steer a judicious course between the factions. Three immediate problems demanded her attention. The parlement had, at Broussel's suggestion, inserted in a new declaration against Mazarin a proposal that no cardinal should in future hold any office of state. Secondly, the assembly of some eight hundred nobles, ostensibly under the protection of both Gaston and Condé, was continuing its meetings in Paris and calling for the regent to convoke the estates-general. In the third place, the disunity of the council threatened to bring the machinery of government to a standstill, and it seemed imperative to re-shuffle the warring ministers and to name one of them to preside at the council table.

In his memoirs Retz chose to select his roles in the first two issues as examples of how he had fulfilled his *devoir*. Nothing, he wrote, gave him so much internal satisfaction as his advice to Gaston to terminate the assembly. He claimed that he had denied his own self-interest and ignored the opportunity to use his friends in the assembly. Similarly, he spoke in the parlement in favour of the declaration against the cardinals. He had expelled Mazarin and freed the princes, and he was content, he explained, to devote himself 'purely and simply to my vocation'. His other actions at the time belied this later interpretation.

The queen eventually agreed to the declaration excluding cardinals from the ministry. Her decision was apparently made on the spur of the moment, for she ordered Châteauneuf, the keeper of the seals, to accept the parlement's request in the presence of the deputation that brought it, without any pretence of consulting Gaston or Condé. Madame de Motteville recorded the embarrass-ment of Gaston and the dismay of the duchesse de Chevreuse at the check to the ambitions of the coadjutor.[13] But in any event the declaration carried no weight. A reaction set in against the ex-clusion of French cardinals, and the edict was first modified, and then allowed to lapse. The regent dealt with the problem of the assembly of the nobility with equal resolution. Its demand for the convocation of the estates-general was regarded by the magistrates as the creation of a rival to their own constitutional role. The queen could not afford to have her authority challenged from a new quarter, but she saw the advantage of using the proposal as a threat to the parlement. Both Gaston and Condé weighed the

profits they would gain from the estates against their corresponding loss of favour in the parlement. Neither, in the end, took any
effective action in one direction or the other. La Rochefoucauld
criticised them both for losing a splendid opportunity,[14] and once
again it was the regent who made the most of the occasion. She
promised that the estates should meet on 1 October, over three
weeks after the king would have attained his legal majority.
Gaston later pressed her to advance the date, but she remained
obdurate, and the estates were never in fact to meet.

The struggle for the ministry was marked by the developing
rivalry between the new Fronde (the party of the princes) and the
old. Their treaty was to have been ratified by the marriage of
Conti and mademoiselle de Chevreuse. Moreover, according to
some, it contained an additional secret clause by which Châteauneuf would have been created first minister.[15] Condé's show of
gratitude to the Fronde for liberating him from prison was
tempered by his aversion for the frondeurs in general and for Retz
in particular. He could not easily forget the conspiracy of December 1649, and he was even less inclined to forgive his supposed
assassins for having evaded justice by plotting with Mazarin to
arrest him in the following January. Retz began to fear that the
prince would not honour the treaty and, when he confided his
concern to his mistress, he was dismayed to find that she did not
share his enthusiasm for the match. In his memoirs he recalled
how he had told her to look upon the alliance with Conti as an
honour, though not one which she should regard as being above
her own rank. But if la coadjutrice was understandably cool about
the proposal, Conti was burning with ardour. He confided in
Retz's friends, Laigues and Noirmoutier, and took precautions
to hide his passion from his sister, madame de Longueville, whose
feud with madame de Chevreuse was as bitter as ever.[16] When
Condé sent président de Nesmond, one of his supporters in the
parlement, to test his brother's feelings, Conti vowed that he
would marry mademoiselle de Chevreuse even if he were abandoned by his friends and if the necessary papal dispensation were
refused. As La Rochefoucauld judged the situation, Condé would
be willing to fulfil the treaty if he saw Châteauneuf firmly in
Mazarin's place. But, if Châteauneuf were defeated, Condé would
ban the marriage.[17]

Although the 'Old Pantaloon', as the coadjutor called Châteauneuf, served as the object of derision for his attempts at gallantry,
he was a shrewd and unscrupulous intriguer who had earned
Retz's respect as a political opponent. At this time he appeared to
be closely associated with Retz and madame de Chevreuse, and
hence to be linked with Gaston. It was known, however, that
Châteauneuf had supported the calling of the estates when Retz
had opposed the project. Among the other ministers Lyonne and
Servien appeared to sympathise with Condé. The princess Palatine
hoped that the superintendency of finance would be transferred
to the father of her lover, La Vieuville, who had held the post when
Richelieu was recalled to the council in 1624. She persuaded the
queen to grant the governorship of Guyenne to Condé and that of
Provence to his brother. Lyonne and Servien were the ministers
who negotiated with Condé on this matter, though neither was
trusted by the queen. Both were anxious to secure the dismissal
of Le Tellier, who, knowing that he, too, lacked the queen's confidence, seemed to Mazarin to be likely to seek the protection of
Gaston.[18] Condé hoped to persuade Anne of Austria to replace Le
Tellier as a secretary of state by président Viole, while Lyonne
and Servien were pressing her to recall Chavigny.[19] The exiled
minister still enjoyed the patronage of Condé but he, like Châteauneuf, was notorious for placing his own interests before those of
his allies. The two constant elements in Chavigny's policies were
his hatred of Mazarin, whom he had introduced to Richelieu's
government, and Gaston's hatred for him, based upon the occasion
when Richelieu had placed him as a watchdog in Gaston's entourage. His ambitions consumed him, and he could never rest
from his intrigues. As Retz put it, he was ignorant of that cardinal
principle of successful living, to 'know how to be bored'.

This was the situation when on 3 April the queen suddenly
announced a change in the ministry. Chavigny was to be recalled
and Châteauneuf required to resign the seals in favour of the first
president of the parlement, Molé. Once again the queen had
consulted neither Gaston nor Condé. She had tilted the balance of
the council slightly towards the princes, and her policy was
designed to divide the new Fronde from the old. The reaction of
the coadjutor and his friends was violent and immediate. Madame
de Chevreuse and her daughter impressed upon Gaston the

enormity of the insult to his position. The king's uncle then called
a meeting of the leading members of both factions and demanded
advice. Retz recommended that Gaston should send an officer of
his guards to seize the seals from Molé, while he and Beaufort
should direct the passions of the mob against the regency. It was
then that the success of the queen's designs became apparent.
Beaufort, suspecting an alliance between the regent and the
prince, and anticipating the ruin of the coadjutor, went over to
Condé's camp and counselled moderation. Retz later believed that
madame de Montbazon and the duchesse de Nemours, Beaufort's
sister, had also been at work to sow division between the factions.
Condé himself was obviously pleased at the turn of events. This
was the occasion when he observed that he preferred not to be
involved in a 'war of chamber pots'.[20] He and Beaufort retired to
the library of the Palais-Royal to discuss their mutual interests,
while madame de Chevreuse was on the point of crying from
vexation. Her daughter implored Gaston to lock Condé and
Beaufort in the library and declare their arrest. Gaston, as might
be expected, endured new agonies of indecision. Retz noted that
he had begun to whistle, always a sign that nothing would be
resolved. Thus a coup d'état was narrowly averted, but the atmosphere of tension remained. Madame de Motteville expected a
new massacre of Saint Bartholomew and recorded how madame
de Longueville had told her that her terror had prevented her
from sleeping.[21] A day or two later, however, Gaston protested
loudly enough to oblige the queen to return the seals to the
chancellor, Séguier, rather than to bestow them upon Molé.

The change in the ministry was followed immediately by the
breaking of the marriage treaty between the factions. The queen
had naturally opposed it from the first, but she had not felt strong
enough to forbid it. La Rochefoucauld observed that Condé had
joked about the virtue of la coadjutrice with Conti, whose ardour
was converted in an instant to extreme aversion.[22] Président Viole
was then despatched with an abrupt message to madame de
Chevreuse and the coadjutor that the marriage would not take
place. Mademoiselle de Chevreuse was the only member of the
faction to be pleased at this *dénouement*. Retz was hardly surprised
at the news, but he was astonished that the princes had not
bothered to find pretexts to cover their disavowal of their

obligations. Nor, when he talked over old times in later years with Condé and madame de Longueville, could he ever discover exactly how the marriage had been broken.

It now became clear that Gaston, for all his assurances to the contrary, was finding his association with Retz an embarrassment. The coadjutor felt so unsafe and so isolated that he decided to withdraw to the cloister. Although the idea of Retz as a religious recluse caused some mirth within the court, the pretence of the retreat was maintained for several weeks. He continued to visit the hôtel de Chevreuse, though he and his squire, Malclerc, took precautions not to be observed. He also kept in touch with the exiled Châteauneuf. But he no longer tried to steer the course of events. He had resolved, he said, 'to wait and see what the next chapter of accidents might produce'. Not that he entirely abandoned himself to providence: several frondeur nobles stood guard in his house, and a group of Scottish officers, who had formerly served Montrose, were on call nearby.

Since the flight of Mazarin the queen had reached many of her political decisions unaided. She had made up her own mind about the assembly of the nobility and the declaration against the cardinals. She had authorised the offer of Guyenne to Condé, and by dismissing Châteauneuf and recalling Chavigny she had driven a wedge between the old Fronde and the new. Mazarin was subsequently to persuade her to change her mind on such issues as the estates-general and the offer of the provinces to the princes, but she had at least demonstrated her capacity to rule alone. She had no one to whom she could turn for dispassionate advice. She knew she would obtain this from Molé, but in his official position Molé was formally obliged to support the wishes of the parlement. She could also confide in old and trusted courtiers such as the marquis de Senneterre, the man who had reported Richelieu's comments on Retz's *Conspiracy of Fieschi*. But Senneterre, a friend of madame de Motteville, tended to garrulity, and Châteauneuf was trying to use him to recover the seals.[23] It was hardly likely that the queen would at this juncture have placed her trust in the coadjutor, whom Mazarin had taught her to revile, and whom Condé had out-manoeuvred in the first phase of the 'war of the chamber pots'. Nevertheless, this was what Retz believed, and what he recorded at length in his memoirs.

He claimed that the queen had first communicated with him before the changes in the ministry, asking for his support. When he had refused to be drawn, she had remarked to marshal du Plessis, the victor of Rethel: 'He wants to be ruined: well, let him be.' During his retreat Retz, by his own account, was visited by du Plessis, who asked him to see the queen, and brought a copy of a letter received from Mazarin as evidence of good faith. The letter, which was not in cipher, opposed the grant of the provinces to the princes, as a measure disastrous to the royal authority. It ended with the suggestion that, rather than surrender to Condé, it would be better for the regent to nominate Retz for a cardinalate and elevate him to Mazarin's place. Nothing in Mazarin's surviving correspondence confirms this assertion in Retz's memoirs, but his papers do suggest that he was negotiating with Châteauneuf, and it was Châteauneuf whom, the memoirs relate, Retz proposed to the marshal as a more suitable candidate than himself. Du Plessis then gave the coadjutor a personal safe-conduct from the queen, which Retz claimed to have raised to his lips and then solemnly burnt.

As in the period when the queen secretly discussed with him the plans to arrest the princes in January 1651, Retz kept his secret assignations with her in the oratory of the church of Saint-Honoré, where he entered by a private staircase. Anne of Austria, he said, entreated him to accept nomination to a cardinalate and to enter the government as a minister, so that he might facilitate Mazarin's return. He answered, again according to his own account, with the appearance of a sincerity intense enough to soften the disrespect of refusal. He argued that the queen could afford to surrender neither to Condé nor to Gaston, who, in any event, had to be prevented from aligning himself with the prince. His own usefulness depended on his maintaining his reputation as an enemy of Mazarin, for without that he would lose his popularity. At first the queen appeared to be offended, but she returned to press the acceptance of her offer. Again, the coadjutor would not commit himself to Mazarin's return, but he proposed a plan to separate Gaston from Condé and to drive the latter from Paris. The queen's affability increased at this, and she began a general denunciation of Chavigny, Servien and Lyonne, saying that Le Tellier was weak and slow-witted, though no traitor like the

others.[24] Retz then suggested that as long as no first minister were
named, Condé might justifiably claim that the post was being held
open for Mazarin. He put forward Châteauneuf's name, and the
queen responded by giving him details of the way in which
Châteauneuf had damaged Retz's career on earlier occasions. The
regent also told him that madame la Palatine had deserted Condé
and was now in her confidence. She promised to consult Mazarin
about Retz's proposal, and sanctioned the continuance of his
public opposition to the cardinal. Retz declared that he could not
pretend he would work for the re-establishment of Mazarin, and
the queen left him with words of mocking gaiety: 'You really are
the devil! Off you go, and be sure to see La Palatine.'

The skilful blend of truth and fiction in the account of this
interview in the memoirs was typical of Retz's narrative at those
points when he enjoyed the imaginative reconstruction of what
might have been. Madame de Motteville confirmed the fact that
Retz had proposed Châteauneuf as first minister, but she said that
it was the coadjutor who took the initiative in arranging contact
with the queen.[25] Retz's primary ambition at this time was to
secure his elevation to the sacred college. It is unlikely that he
would have declined any possibility of being first minister, despite
his later mock modesty in this respect. And while he would not
have accepted a subordinate position in a ministry headed by
Mazarin, it is highly probable that he was willing to connive at
Mazarin's return if he were sure of his own advantage and could
conceal his participation in such an intrigue. Behind such a
manoeuvre lay the possibility of securing his reward and disavowing his own part of the bargain. Châteauneuf, who was prepared
to work for Mazarin's return if it would recover him the seals, had
a similar outlook. Retz was in touch with Châteauneuf. Mazarin,
despairing of Condé's approval for the termination of his exile,
certainly entertained the possibility of making use of Châteauneuf
against Condé.

The distortion of Retz's account becomes clearer in the light of
these elements. He was accurate enough on some issues – the
attitude of madame la Palatine, for example – but he was anxious
to hide his secular ambitions, and, above all, to conceal his association, however indirect, with Mazarin. The queen's motives in her
contact with the coadjutor were solely to secure the restoration of

her first minister. Mazarin hoped that she would make use of Retz against the princes. Perhaps there is a hint of the coadjutor's perception of this in a cryptic comment in this part of the memoirs: 'One should never equivocate with the favour [of princes]: one can never embrace it too firmly when it is genuine: one can never run far enough from it when it is false.' Retz believed, or pretended to believe, that Anne of Austria trusted him. He was later to remark that he had discerned that Mazarin was insincere, and that the cardinal had deliberately concealed his motives from the queen for fear that madame de Chevreuse would discover them if the queen tried to act a part. But the queen was no *ingénue* in conspiracy, and it is more probable that she was fully aware of the implications of her actions. If Retz knew this, his vanity would not allow him to admit it.

By late May, when the queen had her first secret interview with the coadjutor, Mazarin was more in command of her tactics. In a memoir he sent her in the middle of the month he argued that the frondeurs were anxious to gain the queen's support to insure themselves against the hostility of Condé. He specifically suggested that madame de Chevreuse and Retz should be required to prove their sincerity by agreeing to his return. He thought that Gaston was still dependent on the frondeurs and Châteauneuf, and that Condé would never accept Gaston as an ally because the prince feared the queen would use them to restore the cardinal. The messages carried by Ondedei and other agents between Brühl and the court became more frequent, and the code names and numbers designating the various personalities became increasingly complex. The cardinal wrote also to madame la Palatine and to Lyonne. His letters to the queen postulated every possible hypothesis and advised every conceivable reaction. 'I have been deceived and betrayed so much', he wrote, 'that I have learnt at bitter expense to know the most subtle of men when they pretend to be acting openly.' He praised madame la Palatine under the codewords 'the Angel', 'the Diligent' and 'Gabriel', and he warned the queen against Condé ('the Embarrassed', 'the Credulous', 'the Uncertain', 'the Valiant'), Lyonne ('the Cordial', 'the Correspondent', 'the Assured', 'the Unfaithful'), madame de Chevreuse ('the Spirit', 'the Blood') and many others. More especially did he counsel the regent to beware the 'mediocre probity' of the coadjutor, whom he designated by 'the Poltroon', 'the Mute', or, more simply, 'O'. In all his letters he made it clear to 'Serafin' (or, sometimes, 'Zabaot') that his one object was to return to her side. 'I am so alone', he was to write to the queen in July, when he was often sending her two or three letters a day. 'It is necessary for me to work ceaselessly, and affairs are far from pleasant. But, assured as I am of Serafin's friendship, I count the rest for nothing.'[26]

After his interview with the queen Retz was also in a frenzy of activity. He busied himself with the composition of anonymous pamphlets answering his critics and detractors. He worked through the night conferring with Gaston and madame la Palatine. He used Caumartin to spread gossip to his own advantage and the discredit of his enemies. He emerged from his retreat in June and began to challenge Condé in the parlement, where the prince was whipping up opposition to the court by denunciations of Mazarin, together with the cardinal's agents and the ministers alleged to support him. With the aid of the abbé Charrier, Retz set about preparing a favourable response in Rome to the royal nomination he expected. And he continued secretly to meet the queen and to engage her in their elaborate game of double bluff.

The coadjutor proposed that Gaston should be persuaded to arrest Condé on the queen's behalf, but the queen pointed out that Gaston could not be relied upon. There were some, notably Hocquincourt and Harcourt, who were prepared to assassinate the prince if the word were given. Retz scented an attempt to compromise him personally in a number of plans of this kind. Lyonne pressed Retz to act, and at the same time leaked the information to Condé that Retz was organising a coup to arrest him. But the coadjutor had comparable channels of communication, and discovered Lyonne's manoeuvre through madame de Pommereuil and the princess Palatine. The queen was told of this soon after the arrival of Ondedei from Brühl, and, though Ondedei opposed the idea of the arrest with an impertinence Retz greatly resented, she seemed incensed enough to sanction stronger measures. By his own account Retz calmed her with assurances that he was prepared to die in her service, and persuaded her that in the meantime Condé should be dealt with by subtlety and stealth. The queen had agreed to the return of Châteauneuf, as well as to Retz's nomination for a cardinalate but, on Mazarin's advice, she de-

cided to postpone both events until the majority of the king in
September.

Condé had been enraged by the reversal of the decision to grant
him Guyenne. He turned upon Servien and Lyonne and denounced them, together with Le Tellier, as lackeys of Mazarin.
He also opposed the desire of Beaufort's brother, Mercoeur, to
marry the cardinal's niece, Laura Mancini – the match which had
caused his initial breach with Mazarin and which Mercoeur now
sought entirely for reasons of the heart. The agents of the prince in
the parlement pressed for the trial of those who continued to communicate with Brühl, for the dismissal of the ministers, and for a
formal declaration from the queen that Mazarin would never be
recalled. Condé himself kept Gaston hovering between the
prospect of an alliance against the regent and the thought of a
reconciliation between the princes and the court that would lead
to the isolation of Gaston and the frondeurs. Gaston's elder
daughter, la Grande Mademoiselle, whose strong will and
imperious demeanour seemed to deny her paternity, was angered
at the queen's refusal to approve her betrothal with the young
king, eleven years her junior, and pressed her father to join the
prince. Gaston was torn between the two policies and lived in
terror of Condé's dominating personality. 'Of all the passions',
Retz commented, 'fear is the one that weakens judgment most.'
As Condé's agents alternated between menaces and cajolements,
the king's uncle continued to exhibit the irresolution for which he
was so notorious. Gaston's predicament moved Retz to offer
another apothegm. 'Fear which is flattered by subtlety', he wrote,
'becomes insurmountable.'

Yet the prospect of a coup organised by the queen and the
coadjutor deeply disturbed the prince. On the night of 5 July he
mistook the passing of a body of royal troops on their way to the
Porte Saint-Germain for an attempt to surround his house. Leaving a warning for Conti he sprang upon his horse and galloped
out of the city. His pride would not permit him to return when he
learned of his mistake, and he retired to La Rochefoucauld's
country house at Saint-Maur near Vincennes. There he was
joined by a flock of supporters who indulged in a frenetic round of
pleasures. Despite his prestige and the strength of his following
among the great, Condé had difficulty in keeping his faction united.

He regarded the role of *chef de parti* as rather below him, and in any case he had not the patience for the endless intrigues in which the members of the opposing factions delighted. The princess Palatine had already defected. Madame de Longueville did not regard the breach with Mazarin to be as irreconcilable as did the prince, and she was prepared to upset political groupings in order to avoid her husband's demand that she join him in Rouen. La Rochefoucauld necessarily followed in the wake of his mistress, but he also stirred up trouble on his own account. Retz observed that he created quarrels in the morning in order to patch them up in the afternoon. Both Bouillon and Turenne were breaking their links with Condé. Chavigny pursued his own interests in preference to those of his patron, and président Viole was now dependent on Chavigny. The duc de Nemours was pursuing madame de Châtillon and did not want fresh political complications to disturb his love affair.

While Conti continued to press his elder brother's interests in the parlement, Retz tried to rally Gaston, and intermittently sought to persuade the queen that the only permanent solution to her problems was to stop communicating with Mazarin. Despite the consistency of attitude assumed in his memoirs, his objections to Mazarin varied in proportion to his prospect of obtaining his cardinalate. The queen chose to be capricious at times in her midnight interviews with the coadjutor, and Retz was less than frank in his analysis of the motives of the contending parties. It was commonly said by Condé's pamphleteers that Retz was scheming to obtain Mazarin's place, and his denial of this ambition in his own propaganda convinced no one. Condé refused to see marshal Gramont when the queen sent him to Saint-Maur to request the return of the prince. He also refused to accept Gaston's suggestion that he should moderate his attack upon Lyonne, Servien and Le Tellier. It was Chavigny who had incited him to a campaign against these ministers. The coadjutor could not afford to be any less critical of Mazarin and his sympathisers than was Condé. The press of the widow Guillemot, which he usually employed to publish his propaganda, issued the text of a speech he delivered in the parlement on 12 July, suggesting that the judges should ask Gaston to demand from the queen the dismissal of any member of the government who communicated with

Mazarin.[27] It was Molé's moderating influence alone that prevented the radical magistrates from sweeping aside the last vestiges of the regent's authority. The first president's support for Condé diminished in face of the prince's threat to the royal authority. Molé, as Mazarin wrote to the queen, was the one person whose priorities of loyalty were invariable.

The parlement did not mention the three suspect ministers by name in the remonstrance it prepared on 14 July. The proceedings on this day were nearly interrupted by a pitched battle in the Palais de Justice. The Chevreuse ladies had been hooted by Condé's supporters among the crowd at the Palais on the evening before, and they insisted the coadjutor should accompany them with a large armed escort. Both mother and daughter were too angry to listen to reason, and mademoiselle de Chevreuse expostulated that nothing less than the spilling of Bourbon blood would suffice to avenge the insult to the house of Lorraine. Fortunately Conti, who was taken by surprise by such a show of strength, preferred the path of discretion. This affair was a foretaste of a more serious trial of strength a month later.

The queen postponed her answer to a remonstrance requiring a safe-conduct for Condé, saying that she would have to consult the king's uncle. However, Gaston had nothing to suggest save the sacrifice of the three ministers – nor had he the courage to accept the parlement's invitation to appear there when, on 21 July, Condé reappeared in his seat. While Gaston feigned illness at his nearest country estate, Retz came forward to confront Condé in the parlement. To the queen his opposition must have at first appeared somewhat equivocal, since he vied with Condé in the intensity of his campaign against Mazarin and the three ministers. Molé tried to force him to offer an opinion on the rumour that the queen's advisers were pressing for the arrest of the prince. Amid laughter from the benches, the coadjutor passed it off by recommending the parlement to prosecute anyone who might give such counsel. The princes responded later in the day by publishing the text of an alleged agreement between Mazarin, Châteauneuf and madame de Chevreuse, which had supposedly been seized from a courier despatched by Noirmoutier. It contained a clause requiring Retz to conceal the treaty by continuing to criticise the cardinal publicly and secretly to promote his recall. According to the text

G

of this supposed treaty, Retz was to gain his cardinalate and Châteauneuf was to be temporarily first minister. This was precisely what happened later, and madame de Motteville so firmly believed in the authenticity of the document that she included it in her memoirs.[28]

By this time the regent, on Mazarin's advice, was ready to make new concessions. She kept the three ministers from the council, though she did not formally dismiss them, and she allowed the parlement to require an explanation from the unhappy Mercoeur. At this display of weakness opinion began to turn against the regency. Then, by a fortunate chance, the queen discovered that Condé was making overtures to Spain. She determined to recover the initiative, and sent Retz and président Bellièvre to visit Châteauneuf in the country, where they drew up a list of charges against the prince. This declaration began with an affirmation of Mazarin's exile and went on to accuse Condé of conspiracy, assembling troops in the provinces and contacts with the Spanish. On 17 August it was read by the chancellor to deputations from the three sovereign courts and the municipal government. The war of the chamber pots had entered its most critical phase.

It was humiliating for the prince to submit himself to the judgment of the magistrates, but no other course, short of open rebellion, was open to him. He demanded that the parlement should investigate the charges and that it should punish those who had calumniated him. Gaston, of course, kept well away from the Palais de Justice. He was too afraid of Condé not to make some gesture of support, and acceded to Chavigny's demand that he should write to the prince, dissociating himself from the royal declaration and stating that he was unaware of any treasonable association between Condé and the Spanish. Condé submitted this document to the full assembly of the parlement on 19 August, together with a long statement of his family's service to the crown. He turned upon the coadjutor and asked whether one who had recommended riot and carnage merely to wrest the seals from Molé was fit to advise the queen to pour slander on his name. Beaufort, La Rochefoucauld and others, he said, could testify in his support. It was a shrewd enough thrust, and Retz could only reply that the affair of the seals had been misrepresented, and that the king's uncle would support him. The coadjutor was quick to regain the initiative. Referring to the broken treaty between the factions, he remarked defiantly that at least he could not be accused of breaking his word. Both parties had armed men at their call, but nothing more than threats passed between them on this day.

On Sunday, 20 August, the coadjutor began to marshal his forces for the resumption of the proceedings on the following day. The queen was openly pleased at the way in which Retz had honoured his undertaking to confront the prince, and secretly delighted that the policies in which she had been coached by Mazarin had succeeded in setting the two factions at each other's throats. She sent detachments of troops to strengthen the coadjutor's military dispositions. Retz posted the militia and sent word to those elements of the populace who still supported him to defend the bridges near the Palais de Justice. By Monday morning the Palais was practically invested. Condé, too, rallied his forces among the nobility and the populace. When the session resumed, it seemed that the courts of justice were about to become the scene of a wild and bloody encounter.

Uproar ensued almost at once, as Retz and the prince tossed threats and challenges across the floor of the great hall of the parlement. The presidents thrust themselves between the antagonists, pleading that the court should not be profaned by bloodshed. Nicolas Fouquet, the attorney-general, was foremost among those who sought to restore order. Condé sent out La Rochefoucauld to withdraw his men from the ante-chamber, and the coadjutor went out on a similar mission. He spoke to his supporters in an adjoining room but, as he moved to return, he heard a call to arms. La Rochefoucauld, coming through the door in the opposite direction, closed it upon his opponent and pinned him against the jamb. As the clamour increased, La Rochefoucauld called to his assistants to stab the coadjutor, and Montrésor and others moved forward to prevent them. But Retz, with his head facing La Rochefoucauld's two swordsmen, was also in danger from the room at the back. Pesche, the leader of Condé's section of the mob, came up behind Retz, calling out, in the words recorded by Guy Joly: 'Where is that bugger of a coadjutor? I'll cut his throat for him.'[29] Argenteuil, one of Retz's most loyal adherents in fortune and adversity, stepped in front of Pesche and hid Retz with his cloak. Meanwhile Molé's son, Champlâtreux, entered the lobby where La Rochefoucauld was holding the door, and persuaded him to release his enemy. Swords had been drawn on both sides and, even after La Rochefoucauld had stepped back, an affray seemed imminent. At this point a captain of the royal guards intervened and the tension eased slightly.

Retz returned to the *grand'chambre*, thanked Molé for the services his son had rendered, and accused La Rochefoucauld of attempting his assassination. Unabashed, La Rochefoucauld declared that the coadjutor deserved to die for plotting against the state and insulting a prince of the Blood.[30] Retz responded by naming him a coward, and Brissac challenged La Rochefoucauld to a duel, which was eagerly accepted but later prevented by Gaston. The first president appealed first to Condé and then to Retz, saying that as a priest he should not cause a massacre of those entrusted by God to his care. Thus the battle was avoided, and the magistrates promptly dispersed. Retz reflected that the outcome was providential, for, even if he had defeated the princes by force, he would never have been pardoned for leading an assault upon them. Molé persuaded the queen to forbid Retz to return to the Palais. The coadjutor appreciated that a similar ban could not be placed on Condé, and he accepted the command, embracing Molé when he brought the news.

Condé remained in a lower chamber when the parlement resumed its debate next day, and accepted its decision to submit all the documents to the queen and ask her to settle the matter. After the prince and his escort left the parlement, they encountered the coadjutor leading a procession of the clergy in the opposite direction. Some of the nobles in Condé's escort began to raise a hue and cry. Condé stopped them with a gesture and, descending from his carriage, knelt in the street to receive the benediction that convention demanded. Retz replied with a deep bow, and, removing his bonnet, blessed the head of his enemy.

In the days that followed Condé continued to press the parlement to make the queen give him justice. Molé, however, refused to act until Gaston was in attendance, and Gaston had again retired to the country. The chancellor attended the Palais on 1 September to express the queen's satisfaction that the charges against Condé's collusion with the armies of Spain were untrue. This did not satisfy the prince, but once again Molé prevented a crisis by insisting that Condé should pay his respects at the Palais-Royal. The queen granted a new declaration against Mazarin, knowing that the king's majority within a few days would enable a review of the acts and promises made during the regency.

Condé chose to be absent from the parlement on 7 September when, amid a display of pomp and ceremony, Louis XIV was declared of age. At thirteen he could not, of course, be allowed to govern, and his mother, relying on the messengers from Brühl, continued to exercise his authority. She now put into effect the ministerial changes discussed with Retz three months earlier. Chavigny retired angrily to Touraine; Châteauneuf returned to preside in the council; Séguier was deprived of the seals in favour of Molé; and, to the delight of the princess Palatine, the aged La Vieuville became superintendent of the finances once again. Condé recognised his political defeat, and set off for Guyenne to rally provincial support. Le Tellier tried to negotiate with him, and there was talk of convening the estates-general to meet his complaints. The prince had steadfastly opposed war against his sovereign, and in this regard Retz confessed his respect for a man who not only displayed the prejudices appropriate to his birth but possessed the courage to carry them into action. But Condé was now obliged to fight, or to see his own party fight without him. Longueville alone held out for peace, refusing to fight in a war prepared by his wife's lover. Retz described the subdivisions within the faction of the princes as a piece of Italian theatre – a comedy within a comedy.

Yet there was nothing but tragedy in the long war that followed. La Rochefoucauld explained its causes as the outcome of the amours and ambitions of a party that possessed no common ideal.[31] And Retz provided a similar account in his memoirs:

Everyone sought his particular interest in the matter, and no one believed he could achieve it because no one had enough confidence in himself to exclude others from the negotiations. They all wanted war because none of them believed they were able to make peace, and this general disposition, combined with madame de Longueville's interest in remaining estranged from her husband, formed an invincible barrier to accommodation.

NINE

The cardinal's hat

The promotion he had coveted for so long still seemed to elude the coadjutor. Retz had received promises of nomination to the sacred college during his mock reconciliation with Mazarin at the time of the arrest of the princes in January 1650. His claims had again been pressed in September of that year, only to be frustrated in the intrigues at Fontainebleau in the following month. He stated in his memoirs that the queen had finally sent forward his nomination during his struggle with Condé in the summer of 1651, but had subsequently asked Rome to delay his promotion until the king came of age. Here he misled the reader. His correspondence with the abbé Charrier, his agent at the Vatican, did not begin until October. Although Condé and his propagandists pretended that Retz was involved in the supposed treaty between Mazarin, Châteauneuf and madame de Chevreuse, he had then had no express understanding with the queen or the cardinal.

So long as the court remained in Paris it had to submit to the tutelage of Gaston, the frondeurs and the parlement. The head of the government was now the very man who had been responsible for many of the delays and frustrations Retz had experienced with the nomination. As president of the council Châteauneuf had at last secured the opportunity to reveal the quality of his statecraft. He had never been averse to making a bargain, and, if he could withdraw the government from the capital, he intended to prosecute the war against the princes with a firm and vigorous hand. Retz's influence over Gaston and the frondeurs could enable the escape of the court. Thus it was that in the third week of September Retz's nomination was despatched to Rome, and the court was allowed to leave Paris to conduct the war against the princes in Guyenne.

The empire which Mazarin extended over the heart of the queen made his return to France merely a matter of time, once the court had escaped the domination of the two Frondes. Neither Châteauneuf nor Retz was willing to admit this. No contemporary appreciated the nature of the relationship between the queen and her former first minister. Retz was assured by madame de Chevreuse that, while Anne of Austria had been indiscreet with Buckingham in her youth, her affection for the cardinal was quite platonic. Madame de Motteville, who knew every detail of the queen's daily routine, offered the same opinion in her memoirs. Yet the queen's ciphered correspondence with the exile suggested otherwise, and the princess Palatine was later to assert that the only explanation of Mazarin's survival, given the known piety of the queen, was a secret marriage between them.[1] Retz and Châteauneuf could not know that if necessary Anne of Austria would put her lover before any other consideration. Châteauneuf hoped that by demonstrating his capacity he would be able to avert the surrender of his position to Mazarin. At the back of his mind Retz also retained an ambition to sit in Mazarin's place. He had not discounted this possibility in his secret interviews with the queen, whatever he said to the contrary in his memoirs. He was prepared to enter into some kind of negotiation with Mazarin through the medium of the princess Palatine, but, like the cardinal himself, he approached the matter with an entire scepticism of the other's professed objectives. The coadjutor had re-arranged his priorities. The attainment of a cardinal's hat was his primary purpose, and his secular ambitions were vaguely relegated to the background. His was not the mind that could face the daily realities of responsible authority, but the tradition of the cardinal-ministers fascinated him, and he continued to flirt with the prospect.

In the description of this phase of his life in his memoirs, Retz wholly subordinated his attempt to recreate his past experience to the need to conceal his motives. Hence he misdated the despatch of the nomination and said nothing of a bargain with the queen or Châteauneuf. He professed his concern for the public welfare and disclaimed worldly ambitions. He was obliged to represent the departure of the court from the capital as a disastrous error of judgment. It was, he asserted, the consequence of being too much concerned with the present, and too careless about the future. He placed the responsibility for the decision on Gaston, and declared that the duke had subsequently admitted his mistake to Bellièvre and himself. Retz could not in his memoirs confess an entire lack of personal foresight. It had occurred to him, he wrote, that, if the queen left Paris with an army, her determination and the prestige of the crown would prevail over the divisions between her enemies, and might lead to Mazarin's return. He had not, however, taken this opinion seriously until Gaston had sanctioned the court's withdrawal. Moreover, the hand of providence could be distinguished in this error: 'All mistakes are not made entirely by human agency, for there are some that are so gross that no one with a particle of common sense could commit them.' The one fortunate outcome, Retz declared, was that Gaston's hesitant policies allowed the nomination to be confirmed. These were the ingenious arguments with which Retz hid his motives from posterity. His enemies were not entirely mistaken when they accused him of seeking a cardinal's hat as a means of satisfying his other ambitions. In fact the *mazarinades* which Retz wrote in apparent denial of such claims were a surer guide to his motives than the more subtle distortions of the memoirs. The last pamphlets which the coadjutor composed in the first round of these exchanges coincided with the withdrawal of Condé from Paris and the beginning of the new campaign in Guyenne.

When the queen had re-arranged the ministry in April 1651, and Viole had delivered his blunt message to Retz and madame de Chevreuse breaking the marriage treaty, Condé's most prolific propagandist, Dubosc Montandré, had composed a stream of libels against the coadjutor. Retz had replied anonymously with his *Defence of the Old, Legitimate Fronde*. 'The reputation of monsieur le coadjuteur', he had asserted, 'is as far above calumny and imposture as his heart is above fear'. Denying suggestions of a secret understanding with Mazarin, he had claimed full credit for the overthrow of the cardinal's tyranny. Turning on his critics within the new Fronde of the princes, he had denounced them as 'craven imposters and infamous bastards of the legitimate Fronde', who had 'assailed Mazarin's name after having invariably respected his person'. Protesting against the dismissal of Châteauneuf and the appointment of ministers sympathetic to Condé, he had named Chavigny as 'one of the most violent and dangerous instruments of the tyranny of cardinal Richelieu' and superintendent de

Maisons, the brother of Longueil, as 'blackened by countless thefts and betrayals'. It had been a strange and unnatural metamorphosis that 'these scoundrels should in an instant become converted into men of goodwill', while 'our true friends, the ancient protectors of public liberty, should at the same time have been transformed into Mazarins against their own honour, welfare and security'.[2]

There had been little in the coadjutor's *Defence*, beyond his vigorous denunciation of his enemies, to suggest a personal ambition to replace Mazarin. But after the royal declaration against Condé on 17 August 1651 a pamphlet appeared which seemed to assert such a claim. This was entitled *Disinterested Advice on the Conduct of Monsignor the Coadjutor*, which some contemporaries attributed to Retz and others to his pamphleteer du Portail. It took as its theme the coadjutor's courageous defence of the public interest:

> Of all the great throughout the kingdom it was he alone who did not exhibit craven complacency and who condemned the violent measures of the time. He threw himself into the interests of the people when all had abandoned them and when it was customary to regard an attempt to preserve the laws of the state as a crime.

Condé had betrayed the coadjutor by combining with Mazarin before his imprisonment, and, after Retz had secured the prince's release, he had betrayed him a second time. By virtue of their position great princes must inevitably pursue their own interests at the expense of the public welfare and the security of the state. In contrast, Retz had 'risked his own safety to inspire the people with great and prudent maxims and to re-establish their fortune and felicity'. The authority of the government should be limited by honour, convention and public interest, and must proceed through advice and consent. The council was composed of self-interested men and time-servers who had been the friends of the tyrant, Mazarin. It should be changed in favour of a disinterested administration which would inquire into the abuses of the past. Two policies were to be avoided at all costs: that of Condé, who wanted to destroy the authority of the crown and become sole arbiter of the state; and that of Pesche and other popular leaders of a minority in the markets, who had dared to attempt the assassination of the coadjutor. If the populace avoided these false prophets,

the pamphlet concluded, and followed those who would give
them justice, they would become the masters of their own
fortune.[3]

This thinly-disguised advocacy of the coadjutor's claim to direct
the government excited a storm of protest from Condé's writers,
headed by Sarasin's *Letter from a Paris Churchwarden to his Curé on
the conduct of Monsignor the Coadjutor* and the anonymous *Reply of
One who is Genuinely Disinterested to the Advice of the Falsely Disinterested*.[4] Retz answered in September with *The Curé's Reply to the
Churchwarden's Letter* and *The Solitary Recluse to the Two Disinterested
Persons*.[5] He acknowledged his authorship of the latter in his
memoirs, and admitted that a celebrated advocate, Olivier Patru,
had written the former at his direction. Sarasin attempted to show
that the troubles of the preceding years had been largely the consequence of the coadjutor's endless intrigues to procure his own
advancement. His duplicity, cowardice and insolence would have
led to yet greater confusion, were it not for the forebearance and
magnanimity of the prince. Sarasin suggested that the proper station for his former patron would be in the Florentine bank whence
his family had supposedly derived. Retz could hardly complain of
Pesche and the fellow agitators in the markets, for the chorus was
sung by those to whom he had himself been choirmaster three
years earlier. The new civil war was simply the expression of the
coadjutor's frustration at his failure, first, to pass on mademoiselle
de Chevreuse to Conti, and, second, to obtain his cardinal's hat.
Retz's hypothetical 'curé' and his 'solitary recluse' replied in kind
to the 'churchwarden' and the 'genuinely disinterested'. In the
former guise Retz retraced, step by step, the history of the barricades, the siege of Paris, and the exchange of partners with Mazarin
and Condé. He selected his facts to present an interpretation fully
as favourable to his own motives as the distortions of his opponents were prejudicial to them. As the 'solitary recluse', he chose
to be more subtle, and to affect a conciliatory mood which treated
Condé with respect in order to damn him the more effectively. He
professed incredulity that Condé should manifest such ingratitude
after all the coadjutor had accomplished on his behalf, and ended
with a plea to 'abolish faction and preserve the legitimate authority
of our young king'.

A new crop of *mazarinades* sprouted from Condé's presses, including *The Letter of a Bordelais to a Bourgeois of Paris, The Good Frondeur who Frondes the Evil Frondeurs,* and *The Well-Intentioned Frondeur to the False Frondeur.*[6] Retz admitted responsibility for only one of the replies to these libels, *The Free and True Discourse on the Conduct of Monsignor the Prince and of Monsignor the Coadjutor,* which he wrote in collaboration with Caumartin.[7] Once again he protested his own consistent and irreconcilable opposition to Mazarin, and traced the tergiversations and alleged brutalities of Condé. Retz demanded why it was necessary, now that Mazarin had gone, 'to fill reams of paper under pretext of his return, with the sole design of implanting certain empty skulls with the idea that those who were most truly responsible for expelling him are now plotting to re-establish him'. In his sentiments as well as in his metaphors, the propagandist betrayed his fatigue when he complained that 'after more than sixteen years of foreign war and so many consequent afflictions, including all kinds of financial demands intolerably and relentlessly imposed, we are now making manifest our despair by swarms of purveyors of libels, who like the trumpeters of doom, move us with their lugubrious cries to internecine carnage'. This plea at least appeared to be respected, for, after a few sporadic replies to his last libel, the pamphleteers on both sides observed an undeclared truce for the next eight months. But the last phrases of Retz's *Free and True Discourse* made his immediate point, and also revealed a motive far less disinterested than it pretended: 'Let us establish a sound council to lead the state back to its original form and enable us to recall those happy centuries which our fathers once enjoyed under the best princes in the world.' The ultimate aim of the coadjutor was still to establish himself at the head of a reformed council. From September 1651 he was determined first to secure his cardinalate and then to explore the possibility of realising yet more extensive ambitions.

Condé was now openly at war with the government. He could not represent himself as the champion of the rights of the ancient aristocracy, nor would his pride allow him to pretend that he was fighting in any cause other than his own. Nemours and La Rochefoucauld were his principal lieutenants. He hoped for the support of Bouillon and Turenne in Champagne and Picardy, and appointed Tavannes to marshal his supporters in Burgundy. The comte de Marsin, commander of the French army in Catalonia, was soon to join the princes, and the duc de Rohan-Chabot was ready to raise their standard in Anjou. Condé's main strength, however, lay in his own military reputation, in the promise of support from Spain, and in the dissidence of Guyenne. Bordeaux had been the centre of resistance to Epernon in 1649, and in 1650 it had resisted Mazarin's armies on behalf of the imprisoned princes. There Condé took refuge in late September 1651, together with his wife, his brother and his sister. But there were factions in Bordeaux which were as deeply divided as those in Paris. The magistrature was suspicious of the negotiations with Spain conducted by the prince's agent, Pierre Lenet. During the summer of the previous year a Spanish envoy with three frigates and a plentiful supply of money had arrived to strengthen the resistance of the Bordelais to Mazarin's army. In the autumn of 1651 the Spanish undertook to provide a greater contribution, and the parlement became increasingly embarrassed by this alliance. Yet the lower classes knew none of these scruples. A group of popular agitators, named the *Ormée* after the grove of elms where their first meetings had been held in 1650, seemed ready to employ violence against the magistrates and the municipality. Leaving Conti to hold these elements in balance, Condé launched his campaign northwards in Saintonge.

The court moved to Bourges and thence south-west to Poitiers, where its armed strength could be directed either against Condé or any concentration Turenne might effect along the line of the Loire. Harcourt, the royal commander, handled his seasoned troops skilfully, and the prince, whose reputation could not offset the poor quality of the raw levies at his disposal, was obliged to accept a series of minor defeats and withdrawals during the winter campaign. In Paris the parlement maintained a wavering neutrality, while Gaston, seeing the chances of Mazarin's return grow with each of Harcourt's victories, moved steadily towards an open alliance with the prince. Despite his new dignity as keeper of the seals, Molé continued to officiate in the capital as first president. His authority defeated Gaston's manoeuvres and eventually persuaded the magistrates to register the royal declaration branding the princes as traitors. Although the Paris parlement remained intensely hostile to Mazarin, the magistrates lived in constant fear of the intervention of that section of the mob controlled by the agents of the princes.

During the months following the departure of the court from Paris the coadjutor found himself in a predicament which baffled all his ingenuity. While his promotion awaited the approval of the pope he could not afford to act energetically to prevent Mazarin's return, lest the queen withdraw the nomination. It seemed reasonable to suppose that, if Mazarin did return, Retz must abandon hope of a permanent place in the council and expect the immediate revocation of the royal request to Rome. Since Gaston seemed to incline towards Condé, the coadjutor's only means of bringing pressure against the court was to demonstrate his ability to restrain the king's uncle from joining the princes. His own breach with Condé seemed irreparable, and he knew that the latter strove to minimise his influence with Gaston. In any event, the success of the princes' cause appeared a remote possibility. He had, therefore, to pursue a policy of inaction, to keep resistance to Mazarin alive, and yet to offer inducements to the queen so that his promotion might be confirmed. Above all, he had to keep the ear of Gaston and persuade him to take a middle course. The only positive aim that he could advocate in the Luxembourg was the creation of a third party, based upon a league of municipal governments. With the support of the parlements, and secret subsidies from Spain, such a party might prevent Mazarin's return while disavowing Condé's own Spanish alliance. But Gaston was more inclined to side with the prince than to challenge constituted authority in his own name. It was still his constant fear that Condé would come to terms with the court, leaving him in helpless isolation. In his discussions with Retz at the Luxembourg Gaston reiterated that, since no clear plan of action could be distinguished, they must preserve the status quo and wait upon events. The policy was not unfamiliar to the coadjutor, although it was contrary to all his maxims of statecraft. He resigned himself to the exploitation of minor opportunities, while pressing his cause at Rome.

One such opportunity concerned the defection of Bouillon and Turenne from the faction of the princes. In mid-November Mazarin's agent, Bartet, was sent to Paris to negotiate this matter. The cardinal at this time was busy with his correspondence with the princess Palatine, who was now to be numbered among the enemies of Condé, and who acted as an intermediary between Mazarin and Retz.

> I have always had great esteem for Fortune [Bouillon] and the Fugitive [Turenne] and now my passion to serve them is stronger than ever [wrote the cardinal]. I have lost no opportunity to demonstrate this to them, and you may well imagine what pleasure it would give me to see the persons mentioned united with 41 [Retz], the Mute [Retz again], 44 [Mazarin] and 200 [also Mazarin]. I know this has been the subject of negotiations with Rethel [Bouillon] for a greater union by the means suggested to you by the Poltroon [Retz].[8]

Retz attended a meeting between Bartet and the two brothers at the house of madame Palatine. In the course of the discussion Bartet, whose forward manners in such company led Retz to describe him as a 'ridiculous little Basque', declared that the queen was determined to recall Mazarin, and threatened Retz with revoking the nomination for his cardinalate. In his memoirs Retz recalled that he had stated his unalterable opposition to Mazarin and, equally, his intention to fulfil his promise to the queen never to be reconciled with Condé. The first part of this declaration does not accord well with the gist of the letters between Mazarin and the princess Palatine. But whatever Retz actually said, the outcome of this conference was the alliance of the brothers with the court. Turenne was laconic, according to his custom, but Bouillon was both more talkative and less frank. 'No other man I ever knew,' Retz wrote, 'could speak so much and say so little.' Gaston, hearing of the plot, instructed a captain of guards to place them in custody, but Retz sent them warning and they fled from Paris an hour or two before the time appointed for their arrest. According to his own account, the coadjutor admitted his part in the affair during a conversation with Gaston a few days later, and Gaston remarked that, had he appreciated Retz's position, he would not have wished to detain Bouillon and Turenne. If this were true, it betrayed a strange confusion of interests. Turenne was the one commander whose reputation rivalled Condé's. They had been on opposite sides in the first civil war, when Condé had commanded the royal army. Now they were again to be opposed, but it was the turn of Turenne to serve the queen and Mazarin.

Towards the end of November, Condé's agents put into operation a plan to remove Retz from the counsels of the duc d'Orléans. The coadjutor received warning of a plot to assassinate him, but, as it turned out, the scheme was at once less violent and more ingenious. The coadjutor's old enemy, La Rochefoucauld, planned the affair, and his secretary, Gourville, was chosen to conduct it.[9] Gourville recruited a party of adventurers at Angoulême and confiscated the royal revenues there to finance his operation. La Rochefoucauld sent instructions to the governor of Damvilliers in Lorraine that he was to prepare an armed escort to receive the coadjutor, who was to be kidnapped by Gourville's men in Paris and escorted to a place of imprisonment in Damvilliers. Gourville's party secretly entered the capital, and set to work to establish the pattern of Retz's nocturnal activities. They resolved to apprehend him late one night as he left the hôtel de Chevreuse. But on the night they selected Retz was saved by a trivial accident that caused him to reflect how little men really controlled the course of their own lives. Madame de Rhodes, who also visited the Chevreuse ladies on this particular evening, had a new carriage which she did not wish to spoil by the rain which had commenced after her arrival. In consequence the coadjutor escorted her home in his own carriage, and followed a route which evaded Gourville's ambush. On a subsequent night, when Retz was due to visit madame de Pommereuil, the watchers assumed a new vigil. But the coadjutor dallied long with his mistress, and Gourville's sentry impatiently left his post to refresh himself at the nearest tavern. Retz had gone when he returned. The conspirators dispersed after this second failure, but several of them were arrested before they had gone far, and Gourville himself was captured by the coadjutor's squire, Malclerc. Although Gourville was released on the order of Molé, one of the other plotters confessed the full details when interrogated in the Bastille.

The role of the coadjutor was now so equivocal that he could no longer hold the old Fronde together. Fiesque and Brissac were wavering in the direction of Condé; madame de Chevreuse, Laigues and Noirmoutier had been seduced by Bartet, and hoped for personal profit from secret reconciliation with the court. When Noirmoutier was reproached by the coadjutor, he took refuge in ambiguities. Noirmoutier was receiving communications from

Mazarin at this time, but Retz himself was playing an equally devious game, for the cardinal's letters to the princess Palatine had begun to suggest that the secret understanding she had planned between him and the coadjutor was now an accomplished fact.[10] Retz conveyed quite the contrary impression in his memoirs. He observed that the undertaking of madame de Chevreuse, Laigues and Noirmoutier to support Mazarin's return induced him to avoid their company. But mademoiselle de Chevreuse, who had better reason than her mother to turn her back on the coadjutor, still supported him. Three months later she, too, was to abandon him.

Rumours had begun to circulate in Paris about the impending return of Mazarin. Molé had forced the royal declaration against Condé through the parlement, but there were popular demonstrations against the first president, authorised, according to Retz, by Gaston himself. From the middle of December many of the magistrates began to call for a deputation to the court to remind the queen of her promises not to recall Mazarin, and to demand that he be expelled from the electorate of Cologne. The cardinal had actually offered Retz to share the ministry with him, but it seems the coadjutor would not risk acceptance before receiving his cardinalate. Talon recorded in his memoirs that Retz had visited him on the night of 19 December to say that he had refused an invitation from the queen to support Mazarin, and that he intended to persuade Gaston and the parlement to authorise the enlistment of troops to obstruct his passage.[11] By this time Harcourt had taken La Rochelle and Cognac, and driven Condé on to the defensive. Mazarin had already begun to raise a private army and the queen sent Hocquincourt to escort him and his troops to court. Molé was called to Poitiers, leaving président Bailleul to officiate in his stead at the Palais de Justice. The queen had resolved to leave Paris a prey to the factions within it. On Christmas Day 1651 Mazarin and his army entered Sedan. Neutrality no longer seemed a possible course of action.

Gaston's embarrassment and irresolution in the new crisis surpassed all the agonies of indecision he had exhibited in the past. He spent many hours in his study in the Luxembourg discussing possibilities with Retz and whistling through his teeth. He was as much afraid as ever of becoming subservient to Condé, but it did not seem likely that the parlement would take any practical steps to stop Mazarin. It was true that in the storm of emotion provoked by the news of the cardinal's return the magistrates enacted that Mazarin should be declared a traitor, that his goods should be forfeit, his person placed beyond the protection of the law, and a reward of 150,000 livres offered for his apprehension, dead or alive. Two deputies were sent to the towns in the line of Mazarin's march, where they were insulted and roughly handled by Hocquincourt's troops. All these measures appeared directly to deny the authority of the government, which had informed the parlement that Mazarin had been summoned by the king's command. But the magistrates refused to authorise the levying of troops and the seizure of royal revenues, and, although they received an envoy from Condé, they would not enter the general alliance he proposed.

Gaston's problems were increased by the news that the Spanish had at last made available a special force on the Flanders frontier to cooperate with Condé. Nemours, whom the prince had appointed to command these troops, called on Gaston on his way through Paris on 19 January. Retz ridiculed the inconsistency of the behaviour of the parlement, where denunciations of Mazarin were unaccompanied by any effective measures, and where the advance of the Spanish was regarded with horror. Gaston at this point decided to change course. He signed an agreement with Condé, brought by the comte de Fiesque, and recalled his personal regiments from Guyenne so that they might cooperate with Nemours. He even proposed to tell the parlement that the force commanded by Nemours was composed of German rather than Spanish troops.

Meanwhile Mazarin moved slowly and remorselessly towards Poitiers. The secret signs of the affection between him and the queen became increasingly emphatic in their correspondence as their reunion approached. From Arcis-sur-Aube on 7 January the cardinal wrote to declare the intensity of his feeling 'to the very last sigh', and from Pont-sur-Yonne on the 11th he doubled the symbol that expressed his tender affection for the queen, and remarked playfully that his love was much greater than hers for him.[12] Finally, on 28 January, Anne of Austria saw her faithful minister again. It had been nearly a year since he had slipped away from Paris to release the princes and to retire to Brühl. The queen's determination to have him by her side had accomplished the impossible, and the political and military situations were entirely transformed. Despite the support of Marsin from Catalonia, Condé had been forced to retire upon Agen in the south-west, and Turenne had at last assumed command of the royal forces along the Loire. But Nemours had arrived on the upper Seine and Beaufort, commanding Gaston's regiments, was about to join him. In Angers the duc de Rohan had declared for Condé. At the court the ministry was accommodated to Mazarin's return. Servien had already been recalled. Châteauneuf, who had retained to the last his hope that Mazarin's advance could somehow be prevented, withdrew into honourable retirement. His old rival, Chavigny, had defied the order exiling him to Tours, and had returned to Paris to act as Condé's agent and to maintain surveillance over Gaston. Mazarin had many preoccupations, but among them he did not forget the cardinal's hat so anxiously expected by the coadjutor.

Having concealed in his memoirs the manner and timing of his nomination, Retz provided an account of its outcome in Rome which was equally at odds with the truth. The facts are revealed in his correspondence with his agent, the abbé Charrier, whom he instructed to conceal 'any appearance that I have bought this dignity by the sale of my liberty and my honour'.[13] He might well feel confident of the security of his letters to Charrier, since his secretary, Guy Joly, encoded them in five distinct systems of cipher. The memoirs stated that Retz could never stoop to bribery in winning holy office: the letters written in October 1651 referred to the transmission of credit drafts for eighteen thousand, twenty-five thousand and eighty thousand crowns, together with details of the presents he was sending to those who might advance his claims.[14] The coadjutor had found it less difficult than he might have expected to raise so much money, for there were many who assumed that as a cardinal Retz was likely to enter the government, if not to replace Mazarin. Moreover, the Spanish regarded the coadjutor as a firm opponent of Mazarin, and they actively supported his promotion in the belief that it would lead to the conclusion of a peace with France. Whether or not they contributed directly to the sums utilised by Charrier, they certainly exerted their influence in Retz's favour. The coadjutor received open backing from the grand duke of Tuscany, whose principal minister was that Giovanni Battisto de' Gondi who had entertained Retz in Florence fourteen years earlier. Retz told Charrier to suggest that the French and Italian branches of the family might be linked by marriage, and indicated that Tuscan diplomacy might cooperate with the Spanish circle at Rome.

Charrier proved to be an astute negotiator, capable of making the most of unexpected opportunities without first requiring instructions from his master. Innocent x was a timid and ailing pontiff, who made no decision hastily and balanced the conflicting advice he received from his favourites. He detested Mazarin, and sought to heal the breach between France and Spain – attitudes which favoured the candidature of Retz. In the opinion of Claude Joly, the uncle of Retz's secretary, the coadjutor owed his promotion less to the manoeuvres of Charrier and the Tuscan lobby than he did to Innocent's resentment at being obliged to bestow a cardinalate on Mazarin's brother, who had been elevated from his humble status in the Dominican order to the archbishopric of Aix.[15] While the coadjutor had lost a powerful supporter at Rome with the death of cardinal Panciroli, changes in the unofficial power structure within the Vatican helped his cause. Innocent's sister-in-law, the imprudent and self-interested Olympia Pamfili, had recently lost her influential role in the household of the Holy Father. The pope's new favourite was Olympia Aldobrandini, the princess of Rossano, who was reputedly less talented but more venal than her predecessor. Signora Pamfili strove to accomplish the ruin of the princess Rossano, not only because she sought to recover her influence but also because the latter was her daughter-in-law, and their rivalry was intensified by family disputes. The princess Rossano welcomed the jewels, gloves and ribbons which Retz sent her by the hand of Charrier, and very likely accepted large sums of money as well. She kept Charrier informed of the pressures to which Innocent was subjected, and, though her tenure was far from secure (she was displaced by her mother-in-law a year later), she retained her position long enough to win Retz his promotion.

Five months of anxiety elapsed between the nomination by the queen and the approval by the pope. One source of opposition came from the French ambassador, Henri d'Estampes, bailli de

Valençay, who had ambitions to wear the crimson himself, and whose ecclesiastical interests were later to be recognised by his appointment as grand prior of France. Valençay was Retz's enemy. His domineering presence terrified the pope. But, contrary to the belief of the coadjutor, he performed his duties concerning the nomination punctiliously. It was presented to Innocent early in October, before Charrier had received his first coded letter from Retz. The pope had indicated that he regarded it with favour, and that confirmation might be expected in a month or two. It was the practice to elevate all nominated aspirants to the sacred college together, and there were at least ten such possible candidates. At the same time the pope was not unaware that Retz's nomination had been the outcome of the shifting political situation in France, and that delay might ruin his chances. He cherished the hope that, as a cardinal, Retz might take Mazarin's position, but he knew that the nomination might be withdrawn at any time.

Although Retz knew nothing of it, and, if he had heard of it, would not have believed it, Mazarin wrote to Valençay late in October, confirming the queen's instructions and requesting the ambassador to press the case. Valençay obeyed, but at the same time he wrote to the secretary Brienne, through whom his official correspondence with the French court passed, making several allegations of Retz's unsuitability. In later despatches he asserted that the delay was caused by intrigues within the pope's family, and in early December he received an unequivocal command from his government to hold up the promotion. He assured Charrier, nevertheless, that he was continuing to press His Holiness.

As the weeks passed, and the pope still seemed disinclined to call a consistory to elect the waiting aspirants, new obstacles arose for Retz. His uncle, the archbishop of Paris, bitterly opposed the possibility of the coadjutor being elevated to a dignity superior to his own. He first suggested that he himself should enter the sacred college and resign the diocese in favour of his nephew. Retz refused to agree, and warned Charrier of this new source of opposition. The archbishop then wrote to Innocent x to protest against the nomination. A more serious threat was posed by the intrigues of Condé. The prince revived the plan to convert his brother, Conti, into a cardinal, and at the same time launched a campaign at Rome to cloud the coadjutor's name by suggesting he had Jansenist sympathies.

Since proceedings against the *Augustinus* had been initiated in the Sorbonne in 1649, the Jansenists had been losing ground. Several of the Paris curés who had helped Retz throughout the Fronde were of Jansenist persuasion. Retz had several influential friends, such as Félix Vialart, the bishop of Châlons, who approved of the doctrines of Port-Royal. Many frondeurs had links with the Jansenists, and the same was true of some of Condé's partisans. Retz had been entirely opportunist in cultivating an association with Port-Royal. Mazarin, following the example of Richelieu, profoundly suspected the Jansenists. The strangely distorted logic of absolute monarchy led him to view any obstinate adherence to religious principle, however removed from the sphere of practical politics, as a challenge to the state. He concluded that their doctrinal views must necessarily imply political sedition. Their fortuitous connection with the Fronde confirmed his opinion. The French government pressed the papacy for a formal condemnation of the Jansenists, but Innocent x was not to be hurried. He was not to issue his celebrated bull, *Cum occasione*, declaring four propositions ascribed to the *Augustinus* as heretical and one false, until May 1653. The Jansenists were defending themselves at Rome at the very time when Retz's promotion was being considered.

The accusations against the coadjutor's heterodoxy spread by Condé's agents in the Jesuit order were particularly damaging. Fabio Chigi, then bishop of Imola and papal secretary of state, was himself expecting promotion to the sacred college. He was a fervent supporter of the Jesuits in their conflict with the Jansenists, and he was not slow to report to the pope the rumours concerning Retz. In consequence Charrier was discreetly informed that it would be wise for his master to submit a written denial of Jansenist doctrines. But when the abbé reported this request Retz wrote back to tell him to prepare it himself. He had provided Charrier with several blank sheets, containing only his signature, for use in such emergencies. Charrier complied and drew up an equivocal statement which left his master room to manoeuvre. On 2 February 1652 Retz wrote to his agent to say that he doubted whether Rome would seriously entertain the accusations against

his orthodoxy. He added a postscript that if Charrier were pressed
on the Jansenist issue he should say that he did not dare to write to
Paris, since the insult was so great.[16] A week later Retz wrote to
observe that he doubted whether it was worth his while to compose a second declaration, because as soon as he met one objection
his enemies would prepare another. A few lines later he appeared
to change his mind, and promised to send a statement. Then he
added: 'You can represent to these gentlemen, in addition to the
things I have already told you, that the court of Rome should take
care not to light a fire in France which might be difficult to
extinguish, and which, in the end might even involve Rome itself
in a yet more dangerous fashion.'[17]

The coadjutor was prepared to use the charges that had been
made against him to threaten the papacy itself. If he were deprived
of his cardinalate on the supposition that he was a Jansenist, then
he would become a Jansenist to such effect that the schism would
shake Rome as well as France. But perhaps Retz intended no more
than a threat. He found it hard to believe that Chigi's concern
about Jansenism was anything more than a pretext, and he informed Charrier that he was sending a new consignment of jewels
and a further bill of exchange. He was careful, nevertheless, not to
offend his Jansenist friends. The statement he sent Charrier on
16 February was even more ambiguous than the abbé's first version. Retz had actually circulated it to the circle of Port-Royal for
their approval. It proclaimed his respect for Rome and his 'aversion for the quarrels and divisions which warmth of spirit can
produce within the church on the matter of grace'. It went on to
declare the policy he had personally followed: 'I have contained
minds in a gentle and Christian peace. I have employed with
ardour all means which I have thought capable of maintaining the
tranquillity of the church.'[18]

Apart from the Jansenist issue, the correspondence between
Retz and Charrier revealed the way in which the progress of
Condé's rebellion and Mazarin's return could be turned to advantage in Rome. The coadjutor wrote with complete frankness
to his emissary, and his motives, in this as in other respects, were
far more obvious in his letters than he subsequently made them
appear in the memoirs. Towards the end of November he told
Charrier that he thought it unlikely that Mazarin would return for

a considerable time.[19] Then in early January, when Mazarin had reached Epernay on his march to Poitiers, Retz informed the abbé that he should suggest to the pope the probability of a reconciliation between Mazarin and Condé and the revoking of his nomination.[20] Two weeks later he warned Charrier to take care to avoid letting it be known that he and Mazarin were in contact, adding: 'And, in truth it is not so.' Since Mazarin's return, he observed, Gaston was turning more and more towards Condé, but the alliance between them was not expected to last. On Condé Retz remarked: 'As for me I would rather perish than be reconciled with this traitor.'[21] He continued to believe that the court would not revoke its recommendation to Rome while he refused any accommodation with the prince. But Retz's patience was not inexhaustible. On 16 February, the same day on which he sent his own declaration on Jansenism, he composed another letter instructing Charrier to leave Rome at once, since he could no longer endure the humiliating role of a postulant. His wounded pride was barely disguised in this letter. The abbé's departure, he argued, might stimulate the pope to take action, but in any case he refused to be regarded as a dupe by his enemies.[22] A week later another despatch ordered the abbé to remain at his post. He was to tell everyone that he had been instructed to return, but that he had himself decided to stay on in Rome until Easter.[23]

In fact Innocent x had summoned the consistory and approved the coadjutor's promotion on 19 February, between the dates of Retz's last two despairing letters. In their memoirs both Retz and Joly dramatised the circumstances and asserted that Valençay had actually received the revocation from France, and was outwitted by the guile of the pope and his advisers.[24] Another account declared that the couriers carrying the revocation were delayed by Retz's cousin in Florence.[25] But Mazarin never revoked Retz's nomination, for, believing that Valençay would induce Innocent to remain inactive, he still hoped to extract concessions from the coadjutor. The true circumstances were dramatic enough. When Valençay had requested an audience, the pope had deliberately arranged the consistory before the interview could take place. Mazarin's anger was expressed in the reproaches which Brienne sent the ambassador, to which Valençay replied that he could only have stopped the promotion by submitting an official demand for

the withdrawal of Retz's name from the list. Both the grand duke
of Tuscany and the abbé Charrier sent couriers to convey the news
of their triumph. The former was the first to reach Paris, and on
1 March Retz knew at last he had gained his cardinal's hat.

Mazarin and the queen concealed their irritation at the news
from Rome, and had the king send his official congratulations to
the new cardinal. But not only was the letter couched in tones of
the coldest formality: it also suggested that Retz would be expected
to show gratitude for his promotion by his service to the crown.
Retz had sent the faithful Argenteuil to the court, to explore reactions at first hand. There he met Mazarin in a house occupied by
madame la Palatine, and heard new and profuse offers of friendship, together with the repeated suggestion that the cardinal-
coadjutor should join his ministry. Retz could not publicly assume
his new dignity until he had received his cardinal's hat from the
hand of the king. Nevertheless, he would not place himself in the
power of his enemy. He remained at Gaston's elbow in Paris,
persisting in his attempt to separate the king's uncle from the party
of the princes. La Rochefoucauld contended that, if it had not been
for Retz's fear of isolation, so close an understanding would have
developed between Gaston and Condé that they would have imposed a peace upon the court. This view of Retz's motives was not
unjust, but La Rochefoucauld, in his anxiety to blame his old rival
for the continuance of the war, entirely misjudged both Mazarin's
military strength and Condé's willingness to come to terms.

With disarming frankness Retz confessed in his memoirs that
at first he had felt some inconvenience in his new dignity. He
wanted, he explained, to show a becoming modesty, but this was
not easy after the reputation he had acquired as coadjutor. His
modesty was scarcely enhanced by his responding to those who
congratulated him that the earlier cardinals in his family had
taught him not to insist too strongly on his precedence, especially
over princes of the Blood. He asserted that everyone wished to be
reconciled with him, and that he went out of his way to be gracious.

Retz kept away from the Palais de Justice, ostensibly because it
was inappropriate for a cardinal to appear in public before he had
been received by the king, and actually because he was seeking to
establish his neutrality. But he continued to urge his supporters in

the parlement to oppose both Condé and Mazarin. His influence
at the Luxembourg and the Palais de Justice again provoked
Condé's partisans to take overt action against him. Despite his
assertions to the contrary, it was easy to represent the new cardinal
as a secret supporter of Mazarin who had bought his promotion by
deserting his supposed ideals. It was also possible, now that Retz's
popularity among the lower classes had diminished, to turn one of
his own weapons against him. One day, as he emerged from the
Luxembourg, a mob of two or three hundred rioters surged towards his coach, shouting that Retz had betrayed the duc
d'Orléans. Gaston wanted to send out his guards to offer some
protection, but Retz walked forward and threatened to hang the
leader of the demonstration. His sang-froid was attested by other
accounts beside his own.[26] The mob became respectful and even
offered to escort the new cardinal back to the cloister of Notre-
Dame.

Though he welcomed the sycophants who congratulated him
on his new dignity, Retz began to feel his increasing isolation. He
may have been encouraged for a time by those who saw his elevation as foreshadowing his replacement of Mazarin. Yet the difficulties were formidable. He knew the queen to be implacably
opposed to him. He pretended that she had taken a sudden aversion to him because he had ridiculed her appearance to mademoiselle de Chevreuse, and she had repeated his remarks in front
of a servant, who had carried them back to court. Retz lent
probability to the story by claiming in his memoirs that he had
formerly indulged in a mild flirtation with the queen on the
prompting of madame de Chevreuse. The real obstacle was the
indissoluble bond between Mazarin and Anne of Austria. Despite
the assertion in his memoirs that he had renounced the possibility
of becoming first minister, he admitted himself that ambition still
moved him, although most men, he said, would have been content
to be a cardinal and prospective archbishop at the age of thirty-
nine. Yet the ministry, he declared, would have restricted his
pleasures and rendered his glory odious: it was even less to his
taste than to his natural inclination. These protestations were un-
convincing. In the meantime, neutrality left the possibility open,
and could be justified on other grounds. He explained to Bellièvre
on one occasion that he had much to lose and nothing to gain by

positive action. In these times, Retz explained, they were all like
men caught in a tempest and yet impelled to row against the storm.
In his cardinal's mace and the cross of the diocese of Paris he had
two stout oars, and if he lost these his craft would founder.

Bartet and the abbé Fouquet (brother of that Nicolas Fouquet
whose influence after the Fronde was to become second only to
that of Mazarin) had come to Paris to sow new dissension among
Retz's friends with false offers. Noirmoutier, Laigues and madame
de Chevreuse deserted to the court, and la coadjutrice was soon to
follow their example. Retz recorded that she capriciously accused
him of secret negotiations with Mazarin, basing her reproaches on
the fact that one of the queen's valets was staying in his household.
The explanation advanced by Retz was that the valet was a relative
of one of his own servants. In any case mademoiselle de Chevreuse
had cause enough for resentment. The new cardinal had been less
active in the pursuit of his liaison with madame de Pommereuil, but
he was embarked upon a new course of infidelity. He had formed
a 'spiritual and angelic' association with a certain mademoiselle de
la Loupe, whose beauty was equalled only by her modesty. His
friend the chevalier de Sévigné had married a widow, madame de
la Vergne, the mother of that madame de La Fayette who was to
befriend La Rochefoucauld. The house communicated with that
in which mademoiselle de la Loupe resided, and with Sévigné's
help Retz was soon able to introduce himself into her circle. He
thought his hopes were not entirely vain, he recalled, because his
victim neither forbad him to sigh in her presence nor could herself
remove her gaze from his person. Moreover, she appeared to be
impressed by his cardinal's robes. Her extreme modesty tied Retz's
tongue in circumstances where, he admitted, it was usually
libertine, and he confessed that the whole affair scarcely did
honour to his reputation as a gallant.

Retz met Fouquet on several occasions, under pretence of concerting measures to frustrate the activities of Condé's faction in
the city. He claimed to outmanoeuvre the abbé as easily as he
would a schoolboy, but in most respects Fouquet distinctly had
the better of him. Fouquet pursued mademoiselle de Chevreuse
with such ardour that she fell passionately in love with him and
would, Retz recorded, have married him had she been able. Her
German servant warned the cardinal of the affair, and he consoled

himself 'easily enough with the servant for the faithlessness of the mistress'. Retz pretended that Fouquet went in great fear of physical reprisals, and that he had suggested to the queen the assassination of the cardinal. Retz poured salve on his wounded vanity by remarking, 'My anger against him was not very great: it was in proportion to my jealousy, which was only mediocre.' He went on to say that his mistress had earlier lost interest in him when she had conceived an unnatural passion for one of her serving women. For no apparent reason she had suddenly ceased to defend him against her mother's criticism. So fickle was she that she turned against her lovers with the same caprice she exhibited in her wardrobe. Other women simply tired of their clothes and discarded them, but mademoiselle de Chevreuse preferred to burn them, and her women were always trying to save them from the flames. 'I believe', Retz wrote, 'that if she could have consigned her gallants to the fire when she was tired of them, she would have done so with the best will in the world'. For all the bitterness which evidently underlay such statements, Retz was, as always, determined to save appearances. Laigues had gone to court to prepare the way for the Chevreuse ladies, and when their reception was assured the cardinal personally escorted them on the road to Dampierre. In November la coadjutrice fell ill and died of a mysterious malady. Her face turned black and she was thought to have taken poison. Retz, according to Guy Joly, received the news with complete indifference.[27]

During the period of his quarrel with the unfortunate mademoiselle de Chevreuse, Retz found his relations with Gaston complicated by the formidable presence of la Grande Mademoiselle. Gaston's forthright daughter had been in touch with Fiesque when he negotiated the alliance between her father and Condé in January. Her determination to be revenged upon Mazarin, and to oblige the court to marry her to the king, made her a fierce protagonist of the policy of the princes, and she was constantly pressing Gaston for more vigorous action. Before leaving Paris to join the court at Poitiers the princess Palatine had urged her to make use of Retz, but Mademoiselle continued to distrust the new cardinal. When Caumartin had expressed to her Retz's desire to be of service, Mademoiselle finally relented, and accepted an invitation from her father to discuss affairs with him. While the cardinal

might share her aversion for Mazarin, he could not accept her
sympathy for Condé. Mademoiselle pulled Gaston in one direction
and Retz pulled him in the other: yet the cardinal could not afford
to be on bad terms with her. Hence he intervened in the negotiations being conducted by the English queen, Henrietta Maria, for
the marriage of her son, Charles II, with Mademoiselle. Young
king Charles had confessed that he was glad to return to France
after his disastrous endeavour to reconquer his kingdom in the
preceding year. Mademoiselle recorded no very favourable impression of him in her memoirs. He was a timid lover, and followed
his mother's instructions by demanding that she dance with him
whenever opportunity offered.[28] Retz, who had helped the queen
during the winter privations of the first Fronde, was always welcome at the impoverished court of the English émigrés. He acted
as the agent of the widowed queen in discussions with Mademoiselle, suggesting that she consider the match as an alternative
to her design to marry Louis XIV. Mademoiselle chose to decline.
She was far more interested in providing ballets and other entertainments for the officers of the Spanish contingent commanded by
Nemours, whose presence in Paris caused infinite distress to her
father. But if the negotiations failed, Retz had at least been able to
use the affair to improve relations with her.

A few weeks later Mademoiselle provided new testimony of her
formidable powers. Nemours and Beaufort were subjected to contradictory orders. Condé instructed Nemours to relieve his fortress
at Montrond, and then to march to Guyenne, bringing Beaufort
with him. Gaston on the other hand insisted that Beaufort remain
near Paris, and did not want the Spanish troops to reinforce Condé.
This, of course, was also Retz's policy, and it was his advice that
prevailed. The two armies remained close to the Loire and began
to move towards Orléans. The city became of great strategic importance, but the municipal government there insisted on neutrality. The court, escorted by the troops of Turenne and Hocquincourt, moved up the Loire through Tours, Amboise and Blois,
and in mid-March left the river to approach Orléans from the
south. While Gaston hovered in uncertainty at this crisis, his
daughter resolved to act. She insisted that she personally lead a
delegation to the city, and set off with the comtesse de Fiesque and
the comtesse de Frontenac. The three ladies, as madame de

Motteville described them, were clad as though they were ama-
zons, and escorted by the duc de Rohan and a pair of magistrates
from the parlement.[29] Rohan, who had fled in panic from Angers,
had a reputation as a dancing master but not as a soldier. The party
might have assumed a rather ludicrous aspect had it not been for
Mademoiselle. Indeed, Retz's propagandist, Patru, observed that
if the walls of Jericho had fallen at the sound of trumpets those of
Orléans were expected to collapse to the music of violins. When
Mademoiselle was refused entry at one gate, and heard that Molé
and a royal deputation were waiting at another, she carried out a
brief reconnaissance which left her companions breathless and exhausted. Then, commandeering a small boat, she rowed round the
city's defences until she found a side port open, strode into the
city square, and interrupted the municipal authorities when they
were on the point of admitting Molé. No one dared to contradict
Mademoiselle, who ruled Orléans in her father's name for more
than a month.

Once established in Orléans, Mademoiselle was joined by Beaufort and Nemours, and held a council of war. They resolved to
ascend the Loire to Gien and seize its bridges across the river.
Turenne, however, anticipated their plans, and when the attack
was launched at Jargeau at the beginning of April it was repulsed
with heavy loss. The two commanders proceeded to quarrel as to
their future strategy. Beaufort wanted to occupy Montargis and
block the road between Gien and Paris. Nemours, on the other
hand, wanted to carry out a wide sweeping movement to recross
the Loire at Blois and take the royal army in the rear. The fact that
Nemours had married Beaufort's sister (that mademoiselle de
Vendôme whom Retz had once pursued) did not prevent an ugly
altercation. Nemours, as La Rochefoucauld described him, lived
in a fantastic dream-world of his own, and Beaufort, who mixed
extreme vanity with empty-headed bonhomie, was no better
equipped for military command. The quarrel culminated with
Nemours striking Beaufort in the presence of Mademoiselle. She
exerted her authority first to insist upon a form of reconciliation
and then to order the generals to march to Montargis.[30]

While Beaufort and Nemours fought each other with more zeal
than they showed against the enemy, Condé and La Rochefoucauld
were engaged in an epic ride which brought them from Agen to

Orléans in nine days.[31] Condé had left the remnants of his army in
Guyenne under Conti and Marsin. Chavigny's reports from Paris
of the influence which Retz exerted over Gaston had greatly dis-
turbed the prince. Nemours had failed to obey his orders, and
Condé was well aware of the incapacity of Beaufort. For these
reasons he decided to abandon his defensive campaign against
Harcourt and to place himself at the head of his forces on the
Loire. He arrived in the forest of Orléans on 1 April, the day before
Turenne's victory at Jargeau. Concentrating his troops at Montargis he fell suddenly upon Hocquincourt's detachments at
Bléneau and routed them. The road to Gien now lay open, and the
queen, giving way to despair at the news of Condé's triumph,
expected him to seize the court. Turenne alone could match
Condé's tactical genius and inspiring leadership. He left his camp
at Briare and concentrated his available forces to block Condé's
advance. The engagement that followed was indecisive, but it
saved the court and restored the military initiative to the government. At this point Condé felt obliged to heed Chavigny's impor-
tunate demands that he should attend to the political crisis in Paris.
Leaving Clinchamp and Tavannes in command, Condé rode into
the capital on 11 April with Beaufort, Nemours and La Rochefoucauld.

The parlement could not adjust itself to so flexible a political
situation. It had continued to display a policy of vacillation much
ridiculed by Retz. While it remained bitterly critical of Mazarin,
it was also suspicious of Condé, and would not condone his war
against the royal authority. A proposal by the court that the money
for payment of the interest on government stock be diverted to
pay for the upkeep of the royal armies provoked an assembly of
representatives from the parlement, the *cour des aides* and the
chambre des comptes: yet Condé's partisans did not succeed in trans-
forming this body into the Chambre Saint-Louis which had sought
to reform the state in 1648.[32] Many of the more conservative magistrates disapproved of Gaston's moves to support the prince. Gaston could no longer hide his lack of resolution behind a sympathetic parlement, and he was horrified at the thought of Condé's
presence in Paris. Gourville had brought him the news of the
prince's ride from Agen, and at the beginning of April he had
ventured out of the capital as far as Juvisy in expectation of meet-

ing his ally. If Gaston was too frightened of Condé to oppose his entry to Paris, Retz thought otherwise. He knew the city governor, L'Hôpital, to be secretly in favour of the court. L'Hôpital's daughter-in-law was madame de Rhodes, and he owed his appointment to the influence of Retz's friend at court, the princess Palatine. Retz was also in touch with his friend Le Fèbvre, the *prévôt des marchands*, who led the conservative element in the hôtel de Ville. Condé's reputation for terror and popular violence in Bordeaux had preceded him, and it was only upon radical magistrates such as Viole, and upon elements of the lower classes, that he could rely.

The cardinal-coadjutor promoted a meeting of the city notables at the hôtel de Ville to recommend that the prince be refused admission to the city. Gaston was at first secretly delighted, but he soon became alarmed at the reactions of Chavigny and the mobs led by Retz's would-be assassin, Pesche. He reprimanded L'Hôpital and Le Fèbvre, and gave orders that Condé should be allowed to enter the city for a short conference. Once the prince appeared, the mobs openly began to attack those influential bourgeois who had opposed him. Retz hurriedly went into retreat at Notre-Dame. The parlement lapsed into tremulous inaction, and pretended to busy itself with new remonstrances against Mazarin. When the king moved to Saint-Germain at the end of April the parlement and its sister courts sent a deputation which was received with a mixture of firmness and favour. Mazarin was still trying to divide his enemies, but in the meantime Condé and the mob appeared to be masters of Paris, and the new cardinal went in fear of his life.

In his place of refuge Retz turned to his one remaining weapon, his pen. He began to compose a new series of pamphlets to discredit his enemies. His first victim was that ambitious and unscrupulous former minister who had attached himself to Condé, and whose career Retz described in *The Contretemps of the Lord Chavigny*.[33] In a letter to Ondedei Mazarin had repeated Richelieu's opinion that Chavigny could not be trusted to govern a fowl-house. Retz was even less restrained in his pamphlet, dispensing scorn and ridicule in equal proportions. He reported in his memoirs that, when he heard that Chavigny had broken down in chagrin and despair on reading it, he promised to send him a

sequel. From Chavigny he turned to his former ally, the fatuous
Beaufort, whose desertion to the princes had dragged Gaston in
its train. Like Chavigny, Beaufort's vanity was his greatest weakness, and its most susceptible aspect was his belief that he had
inherited the military panache of his grandfather, Henry IV. While
Turenne had protected the progress of the court from Corbeil to
Saint-Germain, the regiments of the princes had occupied
Etampes. Turenne and Hocquincourt had inflicted a sharp defeat
on them, and, when Gaston and Condé had directed reinforce-
ments to the place, the royal generals had trapped the opposing
army in the town and then besieged it. Beaufort was expected to
lead a relieving column, but he refused to leave Paris. Retz
parodied him mercilessly in his *Manifesto of My Lord the duc de
Beaufort*,[34] using the kind of boastful jargon that Beaufort himself
employed:

> I would never say so, but others might think it is better for me to
> stay in the rue de Béthisy [madame de Montbazon's house] than to
> expose myself to cannonades which may blow one quite to pieces, to
> musketry which induces contusions in the head from which one may
> likely die, to pistol shots which break one's bones, to pike thrusts which
> may endanger one's nerves, to sword cuts which are damaging to one's
> tendons. But I can never think so, for I am the great Beaufort, grandson
> of the great Henry. . . .

Apart from buffoonery of this kind, Retz composed a more so-
phisticated justification of his own conduct and a more explicit
vilification of that of Condé.[35] In particular, he examined the
current series of intrigues by which Mazarin, pretending to
negotiate for peace, sought to split the opposing factions.

The first of these moves was an embassy to the court led by
Rohan, Chavigny and Gaston's secretary, Goulas.[36] The queen of
England was said to have initiated discussions when the court was
still at Corbeil. The negotiators went with the strict understanding
that they would have no direct commerce with Mazarin. Their
real purpose was to state the personal rewards demanded by the
princes as the price of peace. Such offers soon rebounded to discredit Condé and his friends. Moreover, Mazarin became a party
to the discussions at the very time when Gaston and the prince
were solemnly assuring the parlement that negotiation with

Mazarin was inconceivable. When these talks broke down, Condé sent Gourville with a peremptory demand for the dismissal of Mazarin and the formation of a general council to be dominated by Gaston and himself. Retz was bitterly opposed to any peace which would leave Mazarin in a position of influence and himself isolated. So, too, was Chavigny, and La Rochefoucauld accused these two enemies of working together to continue the war.[37] Another negotiator was madame de Châtillon, who had first replaced the duchesse de Longueville in the affections of Nemours and had then set her cap at Condé. Nemours, La Rochefoucauld and madame de Châtillon formed an inner group within the party of the princes.[38] Mazarin could not take madame de Châtillon seriously, and, when she returned to Paris from the court with many promises, she found that the government had commenced the siege of Etampes under cover of her negotiations.

Turenne had so completely outmanoeuvred his opponents that they were obliged to seek a fresh ally. Gaston's wife, Marguerite de Lorraine, urged the employment of her brother, who, though deprived of his duchy, controlled an army of eight thousand mercenary troops in Spanish pay. Madame commanded universal respect. Retz was careful not to contradict her opinions; she was the only person who inspired any sense of inferiority in her irrepressible step-daughter, Mademoiselle; Gaston lived in positive dread of her. Thus Madame had her way, and Charles de Lorraine was invited to relieve the beleaguered army of the princes in Etampes. Towards the end of May he arrived in Paris, without his army, amid the applause of Condé's following among the people. Although Retz strove to avoid being compromised, he finally yielded to the pleas of Madame to hold discussions with her brother. They met secretly at a seminary for Jesuit novices, but Retz refused to commit himself. Lorraine left Paris to rejoin his troops, and succeeded in raising the siege of Etampes, allowing Tavannes and the bulk of the prince's army to concentrate at Saint-Cloud. Thereafter Lorraine played a less glorious part. Through the intercession of Charles II of England he negotiated a treaty with the court whereby he promised, for a consideration, to withdraw from France. He was slow in fulfilling the treaty, and for a time Turenne threatened to attack him near Corbeil. Finally he commenced his retreat, his troops following their accustomed

H

practice of rape, pillage and destruction. A month later he was to return in search of further spoils.

The parlement, which had acquiesced in Condé's presence in Paris, roused itself in protest at the incursion of Lorraine's army. The magistrates had sanctioned the establishment of a revolutionary assembly in the hôtel de Ville, despite the king's explicit ban. On the other hand, they had passed a series of formal decrees against the riots and murders by which Condé's partisans had terrorised moderate bourgeois opinion. Since the militia could no longer be relied upon, everyone knew that these ordinances would not be enforced. Condé's policies had lacked consistency and allowed the rallying of that moderate opinion which expressed itself against Charles de Lorraine. A revolutionary leader could not afford to do things by halves. Retz praised him in his memoirs for his magnanimity in not pursuing a defenceless opponent, and criticised him for his political ineptitude. The prince, he said, had prevented his subordinates from attacking the coadjutor when he was unguarded, and had reproached those who desired to take advantage of the opportunity with the remark: 'The cardinal de Retz is either too strong or too weak.' He had read Retz's pamphlets, such as *Truth and Error concerning Monsieur le Prince and Monsieur le Cardinal de Retz*, and observed that it was the only way he could ascertain his faults, since his friends would never tell him. These were gestures, Retz wrote, of which Plutarch would have approved. It is unlikely, however, that the cardinal experienced these sentiments at the time. It is true that some of his propaganda showed respect for Condé, but during the summer of 1652 in Paris the prince remained as dangerous an enemy as he had been in the summer of the preceding year. Retz defied him with the same courage, if not with the same bravura, he had shown in 1651. The coadjutor could not bear to be excluded from the machinations of the Luxembourg, and he ran considerable risks in continuing to wait upon Gaston, while studiously avoiding the prince.

Retz's praise of Condé was the consequence of the altered circumstances of later life: it was also designed to magnify his own actions by stressing the stature of his opponent. His criticism of Condé's politics was less equivocal. If terror was to be employed, it should have followed a more deliberate plan, with less initiative allowed to its instruments. If the parlement was to be used to lend legality to a revolutionary situation, it should have been purged of those who sympathised with the court, and never have been permitted the luxury of voicing criticism. This lack of application to the tactics of revolution was to result in greater bloodshed and anarchy. Retz also had a shrewd eye for some of Condé's personal failings. The birth and disposition of the prince did not fit him to lead the Paris *canaille*. He had an impatient disdain for the *minutiae* of revolution, and, as a prince of the Blood, direct revolt against the king was contrary to all his instincts. When he tried to play the role of Beaufort he exposed himself to ridicule. Towards the end of June, in an attempt to win acclaim from that section of the populace who combined religious fanaticism with revolutionary fervour, he participated in the traditional procession of the 'Chasse Sainte-Geneviève', and presented a sad imitation of Beaufort, the so-called king of the markets. Condé's splendour was on the battlefield, not on the barricades. As Retz justly remarked, he should never have left the command of his armies to novices in order to dabble in political intrigues for which he had neither skill nor application. But, after the relief of Etampes and the withdrawal of Lorraine, he seemed to appreciate his mistake. He joined his army at Saint-Cloud and prepared to challenge Turenne on ground of his own choosing.

Both sides had refrained from campaigning in the immediate vicinity of the capital. Turenne had obeyed Mazarin's injunction to this effect in order to avoid alienating neutralist opinion, and Condé had hoped to gain control of the city before the approach of Turenne's army aroused royalist sympathies within it. He had led the Parisian militia against a small Swiss garrison at Saint-Denis, but had not tried to consolidate his success. Circumstances had now changed so much that both commanders hoped to gain Paris by military action, and only Gaston and Retz among the political leaders were anxious to preserve the capital's apparent neutrality. The king's army concentrated at Saint-Denis. On 27 June the royal council of war resolved to leave Saint-Denis and trap Condé by moving against him along both banks of the Seine. Condé decided to regroup at Charenton. He recrossed the Seine and marched towards the Porte Saint-Honoré by way of the Bois de Boulogne. But Gaston insisted that his troops should not pass through the city. Although the prince obtained permission to send

his baggage through Paris, he was obliged to lead his troops northwards round the walls towards the Porte Saint-Antoine. Turenne
had anticipated his manoeuvre, and sent half of his forces on a
wider arc to outpace Condé and block the Vincennes road ahead
of him. The other half closely pursued the prince's rearguard as he
approached the outer suburb of Saint-Antoine. At dawn on 2 July
he closed his trap and moved from the east and north to pin the
rebel army against the city walls.[39]

Throughout most of that day Condé sustained the courage of
his outnumbered troops by his personal example. Amid a savage
and unprecedented carnage he disputed every street, house and
barricade in Saint-Antoine. Mademoiselle recounted how she had
been awakened at 6 a.m. by Fiesque, who had been sent by Condé
to beg entry at the Porte Saint-Antoine, and had been told at the
Luxembourg that Gaston was too ill to stir from his bed. She
proceeded to the hôtel de Ville to demand permission to send a
body of militia to the prince's aid. She met blank refusal until she
threatened to raise the mob on her own account. Though refuge
was denied to Condé's main force, the wounded came streaming
back into the city, among them La Rochefoucauld who, although
fearfully disfigured by a musketball through both cheeks, continued to rally the fugitives. Mademoiselle, scornfully rejecting
intervention by madame de Châtillon, established herself in the
Bastille. The governor of the fortress, Broussel's son, refused to
cooperate without a written order from Gaston, so Mademoiselle
once more took matters into her own hands. She had the cannon
of the Bastille provide Condé with supporting fire, and organised
a sortie under cover of which the prince could withdraw the
remnants of his army within the city walls. As an ultimate gesture
she had a cannon shot despatched towards the royal party, which
had gathered to watch the battle from the heights of Charonne.
She had saved Condé, but renounced any remaining hope of
marrying the king. That night, while the city accustomed itself to
being occupied by Condé's troops as well as being terrorised by
his partisans, sleep eluded Mademoiselle, for, as she wrote in her
memoirs, her mind was 'full of the faces of the poor dead'.[40] Retz
spent an equally uneasy night. He had remained in his house during
the battle, receiving a flow of despairing messages from Gaston,
who feared Paris would rise against him, and yet was too terrified

to take any step to rescue Condé. The new cardinal now seemed more defenceless than ever.

The prince proceeded to take control of the capital, forcing the unwilling Gaston to associate himself with the extremists. The parlement refused to sit, so Condé arranged for a meeting of the city notables in the hôtel de Ville on 4 July to legitimise the new régime in the capital. Once again Gaston was to be appointed lieutenant-general of the kingdom and the king declared a prisoner in the hands of Mazarin. Condé was to be generalissimo, Beaufort to replace L'Hôpital as governor of Paris, and Broussel to become *prévôt des marchands* in place of Retz's friend Le Fèbvre. Either Gaston had reservations about this plan or he and Condé deliberately sought to provoke the mob against the notables. A large crowd, including many of Condé's troops, had gathered outside the hôtel de Ville, but Gaston did not make his brief appearance at the assembly until late in the afternoon. The crowd had been restive before his arrival. When, after his departure, the notables seemed to remain undecided, word spread from mouth to mouth that the assembly was sympathetic to Mazarin. Muskets suddenly appeared, and shots were fired at the windows of the hôtel de Ville. As the mob surged forward and set fire to the doors of the building, a detachment of militia guarding the notables began to shoot down the insurgents. But the smoke forced them to retire, and the crowd burst into the hôtel de Ville, killing the notables, or holding them to ransom. According to Mademoiselle, the news of the massacre was a complete surprise to Gaston, who emerged from his room in the Luxembourg wearing only his shirt. She had earlier gone walking towards the Place de Grève and had accepted one of the blue ribbons which Condé's partisans had pressed upon passers-by. Condé, she wrote, refused to return to the scene, but Beaufort eventually agreed to restore order. Mademoiselle claimed that she neither knew nor wanted to know who was responsible for the massacre, but she seemed to imply that Gaston, through his passivity, and Condé, through deliberate intent, were both culpable. Retz asserted that Condé had given no specific orders for the killing, and La Rochefoucauld observed that, while both Gaston and the prince had instructed Beaufort to terrorise the city, the massacre was not premeditated. On the other hand, Joly declared that Beaufort was in a house near the Place de

Grève watching the scene, and that he did not intervene until late at night, when Mademoiselle herself brought a command from Gaston to stop the riot.[41]

The presence of Condé's soldiers among the mob convinced moderate opinion in Paris, if it did not convince the memorialists, that the prince had directed the massacre of 4 July. A larger section of the parlement began to swing over to the royalist camp. Although the radical group followed the lead of the revolutionary government now established in the hôtel de Ville, several of the magistrates obeyed Mazarin's order to transfer themselves and their proceedings to Pontoise. The prince continued to hold his position in Paris, although at the end of the month, when Turenne had been obliged to march north to meet the new incursions of Lorraine and the Spanish, he moved his army to Saint-Cloud. New rifts appeared within the party of the princes. Madame de Longueville and Conti quarrelled about the conduct of affairs in Bordeaux, and found royalist military pressure diminished when Harcourt deserted his command and attempted to conquer a private principality in Alsace. Gaston continued to negotiate with the court. Chavigny, who was savagely rebuked by Condé for being privy to these discussions, died of a stroke brought on by rage and frustration. Nemours insisted upon settling his differences with Beaufort, and was killed by his brother-in-law in the resulting duel. On 9 August the death of Bouillon, whom Retz had respected as the most subtle of his former associates in the Fronde, left another gap in the ranks of the leaders. Finally, Mazarin hastened the decomposition of the opposing faction by voluntarily withdrawing into a new but temporary exile on 19 August.

Retz identified himself with the growing movement towards peace in Paris. For three weeks after the massacre in the hôtel de Ville he barricaded himself in his house in daily expectation of an assault by Condé. Many of his friends and servants, including the bishop of Châlons, Brissac, Charrier and Argenteuil, counselled him to retire to Charleville, where Noirmoutier was governor. But both Caumartin and Joly argued against this course on the ground that he would lose what popular opinion still clung to him, and thereby forfeit the respect of the court.[42] So Retz stayed on in Paris, although he admitted his error in his memoirs. Had he withdrawn to the country, he argued, he would have purged himself of faction and yet avoided suspicion of mazarinism. He later explained his decision to remain not by his blindness to the advantages of prudence – for he claimed that he realised these at the time – but by his sense of obligation to his friends, and the pride that forced him not to yield to Condé. Thus he was prepared to 'sacrifice great and solid interests for the tinsel of glory, which is always false when it prevents one from doing something that is greater than appearances'.

While Condé remained in Paris, Retz took what measures he could to defend himself. Caumartin provided the funds to hire a guard of one hundred exiled followers of Montrose, and another hundred swordsmen were drawn from the remnants of Retz's party. Some of the officers of the militia promised their support. Notre-Dame was turned into a fortress, and its towers crammed with makeshift grenades. But the prince and his followers did not attack. They contented themselves with propaganda against the new cardinal, to which Retz, in answer, preached the healing virtues of peace. His appearance in the guise of peace-maker was not welcomed by the court. Mazarin wrote anxiously to warn that Retz should not be allowed to lead the royalist party in the capital. Although Retz still attended the Luxembourg, he no longer enjoyed Gaston's confidence and chose to criticise his defiance of the royal authority. 'I was convinced then, as I am still', Retz wrote, 'that the same laws that permit us occasionally to dispense with exact obedience always enjoin us to respect the title of the sanctuary.'

Retz began to assume the pomp of his new rank, even though he had not yet received his cardinal's hat from the king. The indiscipline of the mobs, the ravages of war, the giddy procession of decrees and counter-decrees between Paris and Pontoise, the variant conditions for peace announced by both the court and the princes, the defeat of French arms in Catalonia, Piedmont and Picardy, all contributed to disillusionment with the methods and aims of faction. Retz caught the prevailing mood in his propaganda.

In virtuous times [he wrote in his pamphlet *Present Interests*] men can be judged by their duty. In times when men are both clever and corrupt, they must be judged by their interests. In times such as our own, when there is much depravity and little light, passion as well as self-interest must be taken into account, and from such a mixture we must fashion a measure for our discernment.[43]

Condé's interests, like those of Mazarin, he argued, were sustained by the continuance of war. After so 'black and tragic a crime' as the massacre of the hôtel de Ville, no one could accept the pleas of those who fostered riot and sedition, and only the cloister remained untainted. His own policy sought to maintain the exile of Mazarin and to restore peace to a suffering people.[44] Retz was not alone in seeking to act as the spokesman of the new public mood, but his ecclesiastical rank gave him an advantage over his rivals. He sent Joly to negotiate with the court, and, when his agent was intercepted by Condé's troops and taken to their headquarters at Charenton, he was fortunate not to have his letters to the princess Palatine discovered and their contents turned against him.[45]

It was Joly who suggested that Retz should lead a clerical deputation to the court at Compiègne, as he had done in 1649. Although the queen would not recognise him as a negotiator, it was difficult for her to refuse him an interview when he demanded no more than the bestowal of his cardinal's insignia. In the second week of September Retz set out for Compiègne at the head of a long cortège of municipal and clerical dignitaries. He had determined to make the most of the ceremony, and had exhausted his remaining credit to provide the deputation with appropriate splendour. He was halted by a royal messenger and informed that no more than twenty-four horses could be accommodated at Compiègne. As there were one hundred and twelve carriage horses alone in the party, he was obliged to leave most of his escort behind. The queen did little to heal his wounded vanity by explaining that the royal guards, customarily sent to escort a new cardinal to his audience, had not arrived because they had lost their way in the forest. It was clear from the queen's attitude that, though she would observe the niceties of convention at the court itself, she had been firmly instructed by Mazarin not to grant Retz any credence as a peacemaker. This did not prevent Retz, when receiving his hat from the king's hand, from delivering an exhortation in favour of peace. 'All your Majesty's subjects can speak to you of their needs', he began, 'but only the church has the right to remind you of your duties. The same power that has established us as mediators between God and man must consequently authorise us to intercede with kings, who are the living images of God upon earth.' He went on to describe the universal desolation in which 'our countryside has been ravished, our towns deserted, our homes abandoned, our temples violated and our altars profaned'. He recalled how Henry IV had consulted his ancestor, cardinal de Gondi, before pursuing the policy that had expelled foreigners and granted a magnanimous peace to his rebellious subjects. He compared the king with Saint Louis, and the queen with the saint's just and wise mother, Blanche of Castile. A parody of this harangue was promptly published by Condé's party in Paris, and Retz on his return was obliged to issue the correct version.

Retz remained in Compiègne for several days after the royal audience on 11 September, but he could make no progress in negotiation and could not afford the expense of his retinue. He found that Le Tellier and Servien were the guests of madame la Palatine, and that they, with Mazarin's other agents, the Fouquet brothers and Ondedei, were everywhere in control. When he returned to Paris he was greeted, according to his own account, with acclamation, and, according to others, with hoots and jeers. However, he was able to claim some of the credit when the king returned to Paris on 21 October. Condé had fled to Flanders a week before, and the court had received delegations from the Paris magistrates, first in their role as officers of the parlement and then in their second capacity as commanders of the militia. Gaston was obliged to withdraw to Limours. For a moment he seemed to contemplate resistance, and told Retz and Beaufort that he would raise the populace against the Louvre. 'But', Retz wrote, 'the threats that would have been terrible in the mouth of Gaston de Foix meant nothing in the mouth of Gaston de France.' To Retz's infinite relief Gaston slipped quietly out of Paris. La Grande Mademoiselle and madame de Montbazon retired with equal discretion. The parlement obediently registered an edict forbidding it to meddle in political matters. An amnesty was granted to those who had not followed Condé into the service of Spain. Beaufort, Rohan, La Rochefoucauld, Broussel and about a dozen other principal members of the old Fronde and the new were exempted from this act of oblivion, and of all the leaders Retz alone was permitted to remain in the capital. He marshalled the Parisian clergy to welcome the royal retinue. It might have seemed, now that he appeared to be forgiven for his political misdeeds and fully confirmed in his new dignity, as though fresh opportunities for glory awaited him. The reality was otherwise. Isolated and bereft of his faction, he was approaching the nadir of his fortunes.

TEN

Imprisonment

Before the court had returned to Paris it had been Guy Joly and Caumartin who advised the cardinal-coadjutor to stand his ground, whereas Brissac and his other friends had counselled him to conduct his bargaining from some place of refuge outside the capital. Now that the king and his mother were installed in the Louvre, Joly stressed the danger that Retz courted by remaining in Paris, and pointed out that his bargaining power was much reduced. Caumartin also held this view, but he was absent in Poitiers, where he was to be married. On the other hand, Brissac and his associates of the old Fronde now urged Retz to stay in Paris and negotiate a reconciliation with the court from which they might profit.

Retz possessed two advantages. The archbishopric of Paris was to be his at the death of his uncle, and he knew that the court would concede much to have him resign his claim. He was also aware that the queen yearned to recall Mazarin, and he guessed that his enemy would not return while Retz might still oppose him. With these counters in his hands Retz explored the likely reactions of the court through his friend, the princess Palatine. She met him late at night at Guy Joly's house, and for a time she seemed to think that he might extract favours for his friends as well as for himself. But it was also apparent that the court might achieve Mazarin's recall by removing the cardinal-coadjutor from the scene. The princess began to pass warnings of the dangers surrounding him. She no longer believed that Retz could secure rewards for his friends, and she ceased to attend their secret trysts.

For several weeks Retz saw no reason to change his style of living. It was true that the civility with which the queen had greeted him on her return turned to coldness and asperity on his next visit to the Louvre, but he ascribed this to the report of a spy that he had been willing to support Gaston before the latter's flight from Paris. In his memoirs Retz pretended that he endured such suspicion with fortitude because he was convinced in his own mind that he had saved the state from further anarchy. 'There are some men', he wrote, 'who prefer to success the satisfaction they find in themselves.' His real satisfaction at this time was expressed in the pomp with which he preached before the court in the great church of Saint-Germain l'Auxerrois on the occasion of All-Saints, 1 November. Marigny, who now served the princes and sent reports on affairs in Paris to Bordeaux, wrote to Lenet that Retz had chosen to speak on ambition, and that he planned to preach again before the king in Saint-Jean de la Boucherie.[1] Retz also found satisfaction in the customary pleasures in which Brissac had now become his mentor. Together they went riding and hunting; together they promenaded in the fashionable gardens of the financier Nicolas de Rambouillet; and together they visited mademoiselle de la Vergne, whom Brissac courted, and her friend the beautiful mademoiselle de la Loupe, whom Retz continued to pursue. Brissac was also conducting an affair with the cardinal's cousin, madame de Lesdiguières. Guy Joly recalled that she and her gallant tried to persuade Retz that he would achieve nothing through his negotiations with the princess Palatine, and should deal direct with the minister Servien.[2] But this, according to Retz's account, was what La Palatine advised herself.

Servien was prepared to offer Retz a lucrative embassy to Italy if he undertook to remain there for three years, but he would do nothing for the coadjutor's friends. Retz's supporters quarrelled among themselves as to the policy to be followed. Some thought he should claim a share in the ministry as the price of Mazarin's return: others that he should merely offer to renounce his claim to the archbishopric. More particularly, they quarrelled about their own perquisites. Montrésor disliked Caumartin, and wished to press for a secretaryship of state for one of his friends rather than for the magistrate. One night, when they were all discussing their expectations at the cardinal's house, Joly read a letter he had received from Caumartin, and Montrésor complained that Caumartin had been dealing directly with the princess Palatine in his own interest. Madame de Chevreuse and Laigues were also trying to reconcile themselves with Retz to gain some share in the spoils. Shortly before her horrible death on 7 November the

former coadjutrice unsuccessfully obeyed her mother's instructions to use her 'beautiful big eyes' upon the cardinal. Retz would
do nothing for the Chevreuse faction, but there were others to
whom he felt a real obligation. He sought the governorship of
Anjou for Brissac, lands for Fosseuse and Argenteuil, an abbey for
Charrier, a secretaryship for Caumartin and money or a post for
Guy Joly. But Servien remained obdurate, and Retz began to
suspect that the minister and the abbé Fouquet were spinning out
the negotiations while secretly advising the queen to arrest him.

   In his memoirs Retz chose to blame his own generosity to his
friends for the disaster which overtook him. Had he accepted
Servien's offers without imposing further conditions on behalf of
the frondeurs, he would, he argued, have reached a satisfactory
settlement. A chance circumstance, he thought, had convinced the
queen that he was secretly in alliance with Condé. When the king
ordered the parlement to assemble on 13 November to register a
new declaration of the prince's treason, sinister inferences were
drawn from the excuses Retz made for his absence. His suspicions
of Servien and the abbé Fouquet deepened. Guy Joly argued that
they were more dangerous enemies than Mazarin, since they
sought their own advancement by counselling his arrest and
preventing his reconciliation with the exiled first minister. Joly
claimed that, whereas Servien wanted to lure Retz to the Louvre
and arrest him there, the abbé planned to attack the cardinal in the
streets, and had again suggested to the queen that he should be
assassinated. Fouquet's plot was not unlike that of Catherine de
Médicis for the assault on admiral Coligny which led to the massacre of the Huguenots on Saint Bartholomew's day, 1572. Retz's
movements were closely watched. His carriage was followed, and
a group of men were posted near madame de Pommereuil's house
in the hope of ambushing him. The queen was more concerned at
the possibility of her complicity being discovered than she was at
the impropriety of assassinating a cardinal. Nevertheless, she
issued a secret order for his arrest, and on one of the three surviving copies a postscript appears in the king's own hand: 'I have
commanded Pradelle to execute the present order against the person of cardinal de Retz, and even to arrest him dead or alive if he
offers resistance.'[3]

   A number of warnings reached Retz. One of his servants

revealed that he had been offered a bribe, and Joly promptly engaged him to play the part of a double agent.[4] The cardinal began
to take a small armed escort with him wherever he went. Except
for avoidance of the Louvre, he curtailed none of his usual
activities. The proximity of danger aroused his customary bravado.
When Brissac received anonymous warning of a plot to arrest
Retz during his promenade in the Rambouillet gardens, the
cardinal insisted that Brissac accompany him with two hundred
gentlemen, and delighted in the discomfiture of the guards officers
he met there at the size of his retinue. He chose to think that
Pradelle, the guards captain who had the king's order to effect
his arrest, was actually pursuing a vendetta against him as the
consequence of a disappointed love affair.

Retz remained uncertain of the determination of the court to use
violence, and this, coupled with his recklessness, ultimately
betrayed him. Believing that Mazarin was unaware of the plans of
Servien and the abbé Fouquet, he tried to open direct negotiations
with his principal enemy. Joly wrote to bishop Vialart of Châlons
to suggest a secret meeting of the two cardinals, but one of
Mazarin's emissaries deliberately misinformed the bishop of his
master's movements, and nothing came of the plan.[5] As the confidence of Retz increased, he began to entertain the suggestions of
madame de Lesdiguières and the king's governor, marshal Villeroy, that he could now visit the Louvre in safety. His cousin and
Villeroy were not deceiving him; rather, Servien was using them
as decoys in his plan to accomplish Retz's downfall. Brissac now
favoured the idea that Retz should see the queen, and argued that
he should do so without waiting for Vialart's reply concerning
Mazarin. Joly protested vigorously, and on 18 December Caumartin came hurrying back from Poitou to dissuade his patron
from so rash a gesture.

Retz went on believing that Mazarin was unaware of the machinations of his subordinates. In this he was mistaken, although both
he and Joly estimated the sensational designs of Servien and the
abbé Fouquet correctly. Mademe de Motteville claimed that the
decision to arrest the new cardinal was taken at about the time
the court returned to Paris. The duplicity of the queen and her
advisers was not quite so calculated as this. Responsibility for the
decision is clearly revealed in correspondence between Mazarin

and Michel Le Tellier.[6] On 26 November 1652 Le Tellier wrote to say that he and Servien had convinced the queen that Retz must be detained, and that the king had given formal authority to arrest him should he come to the Louvre. The same letter mentioned alternative plans to apprehend him in the Rambouillet gardens or the Paris convent of the Carthusians, and explained that Retz's suspicions were being lulled by the negotiations he was pursuing through the princess Palatine. But the queen had insisted that Mazarin's approval should be given before his arrest could be attempted. As if to persuade Mazarin of the necessity for action, Servien reported an alleged threat by Retz to oppose by force any endeavour to evict him from the capital.

Mazarin needed no convincing. He agreed entirely with the plans to imprison Retz, but he answered equivocally, assuming that Le Tellier and Servien would read between the lines. The detention of a member of the sacred college would inevitably provoke strong reactions in Rome, and it was impolitic for one cardinal directly to command the arrest of another. Above all, it was necessary to provide justification. Retz had not been excluded from the October amnesty, and, while it was easy to furnish an indictment of his political crimes before the return of the court to Paris, it was difficult to accuse him of any specific disloyalty or disobedience since this date. Mazarin endorsed the selection of the abbé Fouquet to plan the affair, and he proposed that the princess Palatine, who was throughout the innocent instrument of the plotters, should offer Retz in writing the suggested post in Rome. He would then be obliged to make a formal refusal, and this would serve to justify the arrest. These views were expressed, often in ambiguous terms, in Mazarin's reply to Le Tellier's letter – a reply dated 3 December from Lorraine. He also answered letters received from Ondedei and the abbé Fouquet, and said merely that they should use every endeavour to persuade Retz to go to Rome. But no one in Paris was willing to bear the responsibility, and so on 8 December Mazarin had to write again, this time to Le Tellier and Servien jointly, and specifically to use the word 'arrest'. He revealed a certain exasperation at being obliged to commit himself in such a way. Though he ordered the letter to be burnt after reading, Le Tellier took the precaution of keeping a deciphered version among his papers. It was Le Tellier who wrote out the order to Pradelle. At first the date was left blank, and it was not until 16 December that it was entered.

Neither Caumartin nor Joly could dissuade Retz from going to the Louvre. Even the abbé Charrier felt assured that Villeroy was to be trusted, and Retz declared that the court would not dare arrest him. At dawn on 19 December the baron de Pennacors arrived with a message from the princess Palatine that he should on no account visit the Louvre until he had word from Mazarin. Retz knew he was taking a risk. He burnt his papers, gave Joly his ciphers and placed in his pockets a letter from Charles II of England and part of a sermon he was to preach on the last Sunday in Advent. He was like a gambler making a last throw, and nothing would restrain him. At 9 a.m. he walked across to the Louvre and asked Villeroy when he might see the king. He waited for some time before intercepting His Majesty at the foot of the great staircase. Louis wished him good-morning, pleasantly enough, and passed on to visit his mother, Retz following behind. The queen inquired perfunctorily about the cardinal's health and then ignored him. Retz withdrew to an ante-chamber, where the captain of guards, Villequier, informed him he was under arrest. He was held in Villequier's quarters until the middle of the afternoon, when he was conducted under heavy guard to the château of Vincennes.

Retz saw no evidence of an attempt to rescue him during the slow journey to Vincennes. The marquis du Château-Regnaut had tried to raise the people, and squire Malclerc had thought to block the bridges of Notre-Dame and Saint-Michel. One of the cardinal's mob leaders, a butcher named Le Houx, had assembled others in his trade. But nothing of this sort led to armed resistance. Retz saw detachments of Swiss infantry guarding every vantage point between the Louvre and the eastern wall of the city at the Porte Saint-Antoine. As for his friends among the people of Paris, 'the men were everywhere in dread and the women overcome by tears'.

His aristocratic supporters were scarcely more effective. Brissac hid at madame de Lesdiguières' house, where plans to aid Retz were concerted. The abbé Charrier was to leave immediately for Rome. The abbé de Lameth and Caumartin were to visit Mezières and Charleville to engage the vicomte de Bussy-Lameth and the duc de Noirmoutier, the respective governors of these fortresses, to declare for Retz. Joly was to travel to the seat of the duc de Retz in Machecoul to have him join Conti and the party of the princes in Gascony. Brissac, who wanted to defy the court by holding the mouth of the Loire and Belle-Ile, was to follow Joly. Argenteuil and Montrésor were also involved in these projects, though they were assigned no specific role. The only bases of which the frondeurs could feel in any way confident were those provided by Bussy-Lameth and Noirmoutier, and even Noirmoutier soon showed himself ready to treat with the court.

The elder duc de Retz and his daughter restrained the young duc de Retz, the cardinal's brother, from aiding the prisoner in Vincennes. Brissac, after spending six weeks comforting madame de Lesdiguières (as Guy Joly put it), eventually reached Mache-coul. He and the younger duc de Retz went hunting with about a hundred Poitevin gentry, who after the hunt, again according to Joly's account, talked bravely in their cups of raising regiments, and next day went back to their lands with nothing more to show for their intentions than sore heads.[7] The best that Brissac and Retz's elder brother could achieve was the composition of a joint letter requesting the liberation of the cardinal, which was addressed to the king in March 1653. The letter presented a strong case on Retz's behalf. It represented him as the well-intentioned mediator who had led the rebellious capital back to its allegiance to the crown. It recalled that anarchic summer in Paris in 1652.

Consider the first six months when this new cardinal was resident in the capital [ran the text] and you will see with what courage and vigour he sustained the interests of your crown during Your Majesty's absence. Consider how he undertook enterprises requiring the utmost strength and involving the greatest danger, and with what high-mindedness he rejected all those propositions which he regarded as contrary to the welfare of your affairs.[8]

But most of the letter was far less bold than this, and its general tone was so abject that even the elder duc de Retz was prepared to put his signature to it. The duchesse de Lesdiguières, the unwitting agent of Servien in the arrest, showed a more genuine concern for the cardinal. She asked Villequier to pass him a box of antidotes against poison. Villequier took the box to the royal council, where, as malicious tongues reported, Servien suggested that poisons be substituted for the antidotes.

But the church provided more reliable support. When the queen ordered the arrest of Guy Joly, the latter took refuge in the cloisters of Notre-Dame, where he met nightly with Caumartin to concert the ecclesiastical campaign. The curés of Paris and the chapter of the diocese were almost unanimous in their reaction against the court. If they did not support Retz personally, and most of them did, they united in condemning an outrage by the secular power against the church in general. The chapter ordered forty hours of prayer for the safe deliverance of the cardinal, and the exposure of the host for three days. Le Tellier brought an order from the king forbidding the public display of the eucharist, but the order was ignored. The papal nuncio urged the clergy to support their coadjutor. The canons assembled and demanded of the archbishop that he should intercede. Père de Gondi and the duchesse de Lesdiguières brought the pressure of the family to bear upon Retz's uncle. The archbishop's consuming jealousy for his nephew was balanced against the likelihood that all the clergy of Paris would disown him if he made no gesture. Although he refused the suggestion by the canons and parish priests that the churches be shut until Retz was released, he finally agreed to head a deputation to the court to remonstrate in favour of Retz's liberty. Clearly his heart was not in the mission, and when the queen reproached him for allowing the forty hours of prayer, he responded weakly that the chapter, not he, was responsible.

None of these measures weakened the queen's resolution. Her sole concession to clerical pressure was to instruct the chancellor to justify the court's action. Séguier told the deputation that Retz had had to be arrested to prevent him from executing certain seditious projects upon which he was resolved. But if the stand taken by the clergy produced few tangible results, at least it gave new heart to Retz's friends. Joly went off to the Gondi seat at Machecoul, and Caumartin and Hacqueville, who were the only secular friends of the cardinal not to be exiled from Paris, coordinated plans to secure his release. When the first three days of clerical demonstrations were over, the curés continued to exhort their congregations in his favour and to sing special psalms to mark their unwavering support. The bishop of Châlons spoke vigorously on his behalf, and sympathy for his cause was expressed in the Sorbonne.

Retz believed that the measures taken by the clergy had obliged the court to mitigate the terms of his imprisonment. The duchesse de Lesdiguières wrote to Mazarin imploring the minister to treat his prisoner less harshly. There was good cause for her alarm. For two weeks Retz's room had no heating, and when firewood was supplied it was taken by his guards and used for their own comfort. One of his gaolers stole some of his clothes, and he had to spend a week in bed in consequence. The same man, allegedly a former valet of Servien, appeared intent upon breaking his spirit by a ceaseless mockery. He told the cardinal that he might be allowed to grow a few vegetables in a small garden in the castle keep and suggested that asparagus, requiring several years for the establishment of a bed, would be best suited to his needs. Retz endured insult and discomfort with mildness and fortitude, but he welcomed the relaxing of these conditions. His furniture, bed-linen and church ornaments were sent from Paris. His physician, Vacherot, joined him. He was allowed books, and spent much of his time in the study of classical authors and of Spanish and Italian texts. He composed a work which he called *The Consolation of Theology* in imitation of Boethius, and began a series of notes towards a history of the diocese of Paris, using as his model the history of the church in Milan composed by Saint Carlo Borromeo, whom he had once quoted in his sermons. Neither of these works survived but the latter possibly provided an early draft for certain passages in his memoirs. His gaolers frequently interrupted his studies. He was forced to take exercise at irregular times, and often he was captiously denied it. Retz admitted that there were occasions when he was near despair, though his pride made him affect the stoic. He took pleasure in such small privileges as were granted him. He bred rabbits and kept doves and pigeons in the towers of his prison.

While Retz was experiencing the first shock of confinement, the papacy began to move on his behalf. The abbé Charrier arrived in Rome to find Innocent x outraged at the monarchy's defiance of the Holy See. A cardinal stood beyond the jurisdiction of the secular power. Richelieu had formed a commission of prelates when the political activities of a bishop had required his removal

from a position of influence. There had been no precedent for
direct action by the French crown against a cardinal since Henry
III had had the cardinal de Guise arrested and murdered in 1588.
On that occasion Innocent's predecessor had excommunicated the
king and absolved his subjects from their allegiance. Motives and
responsibilities in the present instance lacked the bloody simplicity
of that earlier challenge from the days of the Catholic League.
Nevertheless, the pope intended to act with vigour. He summoned the French ambassador and denounced the act. He sent
instructions to his nuncio in Paris, Niccolo Bagni, archbishop of
Athens, to demand Retz's liberty from Louis XIV. He despatched
a brief to the king on 20 January 1653, which was translated from
the Latin into French and distributed in Paris. 'We have heard of
the detention of the said cardinal with extreme regret,' Innocent
wrote, 'for by this act against one person the sacred immunities
of all within the church have been violated.' Retz had but recently
been recommended by the crown for elevation to the sacred college. He was coadjutor and archbishop designate of a diocese based
upon a great and illustrious city, the capital of France, and as such
the king should regard him as his pastor and his father. 'We who
have to render account to God for your soul', the pope concluded,
'entreat you by the bowels of Christ to remove this great scandal
from the bosom of the church.'[9]

Yet the fury of the Vatican was not translated into any effective
action. Innocent ordered the archbishop of Avignon to proceed
at once to the French court to reinforce the demands of Bagni.
When the archbishop was halted at Lyon by royal command, he
considered excommunicating Mazarin, but the sacred college
dissuaded him. In March 1653 Bagni presented a formal protest,
to which the queen responded that the pope had not seen fit to
intervene when the parlement had proscribed another cardinal
and put a price upon his head. The incident was promptly por-
trayed in the burlesque verses of Loret's *Muse historique*.[10] In June
Retz smuggled out of his prison a letter in Latin addressed to his
colleagues in Rome, denouncing Mazarin as one who had forgotten his own place as a cardinal and who 'under the mask of
royal authority insults the sacred college by holding one of its
members in chains'.[11] The letter circulated widely, but Valençay,
the French ambassador, who had sought to prevent Retz's promo-

tion to the cardinalate, reported to Mazarin that its effect was considerably diminished by the atrocious Latin constructions its author had employed. Relations with the Vatican improved slightly when the government received Innocent's anti-Jansenist bull, the *Cum occasione*. Mazarin remained the master of prevarication in the conflict with Rome, and the weapons of the Holy See continued to remain sheathed while Retz languished in Vincennes.

The link by which the prisoner had despatched his letter to Rome was established during the second week of his confinement. It was created by one of his oldest and loyalest friends, madame la présidente de Pommereuil, who bribed one of his gaolers, and, according to Guy Joly, pawned her jewels to do so.[12] Retz wrote to her regularly, as he did also to Caumartin and Hacqueville. Though his guards and gaolers were often changed during the fifteen months he spent in Vincennes, his commerce with the outside world through his trusted friends was never interrupted. With it came hope and the possibility of escape. Surveillance was closer for him than it had been for Condé during the imprisonment of the princes in 1650: yet he was kept as fully informed of outside events as ever Condé had been. The channel had its dangers, and Retz took pains to conceal his knowledge of current events in conversation with the officers of the guards. Pradelle, in particular, had been instructed to win his confidence, and often he seemed to impart information in order to test the prisoner's reactions. He elaborated to Retz the details of the triumphant return of Mazarin to Paris in February 1653, the festivities at the court and the applause of the fickle populace. Here there was no need for Retz to hide his feelings. It was otherwise when Pradelle pretended that Retz's distant relative, the vicomte de Bussy-Lameth, had died. The vicomte's cousin, the abbé de Lameth, was a close associate and master of the cardinal's household. The vicomte was a vital link in the plans laid by Retz's friends. He had remained firm in his willingness to hold his fortress of Mézières for Retz against the king. Malclerc was actually concerting schemes with him on the very day when Pradelle reported his alleged death. Retz controlled his features so well that Pradelle could not tell that his prisoner knew the report to be false.

Malclerc was constantly carrying proposal and counter-proposal between one conspirator and the next. Noirmoutier again seemed

ready to offer Charleville and Mont-Olympe as bases for military
operations, although his former confederates, Laigues and madame
de Chevreuse, tried to weaken his purpose. Condé and Spain were
prepared to enter into alliance with Retz's supporters. The government feared such an association and narrowly watched Condé's
agents. One was arrested in Paris, and another, Marigny, escaped
across the roof tops clad only in his shirt.[13] Croissy-Fouquet, the
magistrate who had upheld Condé's cause in the parlement and
had helped to negotiate the 1651 alliance between the Fronde and
the princes, was sent to Vincennes, together with Vineuil, one of
Condé's propagandists.[14] Although Retz's movements in the
château were too restricted for him to meet his fellow prisoners,
Croissy-Fouquet communicated with him by lowering messages
on a string from the room above.[15]

There were dangerous tensions within the network of external
conspiracy. Madame de Chevreuse and her lover were in touch
with Caumartin, but Guy Joly suspected they were tools of
Mazarin. Retz himself showed caution in the face of the conflicting
advice he received from the different factions in his party. This
was taken for a lack of resolution by such advocates of vigorous
action as his father, his secretary and his squire, but it was regarded
by Caumartin and other moderates as necessary prudence. Secretary Joly accused the duchesse de Retz of deliberately subverting
the plans of those who sought Retz's escape. He claimed she had
spies among a group of musicians visiting Machecoul who passed
information to Servien. On one occasion he believed she had
warned the minister of Malclerc's presence in Paris, and he had
narrowly escaped arrest. Madame de Lesdiguières also incurred
criticism from Guy Joly. He said she had falsely pretended that
père de Gondi wanted the cardinal to resign his claim to the archbishopric, and that she had sent a certain canon Bragelonne to join
Retz in Vincennes and give him this advice.[16] Joly spoke with
malice of the Gondi ladies, and his stories of their treachery are
implausible. Bragelonne, the brother of a judge in the parlement,
did act as Retz's chaplain in Vincennes, but he sank into a deep
melancholy under the stress of imprisonment, and finally cut his
own throat with a razor.

The work of the plotters outside Vincennes was linked with
schemes for the cardinal's escape from the fortress. Two general

plans were devised with the aid of Vacherot, Retz's physician, and Carpentier, the gaoler who transported the messages between the prisoner and his friends. Carpentier was no stranger to such affairs, for he had helped Beaufort to escape from Vincennes just before the first Fronde in 1648. The initial plan involved the scaling of various parts of the château by systems of jibs and pulleys. It was hardly to the cardinal's taste and was soon discarded as impracticable. The second required Carpentier to make his fellow gaoler drunk, so that Retz might evade the military guards and climb a tower, where he could conceal himself in a hole beneath some broken masonry. When Retz was safe in his hiding place, Vacherot was to give the alarm and lead the chase in the wrong direction, carrying a bloodied sword as if he had wounded the cardinal while trying to prevent his flight. Retz was to be equipped with bread and wine to enable him to hide in the hole for several days. When the hue-and-cry had diminished, he was to walk out of the château in disguise. This plan was frustrated when the route to the tower was blocked up in the course of renovations. Several variant schemes were discussed, but they came to nothing. At the worst, they were a means of passing the time. As Retz said of the death of the unfortunate canon Bragelonne, it was necessary in prison to come to terms with boredom.

Perhaps Mazarin had assumed that boredom and restraint would soon break the restless mind of his enemy. He used Pradelle to initiate discussions on the resignation of the cardinal's claim to the diocese of Paris. The ill-health of the archbishop made the matter more urgent, and in August 1653 Mazarin decided to make a formal offer of freedom provided Retz submitted his resignation and undertook to reside in Rome. He induced archbishop Bagni to put this proposition to Retz, although the nuncio could not undertake to persuade the prisoner to adopt a course directly opposed to papal policy. In his visit to Vincennes Bagni was accompanied by the secretary-ministers Le Tellier and Brienne. Retz completely turned the tables on the deputation. He had received prior warning of its coming, and Caumartin had smuggled into Vincennes the text of a discourse he thought appropriate to the occasion. Retz delivered it with all the *éclat* he could command. There was no hint of the compliance he had intimated privately to Pradelle. As a cardinal and archbishop-designate, ran the theme of his eloquent refusal, he would suffer every conceivable torment rather than commit an action inconsistent with his rank and his honour. Caumartin had an account of the interview ready for publication in Paris the following day, including the preliminary conversation alleged to have taken place between Mazarin and the nuncio.[17] The incident made the court look foolish, and brought a reproof for Bagni from the Vatican.

Retz did not maintain this pose with constancy. Despondency began to replace his mood of confidence, and he confided his willingness to resign to a young guards officer, Duflos-Davanton. He suggested that he might put the affair in order if he were first allowed to discuss it with Caumartin and Bellièvre, who had succeeded Molé as first president of the parlement. Davanton passed on the message to his suprior officer, the comte de Noailles, whom Retz regarded as his enemy because he had accepted the command confiscated by the queen from his friend, the marquis de Chandenier. Either through prudence or discretion, Davanton withheld details mentioned in confidence by the cardinal which, if known, would have prejudiced his chance of imposing suitable conditions. Retz went on talking of a possible surrender in the early weeks of 1654 without any response from Mazarin. Then the whole situation was suddenly transformed. At 4 a.m. on 21 March the archbishop of Paris died.

Retz and his friends had long anticipated this moment, and when it came they at once put their prepared plans into action. According to Claude Joly, canon of Notre-Dame, the news was conveyed to Retz by a special peal of bells at the cathedral, taken up and repeated in other churches until it could be sounded on the chapel bells of Vincennes. To confirm the news a priest was to mumble the late archbishop's name as he intoned the mass for the cardinal.[18] It was necessary for Retz to know of his uncle's death, but he personally had nothing further to do. A formal procuration had been drawn up on Caumartin's instructions authorising Retz's almoner, Pierre Labeur, to take possession of the diocese on behalf of the cardinal. It had been verified by the apostolic notary and by a doctor of the Sorbonne. Other letters were prepared appointing two parish priests, Lavocat and Chevalier, as grand-vicars to conduct the spiritual government of the see in Retz's name. Another commission nominated an official as the executive administrator, or vice-regent. These papers were made to appear as though they had been signed by Retz before his arrest, on an occasion when he had planned to go to Rouen and wished to provide for the possibility of his uncle's death. Guy Joly claimed that Retz's signature had been forged on some of these papers: his uncle, the canon, recalled that the apostolic notary had himself taken the documents to Vincennes for signature in the disguise of a merchant travelling in tapestries.[19]

Within an hour or so of the archbishop's death, Labeur appeared in Notre-Dame and was installed in possession of the diocese in Retz's name before the dean, the canons and the rest of the chapter. The papers were duly entered in the episcopal register, the *Te Deum* was chanted and the bells of the cathedral announced the advent of a new archbishop. A little later in the morning Le Tellier called upon the dean with a royal order to assemble the chapter to declare the diocese vacant and the reversion of its temporal administration to the crown. The minister was too late. Thus commenced the long struggle between church and state which became known as the ecclesiastical Fronde.

The government continued to maintain that Retz could not be recognised as archbishop because he had not taken the oath of secular loyalty to the crown required of the episcopacy. Arrangements were made for the crown's administration of the revenues of the diocese under the regalian right that applied during a vacancy. The chapter sent a delegation to the Louvre, hoping to offer remonstrances, and was, instead, admonished by the chancellor, who produced an edict of the council requiring the election of two new grand-vicars to conduct the spiritual government. The canons refused to comply, and sent the dean to inform the chancellor that they felt obliged to acknowledge Retz's jurisdiction. The cardinal's grand-vicars, Chevalier and Lavocat, ordered prayers for forty hours for his liberty and the exposure of the sacrament, in the manner of the clerical protest against Retz's initial arrest. These instructions were carried out in every parish church in the capital, and it seemed as if the clergy were united in defiance of Mazarin. The royal council then issued a second edict forbidding recognition of Retz's grand-vicars. Chevalier and Lavocat protested to the chancellor that their spiritual administration of the diocese was unconnected with the secular oath of

loyalty, which, at most, could apply only to the temporal administration. Retz had sent them a procuration authorising them to take
the oath on his behalf, but the chancellor refused to accept it.[20]

Mazarin hesitated to go further. His measures had served merely
to marshal public support for the prisoner of Vincennes, and even
such clerical officials as the dean of the chapter, who would have
preferred to support the government, felt obliged to go with the
majority. There were rumours of the imposition of an interdict
closing the churches. The nuncio was likely to support such a
move, and Bellièvre might rally the parlement against the crown.
Camille de Neufville, the new archbishop of Lyon, would support
Retz with the weight of his authority as primate of the Gauls.
The council of Retz's friends, organised by Caumartin, united the
various centres of opposition, and Condé's supporters fanned the
wind of discontent. Mazarin therefore decided to make fresh offers
to resume the discussions for Retz's resignation. At the same time
Retz was returning to his earlier state of depression. He feared that
he might be assassinated, and, underestimating the strength of his
supporters, he refused to sanction the interdict.

Both Pradelle and Noailles held up to their prisoner the opportunity of reconciliation with the government and suggested a
variety of revenues and dignities to compensate him for the loss
of the archbishopric. At first Retz refused these offers. Bellièvre
then brought an official proposal that, if the cardinal resigned the
see, he would be granted seven abbeys and his immediate release.
Twelve of his friends, including his brother, Brissac, Montrésor,
Caumartin and Hacqueville, were to serve as hostages until the
resignation had been approved by Rome. Retz began to weaken
at this suggestion. In his memoirs he asserted that Bellièvre had
secretly counselled him not to compromise his honour. At the
same time he pretended to see a division within the ranks of his
enemies. He believed, or feigned to believe, that Mazarin alone
was so obsessed by the influence he would continue to possess as
archbishop of Paris, that the first minister was prepared to grant
him liberty and almost any concession if he would resign. On the
other hand, Le Tellier and the abbé Fouquet wanted to keep Retz
in Vincennes, and Fouquet was using Pradelle to make offers he
hoped the cardinal would refuse. This was probably an argument
subsequently devised by Retz to justify his resignation in the eyes

of posterity. Guy Joly recorded the astonishment of Caumartin when Bellièvre told him that his patron was almost ready to resign.[21] Until the last moment Caumartin continued to believe that Retz was playing with his adversaries and would not abnegate his position of strength. When Bellièvre set out to visit Vincennes again on 28 March 1654, it was thought by Retz's friends that he went to fortify the cardinal's resolution, and Joly felt assured that the government would soon be obliged to surrender.

The document of resignation signed by Retz in the presence of Bellièvre was not, however, a simple expression of his weakness and despair after his long imprisonment and the continued disappointment of his hopes. The resignation could not be effective until it was accepted by Innocent x, and it was likely that the pope, wishing to save face, would regard the signature as extracted by duress and, consequently, invalid. Mazarin also feared this outcome. Retz was to be awarded the seven abbeys with revenues amounting to 120,000 livres, nearly twice those of the revenues of the diocese of Paris. Copies of the brevets of nomination and of the letters to Innocent were to be held by Bellièvre. Retz was to be released from Vincennes but held in the liberal custody of his old acquaintance, marshal de la Meilleraye, until the receipt of papal approval for both Retz's resignation and the appointment of his successor had been notified to the marshal by Bellièvre. A further clause required Retz to reside in Rome and not to leave the eternal city without the king's permission. The document was by no means the end of the ecclesiastical Fronde. Retz was to hold tenaciously to his archiepiscopal rights for a further eight years.

Many of Retz's friends were distressed at the news of his resignation. His family at Machecoul and his companions of the Fronde – Brissac, Noirmoutier, Laigues and madame de Chevreuse – betrayed a certain sense of relief that a desperate affair had reached a solution that had cost them nothing. Caumartin, Guy Joly, Malclerc and the chapter of Paris felt justifiably disappointed that their leader had surrendered when victory seemed on the point of attainment. And even if it were not a surrender, in the sense that Retz expected his resignation to be disavowed by the papacy, it was not a move which did him much credit. Père de Gondi, when congratulated at his son's release from prison, declared that he would rather have embraced him dead in Vincennes.[22]

Marshal de la Meilleraye had been instructed to escort Retz to Brittany, where the marshal was lieutenant-general, and to hold him in the château of Nantes. He was obliged to keep his guest under guard but was to permit him privileges inconceivable at Vincennes. He had known Retz from the days of his youthful amours, one of which had even involved madame la maréchale. He had been with him in the street riots of the first Fronde, and regarded him with that mixture of distrust and admiration which a man of limited intellect and unwavering loyalties reserves for one to whom principle is always capable of redefinition. According to custom he took Villequier, the officer who had arrested the cardinal, to Vincennes to assume delivery of his charge. He expected Retz to give his parole, but this was hardly valid when so close a guard was kept on him. Amid a large escort of cavalry and musketeers Retz and the marshal proceeded to Beaugency, where new troops were provided, and the party embarked for the long voyage down the Loire. On 12 April 1654 Retz arrived at Nantes.

The château of Vincennes had few comforts installed since its construction in the fourteenth century, for the new wings added by Mazarin had been scarcely begun during Retz's incarceration: that of Nantes had been built with the Renaissance tastes of the second half of the fifteenth century, but its fortifications had been extended during the wars of religion, and it was as much a fortress as a ducal palace. Retz's room was on the second floor of the so-called Horseshoe Tower. When he retired there at night his door was guarded by four soldiers, and a sentinel was also posted beneath his window. By day he often walked along a terrace escorted by two guards and constantly observed by two others. He could step through a gate on to a bastion overlooking the river, where there was a pleasant garden, but even there he was under close surveillance. However, although La Meilleraye took stringent measures to prevent the escape of his guest, he honoured the Vincennes agreement by allowing Retz entertainments and visits. Brissac and the young duc de Retz called upon the cardinal within a day of his arrival. Caumartin and Hacqueville also visited him. His personal entourage soon joined him, including Guy Joly, Malclerc, and his almoner, Pierre Camus, abbé de Pontcarré. The cardinal gambled with La Meilleraye and watched the comedies that were staged for his benefit. The ladies of Nantes society and from neighbouring provinces flocked to grace his salon. They came from curiosity, and returned to enjoy the pleasure of his conversation. Among them were madame de la Vergne, and her daughter, the future madame de La Fayette, who had entertained Retz and Brissac in Paris. Madame de la Vergne, who in 1650 had married the cardinal's cousin by marriage and fellow frondeur, Renaud de Sévigné, had a country house in Anjou. Retz delighted in this round of gaiety after the restrictions he had endured in Vincennes. The maréchale de la Meilleraye, who joined her husband from Paris after several weeks, was Brissac's sister. Brissac's wife, that Marguerite de Gondi with whom Retz had once tried to elope and who had subsequently become his mistress, was the sister of the duchesse de Retz. Machecoul was only a day's ride to the south of the Loire, and there were times when the château of Nantes appeared to have become a second seat for the Gondi family and their connections.

In such circumstances the reserve which the situation imposed upon marshal de la Meilleraye began to break down, although this did not induce him to relax his security precautions. While his loyalty to the crown was never in doubt, he had never had much respect for Mazarin – an attitude common to many who had served their apprenticeship under Richelieu. On one occasion Guy Joly heard him say to the cardinal that he regarded Mazarin as much more of a frondeur that any in Retz's faction.[23] Nevertheless, La Meilleraye was negotiating at this time to marry his son to Hortense Mancini, Mazarin's favourite neice. Retz thought that he was profoundly afraid of the first minister, but this did not prevent him from making use of any occasion to improve his own relations with the marshal. He showed him reports received from the abbé Charrier in Rome which Joly had deciphered. La Meilleraye responded by allowing Retz to see despatches from the court, and the cardinal realised that he could turn these confidences to his advantage by having Joly prepare his own version of Charrier's letters. The opportunity for this subterfuge soon arrived when the papal refusal to accept Retz's resignation became known at Nantes.

It had been a part of the Vincennes agreement that both Mazarin and Retz should send agents to Rome to press Innocent to recognise the surrender of the Gondi claim to the archbishopric. Guy Joly reported that Charrier, Retz's envoy, had managed to intercept the despatches of Mazarin's agent, the sieur de Gaumont, and to extract the deed of resignation.[24] Yet, if Retz had had any *arrière-pensée* about the pope's reaction when he signed the document, he now appreciated that the crown intended to keep to its intention not to release him until it had received ratification. Accordingly, he pressed Charrier to act in all sincerity. However, Innocent X was no more affected by Retz's pleas than he was by the temporary absence of the actual document. He maintained inflexibly that a deed signed in prison was a deed signed under duress. Retz sent Malclerc to Rome with an urgent request that the pope abandon the struggle and grant him his liberty. Innocent remained unmoved, and intimated that the honour of the entire church was in jeopardy. Retz must, if necessary, suffer for the universal cause. He hinted at the same time that Retz could best serve his own cause if he could somehow manage to come to Rome.

At the French court there were those who suggested that the pope's refusal was prompted by Retz and Charrier. It was asserted that the Vincennes agreement was no longer valid, and that the cardinal should be transferred to some harsher prison, before he could engineer his escape from Nantes. Caumartin and Bellièvre heard rumours of these opinions and sent word to Retz to try to escape while he could. La Meilleraye, too, received word from Paris that his prisoner had been deceiving him and had been secretly counselling the pope to support his authority as archbishop. When Retz provoked his host to reveal his feelings, the marshal added further information. He had heard a report from Paris that Retz had sent word to Gaston at Blois that he hoped soon to make La Meilleraye a member of his faction. The scene in which these recriminations were exchanged persuaded Retz that he must indeed plan his escape. In July 1654 La Meilleraye left Nantes to inspect another fortress, and during his absence Retz received a message from Montrésor that he was shortly to be moved to Brest. When the marshal returned, he tried to lull his suspicions by showing him forged despatches, allegedly from Charrier, indicating that the pope was beginning to change his mind.

Twenty months had passed since Retz had been arrested by Villequier in the queen's antechamber in the Louvre. During this time Mazarin had triumphed over all the forces of dissidence. He had resisted the passionate pleas of the queen to return to Paris until Turenne and La Ferté had driven Condé and his Spanish confederates from Champagne and Picardy.[25] After his arrival in the capital in February 1653 he turned all his military and diplomatic resources against Guyenne, where Condé's brother and sister directed the faction of the princes. Madame de Longueville's love affair with La Rochefoucauld had ended in disillusionment. She had tried to win the duc de Nemours from the influence of the duchesse de Châtillon, and La Rochefoucauld, for his part, had shamelessly conspired with the duchesse de châtillon to turn Condé towards an accommodation with Mazarin. Her younger brother, Conti, no longer accepted her tutelage. He showed impatience with Condé's agents, Lenet and président Viole, and put his own interests before those of the prince. In his household Retz's two former protégés, Sarasin and Marigny, quarrelled with each other. Marigny went to Paris to put his rancour at the service of La Rochefoucauld and to attack the reputation of madame de Longueville. It was during this visit that he was so nearly arrested through the treachery of the duchesse de Retz. Sarasin plotted to reconcile Conti with Mazarin through a marriage with one of the cardinal's nieces, and eventually the project was to win the poet a rich reward from the minister he had so shamelessly libelled.

When the Spanish refused any significant aid to the princes in Bordeaux, there was thought of an appeal to Cromwell, to whom Conti was prepared to offer La Rochelle. But the Lord Protector, who was also negotiating with Condé in Flanders, wanted Bordeaux itself, and ultimately Mazarin excluded the possibility of English intervention by recognising Cromwell's régime. The true masters of Bordeaux were the proletarian faction of the *Ormée*, who terrorised the magistrates and middle classes. La Rochefoucauld accused his former mistress of using the *Ormée* to prolong the war,[26] while Conti connived at the excesses of the radicals and plotted to disrupt their party. The royal forces steadily drew their net tighter about Bordeaux, and in June 1653 the final assault was about to be launched when Mazarin ordered a pause to allow the internal divisions within the city to run their course. At this point La Rochefoucauld's secretary, Gourville, completed his negotiations to reconcile his master with the court, and then

approached the princes with Mazarin's peace offers.[27] The revolt
of Guyenne ended with the treaty of July 1653. The red flags of
the *Ormée* were torn down and replaced with the dismembered
corpse of their leader, the butcher Duretête. Madame de Longueville retired from politics and became the patron of Port-Royal. In
1654 Conti married Anne-Marie Martinozzi, and he, too, became
the friend of Port-Royal. Condé's wife and son rejoined the prince
at Stenay. Retz's friend, the comte de Fiesque, fled to Spain with
Marsin, the commander of Conti's army. The Fronde of the
princes had ended, and only Condé himself remained in opposition.

Mazarin employed the same wiles he had used to disrupt the
family of Bourbon-Condé to win over the other houses of the
aristocracy. His nieces, the 'Mazarinettes', rejoined him in Paris
soon after his triumphant return in February 1653.[28] He deployed
them as though they were engines of war to set against the fortresses of his enemies. Even their mothers, the widowed mesdames
Mancini and Martinozzi, were sought after by those who looked
for marriage to bring them closer to the seat of power and patronage. Marie Mancini was later to awake the precocious instincts of
the king. Olympe Mancini attracted the king's interest even before
her sister, and later married Eugène de Savoie, who was to be
made comte de Soissons by royal decree to mark posthumous
pardon for his uncle, that other comte de Soissons who had been
killed at Marfée in 1641 leading the revolt in which Retz was
implicated. Laure Mancini, who had been pursued by Mercoeur in
defiance of the threats of the Paris parlement, married her lover
only to find her idyll destroyed when she went to join Mercoeur in
his government of Provence and found him in the arms of his
mistress. This hardly mattered to Mazarin, for the Vendôme
family was now secured in alliance with the court. Mercoeur's
father, the duc de Vendôme, commanded the fleet in the Bay of
Biscay. Beaufort had finally denounced the ineffective Gaston, and
consoled himself with the charms of madame de Montbazon. La
Meilleraye's son was eventually to marry Hortense Mancini and to
take the title of duc de Mazarin. In this way Mazarin affirmed his
claim to be the true successor to Richelieu, for La Meilleraye, as
he had indicated to Retz at Nantes, had not previously wished to
support one whose foppery seemed in such contrast to the commanding figure of La Meilleraye's cousin, the great cardinal.

Retz's rival and critic, La Rochefoucauld, recovered slowly from the savage wound and temporary blindness he had suffered in the battle of Porte Saint-Antoine, and moved gradually away from Condé, as he had from madame de Longueville. The gulf between the gallant illusions of those earlier years and the polished cynicism of his present mood was revealed in his parody of some lines from the dramatist du Ryer. The original, which corresponded closely enough to his worship of madame de Longueville, ran:

> To deserve her heart, and please her lovely eyes,
> I fought against the king, and would have fought the skies.

The parody, which mocked his own plight after his blinding, was:

> In this uncertain game, where, learning to be wise,
> I made war on the king, and lost thereby my eyes.[29]

Mazarin showed La Rochefoucauld no bitterness and allowed him to live at Damvilliers, where his brother-in-law, the marquis de Sillery, was governor and where once he had tried to incarcerate Retz. La Rochefoucauld accepted a pension and his son Marcillac became the companion of the king.

The various branches of the house of Lorraine also became supporters of the régime. The romantic duc de Guise, released after five years of imprisonment in Spain, commanded a new expedition to Naples in 1654, which failed as disastrously as the first in 1647. Harcourt, who had deserted his command in Guyenne to set himself up in Breisach, negotiated peace with Mazarin. Elbeuf, with his fellow general in the first Fronde, La Mothe-Houdancourt, obediently served the first minister. Madame de Chevreuse, following the path of such other former frondeuses as the princess Palatine and Retz's mistress, the princesse de Guémenée, also contrived to cooperate with Mazarin. She preferred to live in seclusion at Dampierre and, though she had none of the piety of her sister-in-law, the princesse de Guémenée, she developed several links with Port-Royal nearby. With her companion, Laigues, she helped Mazarin prevent her follower, the duc de Noirmoutier, from supporting either Retz or Condé, and she hoped in return that Chevreuse might be re-erected as a duchy for her son by her first marriage, the duc de Luynes. She defended the Jansenist curé of Saint-Merry, du Hamel, when he was exiled for supporting Retz.

I

Laigues was a particular friend of Port-Royal and a close associate of the Jansenist Arnauld d'Andilly.[30] Charles de Lorraine, the representative of the senior branch of the family, deserted Condé again after his second foray into France. He began to intrigue with Mazarin, and in 1654 was arrested by the Spanish in Brussels, greatly to the distress of his sister, Gaston's second wife.

Marguerite de Lorraine eventually despaired of persuading her husband to pursue any resolute line of action. Gaston's secretary, Goulas, had made his master sign a formula of reconciliation with the court, but the king's uncle remained in isolation at Blois for some years. He took the abbé de Rancé as his almoner, until the gay abbé attended the deathbed of madame de Montbazon in 1657 and underwent the conversion that made him the austere reformer of the monastery of La Trappe.[31] Gaston's entourage tended to maintain the habits of earlier times, and two of Retz's former associates who were in his suite, the comte de Fontrailles and conseiller Coulon, were disgraced in June 1654 for defrocking two monks and insulting the wives of the bourgeois. The old days when Gaston would walk through the Luxembourg palace, whistling through his teeth in apprehension of being forced to make some decision, had gone for ever. He busied himself with his coins and medals, and with his collection of exotic plants and animals. He even developed an interest in mathematics and astronomy.

La Grande Mademoiselle visited him occasionally. She had reproached him bitterly for accepting his exile, and had then herself retired to the sombre fortress of Saint-Fargeau in the valley of the Loing. There, with madame de Frontenac and her old companion madame de Fiesque, she occupied herself with reliving the adventures of the Fronde through their allegorical representation in the romances of the day. That which was most in fashion in 1654 was mademoiselle de Scudéry's *Clélie*, in which Retz was represented as Tarquin, a man of religion with the religious, a libertine with the libertines, and a philosopher with the philosophers. The times had passed when Mademoiselle could occupy Orléans with her ladies, or turn the cannon of the Bastille upon the king's forces. Condé suggested she should throw herself into the fortress of Honfleur, and offer fresh defiance to the upstart Mazarin. Instead, she turned to the law and fought a protracted lawsuit against her father, who, she claimed, was making use of

her lands to help her step-sisters. Madame de Longueville, La
Rochefoucauld, Beaufort, madame de Chevreuse, Gaston and la
Grande Mademoiselle – all the colourful, anarchic figures of the
frondeur nobility – seemed to have submitted to the forces of
piety or convention.

The parlement had gone the way of the aristocracy. Mazarin had
relied upon Molé and the attorney-general, Nicolas Fouquet, to
hold together the royalist party among the judges. He had converted the remainder by clemency and graceful gestures. Only a
few of the magistrates were excluded from the October amnesty,
and no one questioned the suppression of the constitutional powers
of the parlement in the *lit de justice*, just four years since the demands of the reforming party had been granted in October 1648.
Molé led a deputation to the Louvre on 3 February 1653 to pay
homage to the man whom they had branded as an enemy of the
state and disturber of the public peace, whose arrest, dead or alive,
they had decreed in solemn assembly, and whose property they
had sold to the highest bidder. The enemies of the magistrature,
the financiers, had regained their influence over the machinery of
state. Their leader was the attorney-general himself, Nicolas
Fouquet. Fouquet's splendour was such that the republic of letters
was reassembled under his patronage. Abel Servien, his rival in
this respect, was also his rival in the fiscal aspects of government.
After the death of old Vieuville in January 1653 Servien and
Fouquet were jointly appointed to the superintendency of the
finances. The corrupt practices of the past were reintroduced, but,
though Pomponne de Bellièvre, Retz's friend and Molé's successor
as first president, resented the activities of Fouquet and the tax-
farmers, Mazarin carefully placated the magistrates. The parlement
settled down in its role as the judicial support of the administration. The ministers it had once criticised along with Mazarin and
Servien continued to advance in power. Le Tellier, already secretary of state, was granted in addition the post of the late Chavigny
as treasurer of the king's chest. Lyonne was transferred to Rome
to occupy the embassy previously held by the bailli de Valençay,
while the abbé Fouquet continued to act as Mazarin's unofficial
head of secret police.

In everything that Mazarin had attempted since the imprisonment of Retz his subtlety, his patience and his foresight had

brought him an entire mastery of both his friends and his enemies. He had allied himself with most of the great houses of the aristocracy and neutralised the remainder. He had outmanoeuvred the parlement and reduced it to subservience. He had conquered the last stronghold of the Fronde of the princes in Bordeaux, and was sufficiently free of internal distractions to prosecute the war against Spain with vigour. Everywhere Retz's opponents seemed confirmed in their authority, and his former friends among the nobility and magistrature could no longer be relied upon. Only in the church were there still active signs of discontent, and it was here that Retz, when considering his escape in the summer of 1654, hoped to gain some advantage. Caumartin had persuaded the cardinal that if he escaped he should proceed at once to Paris under escort of his friends. The royal army was on the Flanders frontier, attempting to break the siege of Arras by Condé and the Spanish, and the court was absent from the capital. If Retz could reach Paris, he could disown the resignation and register his oath of loyalty with the *chambre des comptes*, where the first president would support him. With the aid of Bellièvre he could begin to exercise his authority in Notre-Dame, or, failing this, withdraw to the safety of Mezières. Noirmoutier had also given assurances that his fortresses were at the disposal of the cardinal.

The first plan to escape from the château of Nantes involved the direct cooperation of Brissac. The duke was a frequent visitor to the castle, and invariably travelled with a large train of baggage containing his extensive wardrobe. It was agreed that a large box should be prepared and brought into Brissac's room immediately beneath that of the cardinal. A hole would be cut in the floor to allow Retz to descend. Brissac would find an excuse for a hurried departure, and Retz would be carried through the gates in the box. A few days before the date set for this attempt Brissac visited Machecoul. When he returned he said that he had decided the plan took too great an advantage of his brother-in-law's generosity. Retz protested that the code of friendship outweighed that of hospitality, but Brissac would not do more than offer to help once Retz was outside the walls of the château. It seemed to the cardinal as though his friend has been unduly influenced by the caution of the family at Machecoul. Guy Joly's account confirms that Brissac raised the question of his honour being compromised, but suggests that the duchesse de Retz was prepared to play the part in which he had originally been cast.[32] The duchess, who was staying in the room below Retz at the time, was the more ready to oblige since she had quarrelled with the duke and wished to demonstrate her independence. Joly was sent in advance to Machecoul, but returned with the unqualified veto of both her father and her husband.

A second plan had already been under consideration. It involved the distraction of the sentinels and the descent of Retz by a rope to the river bank, where horses and an escort would be waiting. The abbé Rousseau, whose brother was Retz's man of affairs in Paris, was summoned to Nantes. The abbé had been that member of Retz's entourage who had knocked the poet Ménage unconscious in a drunken quarrel. He was chosen for his immense strength, for it was he who was to lower the cardinal over the battlements. Vacherot, who had conceived the escape plans of Vincennes, was one of the principal plotters, and both Retz and Joly remarked that his cool judgment was needed to balance the ebullience of the mighty abbé Rousseau. Fromentin and Imbert, Retz's valets, were initiated to the secret and given the task of distracting the guards. Three swordsmen formerly in the cardinal's service, Montet, Boisguérin and Beauchesne, were asked to provide the escort, since after the descent Retz would have to gallop through the suburbs of Richebourg, which was frequented by La Meilleraye's guards when they were off duty. The Scottish priest Salmonet was also summoned as one likely to aid the escape, but he, of all those concerned, alone lacked the resolution needed, and burst into tears when he could not dissuade his patron.

Soon after the duchesse de Retz had left the château to return to Machecoul, Joly met Brissac's squire, La Bade, in Richebourg to arrange final details for the escape. The attempt was to take place at 5 p.m. on 8 August. The escort was to bring the horses below the walls as if they were watering them before departing on a hunting foray. Although the river was low it would not be possible to lead the horses directly beneath the bastion, and the place where they were to be stationed was hidden from the spot to which Retz was to descend. Accordingly the learned Dr. Paris was placed on the far bank, where he would be able to see both the escort and Retz's descent, and instructed to wave his hat three times at the appropriate moment. La Bade assured Joly that Brissac and Renaud de Sévigné would be waiting some ten miles upstream at 6 p.m. Boats would be available to cross the Loire at this point, and a series of relays and escorts would be ready to convey the cardinal to Paris.

Retz informed his entourage of these plans at 2 p.m. Montet, Boisguérin and Beauchesne set out to join La Bade and take delivery of the horse he had brought for the prisoner. Rousseau prepared to hide the rope under his cassock. Salmonet retired lamenting to his room. When the appointed hour came the cardinal was seized with sudden indecision and tried to postpone the attempt. Imbert and Joly besought him to forget the qualms inspired by Salmonet's weakness, and assured him they would not remain in the château if he did not carry through their plan. It was fifteen minutes before Retz was again in command of his emotions. He walked out on to the terrace with Vacherot and Rousseau, and then summoned Fromentin and Imbert to bring him wine. When he had drunk, the valet and the surgeon offered wine to the guards, who retired behind the wall of the Horseshoe Tower to drink it. Retz passed through the door to the bastion, shutting it behind him, and, taking off his red cassock, placed it on a stick between the battlements to delude the distant sentinels into thinking he was praying in the garden. Rousseau produced his rope and lowered Retz slowly over the side of the wall. Swimming in the river below was one of La Meilleraye's pages, who at once began to shout that the cardinal was escaping. By chance the guards on the battlements, who saw the page but could not hear his cries, misinterpreted his signals. A little downstream another swimmer, a Dominican friar, had been caught by the current and appeared to be drowning. His frantic plunges were thought to be the subject of the gesticulations of the page, and his death throes entirely distracted attention from Retz. But a new difficulty arose. The priest Paris had lost his nerve and deserted his post. It was fortunate that the valets of Joly and the abbé Rousseau happened also to be watching events and signalled the horsemen to advance. Retz was hoisted into the saddle by Montet and La Bade, and the group galloped away from the château through the narrow streets of Richebourg.[33]

The streets were wet and slippery. The cardinal's horse was a fresh and vigorous animal and he tried to keep a tight rein to prevent it escaping his control. It was imperative to reach the outer gates of Nantes before they could be closed. Boisguérin called to the party to draw their pistols as he saw two of La Meilleraye's guards ahead, but the guards did not impede their progress. A little farther on, Retz's horse stumbled and threw its inexperienced rider. Retz fell heavily, dislocating his shoulder. A crowd quickly gathered at the scene of the accident. Joly and Montet rode back, brandishing their pistols, but no one showed any desire to interfere. Indeed, there were some who cheered the cardinal when they recognised him. He was helped back into the saddle and the party resumed its headlong gallop. Retz was in great pain, and Joly noticed that from time to time he tore hair from his head in anguish. He swayed in the saddle without responding to the efforts of his companions to cheer his spirits. At the village of Mauves they paused for a minute to allow Retz to drink. The horses of Boisguérin and Beauchesne foundered and they were obliged to turn aside. The remainder reached the rendez-vous with Brissac and Sévigné, and entered the boats, where Retz fainted. He was revived by water thrown in his face, and spoke for the first time since his fall. Two hours behind them La Meilleraye's son was galloping in pursuit at the head of a body of horsemen, 'all the cuckolds of Nantes' as Retz described them, recalling the entertainment his prison had provided for their ladies. The guards on the battlements had been too afraid to pass the news to the marshal. It had taken the page some time to leave the river, run round the castle to the main gate and give the alarm, and there was a further delay before the pursuing party could be assembled. When it reached the place where Retz had crossed, it found the remaining boats had been sunk. La Meilleraye's son wanted to lead a small party of a dozen or so who would swim their horses across the river, but it was pointed out that Brissac would have assembled a strong escort, and the pursuit was temporarily abandoned.

La Meilleraye was infuriated by the escape, especially since he realised that he had been duped by the supposed reports from Charrier. He issued a manifesto disclaiming the suggestion, for which he held the ducs de Retz and de Brissac responsible, that he had connived at the escape.[34] He took vigorous measures to

identify the cardinal's accomplices, and gave orders for his troops
to scour the countryside on both banks of the river. Vacherot and
Salmonet were arrested, but were eventually released for lack of
evidence. Some of the servants of the cardinal's entourage were
maltreated for a time before they, too, were given their liberty.
Doctor Paris was arrested by a detachment of guards which
crossed the Loire near the château and took the south road for
Brissac's domain at Beaupréau. He pleaded his innocence so
vehemently that he was detained for only one day. Beauchesne,
after losing his horse, was nearly intercepted by La Meilleraye's
squire, Coulon, but he held off his assailant with a pistol while he
commandeered a boat and made his escape. He and Boisguérin
made their way to Paris by different routes. Malclerc had not
returned from his journey to Rome. Imbert and the abbé Rousseau
walked out of the château, hid in a neighbouring house, and left
Nantes next day in disguise.[35]

It was nearly 9 p.m. when, a mile or two to the south of their
crossing place, Retz called out that he could endure the pain of his
injured shoulder no longer. He and Montet dismounted and concealed themselves in a haystack beside the road. Sévigné went off
to ask some relatives nearby to provide a secure refuge for Retz,
while Brissac and Joly set off for Beaupréau with hopes of finding
armed protection. Retz grew feverish and thirsty in the heat of the
hay, but horsemen were heard on the road, among them Coulon
and his party. Sévigné's request of his relatives was refused, and it
was not until 2 a.m. that one of Brissac's gentlemen, La Poise-
Saint-Offranges, arrived with a litter and had Retz carried to his
house two miles away. Here he slept during the morning, and was
then obliged to climb through a trapdoor and lie hidden in a dark
cellar. The next day he was concealed under straw in a neighbouring barn. There were several alarms and reports of approaching
search parties and passing horsemen, but they remained undis-
covered. In the late afternoon of 10 August a small escort arrived
to convey the cardinal to Beaupréau. Madame de Brissac behaved
with steadfast loyalty to her husband, but her sympathies were
apparent when she gave Retz some brandy and remarked that she
wished it were poison. By this time Brissac had been able to
assemble over two hundred horsemen. Without further delay the
cortège set out for Machecoul, with Retz in a carriage and servants

carrying torches to light the way ahead. The peasantry were in arms along the route. At dawn they reached the town of Montaigu, where the cardinal's brother was waiting with another large body of retainers. The escort was now so strong that they could afford to take the road past the château of Nantes on the south bank of the river. La Meilleraye did not attempt to launch a serious attack on the column, and they turned southwards to reach Machecoul late in the afternoon of 11 August.

Although the last part of his journey had been eased by placing mattresses in his carriage, Retz was still in extreme pain. His arm was black from the shoulder to the elbow, and he was obliged to retire to bed. An aged and ignorant physician in the duc de Retz's suite, a certain Brocard, inspected the patient and declared that the bones were not displaced and that the cardinal suffered only from severe bruising. This mistaken diagnosis was to leave Retz partially crippled for the rest of his life. Although all the nobility of the province seemed to have gathered at Machecoul to share in the notoriety of the visitor, the cardinal did not feel that his family regarded him as a welcome guest. The hostility of the duchesse de Retz and her father was evident from the moment of his arrival. They reproached him for failing to confide his plans to them, insisted that he ought to have obeyed the king, and had Brissac suggest to Retz that he confirm his resignation with the court. Their attitude was inspired by fear of La Meilleraye, who was rumoured to be preparing a force to besiege Machecoul. Despite his injury, Retz resolved to leave France by sea.

The accident in Richebourg and the misfortunes of the succeeding two days had obliged the cardinal to abandon completely his intention of returning to the capital. But he did not forget his interests there. He had prepared a document, dated 8 August, the day of his escape, to revoke his resignation of the archbishopric, which he declared to have been 'extorted by force and violence in the prison of the keep of Vincennes'.[36] This was taken to Paris by Montet and delivered to the chapter. He sent also a letter of the same date from 'near Beaupréau', addressed to the dean, canons and chapter of Notre-Dame, explaining that he desired 'to use his first moment of liberty' to express his profound gratitude for their support. He wished, he said, to live and die with them in the role of their archbishop.[37] He wrote also to the curés of Paris in similar terms.[38] The news of his escape was received by the clergy in the capital with lively emotion. While the court was close to the scene of operations in Flanders, Séguier had been left in Paris with Servien and Nicolas Fouquet, who were jointly in charge of financial matters. All three thought of leaving the city when they heard that Retz was at liberty and likely to come to Paris.[39] As the first alarm subsided they began to react against the dissident attitude of the chapter. This seemed almost an open contempt for the government:

Their joy was so great and immoderate [wrote an anonymous diarist of the time] that without any thought for the respect they owed the royal authority, they gave vent to their feelings by pealing the great bells, by lighting a fire in front of the cathedral, and by publicly chanting the *Te Deum* there on the 13th of the month with as much rejoicing and solemnity as if the prisoner had escaped from the chains and torments of the Turks.[40]

Some of the curés read the cardinal's letter to their congregations, and the chapter sent Retz a letter of congratulation.[41] After formal registration of the revocation of the deed of resignation by the chapter, it was sent to Rome with the brother of Chevalier, one of the grand-vicars.

As soon as Mazarin heard of Retz's escape, he instructed La Meilleraye to assemble the nobility of Poitou and Saintonge and set siege to Machecoul. He responded to the defiance of the Parisian clergy by summoning the grand-vicars, together with Claude Joly, two other canons and two curés, to appear before the council at Péronne.[42] On 20 August the council issued an ordinance for the arrest of the cardinal, in which Retz was denounced for breaking faith and organising revolt, both in the provinces and in Paris, by illicit assemblies and the incendiary acts of his agents.[43] Letters signed by the king and Le Tellier were sent to L'Hôpital, the governor of Paris, and to the *prévôt des marchands*, instructing them to prevent the rebellion of the people. Another ordinance dated 22 August required all Retz's servants, agents and supporters to leave the capital within twenty-four hours on pain of imprisonment. There followed an edict declaring the diocese of Paris vacant.[44] At first the grand-vicars were not to be cowed by this flagrant deposition of their archbishop. On 23

August they published an instruction, or *mandement*, supposedly from Retz, threatening the excommunication of anyone who recognised any jurisdiction save his own.[45] However, the chapter capitulated five days later and nominated four new grand-vicars.

There was no likelihood of armed resistance to the government in Paris, but it was certainly true that Retz's friends there were active in his cause. Bellièvre refused the demand of the abbé Fouquet that he should surrender the duplicate copy of the cardinal's resignation. On a blank sheet of paper signed by Retz, Caumartin had composed a letter to the king and the queen mother offering the cardinal's obedient respects in his capacity of archbishop of Paris.[46] Although this letter was ignored there were some hopes of a settlement when the princess Palatine wrote to say Mazarin might conceivably negotiate when the campaign at Arras was over. The unreliable Noirmoutier indicated that he was ready once more to offer Charleville as a refuge. In a letter to Retz he criticised the cardinal's friends in Paris as incompetent, untrustworthy and of inadequate status. If Retz went to Rome, Noirmoutier argued, he would find nothing but prejudice and hypocrisy, and he might as well plan to go to China for all the good it would do him.[47] Others, more influential than Noirmoutier, hoped to profit their own cause by association with Retz. Condé hoped to reach an understanding with him, and suggested that Fuensaldagne might order the Spanish army to march on Paris on his behalf. The fortunes of war soon put an end to this possibility. On 25 August Turenne, Hocquincourt and La Ferté broke Condé's siege lines round Arras, and obliged the Spanish to retire. At Péronne Mazarin was now free to devote more attention to the problems created by the escape of his enemy.

While his supporters were receiving the first news of his flight, the cardinal was preparing to leave Machecoul. Even before the receipt of his orders from Mazarin, La Meilleraye had taken measures to guard the Breton coast and to prepare his forces to attack the duchy of Retz. Only a few miles of flat sandy country separated Machecoul from a tidal inlet where the coastal village of La Roche-Bernard was situated. There was no vessel there large enough to take Retz to Spain or Holland, but there were several shallow-drafted boats which could transport the fugitive to some more convenient place of refuge. Belle-Ile was securely in the

control of the Gondi family, having descended to the elder duc de
Retz from his father, that marquis de Belle-Ile who died in an
assault on Mont Saint-Michel during the wars of the League. It
was decided that, if the cardinal could reach Belle-Ile in safety,
arrangements could be made for a ship to transport him abroad.
On the night of 14 August Retz was carried in a litter to La Roche.
There he embarked with Brissac, Sévigné, Joly and Brocard,
while a retinue of some thirty gentlemen boarded three other small
boats. They set sail at once, and put in next day in the bay of Le
Croisic, just north of the mouth of the Loire, to shelter from bad
weather. They feared not only an encounter with one of the
patrolling ships of La Meilleraye but also an attack from armed
Biscayan barques. These Spanish vessels frequented the Breton
coast, and, after the fugitives had left Le Croisic, one such barque
sighted the small fleet and gave chase. The Spaniard fired several
cannon shots but did not follow them inshore. They were forced
to land near a ruined church, and as Retz feared capture by the
local forces they spent the day in hiding. They put to sea again
that night. The rest of the voyage was less eventful, and they
arrived at Belle-Ile under cover of a thick fog on 18 August. On
the same day Mazarin received a report that La Meilleraye had
reached Machecoul, where the elder duc de Retz had promptly
surrendered, and the secret of Retz's destination had been revealed.

Retz remained on the island for ten or twelve days. His shoulder
improved gradually, despite the attentions of the doctor. The
younger duc de Retz joined the party and busied himself organising the defences. There was a garrison of one hundred and fifty
men, in addition to Retz's entourage and a makeshift militia, who
were to rally to the fort on the sound of a cannon shot. Reports
arrived that La Meilleraye was fitting out an expedition to attack
them, and every passing sail that was sighted brought a new alarm.
La Meilleraye had indeed been ordered to assault Belle-Ile in
cooperation with a fleet supplied by the comte d'Entragues in La
Rochelle. But here the marshal proved more dilatory and on 25
August, when he wrote to the comte d'Estrades in Bordeaux to
say there was no need for further troops to be sent to Saintonge,
he gave no indication of any plan to attack Retz's place of refuge.[48]
It was difficult for the fugitives to decide upon their future action
until news had been obtained about reactions in Paris. This was

brought by the faithful Boisguérin, who had evaded La Meilleraye's troops and had even succeeded in calling on mesdames de
Retz and de Brissac in the course of his return journey from Paris.
Retz began to find that his associates were now anxious to be rid
of him. Sévigné was afraid his estates would be seized; Brissac
seemed to think he had done more than enough to compensate for
his inactivity during Retz's imprisonment; while the young duc de
Retz was constantly receiving admonitions from his wife and
father-in-law.

Three courses seemed open to the cardinal. He might go to
Charleville, join Condé in Flanders, or take ship for Spain. Joly
alone favoured the idea of using Noirmoutier's fortress. The ducs
de Retz and de Brissac opposed it, and wanted Retz to embark on
a Hamburg ship, bound for Holland, that was standing offshore.
The cardinal refused this suggestion, for he feared the ship's
captain might prefer to deliver him to La Meilleraye at Nantes. He
wanted to board a Biscayan corsair that was watering on the other
side of the island. Both his brother and Brissac stood firm against
this proposal on the ground that contact with a Spanish warship
would incriminate them. Retz became increasingly impatient at
the delays and alarms. It was finally resolved that he, Joly,
Boisguérin, another gentleman named Sales and a valet should
disguise themselves as army deserters and sail for Spain on a small
barque manned by five sailors. They gave out that Retz had
boarded a Dutch vessel, and for two nights after this ship's
departure the cardinal remained in hiding until his own barque
was made ready. Preparations for the voyage were exceedingly
meagre. Little money was available, so the duc de Retz bought a
consignment of sardines which were loaded on board as a cargo
that might be sold on arrival. Thus Retz left his influential friends,
and set out on a long and perilous Odyssey dressed in rags,
accompanied by only four retainers, and equipped with nothing
to provide for the future save a cargo of rotting fish.

ELEVEN

Exile

The fishing boat in which Retz and his four retainers left Belle-Ile took three days to reach the Spanish port of San Sebastian, where they landed on 12 September 1654. The voyage was full of incident. They ran before a storm, lost the ship's compass overboard and were quite unable to determine their position. They were pursued for a time by a Moroccan pirate and escaped by sheltering off a coast which they could not identify. On the following day they found themselves well to the west of Bilbao, and, with adverse currents and poor navigation had the greatest difficulty in reaching San Sebastian. Eventually they were taken into port by another vessel, and left their cargo of sardines to follow the next day. When they came ashore their tattered military dress and lack of papers aroused such suspicion that the port authorities promised them a hanging. Retz insisted that he was known to the baron de Vatteville, a nobleman from Franche-Comté who had cooperated with the princes in Guyenne and was governor of the region where Retz had landed. Joly was granted an interview by Vatteville, who was at first incredulous of the story he heard. After a short delay the governor called on Retz in the primitive hostelry where he was lodged. He remained unconvinced of the identity of his visitors for a day or two, but he did transfer them to the comfort of his own residence. Retz remained in bed for some time, recovering from the fatigue of the voyage and the injury to his shoulder. A surgeon who examined him declared that it was too late to put the joint back in. The party was not entirely dependent on Vatteville's hospitality, for the cargo of sardines had been sold and a second cargo, sent from Belle-Ile, was also disposed of. Beauchesne arrived in the second ship with news of Condé's retreat from Arras and the capitulation of the chapter in Paris.

Retz had sent off Boisguérin to Madrid to obtain permission to

cross Spain and embark for Italy. Boisguérin returned bearing as a
gift a heavy chain of gold from Luis de Haro, the principal minister of Philip IV. Further Spanish gold and armed protection were
promised, but Haro had made it clear that he wanted Retz to visit
Madrid and then to proceed to Charleville. Although the Spanish
desired an alliance between Retz and Condé, the cardinal had
decided to concentrate solely on his ecclesiastical rights and not to
involve himself in the treason of his old enemy. He wrote in his
memoirs that he managed to avoid Condé's agents to Vatteville in
San Sebastian, and that he had instructed Boisguérin not to involve
himself too deeply with Fiesque, the prince's representative in
Madrid. Nevertheless, it is likely that Retz did talk with Mazerolles,
Condé's envoy to Vatteville. Mazarin's intelligence service reported that such discussions had occurred, and also that Trancars,
Condé's envoy to Cromwell, had travelled from London to San
Sebastian to see Retz, and had called at Belle-Ile on his return
journey.[1] Mazarin tended to sneer at Retz's presence in Spain. On
22 September he wrote to the duc de Gramont to say he had had
news of Retz's arrival in San Sebastian: 'It is a mark of the charity
of this great luminary of the church that, having spread such light
in France, he should choose to extend his illuminations to Spain
also . . .'[2] He pursued Retz with a malevolence markedly in contrast with his attempts to mollify his other opponents. As soon as
he received the information of Retz's arrival in Spain, he had the
parlement prepare an indictment of treason.

Towards the end of September, don Christoval de Crassembach,
Haro's secretary, arrived in San Sebastian with a litter which he
placed at Retz's disposal. The secretary also brought a large sum
of money and letters of credit for 50,000 crowns. He intimated
that more would be available if Retz agreed to proceed to Charleville, but he also made it plain that, if the cardinal insisted on
crossing Spain and taking ship for Italy, the Spanish government
would assist him in his journey. Joly tried to persuade his patron
to accept both the money and the advice. Little could be achieved
in Rome and, even if the pope did provide vigorous support,
Mazarin would marshal Gallican sentiment against him. Joly
agreed with the Spanish that the only way for Retz to recover his
diocese was to join Condé and to force Mazarin to negotiate.[3]
Retz would have none of this. Like his friends in Belle-Ile and

Paris, he believed that the proper place for a clerical supplicant of his status was in Rome. The French, he commented, might be over-sceptical, but the Spanish were too inflexibly attached to general principles to see how particular circumstances might vary their application. He refused Crassembach's gold and asked only that the Spanish should defend his brother and Brissac in Belle-Ile if La Meilleraye attacked them. Beauchesne was sent back to Belle-Ile to report this promise and indicate Retz's future intentions. On 1 October the exiled cardinal set off in the litter on the long journey to Valencia. He adopted the style of a Burgundian nobleman, the marquis de Saint-Florent, who was on his way to Milan to serve Philip IV. Behind this supposed marquis rode his retainers upon mules, together with don Pedro, the master of Vatteville's household, who was to disburse expenses which Retz had undertaken to repay to the governor.

The disguise adopted by the cardinal was far from effective. Mazarin was accurately informed of Retz's plans, although he chose to pretend that Retz was going to Madrid to inspire a Spanish invasion of Guyenne. Moreover, two days after leaving San Sebastian the cortège encountered a group of French merchants, who recognised Retz and subsequently reported the fact to the investigating tribunal in the parlement. There were no further incidents until they reached Tudela, a town on the river Ebro forty-five miles south of Pampeluna. The peasantry and town labourers had risen against the authorities in a series of riots reminiscent of those in provincial France. Retz was mistaken for a visiting official and found himself besieged in his hostelry by a noisy crowd, who shouted and sang throughout the night and seemed likely to burst through the guard of militia posted outside the inn. The militia itself was thought to be disaffected and the municipal authorites expected a massacre. The cardinal remained in his quarters for three days until a detachment of musketeers arrived from the viceroy of Navarre at Pampeluna. When the party resumed its journey it was accompanied by the musketeers to the frontiers of Aragon. Travel in Spain had its discomforts. By night they stopped at local inns which, according to Guy Joly, were seldom furnished with beds. When they reached Saragossa, the capital of Aragon, they were received with some ceremony and shown over the town by gentlemen from the viceroy's suite. Retz

noticed that there were many French artisans in Saragossa. It
touched his sense of irony that the Alcazar of the former Moorish
kings now housed the office of the Inquisition. He was addressed
as the marquis de Saint-Florent, but it was obvious that his hosts
were aware of his identity. In the church of Our Lady of the Pillar
he was granted a privilege reserved only for cardinals and princes:
he was allowed to see the sanctuary where the Virgin had appeared
on a pillar to Saint James. Retz was inwardly sceptical of the local
miracles celebrated in the place: he much preferred the visits of
the ladies of the city to his establishment, and was particularly
pleased when he was mistaken for Charles II of England.

From Aragon they travelled through Valencia where the fruit
and flowers made the cardinal reflect that it was the finest garden
in the world. On 14 October they entered the port of Vinaroz,
and were welcomed by don Fernando Carillo, commanding a
squadron of Neapolitan galleys. The viceroy's representative
arrived soon afterwards with gifts of cases of Valencia preserves,
Spanish gloves and a scented purse heavy with gold. Retz gave
the preserves to the captain of the galley on which he embarked,
the gloves to Carillo and the money to Vatteville's major-domo
with instructions to repay his master. The galley was the flagship
of the squadron, manned by one hundred and twenty soldiers,
eighty sailors and some two hundred and fifty slaves. They put to
sea at once and, assisted by a tail wind, arrived at Majorca within
twenty-four hours. A system of quarantine was in force because
the plague was raging in Aragon. However, the viceroy allowed
them to land, provided they slept on board. They were welcomed
by a procession of all the carriages of the nobility on the island,
and fêted for three days while contrary winds delayed their
departure. At night they would return to the galley with the torch-
light dancing on the water and the sound of trumpets and the
salute of cannon ringing in their ears. Retz dined with the viceroy
in a tent of gold brocade, attended balls and was serenaded by a
choir of nuns in a convent. His libertine instincts made him descry
a passion more human than divine in the singing. The abiding
impression which both he and Joly retained was of the astonishing
beauty of the local ladies.

On 19 October the galley sailed for Minorca, reaching Port
Mahon in twelve hours. There they remained for six days,

although the strict enforcement of the quarantine regulations prevented their landing. The harbour was a striking one with a narrow entrance, broadening to a wide basin surrounded by mountains on all sides. The steep slopes, tall trees and cascading streams impressed the cardinal, not because of natural beauty in itself but because, he wrote, it surprised him that it could surpass the contrived perspectives of the Italian stage scenery to which he was so much more accustomed. They took on provisions and engaged in fishing. The captain provided some entertainment for his passengers by having the slaves dive for a particular kind of shellfish embedded in rocks. There were four false starts before the wind turned sufficiently in their favour. Their crossing of the Gulf of Lion was fast and smooth, and within thirty-six hours they sighted the coast of Sardinia. They considered putting in at the harbour of Porto-Conte but decided against it. It was as well they did not land, because the duc de Guise was sheltering there with his fleet on the way to Naples. The Genoese fortress of San Bonifacio fired four cannon shots as they passed, which were assumed to be a signal of the presence of the French at Porto-Conte.

Soon after this incident they sighted a small Barbary corsair. Carillo, a young nobleman of twenty-four who was constantly in search of excitement and adventure, immediately proposed to his guest that he should have the pleasure of watching an engagement. They gave chase, and, as the Turkish frigate had a good lead, a course was set close in shore to intercept her. Carillo withdrew to the poop to play piquet with Joly until they were within closer range of their prey. Suddenly the galley shuddered and stopped. She had run hard upon a sand bank. In the belief that they were sinking, the galley slaves clamoured to be released, and some of them began to break their chains. Carillo threw a sword to Retz and led his soldiers between the rowing benches, striking out on either side until order had been restored. He was anxious to ensure the safety of his guest while he tried to refloat the galley, so he had Retz placed in a long boat with thirty Spanish musketeers for protection. The party rowed to a small reef some fifty yards away. There Retz stood awkwardly upon the few square feet of dry land while his escort surrounded him up to their waists in water. They could not be persuaded to return to the galley and end that un-

comfortable vigil because at any moment an attack was expected
by the bands of Corsicans who descended on any wrecked ship.
After two hours their vessel was refloated and discovered to be
sound. The party on the reef reboarded the galley, and they once
more gave chase to the Turkish frigate. Eventually they caught
up with their quarry, and found her to be manned by Genoese
sailors, who had captured her from the corsairs and were taking
her to port. Retz felt a certain sense of relief, for to have
been wounded in such an imprudent affray would have invited
ridicule.

They watered at Porto-Vecchio, but a report that the French
fleet had sighted the galley decided them to abandon their shelter
rather than risk being trapped by a night attack. They put out from
the Corsican coast in darkness, fearing the currents and reefs in
the vicinity. The weather was bad and the ship's officers submitted
written protests against Carillo's decision. The waves rose to such
magnitude that the oldest seaman on board told Retz he had never
encountered such a storm in fifty years at sea. Some of the ship's
complement threw themselves at the feet of the priests, praying
and offering confession, while others sought to jump overboard.
Amid the confusion Retz admired the sang-froid of young Carillo,
who remained on the bridge giving orders, and told the cardinal
that he imagined a confession extorted by fear was worthless in
any event. The galley's captain also set an example. He dressed
himself in his most splendid clothes, saying that a subject of the
king of Spain should know how to die in His Majesty's uniform,
and, seating himself in a chair in the most dangerous position he
could find, he occupied himself by kicking aside the sailors who
came crawling in terror along the deck. The horror of the tempest
made the most vivid impression upon Retz, but, while he described the reactions of his companions, he was silent about his
own conduct. After some hours the galley was manoeuvred into
calmer water in the lee of a small island, and two sea anchors were
cast overboard. Carillo reported to Retz that they were out of
danger, though he insisted on personally remaining on watch
despite his fatigue.

When the storm had blown itself out they moved forward
again, and later in the morning they sighted the island of Elba.
They landed at Porto-Longone, only to find that the wind had

risen again, and it was impossible to reach Piombino on the Tuscan coast. Retz spent three days on the island, receiving every civility from the Spanish governor. He rode over to inspect the impregnable fortress of Porto-Ferrajo, which La Meilleraye had described to him in the château of Nantes. At last the wind changed, and on 3 November the galley made the crossing to Piombino. Retz distributed to the ship's company nearly all his money, including a sum he received for the sale of Boisguérin's Spanish gold chain. After the dangers they had shared on the voyage Carillo and his men regarded the cardinal with considerable affection, and some of them wept as Retz stepped on shore. He stayed to dine in Piombino and then set out with his four retainers on the road for Florence.

Ferdinando II de' Medici, grand-duke of Tuscany, was well disposed towards the family of Gondi, and Retz's distant cousin was still the duke's secretary of state. The news of the cardinal's approach had already reached Florence from Elba, and the grand-duke's major-domo met the party some ten miles west of Volterra. The plague in Aragon necessitated a short period of quarantine. Retz was taken to a house close to the battlefield where Catiline had been defeated and killed by the army of the Roman republic. There was plenty of time for Retz to muse on the fate of conspirators, for he stayed for two weeks in the mountains near Volterra. Charrier arrived there from Rome on the fifth day. According to Joly, the abbé was convinced that Retz could only succeed in Rome if he re-affirmed his resignation from the diocese of Paris.[4] But Retz was confident that his clerical friends in the French capital would continue to defend his rights, and he was soon to receive from them an offer to contribute to his expenses which confirmed his belief. Though Charrier offered to go to Paris to persuade the cardinal's supporters of the wisdom of resigning, he had to be content with the decision to reconsider the matter when Retz arrived in Rome. The abbé called in on Giovanni Battisto de' Gondi in Florence to obtain money for his master before returning to his post.

At the conclusion of the period of quarantine, a litter arrived to convey Retz on the next stage of his journey. He was met by his cousin and taken to Camagliano. On the following day they set out for Ambrogiano, where the grand-duke was hunting. Retz stayed

in Ambrogiano for three days, discussing his future with Ferdinando and the likely course of French policies in Italy. The duke
pressed money on his guest and suggested to him that, if the ailing
Innocent x were to die, he should support the secretary of the
papal chancery, Fabio Chigi, as his successor. During their discussions the news arrived of the landing of the duc de Guise in
southern Italy. Ferdinando did not conceal his contempt for
Mazarin's policies, and scorned the threat he had received that
France would sever diplomatic relations if he entertained Retz.
Assured of Tuscan support, Retz proceeded to Florence, where he
was entertained for two days by the duke's two brothers, prince
Leopold, subsequently to be made a cardinal, and cardinal Giovanni Carlo de' Medici. He went on to Siena, where a third brother,
prince Maffeo, extended the same splendid hospitality. He then
took the road to Rome by Radicofani. During this journey Retz
encountered a storm at Ponte-Centino on the right bank of the
river Paglia, where his mules took fright and he was nearly
drowned when his litter overturned. On 28 November, a few
miles north of Rome, he was met by the muscular abbé Rousseau,
who had been awaiting his master in the Holy City since his own
escape from Nantes. Rousseau brought a report that the French
faction in Rome were planning to prevent his entry, but no
obstacles were encountered when Retz passed through the Porta
Angelica. He went to Saint Peter's to pray, and then made his way
to the lodgings of the abbé Charrier.

Innocent x had made a number of vigorous protests against the
French government's arbitrary imprisonment of Retz, and he had
refused to accept the act of resignation signed at Vincennes. There
was every reason to expect the continued support of the pope.
A papal brief had been issued on 30 September to congratulate
Retz on his escape, and it had praised both his virtue and his
constancy in most generous terms.[5] Yet in other respects the last
phase of Innocent's pontificate had been marked by a spirit of
indecision, and the petticoat influence of his family in Roman
politics had produced a series of vacillations. Moreover, the
French faction in Rome was far from inconsiderable. Cardinal
d'Este was its leading representative within the sacred college, and
cardinal Antonio Barberini, whose family had for long enjoyed
the support of Mazarin, had made his peace with the pope in the

preceding year. Hence it was important for Retz to establish a personal link with Innocent as early as possible. He felt some relief on his arrival to find the pope's master of ceremonies waiting to ascertain his needs, and the papal treasurer on hand to deliver a purse containing 4,000 gold crowns. On the same evening Retz called, incognito, first on signora Olympia and then on the princess Rossano, hoping to secure the support of one or both of these powers behind the throne.

Next morning Retz was still in bed when he received a caller who gave him a foretaste of the kind of opposition he was to encounter. The visitor was one of Mazarin's agents, the abbé de la Rocheposay, who was related by marriage to the Gondi family. He came to deliver a warning that the French interest in Rome had received 'terrible orders' from the king, and was at that moment deliberating on the best means to expel Retz from Rome. The cardinal was delighted by the naïvety of this threat. He expatiated to the abbé on the scruples he would feel about employing the kind of defensive measures he had been obliged to use in Paris. He was now in such extremities that he would have to rely upon providence rather than barricades. La Rocheposay had the wit to perceive he was being mocked, and returned to his masters. Retz immediately sent word of the French threats to the pope, who despatched an officer of the papal guards to tell Charrier that armed protection would be afforded against any violence. Retz saw to it that cardinal d'Este was fully informed of this assurance. On the following day he was admitted to a secret audience with Innocent. The pope apologised for the ineffectiveness of his endeavours to free Retz from Vincennes, and explained that the royal version of the arrest, alleging that Retz was implicated in fresh conspiracies against the crown, had reached Rome before Charrier. To demonstrate publicly his support, Innocent undertook to bestow upon Retz his cardinal's hat at a forthcoming consistory. Retz was suffering from the pain in his shoulder, and an unsuccessful attempt was made to put the joint back in. As it was not expected that he would be able to attend the consistory, the pro-French group of cardinals arrived there in force, and when Retz presented himself they were obliged to leave in shamefaced confusion.

The pope insisted that the French faction in Rome show formal courtesy to Retz, but instructions to Lyonne from Paris required them to have no communication with the exile. In these circumstances Retz eventually resolved to display his own strength and status. He believed that in Rome appearances were all-important, and thought it necessary to show the pope that he was not abandoned. His revenues in France had been seized, and his friends there wrote that they expected a persecuted cardinal to live as a private person, so that attention could be drawn to his plight. A modest style of living, they argued, would impress the clergy in Paris and maintain their loyalty to their archbishop. At first Retz lived in the house of the fathers of the Mission founded by Saint Vincent de Paul. The superior tried to excuse himself from entertaining the cardinal in his establishment, but Innocent enjoined him to comply. In February 1655 the French government ordered the priests of the Mission to return to France because of their hospitality to Retz. In the spring of this year the cardinal moved into the palace of Santa Maria de' Loreto, and resumed the habits of conspicuous display natural to his temperament. He maintained an armed escort of twenty gentlemen, and dressed the eighty servants of his household in grey livery. He kept three personal carriages, supported a large table and generously distributed alms. He gathered his own particular circle round him, including the abbé Robert de Courtenay and the abbé de Sévigné, a son of his old companion, Renaud de Sévigné. Inevitably, Retz was soon heavily in debt, and his friends in Paris, who sent him money, grew critical of his conduct.

In his first weeks in Rome, when he was living with the congregation of the Mission, Retz depended entirely upon the support of Innocent x. Guy Joly maintained that the warmth of the pope's personal favour towards Retz was offset by the enmity of Fabio Chigi. It was Chigi who had attempted to frustrate Retz's elevation to the sacred college by carrying tales of his affiliation with the Jansenists. Joly thought that Chigi was anxious not to spoil his own chance of occupying the see of Saint Peter by offending the French lobby. He claimed that Chigi had reduced the money given to Retz to a fifth of the sum proposed by Innocent, and that he had persuaded the pope not to allow his guest to live in the papal palace of Montecavallo.[6] Perhaps the greatest harm that Chigi did Retz's cause was his advice to refuse papal approval for a circular letter which Retz addressed to the bishops of France.[7] This letter created a great stir and set the tone of the cardinal's policy in the ecclesiastical Fronde. According to Joly, it was composed at Port-Royal and the draft brought to Retz at Ambrogiano by the abbé de Verjus, who was later to become the cardinal's secretary. There was even a rumour current later in the century that the abbé de Rancé was the author, and that Mazarin had refused Rancé preferment because of it. But Rancé disclaimed responsibility, and Retz, in another circular addressed to the bishops in April 1660, claimed that he had composed it in Rome in December 1654.[8] When the printed version of the letter appeared in the streets of Paris in January 1655, Mazarin had the *châtelet* condemn it to be burnt by the public executioner, and at least six published replies to it were composed by his pamphleteers.[9]

The letter to the bishops began with a general denunciation of 'the atrocious and scandalous injuries through which, in my person, the holy dignity common to us all has been dishonoured', and of 'the unheard-of undertakings, violating the rights and majesty of the church, which our status obliges us to defend even at the expense of our lives'. It proceeded to list all the attacks on Retz's character and his office, and to describe his suffering and humiliation during his imprisonment. It pointed out that he had not been excluded from the amnesty, and that no attempt to bring charges against him had been made until after his escape from Nantes. It held up the attempt by the secular power to deprive him of his diocese as a warning to all his colleagues. It traced the persecution of his family and the suppression of the authority he had committed to his grand-vicars. It reminded the bishops of an occasion in 1646 when Retz, as the spokesman of the clergy, had quoted to the king the words of Saint Martin, the fourth-century bishop of Tours: 'It is an inexpressible impiety for lay powers to interfere in the concerns of the church', and added the view attributed to Constantine two generations earlier: 'It is not permitted for me, who am of merely human condition, to judge the causes of bishops.' Argument, precedent and fact were piled together to reach a crescendo of outraged indignation. The acts of Constantine against Saint Athanasius, Arcadius against Saint Chrysostom, Valens (Retz said Theodosius) against Saint Cyril, Henry II of England against Thomas Becket, and Louis VI against bishop Etienne de Senlis of Paris (a persecution invented by Retz for the occasion) were not more gross than those from which Retz had suffered. And it was not the king, to whom no disloyalty was intended, who was responsible, but those evil ministers who usurped his authority. Few more eloquent or skilful polemics were advanced in Retz's cause than this. His pose was that of a bishop of the early church defending his rights and his flock, and thundering his anathemas against the illegalities of the ungodly.

His letter to the bishops was not the only piece of propaganda issued in his name at this time. He also arranged the publication of letters to the king and the queen mother, protesting his loyalty and proclaiming his innocence.[10] He published a fictitious account, dated 30 December, of the pope's reactions to the indictment against Retz which Mazarin had published in Paris and sent to Rome.[11] Here Innocent was depicted as rallying momentarily from the illness of which he was dying to refute Mazarin's accusations. There was a wry twist to the exaggerations in the pope's supposed responses, especially when he declared Mazarin was moved by a bitter envy for Retz, who was as 'pure as a newly-baptised child'. Another letter, published in January 1655, and more certainly from Retz's own hand than the preceding one, sarcastically congratulated the elder duc de Retz on his desertion of the cardinal's cause and his reconciliation with the court.[12] By this time Retz's one major hope for the future had been gravely attenuated. His protector, Innocent x, had died, and he was engrossed in the conclave which, in choosing a successor, could ruin or revive his chance of regaining his country and his diocese.

At Innocent's death on 7 January 1655 his servants deserted his household, and the rumour spread that his corpse was so neglected that the rats had disfigured it.[13] The contrast between the majesty of the living pope and the degradation of his lifeless body was not more remarkable than the gulf between the sacred ideals he represented and the cynical realities of Vatican politics. It was the latter which prevailed in the conclave which began on 18 January, and found itself unable to elect a new pope until 7 April. Retz was permitted to have Guy Joly as well as his valet, Imbert, as his attendants. Both Joly and Retz included in their memoirs long analyses of the manoeuvres of the contestants and their supporters, and both were quite disenchanted as to the personal and national motives of the individual cardinals and the cliques they formed.

But Joly paid some lip service to the mystique of the occasion. Human passions, contradictions and caprices were, he claimed, the dominating factors that impressed an observer, and yet it seemed to him as though some invisible power frustrated the sordid intrigues in which the members of the sacred college were engaged for nearly three months.[14] Retz discerned no such operation by the hand of divine providence. Instead, he took personal credit for the outcome.

The cardinals grouped themselves into five principal factions. The largest consisted of the twenty-two cardinals who supported the Spanish interest, and whose general concern was to prevent the election of a pope favourably inclined towards Mazarin. At their head were the two Medici cardinals, Giovanni Carlo, who had entertained Retz in Florence, and his uncle, Carlo. The principal source of disunity in this faction was the suspicion of the Spanish ambassador that his sovereign's interests were being subordinated to those of Tuscany. The next largest group, of nineteen, was loosely controlled by the Barberini cardinals, Francesco and his uncle Antonio. The former was the nephew and the latter the brother of Urban VIII, Maffeo Barberini, who had died in 1644. Antonio's close friendship with Mazarin excited the suspicions of the Spanish party. The house of Medici had opposed his candidature at the conclave which elected Innocent X, but he still hoped that he might be chosen. There were many in the faction of comparable age and seniority who treasured a vague expectation of receiving nomination and a corresponding urge to exclude each other. For that matter, there were few in the conclave who were not possessed by what Retz termed the *rabbia papale*, the madness of ambition to rule the church. For some time the Barberinis did support one of their number, cardinal Sachetti, and in consequence the Spanish-Medici faction opposed him. It was this circumstance that deadlocked the conclave. A two-thirds majority was required and either of the two major factions could successfully block a candidature.

The Barberini represented the tradition of Urban VIII. Innocent X had failed to leave either a faction or a tradition it could defend. He had shown an unusual reluctance to promote his relatives to the sacred college. His only significant lapse in this respect was to confer a cardinal's hat on his nephew Francesco Maidachini under pressure from signora Olympia: but Maidachini was still a child. He had, it is true, elevated his nephew Camillo Pamfili, but the latter had resigned his cardinalate to marry the princess Rossano. A third possibility as his heir, cardinal Astalli, whom Innocent had adopted in 1650, had been degraded for his own shameless nepotism in 1654. There were, however, a number of comparatively young, uncommitted cardinals who owed their advancement to Innocent, and among these Fabio Chigi had been recommended by the pope as his successor. Chigi had the support of the Jesuit order, which was a strong, if unseen, force within the conclave. Before his appointment as secretary of state in the Vatican he had served as inquisitor in Malta and as papal envoy to the conference at Münster, where negotiations had taken place to end the war in Germany. He had been critical of the French envoy, Servien, during the peace talks, and was strongly disliked by Mazarin. Several cardinals whose moral conduct was more than questionable were suspicious of Chigi's rigid severity and narrow doctrinal opinions. Antonio Barberini, whose life was as blameless but whose mind seemed less bigoted, feared the opposition to Augustinian theology which Chigi had revealed in his campaign against the Jansenists. The Medici opposed Chigi because he came from Siena, and must consequently be regarded as anti-Florentine. But Chigi was not immediately a candidate, nor even the leader of the third faction, to which he belonged.

The number of cardinals in the third group varied from ten to thirteen, and at first a certain idealism prevailed among them. They talked of reforming electoral conventions and of making a free choice, uninfluenced by faction or the secular powers. They became known as the 'Flying Squadron' and, like any group which claims a higher moral tone than its fellows, they met with severe criticism, especially from the Medici clique. Retz himself joined the Squadron, less, perhaps, for idealism than for the advantages of an independent position. As it might be expected, the Squadron was also opposed by the French, who formed the fourth group, consisting of cardinals d'Este, Grimaldi, des Ursins and Bichi. The French faction had links with the Barberini and gave strong support to Sachetti. Despite its dislike of the Squadron, one of its members, Bichi, was related to Chigi, and had contacts within the anti-French parties. Bichi, alone of the French group, preserved courteous relations with Retz. The fifth faction, the 'Little Squadron', consisted of six cardinals linked with Pamfili and the princess Rossano, who tried to promote the claims of Chigi even before he himself would admit to them.

The stage was one where all Retz's political skills could be displayed to advantage. He enjoyed the endless lobbying and negotiating. His ability to judge men and their motives enabled him to reconcile conflicting interests and to encourage defections from one cabal to another. He used theatrical imagery in his account of the conclave: 'All the actors played well; the scenes were all much to the same pattern but the piece was finely contrived, and it possessed a fundamental simplicity, whatever the chroniclers have written to the contrary.' The simplicity was in Retz's mind, not in the politics of the conclave as a whole. It stemmed from the policy of the Squadron alone, as devised by one whose intellectual gifts and similar tastes strongly attracted Retz – cardinal Azzolini. Azzolini saw that Sachetti was a mediocre candidate of good reputation who could never succeed in the face of Spanish opposition. He therefore persuaded the Squadron to vote for Sachetti while secretly working in the interests of Chigi. The French faction supported Sachetti in the belief that he would win, and the Spanish devoted all their energies to defeating him. Thus the national parties were engrossed with the first round of the conflict, while the Squadron, knowing that it would be inconclusive, made their preparations for the second. At six in the morning and two in the afternoon the voting bells rang with monotonous regularity, and, day after day, Sachetti would receive sufficient votes for his genuine backers to persist with his candidature. Meanwhile, the inner group in the Squadron detached certain of their colleagues from the cabals to which they belonged, and prepared for the time when they would enrol them in the promotion of Chigi. As secretary of briefs, Azzolini had worked beside Chigi in the chancery and persuaded him to fall in with their plans. Chigi appeared disinterested, but Azzolini warned Retz that he knew him to be less than candid. Nevertheless, Chigi filled to perfection the part in which he was cast. He prayed in his cell while others lobbied and gossiped. Retz, who acted as a scrutineer for a time, talked to Chigi when he came to cast his vote, and felt convinced that the cardinal would take up his cause if he became pope.

Two principal obstacles to Chigi's candidature were the attitudes of the Medici and Barberini cardinals. The elder Medici was tired by the length of the conclave and critical of the impetuosity of his nephew. Retz caught him at the right moment and, relying upon his personal friendship, revealed his plans for Chigi. On this occasion 'sincerity was more useful than artifice', and Carlo de' Medici began to tolerate the prospect of Chigi as pope and, what was more remarkable, to entertain the possibility of agreeing with Barberini if he proved of the same opinion. The greatest care was needed to prevent Antonio Barberini from catching a whisper of their plans before they were ready to divulge them. First it was necessary to convince him that neither Sachetti nor any other member of the entourage of Urban VIII could secure general approbation. In the end it was Sachetti himself who opened Barberini's eyes. Respect for Chigi's piety overcame Barberini's distrust of his theology. The Squadron now put into operation the second phase of its plan. The unity of the French and Spanish factions was shattered. Bichi declared for Chigi, and Sachetti sent a courier to Mazarin suggesting that French opposition should be withdrawn. The Medici and Barberini cardinals instructed Retz to tell Chigi they would support him, and Chigi, according to Retz's account, fell upon his informant's neck when he heard the news and regarded him as responsible for his election.

Guy Joly did not give his master as much credit for being the manipulator of the conclave as Retz gave himself. In Joly's view it was Bichi who persuaded Sachetti that his cause was hopeless and then advised him to reconcile Mazarin and Chigi.[15] Retz himself had tried to use the conclave to regain the graces of the French court. When he was refused entry to the French cabal, he had not aligned himself with the Spanish but had preserved a position of independence. He had entered into discussions with cardinals Grimaldi and Bichi, and des Ursins had at least exchanged greetings with him when no one was looking. There had been several personal clashes during the conclave, and one of them, at least, Retz had tried to turn to his advantage. The Spanish ambassador had presented a memorandum in which he gave the king of Spain the customary title of eldest son of the church. Retz signed a formal objection which he presented to Carlo de' Medici, the cardinal-dean of the college, in favour of the status of the king of France. Joly recorded that Retz and Chigi arranged this together as a device to persuade Mazarin to withdraw his ban on Chigi's candidature. But, according to Retz, Mazarin publicly denounced the protest as a scheme planned in concert with the Spanish ambassador. In another scene at the conclave Giovanni Carlo de' Medici criticised Retz for joining the Squadron and forgetting the obligation of his family to the Medici. Had it not been for the favour shown his ancestors by Catherine de Médicis, said the cardinal, Retz would be enjoying the status of a mere Florentine gentleman. This was the occasion when Retz formally announced before a large group of cardinals that the Gondi were a more illustrious family than the Medici, and had been so four centuries earlier. Retz observed in general that, although the conclave contained many more acrimonious personal differences than any other he had known, it was marked by a general familiarity and an apparent spirit of charity. No cardinal had exceeded the bounds of propriety in dispute and, whatever the political manoeuvring, the rules for the casting of ballots and the secrecy of votes had been scrupulously observed. But all this was a little beside the point. In supporting Fabio Chigi, Retz had made a serious error of judgment.

Joly believed that the new pope had betrayed Retz's interests when he had been secretary of state.[16] Retz thought that he had sincerely helped his cause during his imprisonment, and that he had done nothing before or during the conclave which indicated any lack of sympathy. He had published a book of verse and had shown himself a man of culture, if not of learning. As Retz put it, he 'knew enough of the humanities to make it appear that he had a sprinkling of other subjects'. He had dissociated himself from the intrigues of signora Olympia in the pontificate of his predecessor, and 'passed in the world as a man of invincible virtue and inflexible rigidity'. During the conclave he had kept to himself, and was remarkable for a discretion that concealed the least hint of ambition. His interest in trivial detail rather than general concepts was to Retz a sign of 'a lack of genius and a base heart'. Joly repeated a saying about him that he was *maximus in minimis, minimus in maximis*.[17] Nevertheless, with the exception of Azzolini, Chigi convinced his supporters in the Squadron that a saint had ascended the throne.

The behaviour of the new pope, who took the title of Alexander VII, seemed more eccentric than saintly. He betrayed such extreme modesty at his installation that he would not occupy his proper place in the ceremony, but sat near a corner of the altar. He refused to summon his relatives, and he had a coffin kept by his bedside, as a constant reminder of mortality. But as yet Retz had no personal cause for complaint. The pope publicly embraced him at the installation, and said to him in front of the Spanish and Venetian ambassadors and the constable of Naples: '*Ecce opus manuum tuorum* – behold, this is the work of your hands.' Retz recalled that when the news of this spread everyone confidently expected him to dominate the Vatican, and one hundred and twenty carriages escorted him back to his residence. This was also the period when Chigi encouraged Retz to defy his enemies and maintain his ostentatious style of living. In June 1655 he acceded to his request to bestow publicly upon him the *pallium*, the stole of white wool sewn with black crosses which was the symbol of his authority as archbishop of Paris. When Retz began to press His Holiness to have d'Este refrain from provocative acts against his fellow cardinal, Alexander began to equivocate. He was prepared to discuss generalities but he refused to take any specific action to restrict the activities of the French circle. He was limited in such matters, he explained, by the precedents established by his precursors.

Retz was unwise to publicise the claim that he was responsible for the pope's election, and imprudent to assert that he ruled the pope's policies. When Retz pressed Alexander to suggest what attitude he should adopt towards the French government, the pope replied that he did not want Retz to imagine he would abandon him but that he must proceed with circumspection. Retz heard from the Tuscan ambassador that Alexander had wished to push him into the position where the pope might placate the French envoy by saying he had exhorted Retz to obey his king. At the same time Lyonne was taking a high hand in directly admonishing Alexander for granting Retz the *pallium*. Faced with threats of the exclusion of papal diplomacy from the exploratory peace talks between France and Spain, the pope offered abject excuses and agreed to convoke a congregation of cardinals, acceptable to the king, to investigate the charges against Retz. It became clear to the cardinal that the pope was turning against him, and in late June he left Rome to spend a month at Grotto Ferrata, some twenty miles distant.

Retz stayed at an abbey at Grotto Ferrata controlled by the elder Barberini, and enjoyed some relaxation of mind and body as he walked along the white marble cloisters and listened to the monks singing the psalms in Greek. But he remained closely in touch with his affairs. Conseiller Croissy-Fouquet, Condé's former agent and Retz's fellow prisoner in Vincennes, arrived from Rome bearing indisputable evidence that Lyonne had been following instructions from Mazarin to press the pope to prosecute Retz. Since his arrival in Rome Lyonne had conducted himself with moderation and at the end of the conclave he had even passed a hint to Retz that he might secure his reconciliation with the court without the necessity of his resigning his archbishopric. The suggestion, which may well have been a trap, was conveyed to Retz by a member of the French circle in Rome, Barillon de Châtillon. When Croissy-Fouquet arrived he lodged with Châtillon, and the two were frequent callers at Retz's establishment, though the French ban on contact with the exile required them to visit him secretly by night. They developed an association with Louis Fouquet, who was a younger brother of Nicolas and the abbé Basile Fouquet, and was later to become bishop of Agde.

Louis Fouquet was conducting an affair with Lyonne's wife, and he and his two companions regaled Retz with accounts of this, as well as of Lyonne's involvement with one of his wife's servants. This was the sort of situation which appealed to Retz, and he soon found that his visitors were prepared to provide him with information of another kind. Louis Fouquet derived valuable reports of affairs in the embassy from madame Lyonne, and even began to intercept despatches to and from Paris and to pass Retz copies. Joly was extremely suspicious of these proceedings. He believed that Lyonne was simply fulfilling his instructions, and that such actions as his sending an officer to convey to Retz's servants an order from the royal council to abandon him and return to France were not inspired by any personal malice. He thought that Louis Fouquet, and possibly Croissy-Fouquet (the two families were not related), had been sent to Rome to spy on Lyonne and to trick Retz into resigning. Joly also believed that

Charrier himself wanted Retz to resolve his problems by resignation, and hence tried to allay any doubts in Retz's mind.[18] Joly was partially correct in his analysis of these strange cross-currents. The full explanation lay in the division within the royal council between Servien, Lyonne's uncle, and the elder Fouquet brothers. Louis Fouquet was in fact receiving instructions from Nicolas Fouquet as to the manner in which Lyonne could be discredited. At the same time Servien was writing to his nephew to warn him against the machinations of his enemies.[19] Neither faction wished in any way to help Retz, but their rivalry was certainly to his advantage. He was able to see genuine copies of the French despatches and was forewarned of papal attitudes. The report that Croissy-Fouquet brought to Grotto Ferrata gave him a full understanding of the manner in which Lyonne's diplomacy was playing upon the pope's weakness.

Retz did not forget his friends in France while he was occupied with the politics of the Vatican and the French embassy in Rome. His family in the west considered their obligations to him discharged as soon as he left Belle-Ile. The ducs de Brissac and de Retz had no intention or resisting La Meilleraye in Belle-Ile, and the prospect of a Spanish fleet being sent to their aid filled them with alarm. Like the elder duc de Retz, they offered their complete submission to the crown, and were gratified by its acceptance and the return of their wives from exile. The cardinal's supporters in Paris proved more resolute. The residence of the archbishop was occupied by a detachment of royal archers. Another group of soldiers searched for Caumartin, who hid behind a tapestry for over an hour while his house was ransacked, and then escaped to Franche-Comté.[20] Bellièvre subsequently obtained permission for him to live near Paris. Père de Gondi was apprehended and despatched to a lonely exile in Auvergne. The nucleus of Retz's friends in the chapter had been summoned to Péronne and then forbidden to return to Paris. Those remaining in the capital had at first forbidden the recognition of any jurisdiction save that of their archbishop, but had eventually surrendered to the threats presented by Séguier. However, their capitulation was not complete. Their instruction to the diocese of 31 August 1654 named vicars to conduct the general administration, but declared this was because of Retz's absence, not because of a vacancy.[21]

K

The violence Mazarin employed against the Parisian clergy and against Retz himself excited wide sympathy for the exiled cardinal. In the face of clerical opposition the council decree declaring the diocese vacant was not taken further. No charges had been preferred against Retz at this stage, and the act appeared to be a flagrant interference with the procedures of the church by the secular power. No bishop had ever been deposed except by a commission of his colleagues. Mazarin made a great mistake by having the council, on 21 September 1654, instruct the parlement to investigate Retz's conduct with a view to an indictment for treason. The error was magnified by the publication of the terms of reference sent to the magistrates.[22] The parlement was delighted to receive this remarkable extension of its jurisdiction, but an explosion of discontent occurred among the prelates who now, it seemed, could be tried by a secular court on the arbitrary whim of the government. The council could not revoke the commission of the parlement without the humiliation of holding a *lit de justice*, so it temporised by sending a second decree restricting the authority of the tribunal to the simple gathering of information.[23] Then, when Mazarin decided to have the pope try Retz by a commission of cardinals, the plan of judicial proceedings against him in France was quietly dropped. When Innocent x did not respond to the royal request dated 12 December, Mazarin's motives were exposed in the worst possible light by the publication of Retz's letters to the king, the queen and the French bishops, together with the reply to the royal letter issued in his name on 30 December. On 16 April 1655 the royal ordinance appeared requiring Retz's servants in Rome to leave him and return to France, and shortly afterwards Lyonne was instructed to oblige Alexander vii to institute the commission of cardinals.

After his election, Alexander proclaimed a jubilee, and Retz made use of the bull to reassert his claims to the archbishopric. He did not send the bull to Bagni, the nuncio in Paris, but to the former grand-vicars, Chevalier and Lavocat. On 22 May he addressed a letter to the chapter of Notre-Dame and had a printed version distributed in Paris.[24] The letter complained in vigorous terms of the usurpation of his spiritual government, and explained that he had nominated two new grand-vicars, Jean-Baptiste Chassebras, curé of La Madeleine, and Alexandre Hodencq, curé

of Saint-Séverin, who would execute the bull of the jubilee if
Chevalier and Lavocat were still in exile.[25] Retz displayed in the
letter a shrewd indulgence to those members of the chapter who
had been sufficiently frightened by Séguier's threats to appoint
the vicars required by the council. He noted that they refused to
admit the existence of a vacancy, and instead performed the election because of the absence of their lawful pastor. At the same time
he resumed the pose of a persecuted bishop of the primitive
church, and reminded his readers that when Saint Cyprian, the
bishop of Carthage, heard of an intended persecution of Christians
and the demand that they be fed to the lions in the amphitheatre,
he had gone into hiding so that his absence might avert the fury
of the pagans against his flock. But, because Saint Cyprian had
withdrawn, the diocese had not become vacant. In fact he had
administered it from his retreat with more firmness and vigour
than ever before. Retz added an even more surprising precedent.
He referred to the occasion in 1617 when cardinal Richelieu, then
bishop of Luçon, had fled to Avignon after the assassination of his
protector, Concini, the favourite of Marie de Médicis. Though
Richelieu had been in disgrace, his grand-vicars continued to
govern his diocese in his name, and no one suggested that his see
was vacant and should be governed by the chapter. Retz concluded
by announcing that the pope had bestowed the *pallium* upon him as
final confirmation of his episcopal power. This clever polemic did
not go unanswered, but the replies were so violent and so clumsy
that they enhanced Retz's cause. One such accused him of waging
a personal war in the Fronde, attempting to hold the king and
queen mother prisoner, and plotting the assassination of both
Molé and Condé. It tried to prove that Retz was no longer archbishop, and that the king had full power to depose him.[26]

The chapter's appointment of vicars lapsed when Retz nominated Chassebras and Hodencq. The government responded by
ordering both the new vicars to appear before the council. Hodencq obeyed, but Chassebras went into hiding, and for long
continued to issue instructions on behalf of the archbishop. He
concealed himself in the tower of the church of Saint-Jean-en-
Grève, where all the efforts of the abbé Fouquet and his army of
informers failed to find him. Chassebras went out at night in secular disguise to discuss his plans with those among Retz's supporters

whom he could trust. He composed and secretly printed a series
of manifestos and monitions in the name of his archbishop,
sometimes with the aid of the principal of the collège des Grassins.
The principal's brother was one of Retz's former mob-organisers
of the Fronde, the butcher Le Houx.[27] Le Houx employed a gang
of youths to placard the declarations of Chassebras on the doors
of the churches. Their favoured method, according to Claude Joly,
was to conceal the leaflets in a loose fold at the back of their
clothing and, having leant against a wall or door, to move away
leaving the placard behind them.[28] Claude Joly described the
heroic Chassebras as an invisible man who, though he was one
of the lesser curés of Paris, held the whole court at bay with his
firmness and constancy. The first of his placards appeared in
August, and on 8 September he posted his first monition, listing
the illegal attacks made on his own jurisdiction and that of his
archbishop. The government threatened to execute the printer if
once he was identified. The first monition, and all its successors,
were publicly burnt. On 27 September the *châtelet* proclaimed
sentence of banishment against Chassebras and the confiscation
of his goods. Ten days later Chassebras issued a *mandement* received from Retz forbidding the bishops of Dol and Coutances to
interfere with his jurisdiction. A second monition followed with
a new list of the outrages of the secular courts against the authority
of the church. For all its threats and sentences, the government
could not prevent the indomitable grand-vicar from serving his
master.[29]

With the suspension of the chapter's vicars, and the proscription
of those appointed by Retz, the spiritual administration of the
diocese lacked official direction. Bishop Cohon of Dol and bishop
Auvry of Coutances for a time performed episcopal services in
Notre-Dame, but many of the clergy regarded their activities as
illegal. When they sanctified the holy oil, several curés refused to
receive it, and Bagni, the nuncio, supported them. The court was
doubly embarrassed because the anarchy in the diocese of Paris
prevented the convocation there of the general assembly of the
clergy. The assembly had first been set down to meet in May 1655.
The date was advanced to August and then to October. In the
provinces the government tried to influence the election of the
clerical deputies to prevent the appearance of a party sympathetic

to Retz in the assembly.[30] In the diocese of Paris the placards posted by Chassebras forbad the election of any deputies without Retz's authority. The bishop of Meaux, who was Séguier's brother, wisely refused to intervene. There was already strong feeling within the episcopacy against the methods employed by Mazarin. The archbishop of Rouen had forbidden the bishop of Coutances to perform any ecclesiastical function in the province. The bishops of Chartres and Orléans had earlier refused to recognise the vicars appointed by the chapter of Notre-Dame.[31] In the province of Paris there was a dispute between the bishops of Meaux and Chartres as to which of them should assume the presidency of the preliminary provincial assembly. No progress could be made until the province had settled its problems, and until official approval from some constituted authority within the diocese of Paris had been given for the general assembly to meet there. The government needed the finances it expected the assembly to vote, and in the circumstances it was forced to yield ground. Hodencq was allowed to return to the capital and it was he who, despite Chassebras, authorised the meeting of the assembly at the great abbey of the Augustins.

When Retz returned to Rome late in July 1655 he could not predict the trend of events in either Paris or Rome. Though Chassebras had not yet begun his campaign, Malclerc had reported the final defection of both Noirmoutier and the vicomte de Lameth. While Retz was in the conclave Malclerc had been sent to Paris with a double mission. He had to convince his friends that the cardinal was in need of further revenues, and to persuade Noirmoutier to postpone his negotiations with Mazarin, at least until the result of the papal election was known. Caumartin and the bishop of Châlons warned the squire that it would be dangerous to visit Charleville, but Malclerc obeyed his master's orders, and was fortunate to escape a trap which madame de Noirmoutier had prepared for him in expectation of forcing her husband's reconciliation with the court. Retz was hurt by the methods used by his former friends in Charleville and Mont-Olympe, but the cynicism that now dominated his attitudes also made him reflect that it was the custom of those who wished to escape an obligation first to destroy the reputation of those to whom they were indebted. When Noirmoutier went to Paris to sign that agreement with Mazarin towards which madame de Chevreuse and Laigues had been working for so long, he heard that Malclerc was still hiding in the city. He expressed a certain shame at his own conduct, and made out that he was trying to reconcile Retz with the court. He even offered to make a personal contribution to Malclerc for Retz's expenses. Retz reflected that the gospel required one to give favours to those who had done one an injury, but it certainly did not enjoin the acceptance of gifts by an injured party. Caumartin did not trust Noirmoutier, and told him that Malclerc had already returned to Rome.

Affairs in Rome gave little cause for optimism. It was true that Alexander VII had not accepted Lyonne's demand to institute the commission of cardinals. Lyonne had submitted a new list of specific charges against Retz drawn up on 9 July 1655.[32] The pope had consulted a consistory and thankfully postponed his decision when he received the advice that it would be wrong to proceed against Retz before he had been re-established. The French circle brought every conceivable pressure to bear on Retz. Cardinal Bichi reported to the pope that he was defying the king's orders by declaring that no secular power should divide churchmen bound to each other in the spirit of charity. Alexander actually reproached Retz for his attitude, and Retz responded that his conduct would be as the pope commanded, and he would inform the sacred college accordingly. When the pope abruptly told Retz that this was to misinterpret him, the cardinal replied that he therefore presumed the pope condoned his policy. This incident was typical of Alexander's relations with Retz. The pope could not abandon him without humiliating the church, but he was determined to avoid any direct clash with the French court. Retz then tried to force matters by attending the fête of Saint-Louis, an annual celebration on 25 August to which the French community invited the college of cardinals. The pope tried to dissuade him, but ended by allowing him to make his own decision. Retz was snubbed at the service, but he maintained his dignity and refused to leave until the ceremony was completed.

A week later Retz left Rome to take the waters at San Casciano, south of Florence on the road to Siena. He was still suffering from his shoulder, but neither the painful resetting of the bone in the socket nor a lengthy course of bathing at the spa provided any

relief. He remained at San Casciano for a month, and while he was
there troubles which had been simmering for some time in his
own entourage came to the surface. The members of the cardinal's
household in Rome had been under pressure from the French
embassy. The uncertainty about their master's future, and the
tension produced by continual changes of front, magnified the
petty jealousies among them. The abbé de Lameth, master of
Retz's household, tended to disagree with Guy Joly, and both were
jealous of Charrier. There was a clash between the abbé Bouvier,
the cardinal's financial agent in Rome, and the abbé Rousseau,
who claimed that this function should be his because his brother
had been Retz's intendant in Paris. Charrier supported Bouvier
and Joly backed Rousseau. The new secretary, the abbé de Verjus,
apparently managed to work without antagonising anyone.
Malclerc, who was constantly travelling on one mission or another
for his master, received so much praise from Retz for his selfless
service that the others resented the confidence Retz placed in him.

The cardinal blamed his own habit of affecting an easy familiarity
with his servants and supporters. In times of good fortune this
might be no great fault, but in times of anxiety the custom of
allowing anyone to speak his mind often led to bitter disputes
between advocates of conflicting policies. Guy Joly seemed to
disagree most frequently with his master, and time after time he
appeared in the party whose advice was rejected. Retz indicated
his own view of his secretary's attitude when he said that Joly was
inspired by a spirit of contradiction. It was Joly who pressed Retz
to go to Charleville, and, later, to accept the Spanish suggestion
to join Condé. It was Joly who warned against Louis Fouquet and
Croissy-Fouquet, and Joly who opposed Charrier on the issue of
resigning the archbishopric. And on each occasion Joly felt himself slighted. He was to remain with Retz for several further years
of exile, but he became increasingly discontented, and when he
came to write his memoirs he took care to show that it was always
his opponents who were in the wrong. There were also quarrels
and complaints about Retz's unequal distribution of rewards and
favours. At San Casciano Retz found it necessary to draw up a
detailed list of the money and gifts he had presented to each of his
gentlemen since his arrival in Rome. Some proved particularly
expensive. Boisguérin became ill, and had to be left behind in San

Casciano and subsequently sent back to France. Retz remarked
that Boisguérin had received more than any servant of Mazarin
might expect, but he showed no gratitude for his patron's liberality.

In early October Retz moved to the Farnese fortress of Caprarola
near Viterbo, where he was the guest of the duke of Parma for six
weeks. There he heard of the activities of Chassebras and of the
sentence passed against him. In Rome the pope concluded that
Retz's party was becoming weaker in France. He offered Lyonne
to make Retz choose new grand-vicars from a list to be sent by the
king. Lyonne refused because this would publicly recognise Retz's
claim to the diocese. The pope then considered that a suffragan
bishop might be appointed to officiate temporarily in Paris.
Dominique Séguier, the bishop of Meaux, was approached but
refused to act in any capacity. A number of bishops in the assembly
of clergy also made it clear that they would regard this solution as
an infringement of Gallican liberties. At this point Joly pressed
Retz to leave Italy and reside in the Low Countries or Franche-
Comté, whence he might impose an interdict upon Paris, and rely
on Chassebras and his friends among the parish clergy to execute
it. But Charrier had arrived from Rome to say that the pope
seemed more favourably disposed towards him, and Retz returned
with the abbé to the Holy City.

In Rome Retz found Alexander VII to be totally transformed.
Instead of extreme diffidence, he engaged in the most opulent
display and self-advertisement. He quarrelled openly with members of the sacred college where previously he had taken refuge in
ambiguity. He engaged in puerile word games, and offered a prize
for the best suggestion for a Latin word to describe his new
phaeton. He obliged the cardinals to accompany him on a tour of
inspection of all the major churches in Rome on the same day.
His most remarkable antics concerned the reception in Rome of
Queen Christina, who had abdicated the throne of Sweden a year
earlier and had accepted conversion to Catholicism. A mixture of
amazon and blue-stocking, Christina was as wilful as the pope
himself, but she had a livelier sense of humour. The spectacle of
the pope presiding at the fêtes, balls and comedies which were
staged in her honour caused her a good deal of amusement. Retz
took the trouble to insinuate himself in her good graces, but there
was little she could do for his cause. With the pope in such a mood

Retz was uncertain where to turn. When the French embassy arranged a special service on 13 December to commemorate the king's grandfather, Henry IV, cardinal d'Este announced that Retz was specifically excluded. Retz demanded an audience with Alexander, but the pope feigned illness and refused to see him. Retz then attended the service in the Lateran church of San-Giovanni. He took with him a strong escort and was prepared to defend his status by force. As on the occasion of the fête of Saint-Louis, he was ignored by the French community, but he felt he had made his point.

As the months passed and no solution appeared in sight, even Retz began to feel embarrassment at the expenses of his household in the palazzo Santa-Maria. Nearly all his French revenues were frozen, and few French financiers dared to disobey the royal injunction against advancing him money. His creditors in France began to press for repayment of earlier debts, and some lodged suits against him in the Roman courts. In the past, when there seemed at least a possibility that Retz might secure some high office of state, there had always been investors ready to speculate in his political fortune. Now that the court remained inflexible and papal support had clearly become less than lukewarm, it seemed unlikely that Retz would even regain his archiepiscopal status. Consequently he was obliged to rely entirely upon the generosity of his friends. The bishop of Châlons, Caumartin and Hacqueville gave generous support. La Houssaie and the Jansenist Bagnols, who were both related by marriage to the marquise de Sévigné and had aided Retz on several occasions, advanced substantial loans. So, too, did the duc de Brissac and the younger duc de Retz. Further help came from the marquis de Crève-Coeur, who was the receiver of clerical taxes. In his memoirs Retz reproached other friends for using the royal ban as a pretext to refuse him any money. The duc de Liancourt, first gentleman of the royal bedchamber and an old Jansenist associate of the cardinal, had offered twenty thousand crowns to help père de Gondi, but would offer the bishop of Châlons no more than two thousand crowns towards the fund for Retz because he had promised the queen not to support him at all. It was surprising that Retz was able to borrow as much as he did, but it was quite inadequate to maintain the style of living he affected. One of Mazarin's correspondents in Rome, the Jesuit father Duneau, reported to Paris that it was commonly assumed that Retz was supported either by the Jansenists or by Spain.[33]

The pope's lack of sympathy for Retz was apparent from his brief allowing the nomination of a suffragan bishop to administer the diocese of Paris, and, had it not been for the objections of the French clergy, this brief would have ended all Retz's hopes, even though it acknowledged him as archbishop. The Jesuits were said by Guy Joly to be carrying tales to the pope of the links Retz had with the Jansenists.[34] In fact père Duneau regularly reported to Mazarin Jesuit endeavours to this end. The pope evidently had not taken them as seriously as he had when, as papal secretary of state, he had tried to oppose Retz's candidature for the cardinalate. Soon after his election he had commented on these accusations and observed that Retz had no sympathy for the doctrines of Jansenism, but regarded individual members of the sect as men of good will. Alexander VII remembered the opinion of père Annat, now the provincial of the Jesuit order in France, that Retz kept on good terms with Port-Royal for political reasons.[35] In any event Mazarin had good reason not to raise the Jansenist issue, which had been quiescent since the reception of the bull *Cum occasione*. In the winter of 1653–4 he had come to an understanding with Arnauld d'Andilly at Port-Royal to leave the Jansenists in peace. Bishop Auvry of Coutances had been the intermediary between d'Andilly and the court in this matter.[36] In January 1655 Mazarin interviewed a number of Jansenist curés, and asked them, with every appearance of amiability, to preach obedience to the king. It was a matter for regret, he said, that the curé du Hamel should be in disgrace for supporting cardinal de Retz.[37] The truce lasted for over a year, when Antoine Arnauld could no longer prevent himself from criticising the bull *cum occassione*. Antoine Arnauld's tract, *Letter to a Duke and Peer*, was examined by the Sorbonne for heterodox opinions, and in November 1655 Arnauld narrowly failed in an attempt to have the parlement prohibit the Sorbonne's censure. Thus, despite Mazarin's desire for peace, the French church was again embroiled in a factious conflict, from which the only positive gain was the ironic prose of Pascal's *Lettres Provinciales*. When Duneau received detailed information from Annat of Retz's contacts with Port-Royal, he had it submitted to the pope, and received in return the assurance that Alexander was anxious to satisfy the king.[38]

Lyonne was anything but satisfied, but he kept up the demand for Retz's trial. The cardinal entered a mood of depression, and told Joly to lock away his papers in expectation that he would be imprisoned in the papal fortress of San Angelo. On 27 July 1655, soon after Duneau's second attempt to raise the issue of Retz's Jansenist affiliations, Lyonne wrote to his uncle, Servien, concerning a report that the pope had threatened Retz to his face with imprisonment and that Retz had continued to show an 'invincible obstinacy'. But the pope's refusal to act eventually drove Lyonne to despair and in December 1655 he was suggesting in his correspondence with Servien that he should resign his commission.[39] At the same time difficulties encountered by the French government over the administration of the diocese of Paris and the assembly of clergy persuaded Mazarin to seek a way out of the deadlock. He had a list of six possible vicars sent to the Vatican and suggested to the pope that Retz be required to name one of them. All were known to be unsympathetic to the cardinal, but his spirits were so low that he accepted the proposal. The government's offer implied, at least, that his title was recognised. He chose du Saussay, the curé of Saint-Leu.[40] Charrier applauded this decision, but Joly argued that Retz should not agree until his revenues as archbishop had been restored to him.[41] Early in January 1656 Retz wrote to du Saussay asking him to take the archbishop's oath of loyalty, and at the same time he wrote to the king and the queen mother, begging to be allowed to exercise his functions.[42] He wrote also to the assembly of clergy announcing his nomination of du Saussay, and requesting the assembly to intercede on behalf of Chassebras and his disgraced supporters among the Parisian clergy.[43] These letters had no effect. Those to the king and queen were returned unopened by way of Lyonne. That to the assembly, which was addressed to the three suffragan bishops of Paris, the bishops of Meaux, Chartres and Orléans, was handed to Mazarin. Du Saussay ignored the demand to take the oath, as he did two further letters from Retz to the same effect. He also refused to publish the *mandements* which Retz sent him.

Retz's sympathisers within the assembly of the clergy began to take up his cause, and the threat of intervention by the assembly

obliged the government to relax some of its measures. The exiled
clergy, including Chevalier, Lavocat and Claude Joly, were allowed
to return to Paris, and père de Gondi was permitted to leave the
snows of Auvergne for the Gondi residence at Villepreux. This
moderation did not apply to Retz personally. On 28 March a new
ordinance was issued forbidding any contact with him, and requiring once again that all his servants should return to France
under pain of the confiscation of their property. Retz responded
with one of the most eloquent of his polemics, his *Important and
Disinterested Advice on the Affair of Monsignor the Cardinal de Retz*.[44]
It justified his conduct during and after the Fronde, argued con-
vincingly that Mazarin was moved only by personal animus, and
pointed out that since the nomination of du Saussay no one could
doubt Retz's claim to the archbishopric. The latter point was
reiterated in a document[45] composed at about the same time and
presented to the assembly of clergy in June by one of Retz's agents,
the abbé Dorat, who attended the meeting at the Augustins under
an assumed name, and went into hiding as soon as his mission was
accomplished. This manifesto recited the burning of the monitions
and *mandements* published by Chassebras and concluded: 'My
imprisonment . . . and these excesses render the secular power the
absolute master of the whole Gallican church.' The sympathy
which it excited was increased when a detachment of troops
searched the cloisters of the Augustins for Dorat.

Both Mazarin and Retz were now determined to force the issue.
Lyonne had been in Rome for eighteen months, and throughout
this entire period he had been pressing the pope to convoke a
tribunal to try Retz. Mazarin now recalled him. Mazarin's treaty
with Cromwell of the preceding November had already been taken
as a deliberate affront to Rome. Alexander VII feared that France
would break off diplomatic relations with the Vatican, and he
resolved to disembarrass himself of Retz and his problems. Retz,
for his part, had lost patience with du Saussay after so many
instances of disobedience, the last, and most flagrant, being the
vicar's invitation to the bishop of Coutances to officiate in Notre-
Dame during Easter. Disregarding the pope, he revoked du
Saussay's commission on 15 May 1656,[46] and left Rome for the
waters of San Casciano. There he despatched an instruction restoring Chevalier and Lavocat as grand-vicars, and made provision

for Chassebras and Hodencq to act if the government proscribed the former.[47] This document was placarded in Paris, where it was accepted by the Parisian clergy. Retz also wrote to cardinal Rospigliosi, the papal secretary of state, to explain that, having told Alexander VII of du Saussay's disobedience, he had presumed the revocation met with the pope's approval. The pope, who was at Montecavallo because of the plague in Rome, despatched a courier to Retz demanding the restoration of du Saussay, but Retz would not respond. Du Saussay himself had just received his bull of institution to the bishopric of Toul. He hurriedly recog- nised the revocation of his commission, and sought Chevalier's permission to be consecrated at Saint-Denis. Mazarin promptly had Chevalier consigned to the Bastille, where he continued to affirm his right to be grand-vicar. Lavocat went into hiding. When the government claimed that du Saussay could not be dismissed after his appointment had been approved by both pope and king, the clergy of Paris declared that they would recognise no authority save that of their archbishop.

In July the council published a further ordinance in the series of edicts forbidding any subject of the king to have any commerce with Retz.[48] Retz had already composed a letter to Chevalier and Lavocat explaining his reasons for revoking the powers of du Saussay.[49] Du Saussay, who had managed to have his consecration as bishop of Toul performed at Poissy, began to boast that the pope was about to make him suffragan bishop of Paris with authority to resume the administration of the diocese. As nothing was heard from Rome to substantiate his hopes, he appealed to the archbishop of Lyon. While the archbishop pondered over the case it was tacitly agreed that Hodencq should act as grand-vicar in the interim. Mazarin sought to check any sympathy for Retz in the assembly by having the king sign a letter to that body de- nouncing the revocation of du Saussay as an affront to the pope as well as to the crown. The letter recited the details of Retz's 'criminal and seditious conduct' and promised that any delegate acting in his cause would incur the royal displeasure.[50] These were almost the last shots to be fired in the ecclesiastical Fronde. It seemed that Retz had lost the battle in France as he had lost it also in Rome.

Retz had decided to leave Italy. He had arrived as a supplicant

eighteen months earlier and had been given every expectation
that the pope would insist upon the restoration of his rights.
Innocent x had confirmed his favour by bestowing on him his
cardinal's hat: Alexander vii had granted him the *pallium* as archbishop of Paris. A long sequence of disappointments had ensued
in which the inexplicable vagaries of Fabio Chigi had tried his
patience beyond measure. In France his clerical friends had supported him staunchly: in Rome he had himself to brave the venom
of Mazarin's agents while his own entourage squabbled about
trifles. In all his travail he had consistently maintained his stand
as a bishop defending his church against the wilful persecution of
a tyrannous minister. Even in his most eloquent public indictments of his persecutors he displayed a moderate and charitable
air that set off his pose to perfection. But in the end Retz realised
that he could hope for nothing from Alexander vii. As a final
gesture he sought the pope's permission to return to Rome to
serve the victims of the plague as Saint Carlo Borromeo had
ministered to the afflicted in Milan a century before. The pope
refused and Retz made his final preparations to depart. He fled
from papal territory with Joly, Lameth, Malclerc and two valets,
and thus returned to Tuscany with a retinue no larger than that
with which he had entered it in the autumn of 1654. He stayed
briefly at a place named Marena, and then for two days at a summer
resort belonging to cardinal Giovanni Carlo de' Medici. On 5
August 1656 he wrote the pope an ironically reproachful letter
from Marena declaring that he was about to leave Italy, and hoping
for the continuance of papal protection.[51] Then he took the road for
Franche-Comté by way of Milan and Lausanne. The first phase of
his exile had ended, and he entered upon a humiliating, vagabond
life where neither dignity nor self respect remained to him.

TWELVE

A fugitive and secret life

Retz closed his memoirs with his flight from Italy when he was working on their final draft some twenty years later. His departure marked another break in the continuity of his life and another plunge into a fresh mode of existence. The transition from the heroic ideals of his youth to the cynical realism of the frondeur had not been a gradual response to the pressures of betrayal and deceit which he had experienced in his early duel with Mazarin. It was an abrupt change, following from his decision 'to do evil by way of design' and play the hypocrite in his ecclesiastical career. It was true that elements from his youth continued to reappear in the years when he marshalled the dissident factions in the Fronde. The intrusion of *Astrée* into the scene at the hôtel de Ville during the first civil war revealed the persistence of the romantic ideal. The impulsive urge to act for the sake of action, the affirmation of the self through the singularity of the deed, continued to be manifest in the contest between the old Fronde and the new. But for Retz the calculation of interest and motive came to eliminate the romantic illusion and the noble gesture. In the extraordinary vacillations of his career in the period when he acquired his cardinal's hat he found himself less able to dictate the march of events and more inclined to wait prudently upon opportunity. It was as if he anticipated La Rochefoucauld's maxim, 'in affairs of importance we should concentrate less on making opportunities than on taking advantage of those that present themselves'; and yet this was the very reproach he levelled against Gaston. Thus the identity of the youthful Retz became entirely submerged by the personality of the middle-aged and disillusioned frondeur.

The months of imprisonment had again broken the continuity of attitude and experience. Though there were moments when he was reduced to despair, he bore his confinement with astonishing fortitude. In this period of enforced inactivity, reflection bred a gift of self-analysis and a preoccupation with what might have been, which were later to be revealed in the memoirs. Captivity also revived the Stoic element he had encountered in classical antiquity, and with it a dependence on the controlled will to shield the self from the caprice of fortune and the malice of other men. It was in this mood that he recorded Bellièvre's advice in 1654 to refuse the resignation of his archbishopric with the words: 'I count as nothing the poison and steel my enemies direct against me. Nothing can touch me save what is in me. Everywhere death is waiting.'[1] The stoicism he exhibited helped him to assume his pose as the persecuted bishop when the long struggle to deprive him of his diocese began. In the course of this contest he had made his dramatic escape from the château of Nantes, and his pent-up energies were suddenly released into a bewildering series of adventures. Two years of intrigue and anxiety had followed in which the politics of the Vatican had proved as shifting and uncertain as those of the Louvre. In his memoirs Retz endeavoured to rediscover himself and his attitudes in all these discontinuous phases of his life, but as he approached the period when he gained his cardinalate he became more concerned with rationalising and re-interpreting his past actions to satisfy the demands of *amour-propre*, and less concerned with the immediacy of past experience.

In his account of affairs in Italy he did not display his earlier anxiety to rediscover his past identity. There was no point in continuing the memoirs beyond this phase. The years that followed contained little he would wish to communicate either to his contemporaries or to posterity, and less that he would wish to justify. La Rochefoucauld, whose life, like his posthumous literary reputation, ran so curiously in parallel with that of Retz, described this phase of his career as '*une vie errante et cachée*'. When Retz was leaving Italy in 1656, La Rochefoucauld was arranging his return to Paris. His life in the capital became as brilliant and rewarding as that of the wandering exile was harsh and degrading. The misanthropic author of the *Maximes* had made his peace with Mazarin: Retz met the implacable opposition of the first minister in every place where he sought refuge. The favour of Mazarin allowed the one to shine in the literary salons of Paris, and his hatred condemned the other to a sordid and fugitive existence.

Secure in the affections of Anne of Austria, Mazarin could survive occasional setbacks at home and abroad. In the autumn of 1655 marshal d'Hocquincourt had followed the precedent set by Harcourt and used his possession of the fortresses of Ham and Péronne to defy the court. The duchesse de Châtillon, whose charms had inspired the marshal's treason, had tried to arrange the surrender of the fortresses to Condé and his Spanish allies. So feeble an imitation of the intrigues of his feminine adversaries of the Fronde scarcely ruffled Mazarin's calm. The relentless intelligence service of the abbé Fouquet had for some time been intercepting the correspondence of the duchess, and at the appropriate moment the abbé had her arrested. She was released because of his own amorous ambitions, and as his mistress she no longer proved a threat to the régime. The loyalty of the traitor Hocquincourt was assured by the gift of 600,000 livres.[2]

The war with Spain caused greater anxiety. Conti had proved a failure in Catalonia. In the summer of 1656 Mazarin sent Lyonne to Madrid to negotiate with Luis de Haro. In July Condé relieved Valenciennes and forced Turenne to retreat. Soon afterwards the Spanish negotiations were broken off, as Mazarin moved towards a military alliance with Cromwell. The Stuart cause was finally abandoned. Since the commercial treaty of Westminster with the English republican government, Charles II remained in Cologne, while his brother, the duke of York, was serving in Italy with the duke of Modena's army. The exiled English king was in turn to seek the support of Spain, and to find a sympathetic ear in cardinal de Retz, the critic of Mazarin's foreign policy.

Problems other than that of the archbishopric of Paris disturbed the peace of the church. The Jansenists were on the defensive after Antoine Arnauld had been condemned by his colleagues of the Sorbonne. The caustic brilliance of Pascal's pen discredited the Jesuits, and the miraculous healing of his niece by the Holy Thorn of Port-Royal in March 1656 sustained Jansenist conviction of divine favour. It was a conviction shared neither by the papacy nor by the majority of the assembly of the clergy. The latter were prepared to sanction the imposition of a formulary requiring Jansenist submission to the bull of Innocent X, which condemned the five propositions supposedly extracted from the *Augustinus* of Jansenius. The Jansenist denial that the propositions were to be found in the book, and their obstinate adherence to the legal quibble that the pope had the right to pronounce on doctrine but might yet err in terms of fact, were rigorously forbidden by a new bull issued by Alexander VII in October 1656, three months after Retz's flight. The Jansenists did not wish to subvert Mazarin's authority, but they were prepared to seek out Retz in exile as a possible ally. Mazarin had no desire to persecute the Jansenists because of their religious doctrines but, now that his understanding with d'Andilly had broken down, his suspicions of their political disloyalty were revived, and his obsession with Retz's supposed intrigues intensified his antipathy for Port-Royal.

If the political threat of Jansenism was chimerical, there was, at least, no sign of any more realistic internal opposition. Mazarin's administration floated on a sea of corruption, but there were few to challenge his authority. Molé was dead and some incipient antagonism from the parlement in the spring of 1655 had been smoothed by an agreement between Pomponne de Bellièvre and Turenne, acting on behalf of the government. As joint superintendent of the finances, Nicolas Fouquet continued to amass a vast fortune in his dealings with the tax-farmers. The limiting measures instituted by Mazarin's German banker, Herwarth, no longer proved effective, and Herwarth was obliged to join Fouquet in providing personal guarantees for government borrowing, which inextricably confused the finances of the state with the personal fortune of the superintendent. Fouquet's brothers rose with him. François became first count-bishop of Agde (a dignity which passed later to that Louis Fouquet who visited Retz in Rome) and then archbishop of Narbonne. Those who sought the superintendent's friendship were often permitted to share in the profits as the price of their support. La Rochefoucauld's secretary, Gourville, who had negotiated the accommodation of his master with Mazarin, was granted the receivership of the poll tax in Guyenne. His newly acquired wealth enabled him to advance money to La Rochefoucauld and to restore the latter to solvency.[3]

In the salon society which La Rochefoucauld re-entered at this time government corruption was an acceptable source of pensions and patronage, while the theological disputes of the Jansenists provided an entertaining intellectual exercise without political connotations. Mazarin was content enough with this diversion of aristocratic energies, as his predecessor had been with the hôtel de Rambouillet. The old marquise de Rambouillet, now well into her seventies, even reopened her celebrated salon after the Fronde, but the former habitués were dead or dispersed, and their glamour had passed to the circle of her younger rivals. The new luminaries shone in the hôtel d'Albret and the drawing rooms of la Grande Mademoiselle, the marquise de Sablé, mademoiselle de Scudéry and madame de La Fayette. Madame de Sévigné and her cousin, the comte de Bussy-Rabutin, were members of this circle and frequent visitors at La Rochefoucauld's own hôtel in the rue de la Seine. Each salon came to develop its own brand of preciosity. At mademoiselle de Scudéry's one concentrated upon madrigals: at la Grande Mademoiselle's one developed the art of the pen portrait: and at madame de Sablé's one played the game of composing epigrammatic maxims, the genre in which La Rochefoucauld became the master. La Rochefoucauld spent much of his time with madame de Sablé until the latter, who lived near Port-Royal de Paris in the faubourg Saint-Jacques, became a convert to Jansenist piety. The trend dismayed La Rochefoucauld, who followed the gradual conversion of madame de Longueville with mingled curiosity and raillery. But the devout Arnauld d'Andilly was as close to the circle as the celebrated courtesan, Ninon de Lenclos, and La Rochefoucauld's cynicism towards the weakness of reason and the strength of passion was paralleled by the pessimist outlook of the Jansenists on human nature. Even Pascal owed something to the literary form of the *maxime* in recording the religious insights of his *Pensées*. La Rochefoucauld admired the romances of mademoiselle de Scudéry, and saw the heroes of the Fronde thinly disguised in the characters of the interminable volumes of *Clélie*, the successor to *Le Grand Cyrus*. In later years he was to collaborate with madame de La Fayette in the less stylised historical romance, *La Princesse de Clèves*. The surviving frondeurs were reliving the past in the salons which became established in Mazarin's last years. But Retz was not among them. His life became in every way a contrast to the gay society of his former friends and rivals.

When Retz left Tuscany early in August 1656 he was provided with an escort by the Spanish governor in Milan, count Fuensaldagne. The escort was necessary because the duke of Modena, secure in the French alliance by the marriage of his son with yet another of Mazarin's nieces, had launched an invasion of the duchy. Retz had negotiated with Fuensaldagne when the latter had commanded the Spanish army in Flanders during the Fronde. The count pressed advice on Malclerc that Retz should join Condé in the Netherlands, and the cardinal felt obliged to feign acceptance of this proposal. To induce Fuensaldagne to grant him passports to Franche-Comté, he had Malclerc exchange a cipher with the count. This, as Joly observed, was not the first time Retz had left a cipher which he had no intention of using, but it created the confidence he sought. He continued his journey with his Spanish escort, passing within twenty miles of a town besieged by Modena and Mercoeur. Travelling through the Swiss passes, he paused at Lausanne, and finally reached Besançon at the end of the month. Here he sent Malclerc to find the abbé de Vatteville, the brother of the governor who had entertained Retz at San Sebastian. The abbé, who was now living quietly enough, was a man of some notoriety. As a young Carthusian monk he had been guilty of a double murder, and had taken service with the Turkish army fighting the Venetians in the Morea. He had then sold Turkish military secrets to Venice in exchange for papal absolution from his crimes and his apostasy.[4] The abbé at first did not wish to be compromised by association with Retz, but he subsequently saw that he might gain some personal advantage from the Spanish desire to negotiate with the cardinal. He found Retz a hiding place in the house of a relative, the marquise de Conflans, whose husband was fighting for Spain in Flanders. Retz charmed her by recounting his adventures, and used her home as a base while he tried to discover the reactions of the French government to his departure from Italy. He sent some of his entourage to Strasbourg and despatched the abbé de Verjus to Paris to gather news.

So far as Mazarin was concerned, Retz had disappeared. One agent reported that he had embarked at Genoa, another at Livorno, and a third repeated information that he had landed at Monaco.[5] Spies were sent to Brittany and Machecoul, and a watch maintained on the house of madame de Pommereuil. On 14 September a royal ordinance required the arrest of Retz as a traitor in Spanish pay who had disobeyed the pope by revoking the authority of du Saussay.[6] Like the edict issued on 20 August 1654 after his escape from Nantes, it forbade any subject of the king to shelter him or communicate with him. A week later it became known that the cardinal was at Besançon, and Le Tellier's protégé, Colbert, proposed a plan to kidnap him which Mazarin rejected. On 15 September Retz despatched a letter to the assembly of the clergy headed 'from the place of my retreat which, as you can well understand, I cannot divulge'.[7] It explained that he had been obliged by the plague to leave Rome, complained about the imprisonment of Chevalier, and demanded the restoration of his episcopal revenues and privileges. It also contained a hint that Retz was about to place his diocese under interdict, suspending the administration of the sacrament. 'The respect I possess for your assembly', he wrote, 'and my constant preference for the ways of moderation have, until now, restrained me from employing those spiritual weapons which all the power of my enemies cannot wrest from my hands.' The threat was a serious one, and the court responded by releasing Chevalier from the Bastille and banishing him to Issoudun. But Mazarin would offer no genuine concession to his enemy, and disdained a new letter sent by Retz to the king on 22 September professing the cardinal's 'inviolable fidelity'.[8] Rumours that Retz was planning some new démarche circulated freely in Paris. On 6 October, Guy Patin, the dean of the faculty of medicine, wrote flippantly to a friend: 'It is said here that the cardinal de Retz is in Franche-Comté, and that he intends to place his archbishopric of Paris under an interdict and to excommunicate everyone. He has already made us eat meat throughout Easter without offending God. Perhaps by this new move he will exempt us from going to mass.'[9]

Receipt of Retz's letter of 22 September coincided with the ruling of the archbishop of Lyon on the claim of du Saussay, now bishop of Toul, to exercise jurisdiction in the diocese of Paris.[10] The archbishop declared that Retz's former grand-vicar might submit his case to an appropriate tribunal. Stung by this new assault upon his episcopal rights, Retz addressed a sharp appeal to the assembly, which Hodencq boldly submitted on his behalf on 24 October.[11] Opinion seemed to swing in favour of the exile as soon as Louis de Gondrin, archbishop of Sens, defied Mazarin and defended his cause. When the president of the assembly, the archbishop of Narbonne, voiced the attitude of the government, the

dispute became so intemperate that the delegates, having set aside
the pronouncement of the archbishop of Lyon, decided it would
be unseemly to include the speeches of the parties in the transcript
of the proceedings. Mazarin adjusted his tactics and accepted a new
proposal to solve the problem of the grand-vicars. On 25 October
the assembly resolved that the bishops of Châlons and Le Mans
should write to Retz asking him to rename acceptable grand-
vicars from a list which included Hodencq. Retz was told of this
offer by Verjus before receiving it in its official form. He wrote at
once to the king, the assembly and the dean of Notre-Dame,
nominating Hodencq together with the dean of the chapter.[12]
These letters, dated 31 October and addressed from 'Du Plessis',
were received in only three days, and it was rumoured that Retz
must be hiding in the capital. The royal guards searched first
the towers of Notre-Dame and then the homes of his friend Le
Houx, the butcher, and Crochet, a canon of Saint-Germain
l'Auxerrois.

   Retz was still in Besançon, and, despite the evident determination of the court to complete his ruin, his supporters prepared a
new attempt to sway the assembly. Mazarin had Le Tellier despatch
a *lettre de cachet*, phrased much more strongly than its precursor in
July, to forbid any debate on the matter in view of imminent
proceedings against Retz for treason.[13] Nevertheless, the lobby
supporting Retz proposed in mid November that the assembly
should send remonstrances to the king demanding the restoration
of the cardinal's temporal revenues. Typically enough, Mazarin
preferred to influence the course of the debate rather than to provoke sympathy for Retz by attempting to enforce the ban. His
agent in these manoeuvres was Pierre de Marca, archbishop of
Toulouse and one of Retz's most determined enemies. The
suggested remonstrances were narrowly defeated, and, as a compromise, the assembly resolved that the king should be asked to
arrange the trial within six months, to ensure that the judges were
ecclesiastics and to respect the immunities appropriate to a bishop
of the Gallican church. If the trial was not settled within six
months, the revenues of the see of Paris should be administered
by the financial agents of the clergy. There the matter rested. Retz
had been no more successful in Besançon than he had been in
Rome. Mazarin's concessions had been purely tactical, and his

implacable hostility barred the way to any prospect of an accommodation. The revival of the plan to bring him to trial would have seemed yet more ominous to Retz, had he known of a new list of indictments sent to Rome in October.[14] It was clear that his colleagues within the assembly would go no further in defence of his cause. Once again, the victory lay with Mazarin.

During his exile in Italy Retz had delighted in comparing himself with the bishops of the primitive church persecuted by the pagan emperors. His friend Vialart, the bishop of Châlons, expatiated upon this theme in one of the letters he sent Retz in Besançon, and recalled how the saints had hidden from their enemies in the desert. According to Guy Joly, Retz began to consider a plan to disappear from the public gaze and to travel incognito from place to place. Joly believed that his master was influenced partly by the *éclat* of such action and partly by a taste for libertine pleasures in the hostelries of the Low Countries and the Rhineland. As a judge of Retz's motives, Joly was a biased witness. La Rochefoucauld declared that Retz disappeared simply from fatigue at the thought of maintaining the struggle and the public character it obliged him to assume.[15] Lassitude, sensual indulgence and a thirst for sensation may all have influenced the cardinal, but fear provided an additional motive. There were constant rumours in Besançon of plots to kidnap him, and Joly recorded that a body of Mazarin's guards arrived in the city a few days after his own departure. A solution had been found to the problem of the expenses of Retz's household. The cardinal had Verjus solicit funds from his friends in Paris. Joly had suggested that collection boxes be placed in the churches of Paris for his support, but Retz had objected that his honour forbad him to become a beggar. It did not, however, prevent his borrowing. Bishop Vialart arranged for the sum of 8,000 crowns to be made available annually, and this was sufficient to provide for the expenses of Retz's travels, together with the upkeep of a modest entourage of three or four servants. Retz laid his plans with Malclerc, Joly and the abbés Charrier and Lameth, that they would travel disguised as cavaliers under assumed names. The cardinal sent Vacherot to Strasbourg, and set off for Constance with Malclerc and Charrier. Lameth and Joly arranged his affairs in Besançon and left at a later date, narrowly avoiding the party sent by Mazarin.

Retz remained in Constance throughout the winter. Joly and Lameth secretly visited France to obtain news and reported that the government had arrested a number of the cardinal's friends, including the marquis de Fosseuse and Retz's intendant, Rousseau. The one man upon whom Retz and his friends could depend for a modicum of justice against the activities of the abbé Fouquet, Pomponne de Bellièvre, had recently died, and the loss of the first president deprived them of a channel to seek legal redress. Joly arranged for the exchange of ciphered letters with Bellièvre's secretary, who was to pass them on to Caumartin, Vialart, La Houssaie, Hacqueville and canon Stuart d'Aubigny, and sometimes to Montrésor and Laigues. Joly also arranged for the supply of money through letters of exchange on Frankfurt-am-Main and Cologne. It was Malclerc who controlled the cardinal's own purse and arranged Retz's pleasures. Joly felt aggrieved at being excluded by Malclerc from his master's confidence, and there was a succession of unpleasant scenes between the two. Verjus was occupied on a variety of missions, while a second secretary, Gaultray, served Retz's interests in Rome. The entourage of the cardinal was scattered, and for several months Mazarin's agents were unable to pick up the trail they had lost at Besançon.

In the early spring of 1657 Retz travelled from Constance to Ulm, and thence to Augsburg and Frankfurt, where he was joined by Lameth and Joly. He wrote again to the assembly of clergy on 28 March to indicate, in moderate terms, his disagreement with their November decision and his intention never to resign his rights as archbishop of Paris.[16] His tone implied that the letter was meant more as a gesture than as a lever to his successful restoration. There was the same air in his publication of two new appeals addressed to the king and queen mother two weeks later.[17] Certainly, the request to re-establish him in his diocese was so regarded by the court. On 6 April Mazarin had the king sign a new demand to the pope to appoint the commission to bring Retz to justice.[18] Mazarin was relentless as ever in his persecution, and on 26 April, in an endeavour to hasten the papal decision, the council issued a royal declaration guaranteeing clerical immunity from the secular power, and formally revoking the powers granted the parlement with respect to Retz in September 1654.[19] Retz was again on the move before he heard of these measures. He sent

Lameth to Münster, where the abbé, disguised as a soldier, was nearly pressed into military service. He himself took Malclerc to Holland, and stayed there for much of the summer. According to Joly, his indulgence in his pleasures obliged him to visit Dr Vacherot in Cologne for the treatment of 'a certain inconvenience which he did not catch from saying his breviary'. Joly was sent to Amsterdam where he was joined by Verjus. Gaultray, recalled from Rome, went with the abbé Rousseau to Liége to collect certain packages from France on Joly's behalf.

Though apparently absorbed in his private pursuits, Retz continued to follow the course of international diplomacy with a sharp interest, and looked for an opportunity to damage Mazarin's reputation. In March 1657 the first minister had concluded the treaty of Paris with Cromwell, promising to cede Mardyke or Gravelines and, later, Dunkirk to the Protectorate in return for the support of an English army in Flanders. Cromwell's soldiers arrived in May, and were reviewed by the king at Montreuil. On 3 October Turenne captured Mardyke from the Spanish and duly transferred it to English possession. Against this background Retz published his best known pamphlet, *A Most Humble and Important Remonstrance to the King concerning the Surrender of the Maritime Town of Flanders into the Hands of the English*.[20] A second French edition was issued in 1658, and the work was translated into several languages. Joly also composed an attack upon the alliance, the *Letter from an English Gentleman to One of his Friends in the Hague*, but it was the cardinal's *Remonstrance* which influenced opinion and caused Mazarin to have Lyonne write a refutation entitled *Remarks on the Transfer of Dunkirk into the Hands of the English*.

There were hints in Retz's memoirs that his attitude to the Protector had been more ambiguous than he pretended. He had assumed embarrassment when the younger Henry Vane had called on him during the imprisonment of the princes and had conveyed Cromwell's request for an understanding: but he was obviously flattered by the incident and impressed by the ability of the republican envoy. Then, when Mazarin had used the tactic of comparing his political manoeuvres with Cromwell's ruthless overthrow of the crown, Retz had publicly defended himself in the parlement, and forced Mazarin to free the princes and retire

into exile. In August 1651 there had been a third occasion when
the names of Retz and Cromwell had been associated. Retz had
asked Bellièvre where his rivalry with Condé to control the court
was likely to lead him, and Bellièvre, who had met Cromwell in
England, replied that it was a maxim of the Protector that no one
climbed as high as he who knew not where he was going. Retz
had indicated his aversion for all that Cromwell represented and
described him as a madman. Bellièvre had repeated the comment,
and Cromwell, hearing a report of the incident, told the French
ambassador that Retz was the only man he knew who distrusted
his intentions. Then, at the time of his arrest, the report was spread
that the letter from the exiled Charles II which Retz happened to
have in his pocket was a communication from the leader of the
English regicides.

Now that Mazarin was Cromwell's ally, Retz delighted in
reversing the reproaches with which the first minister had tried to
discredit him. If he had any lurking admiration for the achievements of the Protector, his own common interest with the Stuart
cause and the opportunity to blacken Mazarin through the association, obliged him to suppress it. Cromwell was represented as
a man of low birth whose diabolical and passionate ambitions
had caused him to murder the grandson of the great Henry IV.
'The ulcerated soul of this tyrant' was 'poisoned by the furies that
always stir the minds of such parricides', and moved by 'hatred of
the Bourbon blood he had outraged'. Cromwell knew that he had
most to fear in the just indignation of the king of France. A minister of France who had given him what 'he would never have dared
to claim through all the endeavours of his powerful forces' was 'a
monster that nature had never before produced throughout all
the centuries'. Mazarin had so deceived his king that Louis XIV
was now acting in concert with the bloodstained murderer of his
cousin, and had been compelled to turn his back upon his unfortunate aunt, the English queen, and her sons. By the surrender
of the Flanders ports Mazarin was reviving the spectre of the
Hundred Years' War, when the English possession of bases in
France had threatened to dismember the kingdom. Little more
than a century had passed, Retz reflected, since Calais had been
regained. Moreover, English Protestantism was likely to inspire
Huguenot disaffection, and English republicanism was a threat to

all the monarchies of Europe. The alliance of the most Christian king of France with this regicidal heretic was a blow in the face of the papacy and a shameful dishonour to both his ancestors and his Stuart cousins.

Having attacked the treaty in terms of religion, honour and the traditions of the monarchy, Retz tried to show that it was indefensible in terms of 'necessity of state' and the 'maxims of Machiavel'. The union of Spain and republican England was little to be feared. The Dutch, who had recently fought a war against Cromwell, would be alarmed by the establishment of English bases in the Netherlands. Cromwell's aggressive designs in the Baltic had alienated both the Swedes and the Danes, and their friendship would be lost to France. Some of these arguments were by no means consistent with the precepts that Retz had advocated earlier in the pamphlet, and he chose to conclude that Mazarin was as clumsy as a Machiavellian as he was shameless as a betrayer of national tradition: 'Monsieur le cardinal Mazarin, Sire, did not take early enough the right sort of nourishment for a politician, and from his infancy he has imagined that the principal attribute of a clever man was never to do good.' Mazarin, like Richelieu, believed in conflict for its own sake. But Richelieu had known how to use Sweden to check the growth of Hapsburg power in circumstances very different from those in which Mazarin had designed a role for Cromwell. The opportunity existed to conclude a favourable peace, but Mazarin wilfully opposed the peacemakers and had become the dupe of his English ally. The same kind of Catholic sentiment that had animated the opposition of the party of the *dévots* to Richelieu was mingled in this polemic with a clear-sighted analysis of the realities of European diplomacy. Retz wound these threads together with the careless bravura of his writing, and discharged a sizeable portion of the animus he felt for his enemy.

Even before Retz published his indictment of Mazarin's policies, the agents of the first minister were plotting to dispose of his critic. He received a report of the presence of Retz in Cologne in the middle of September 1657. An adventurer named Bracq, a relative of the Fouquet family, was engaged to lead fifty cavaliers to Cologne and hide them in the city until an opportunity came to kidnap the cardinal, preferably when he was walking outside the walls. It took some time to make these preparations and rumours of them reached the ears of Retz's friends in Paris. According to Guy Joly, Retz treated the warnings they sent him so lightly that he did not bother to read their letters. Joly recorded that his master was engrossed in the pursuit of pleasure at the house of a Liégeois named Daudrimont. It would have been quite feasible to apprehend Retz because, as his Paris friends pointed out, the elector of Cologne was an ally of Mazarin, and the bishop of Strasbourg, through whose territory Bracq's party would probably withdraw with their prisoner, was also favourably disposed. The danger seemed yet more pressing when Lameth and Vacherot brought word that Croissy-Fouquet had arrived in the city. Retz abruptly changed his attitude, and chose to believe that Croissy was corrupting his servants and intended to assassinate him. Croissy's role in Rome, either as a spy against Lyonne or as a double agent against Retz, had been mysterious enough. The motives for his presence in Cologne were still more impenetrable. Joly said that he had come there from Florence on his own account to try to obtain the resignation of the archbishopric from Retz, and thereby secure permission from Mazarin to return to France. Yet Joly also recorded the fact that Croissy frequently visited Bracq.

Suspicion preyed upon Retz's mind. His balanced judgment deserted him, and he turned upon his servants and accused them of trying to murder him. Noël, his cook, who had served him in Vincennes and rejoined him in his exile, appeared to be watching his master's movements. He was reported to have been visiting the house where Croissy lodged. Retz told Lameth to keep Noël under surveillance and see whether he behaved furtively. Lameth found that the cook did act as though he were trying to avoid observation, but when Noël was taxed with his behaviour he explained that Malclerc had instructed him to discover Croissy's intentions. Imbert, Retz's faithful valet, who had come from Paris to join him in Besançon, was accused by his master of selling secrets to Lyonne and plotting his assassination with Croissy. Joly claimed that Malclerc's jealous hand was behind these accusations. He thought the squire had resented Retz's confidence in Imbert and Noël and had conspired to discredit them. But the truth is difficult to determine, since Joly himself envied Malclerc.

On Retz's orders the abbé Lameth sent the two unfortunate servants on bogus missions and arranged for their arrest and detention in a Spanish prison. Verjus interrogated them and told Retz he believed them innocent, but the cardinal would not be convinced. They remained in prison at Retz's expense for three years, until Noël escaped and persuaded Vialart to have the cardinal give Imbert his liberty. Retz himself left Cologne under a strong escort provided by Condé, which Malclerc had obtained after an urgent ride to Brussels. Bracq, who seems to have been an ineffective conspirator, did not learn of the departure of his quarry until the following day. He assembled his band of adventurers and set off in pursuit, but he did not overtake Condé's soldiers. The escort left Retz at Gemap, whence he travelled to Nimwegen and then to Leiden, where Joly joined him again.

The cardinal seemed to be losing his self-respect. He made no attempt to preserve his dignity, let alone his desire to make his mark in the world. But while he deliberately sank into obscurity, his life, as Joly said, was hardly that of an anchorite in the desert. He took pleasure in acting each part for the various disguises he assumed. Malclerc arranged the sordid entertainments he sought in the inns they frequented, and on occasions the squire's familiarity led him to treat his master with contempt. Nothing seemed to lift Retz from his apathy towards his political interests. Moved to despair, Malclerc once remarked to Joly that no one could transform a buzzard into a sparrow-hawk. Some hopes were briefly raised when Retz decided to visit Condé in the spring of 1658 and thank him for rescuing him from his predicament in Cologne. He passed through Liége and Antwerp in early April before arriving in Brussels. Retz had resisted Spanish pressure to have him ally himself with Condé, not because he still preserved the defiant attitude that had led him to oppose the prince's faction in the last phases of the Fronde, but because he did not wish further to compromise his ecclesiastical status and give substance to the allegations about his treasonable commerce with Spain. He had always treated Condé with the respect due to his rank and reputation, and Condé, in turn, had held his hand when Retz was at his mercy after the massacre at the hôtel de Ville. Their meetings in Brussels were amicable, and their conversation about past rivalries provided mutual understanding of many manoeuvres during

the Fronde which previously had been unexplained. Apparently
there was an informal agreement that neither would come to terms
with Mazarin without informing the other. But Retz disappointed
many of his friends by refusing to tie himself closely to Condé or
to suggest any vigorous action, such as the declaration of an
interdict. He left the prince a cipher, just as he had left ciphers
with Haro and Fuensaldagne. Before returning to Holland he
called on Charles II of England and gave the duke of Ormonde
Joly's address in Amsterdam.

The cardinal resumed his sordid existence in the hostelries of
The Hague, Rotterdam, Utrecht and other Dutch towns. Mazarin's agents continued to follow their instructions from Paris to
trace Retz's movements regardless of expense. To this end the
French ambassador to the United Provinces employed madame
de Pons, a former mistress of the duc de Guise, to gain news of
Retz.[21] His visit to Brussels was known to the French government,
but after he had left Condé he shook off Mazarin's spies and completely disappeared. He lingered for some time in Utrecht, where,
according to Joly, a servant girl called Annetje occupied a particular place in his affections at an inn named the Kleine Poortje.
Charrier came to find him in Utrecht and suggested he should
negotiate Retz's resignation with marshal Villeroy. Retz refused
to consider the proposal. He visited Condé again in Brussels and
discussed with him a project for a rising in Normandy. Marshal
d'Hocquincourt, who was again in revolt against Mazarin, took
part in the plans made at Brussels. He was to lead an invasion
force of four thousand men to cooperate with the discontented
Norman nobility, while Condé was to advance on Paris with a
Spanish army. Nothing came of these schemes. The Spanish gave
first priority to the relief of Dunkirk, now besieged by Turenne.
On 14 June the combined French and Cromwellian armies destroyed the Spanish force and its royalist British auxiliaries at the
Battle of the Dunes, Hocquincourt being slain in the course of
the engagement.

Mazarin had received warning of the plans for the Norman uprising. He saw Retz as one of the instigators of the plot, and sanctioned a new attempt to eliminate his enemy. Retz was fortunate
in possessing an intelligence service which proved as effective as
Mazarin's. The dozen bravoes hired by the abbé Fouquet were

discovered by Joly hiding in a tavern in Amsterdam. Joly employed a spy to drink with Fouquet's men and acquire their plan of operations. He sent word to Retz, who was at Naerden with the abbé Charrier, and the cardinal hastily moved with his entourage to the greater security of Utrecht. He was there in September 1658 when he received a letter from Vincent de Paul, requesting his archbishop's approval for a new set of regulations for the priests of the Mission. Saint Vincent was always mindful of the debt he owed Retz's parents, and showed every respect due to the rank and person of their son. It was ironic that the cardinal should receive such a letter when he was enjoying the charms of Annetje. Saint Vincent felt the approach of death, and in January of the following year he wrote to Retz again, asking him for his blessing and requesting his continued protection for the Mission after his own departure.

The Battle of the Dunes foreshadowed the final defeat of Spain and the coming of peace. The French court itself experienced a new crisis at this time. The king became gravely ill when reviewing his victorious troops at Mardyke in early July. A cabal formed at court which intrigued to overthrow Mazarin and make peace with Condé. Mazarin once again turned the tables on the plotters.[22] Among those who were exiled were the duc de Brissac and his wife and the splendid figure of Jarzé, who had opposed Beaufort in the affair of *la nappe renversée* at Renard's and had once been bold enough to declare his love for the queen. Although Mazarin was himself ageing and sick at this time, he grasped the reigns of power as tenaciously as ever. His plans to wrest the German Empire from the Hapsburgs failed on 18 July, when Leopold of Austria was elected emperor: but in August France became associated with the League of the Rhine, an alliance of Catholic and Protestant princes to impose limitations on the emperor's power. Mazarin's success in this direction was offset by the simultaneous death of his English ally, the Lord Protector. Gravelines fell to Turenne two weeks later. Spain was ready to seek peace. England returned to instability, and the restoration of the Stuarts became more than a possibility. The balance of European power was shifting and Retz was anxious not to be left isolated in any general peace.

The duke of Ormonde called personally on Retz to tell him of the death of Cromwell, and asked for the cardinal's help in obtaining money to effect Charles II's restoration. He suggested that Retz should solicit the pope to lend money to the English king in return for special measures which Charles would take to protect Catholics in England. Retz welcomed this approach, though he knew his own standing in the eyes of the papacy would impede the negotiation more than it advanced it. He sent Charrier off to Rome, accompanying him from Rotterdam as far as Augsburg. Charrier did not see Alexander VII, but he was able to discuss his mission with cardinal Azzolini. The latter made it clear that Charles could expect no assistance from the Vatican, and that the pope was not prepared to embitter relations with France by defending Retz. The only encouraging aspect of Charrier's visit was the fact that Alexander appeared to have done nothing in response to the French request to bring Retz to trial.

Retz's relations with the pope were complicated by his continuing link with the Jansenists. At about the time of Ormonde's proposal he received an envoy from Port-Royal, Saint-Gilles d'Asson. Saint-Gilles was an unlikely inmate in the Jansenist abbey. He was a swordsman from Poitou who, like his brothers, was distinguished by his courage and his physical strength. He had been converted by reading Antoine Arnauld's *Frequent Communion* and had introduced to Port-Royal the young and pious abbé de Pontchâteau.[23] In the autumn of 1658 he set off for Stenay, ostensibly to distribute alms in fulfilment of madame de Longueville's wish to repair the effects of her earlier activities as a frondeuse. He brought to Retz in Rotterdam an offer of monetary support if the cardinal would use his ecclesiastical influence in the Jansenist cause. Retz had received several communications from the Jansenists after his flight from Italy. His friend bishop Vialart was an active supporter of Port-Royal who had stimulated the *solitaires* to write consolatory letters to the exile. Arnauld d'Andilly, whose reputation for candour and sincerity was respected in the salons as it was at the council table, wrote to Retz with an excess of admiration which in another man might have been mistaken for sycophancy: 'Your reward in heaven, Monsignor, is assuredly well-deserved, since you seek no other recompense in the zeal that leads you to employ all the authority that God has entrusted to you for His service and His glory.'[24]

Retz's grand-vicars in Paris possessed Jansenist sympathies, and
had obeyed his instruction to institute the pious Singlin as superior
of Port-Royal. According to the hostile pen of the Jesuit père
Rapin, Retz, knowing that Port-Royal could never afford to take
the risk, had actually suggested that he should secretly live in the
abbey.[25] The cardinal was entirely opportunist in his use of the
Jansenist issue. In 1658 he allowed his vicars to issue an official
censure of the extremist Jesuit answer to Pascal, Pirot's *Apology
for the Casuists*. This measure did not appear to offend Alexander
VII, who himself condemned the book in the following year. The
pope did not always take Retz's connections with the Jansenists
seriously, and he did not forget that Retz's deprivation by the
secular power was a standing affront to the church. On 25 October
1658 Guy Patin reported in one of his letters that the nuncio had
asked Mazarin to restore the temporal fruits of the diocese of
Paris to the cardinal. Yet, as Patin reflected, the pope would be
unlikely to insist in the matter while Mazarin was first minister,
for he was unwilling to endanger relations with France.[26] From
time to time the Jansenists had assisted the cardinal in the publication of his manifestos and pamphlets. Retz asked Antoine
Arnauld to write on his behalf, but Arnauld who, like Retz, was
hiding at this time, would not accept the commission. In 1659
Retz prudently refused to intervene when some thirty curés of his
diocese demanded that the vicars censure another Jesuit work.[27]
He was anxious lest the support which Hodencq and the dean,
de Contes, gave the Jansenist movement should worsen his own
relations with Rome, or lose him the support of his colleagues
within the French church. While he was prepared to use his
Jansenist friends to disturb the government and excite criticism
of Mazarin, he knew also that Mazarin could use his links with
the movement to discredit him. When the opportunity came, he
was quite ready to turn on Port-Royal if it would aid him to reach
an understanding with the court. Père Rapin was probably not
unjust in repeating a story that Retz had described the Jansenists
as being a more absurd cult than any Protestant sect in England.[28]
For their part, the Jansenists invited retaliation when they tried to
make political use of Retz, and they were prepared to disavow
him when they believed the association would do them more harm
than good. The mission of Saint-Gilles, to which, as père Rapin

L

said, Retz seemed too lethargic to respond, marked a phase in the
Jansenist tragedy where religious ideals were tarnished by their
contact with the kind of cynicism habitual to the cardinal.

Charrier returned from Rome to report the failure of his mission, and then made his way to France to gauge the present attitudes of the court. He found that the prospect of peace with Spain
had engrossed the attention of the government. Retz heard rumours of imminent negotiations when he was in Ratisbon and
hurried back to Holland. Verjus was there with news from France,
so Retz promptly visited Brussels to confer with Condé. There was
some opposition to the peace at the Spanish court, and the marquis
de Carcena, the commander of the Spanish army in Flanders,
seemed to be in touch with this circle. He wrote to Haro saying
that if Condé and Retz were able to come to terms with Mazarin
they would try to overthrow him when they had returned to
France.[29] But the Spanish could no longer hope for another
Fronde. The full extent of the Norman conspiracy had been uncovered. One of the local plotters had been decapitated in Paris
and others had fled to Holland. Haro judged that Mazarin would
exclude Retz from the terms of the treaty, and he instructed Carcena not to communicate with the cardinal lest the negotiations be
endangered. Retz continued to confer with Condé, who advised
him in May 1659 that an armistice had been agreed. In August the
prince told his negotiator, Lenet, that Retz should not be included
in his discussions. Mazarin met Haro at Saint-Jean-de-Luz to
decide the final terms. He wrote to Le Tellier at this time reminding him that Retz's association with the Normandy plot was only
the most recent of the long series of intrigues in which Retz had
fostered sedition in the parlement, in Port-Royal and among the
curés of Paris.[30] The cardinal was a blind spot in Mazarin's lucid
analysis of the national advantage. So great was his obsession that
it seemed he was ready to continue the war rather than pardon his
enemy. The treaty of the Pyrenees was signed on 7 November
1659. Condé returned to France to be fêted and forgiven. Retz
went back to Holland to feed upon his chagrin.

Joly suggested to his master that it would be more consistent
with his purse, his dignity and his vocation if he retired to a
monastery under the protection of the emperor Leopold. Retz
refused to listen. He visited Brussels early in 1660 to see Charles

II, who had attended the peace conference. Then he resumed his life in the wayside taverns of Holland. 'He spent his time', wrote Joly, 'watching comedies, rope dancers and puppet shows, and read nothing save empty trifles and mawkish nonsense.' In the disappointment of his hopes of inclusion in the peace he relapsed into that mood of empty despair where his mind would respond only to trivial amusements and the titillation of his senses. Sometimes he turned with idle malice to exacerbate the petty jealousies within his own household. Joly claimed that he tried to excite envy between himself and Verjus. There were endless minor quarrels and a deepening atmosphere of distrust. Joly bitterly resented the ascendancy of Malclerc, and the account of this period in his memoirs was clouded with his discontent. Malclerc, he asserted, came to control the cardinal's mind in all things by providing him with women. There was one occasion when Vacherot and the servants burst into a room in an inn in Antwerp to find Retz and his squire panting after an affray from which both emerged with bloodied noses. The cardinal, according to Joly, had been beaten by Malclerc, and thereafter became completely submissive to him. Malclerc lorded it over his companions and insulted them in Retz's presence without any protest from the cardinal. He sent his own ciphers to Paris, and would have taken control of all his master's political affairs if Caumartin had not insisted upon dealing with Joly. Malclerc then attempted to damage Joly's reputation, and in his search for evidence he secretly entered his room at night to turn out the secretary's pockets when he thought him asleep. Though Joly continued to work assiduously for his master, he saw that Retz only pretended to repose confidence in him, and that his mind had been poisoned against him. Such, at least, was Joly's version of affairs. Malclerc would doubtless have presented a different account.

In the spring of 1660 Retz momentarily shook off his despondency. Mazarin's diplomacy had been everywhere triumphant. Having ended the war with Spain, he had healed the breach with the Stuarts and supported the measures taken by Charles II for his imminent return to his kingdom. As the foremost power in Europe, France had little to fear from the Hapsburgs. The young Louis XIV, whose wilful flirtation with Mazarin's niece, Marie Mancini, had been ended in August 1659 by both his mother and

his first minister, was about to consummate the new alliance with
Spain by his marriage with the Infanta, Maria Theresa. After a
long series of wars in the Baltic, peace had been restored among
the northern powers through the endeavours of Mazarin's peacemakers.[31] But, though Mazarin was at the height of his success,
his health was failing and the end of his régime was in sight. The
decline of his vigour inspired the hope that by a last act he might
restore peace to the Gallican church as he had restored it to the
nations of Europe. The bishop of Coutances made some tentative
representations for the settlement of Retz's status. The bishop had
recently persuaded the authorities to drop an impending prosecution against Saint-Gilles. He had been an intermediary between
Mazarin and the Jansenists before the Jansenist conflict had been
intensified by the Sorbonne's condemnation of Antoine Arnauld.
Although he had performed episcopal functions in Paris while
Retz was in Italy and incurred a ban on his jurisdiction from the
cardinal's vicars, his intentions had been those of a peacemaker.
Mazarin, who, despite his illness, was not inclined to listen to new
overtures, commented acidly that Retz would disrupt any kind of
peace. Nevertheless, the Jansenists saw an opportunity to take the
initiative. If Retz could be installed as archbishop of Paris, he
would be able to shield them from their enemies. Hence they
suggested that the cardinal should issue a new manifesto to bring
pressure against the government. According to Joly, the Jansenists themselves composed the appeal *To all the Bishops, Priests and
Children of the Church from Jean-François-Paul de Gondi, Cardinal de
Retz and Archbishop of Paris*,[32] and Retz merely retouched the text.
The pamphlet contained many citations from the fathers, and the
Jansenist contribution may well have been a major one, but the
characteristic style suggests that the cardinal did more than retouch
the manuscript. The learned abbé Verjus, who probably produced
the Latin version, may also have had a hand in its composition.
Retz had the letter published by a Dutch press in French and
Latin. He dated it 24 March 1660, and had Joly despatch signed
copies to the bishops of Italy, Germany, Spain and Poland. On the
advice of Vialart, he had second thoughts as to the effect this open
letter would produce if Mazarin were to die, and he considered
the possibility of suppressing it. Only a few copies circulated in
Jansenist circles in France, and when the authorities in Paris were

instructed by the government to burn the pamphlet they reported that they could not trace any examples.

The publication merely renewed the resolution of Mazarin and Anne of Austria never to come to terms with Retz, and the young king apparently shared their attitude. Retz wrote to the pope at the same time, and shortly afterwards he had printed two short but eloquent addresses to the king and to the vicars of the diocese.[33] These were equally without effect, but Retz continued to sustain his new interest in public affairs. His activities remained the subject of speculation in the salons, the church and the university in Paris. Guy Patin wrote to a friend on 19 September 1660 that Retz's pamphlets remained a source of personal irritation to the king, and it was believed that the cardinal, exasperated beyond endurance by the failure of the court to respond to the overtures of his friends, was at last on the point of launching his interdict on the diocese. Three months later Patin wrote that Retz was rumoured to be hiding near Paris, awaiting the death of Mazarin.[34] But in fact the cardinal was at this time enjoying the hospitality of the restored king of England.

The restoration of Charles II to his kingdom in May 1660 provided the cardinal with a fresh source of influence. He had persuaded the English king that he might be able to assist in the promotion of his cousin, Stuart d'Aubigny, to the sacred college. D'Aubigny, the son of the duke of Richmond, had been educated at Port-Royal and, as a canon of Notre-Dame, had proved to be one of Retz's most consistent supporters among the clergy of Paris. In return for his offer to support a cardinal's hat for d'Aubigny, Retz obtained from king Charles the gift of four thousand guineas, which Malclerc, according to Joly, promptly appropriated. Retz chose to keep this matter secret, since Vialart and his friends in Paris might reduce his pension if they thought he had access to English gold. He did, however, make some gestures to carry out his own side of the bargain, and visited queen Christina in Hamburg during the summer of 1660 in the hopes of securing her support for d'Aubigny's candidature. Mazarin had sent his agent Bartet to England to explore the possibility of a marriage between Charles and his niece, Hortense Mancini. D'Aubigny suggested that Retz should go to the English court to help conclude this match, and thereby earn Mazarin's gratitude. Retz spent some

time in England in the winter of 1660–1. Although Charles had
hinted he might entertain the possibility of the marriage when he
had attended the conference at Fuentarrabia before the peace of
the Pyrenees, Retz now found that the proposal was regarded by
the English government as a gratuitous insult. He rapidly changed
front, and denounced the scheme as yet another instance of
Mazarin's crass effrontery. This grossly misrepresented Mazarin's
actual policies, as the English government was well aware.
Mazarin had abandoned the match as soon as he became conscious
of its difficulties, and its advocates were the English queen mother
and her adviser, the abbé Montagu, rather than Bartet. On 17
November 1660 Mazarin wrote to Montagu to dissociate the
French government from the scheme, and declare French support
for the marriage of Charles with the Portuguese princess, Catherine of Braganza.[35] Yet Retz's royal host was too mindful of the
help the cardinal had given him during his exile to make his guest
feel foolish. Though no one, not even Mazarin himself, was more
realistic in his statecraft than king Charles, he could not easily
efface the memory of the French alliance with Cromwell. He took
a personal interest in Retz's cause, and deliberately concealed his
movements from the inquiries of Mazarin's agents in England.

In his last months Mazarin seemed haunted by the possibility of
the return of Retz after his death. He remembered Retz's ambitious
designs during the Fronde to occupy his own place, and he could
conceive a situation where the cardinal, restored to his archbishopric and pardoned by the king, might somehow inveigle himself
into the royal confidence. It was not that Mazarin's vindictive
distrust for Retz was based on the memory of all the occasions
when Retz had deceived him: he was too much of a realist for that,
and he had himself resorted to the same kind of manoeuvre. It
was rather that he saw in Retz a supreme egoism that subordinated
national interests to personal whims. He discerned in his rival a
congenital instability, a lack of fixity of purpose, that would
destroy all that he and his predecessor had created. More than this,
his antipathy for Retz was based upon emotion – the one remarkable piece of irrationality in what was otherwise so patient and
balanced a mind. His own hatred was abetted by that of the queen,
who was incapable of forgiving Retz for his role in the Fronde.
In January 1661 the dying minister was taken to Vincennes, where

formerly he had imprisoned his enemy, and where now his treasure was secreted. During these last weeks Mazarin did all he could to prevent any future accommodation with Retz. Early in March 1661 one of Charrier's informants reported that Mazarin had exhorted the queen and her son never to pardon him. Rapin recorded that the king had promised his dying minister he would never allow Retz to return to Paris as archbishop.[36] On 3 March Louis XIV signed an edict renewing the ban on communication with the exiled cardinal.[37] Four days later Mazarin summoned Michel le Tellier, Hugues de Lyonne and Nicolas Fouquet and commended them to the king. On 8 March the edict against Retz was proclaimed in the capital to the sound of trumpets, and on the following day Mazarin died. The memoirs of canon Hermant recorded how a priest had exhorted the minister to forgive his enemies, and how Mazarin had replied that he could not forgive the cardinal de Retz, for that was a matter of state.[38] His obsession dominated his last thoughts.

Retz came hurrying back from England as soon as he heard of the passing of the man who had for so long frustrated all his hopes. He approached as near as was prudent to the frontier and reached Valenciennes, where he wrote to Guy Joly and Jean Verjus in Amsterdam to follow him. When he was told of the edict of 3 March, he withdrew to Brussels, where he met his two secretaries. The king had announced in the council that henceforth he would be his own first minister, although it was generally anticipated at court that Nicolas Fouquet would exercise a preponderant voice in the government. Fouquet's great wealth, and the patronage he exercised among the nobility, provided him with a formidable power. He also possessed military resources. He had recently acquired Belle-Ile from Retz's family and was engaged in fortifying and extending the port where the cardinal had spent his last days before his departure into foreign exile. But the extent of Fouquet's influence created resentment within the council and in the mind of the king. Colbert was already planning his ruin. As early as October 1659, eight months after the death of Abel Servien and Fouquet's installation as the sole superintendent of the finances, Colbert had sent Mazarin a memorandum criticising his administration.[39] Mazarin on his death-bed was persuaded by Colbert to give the king a warning against the minister he had

recommended two days before. Shortly after his accession to
personal power, Louis xiv taxed Fouquet with his errors and
extracted an emotional confession from him before confirming
him in his office. But Colbert continued to gather evidence against
him, and Colbert's original patron, Le Tellier, supported his
campaign in the hope of stepping into Fouquet's place. Retz's
own endeavours to negotiate a settlement were complicated by the
rivalries within the government.

According to Guy Joly, Bartet, who felt himself isolated in
England at the death of the first minister whose schemes he had
served so well, conspired with Stuart d'Aubigny to secure Retz's
pardon and his elevation to the royal council. Bartet must have
been singularly uninformed of the personal attitudes of Louis xiv.
When he returned to Paris with d'Aubigny's agent, Meade, he
was promptly incarcerated in the Bastille. Malclerc, who was also
in Paris at the time, narrowly escaped arrest, and Meade also
effected his escape. Others who tried to negotiate a settlement for
Retz were equally unsuccessful. Charles ii asked his mother to
intervene with Louis, but the king did not even reply to his aunt's
letter. The English queen mother then requested Hardouin de
Péréfixe, bishop of Rodez and the king's former tutor, also to
speak to Louis on behalf of the cardinal. He was immediately sent
to the provinces. The king was bent upon fulfilling Mazarin's
policies against Retz, and hoped to procure from the pope the
commission to try Retz which the first minister had sought in vain.
There had been no ambassador in Rome since the recall of Lyonne.
Colbert was sent on this mission, but Alexander vii was shocked
by the origin of such an emissary – he was the son of a draper of
Reims – and gave him a cold reception.[40] The king's attitude was
quite unambiguously expressed in a letter to the pope dated 3
May:

Most Holy Father, the cardinal de Retz continues more than ever
to show through his conduct and actions, even in the obscurity of his
retreat, the evil intention he has always manifested to disturb the
tranquillity that we have had the good fortune to establish in our
kingdom, and he forgets nothing that is within his power to destroy
the peace and to seduce our subjects from their loyalty and from the
obedience they owe us. Thus we have esteemed it our duty, in view of
our obligation incessantly to watch over the welfare of our people,

not to conceal any longer the many endeavours undertaken by the said cardinal, our subject, with such invincible obstinacy, against our sovereign authority and service.[41]

When Colbert failed to convince the pope of these sentiments, Louis despatched the sieur d'Aubeville, a gentleman of obscure but irreproachably aristocratic lineage, to demand the prosecution of the cardinal. Lyonne, who held the secretaryship for foreign affairs following the disgrace of Brienne, was able to brief d'Aubeville from his own experience of his mission to Rome to instigate Retz's trial, and his instructions were consequently better informed than those he had received from Brienne six years earlier. Alexander VII, who remained as firmly opposed to Jansenism as he had been when he was papal secretary of state, was more concerned with the resistance of Retz's grand-vicars to the anti-Jansenist formulary than he was with the king's accusations against Retz's treason. While Louis sought to take advantage of this by instructing d'Aubeville to represent once more that Retz was himself a Jansenist, the cardinal himself was busy disclaiming any such sympathies.

For a time the reappearance of the Jansenist issue seemed likely to block any chance Retz might have of negotiating with the court. His denial of Jansenism was conveyed to the king by the Jesuit provincial, père Annat, who received it from the duchesse de Brissac. The latter evidently had forgiven Retz for the anxieties he had caused at the time of his escape from Nantes. Her sympathy cost her a new exile, for she was ordered by the king to retire to Bourges. The cardinal's disavowal of Jansenism met a better reception in Rome. He wrote to His Holiness 'in order to take full advantage, before the entire world, of the one glory that remains to me, the glory of my obedience'. He had sworn his submission, he said, to Innocent X's bull of 31 May 1653 and to that of Alexander VII dated 15 October 1656. He pronounced 'anathema to the doctrines of the five propositions of Jansenius as condemned by the said bulls'. He had always repudiated Jansenist attitudes and in his youth he had denounced the ideas of the *Augustinus* when he had been at the Sorbonne. 'What more can I say, Holy Father?' he concluded. 'While I have breath in my body, I shall continue to obey the decrees of the Holy See, and your particular pronouncements will rule my thinking.'[42] There could be no greater contrast between this unequivocal and far from accurate account of Retz's past and present views of grace and the carefully contrived statement on Jansenism he had prepared at the time when he was seeking his cardinal's hat. The pope welcomed his letter joyfully. Retz had feared that Alexander VII would not be able to resist the demands of Louis XIV for his trial as effectively as he had resisted those known to have been inspired by Mazarin, and he had been anxious to remove a barrier against his eventual reconciliation with the French court. Thus he renounced his friends at Port-Royal whose assistance he had for so long exploited. Indeed he indicated his willingness to suppress Jansenism if he were reinstated.

The theological turmoil continued to perplex the diocese of Paris. On 8 June 1661 de Contes and Hodencq issued a *mandement* allowing a distinction to be made between *droit* and *fait* by those subscribing to the formulary which had been approved by the assembly of clergy in 1657. They suggested that 'respectful silence' be maintained on the question of whether the five propositions were actually contained in the *Augustinus*.[43] The council referred the *mandement* to the assembly of clergy, and the assembly declared it void. Those curés who protested in favour of the grand-vicars were admonished by the court. The pope wrote to the vicars on 1 August accusing them of creating a new schism and threatened them with reprisals. He instructed his nuncio in Paris to proceed against de Contes and Hodencq if they refused to withdraw the *mandement*. De Contes said for a time that he would rather be hanged, but in October both he and Hodencq finally complied.[44] Retz, however, refused further comment on the continuing struggle. He thought only of his own interests and, having declared himself, he remained aloof from the dispute.

At this point two of Retz's supporters and distant family connections, Montrésor and François de Vaillan, baron de Pennacors, persuaded bishop Auvry of Coutances to make a further approach to the government on his behalf. A letter, dated 4 July, in which Retz had once more declared his loyalty to the queen, had been returned unopened. Colbert had finally convinced the king of the necessity to dismiss Fouquet and to bring him to justice. Louis awaited a favourable opportunity, and in the meantime he followed

Colbert's advice in lulling Fouquet into a sense of false security. It was necessary for Colbert to destroy the queen mother's confidence in the superintendent, and to this end he engaged her former confidante, the ageless madame de Chevreuse, together with her paramour, Laigues, to launch an intrigue against him. They were joined by the sinister abbé Fouquet, who had quarrelled with his brother four years before.[45] Fouquet heard whispers of the machinations of his enemies, and made the mistake of confiding in the king's mistress, mademoiselle de la Vallière. It occurred to him that if he could solve the continuing problem presented by the cardinal de Retz he might regain the king's favour. Moreover, he had hopes of obtaining the archbishopric of Paris for one of his brothers. With these objects in mind he made contact with the abbé Charrier. Meanwhile the bishop of Coutances approached Le Tellier, observing the utmost caution in view of the royal attitude to the exile. Le Tellier himself saw the advantage he might gain from procuring Retz's accommodation. He knew the king would not accept conditions for Retz's resignation of the archbishopric, but he gave the bishop to understand that negotiations were not impossible. During the summer the cardinal had removed himself as far as possible from the theological dispute in Paris by seeking a second refuge in England. Le Tellier had sent the baron de Pennacors to see Joly at The Hague. Retz crossed the channel and began deliberations with Pennacors, whom he had last seen when the baron had brought him a warning on the day of his arrest. Pennacors suggested that if the cardinal resigned the archbishopric unconditionally, the king might respond to the gesture by restoring him. If the king did not restore him, Le Tellier could, at the least, procure a reasonable compensation. Retz was understandably suspicious of this proposal. On 28 August he wrote to Le Tellier in ambiguous terms which implied a desire for more definite assurances.[46] Pennacors, however, was prepared to offer a secret guarantee that Retz could expect generous terms.

Meanwhile Fouquet had been providing lavish hospitality for the king at his magnificent château of Vaux-le-Vicomte, and felt reasonably confident that he was in no imminent danger. He had resigned his additional post of attorney-general in the parlement, the office in which he had once participated in the dramatic

confrontation of Retz and Condé on 21 August 1651. His last act
in this capacity had been to register the title of duc de Mazarin
for La Meilleraye's son, who had become the late cardinal's heir
through his marriage with Hortense Mancini.[47] This was the
match mooted during Retz's enforced stay at Nantes. Now, as
Fouquet entered the negotiations, many threads from Retz's past
began to draw together. Pennacors had hardly left The Hague
when Charrier arrived with promises that Retz would receive
lucrative revenues if he reposed the negotiations for his resignation in Fouquet's hands. The cardinal preferred Le Tellier's offer,
since it left open the possibility of his retaining his diocese. He was
also imprudent enough to tell Charrier of the mission of Pennacors, but the arrest of Nicolas Fouquet at Nantes on 5 September
saved Le Tellier's negotiation from exposure. At the same time
the fall of the Fouquet family made Le Tellier less anxious to conclude his plans for Retz. The approval of the pope was a necessary
part of the settlement, and Aubeville was still vigorously pressing
Alexander VII to commence the trial. The pope refuted the French
envoy's allegations that Retz was a Jansenist and pointed out, with
a candour suggesting he did not take Retz's declarations at their
face value, that the cardinal's affiliations with Port-Royal had
always been founded in political opportunism. However, Alexander did not refuse to institute the commission: he merely
delayed matters by saying that the charges were not in their
proper form. Aubeville revised the indictment and prepared drafts
for Lyonne's approval. The selected draft was not returned to
Aubeville until late in October. The king expressed his pleasure
at the pope's anticipated agreement by appointing the duc de
Créquy as permanent ambassador to the Vatican.

   While the king was continuing to press Alexander VII to bring
Retz to trial he was also reviewing Le Tellier's negotiations. There
was an obvious advantage in threatening Retz with absolute ruin
on the one hand and offering him minimal terms for his resignation
on the other. As he was expected to do, Retz became fretful at the
long delay and increasingly anxious of the possibility of the pope's
accepting the demand for the commission. Pennacors had written
to explain the slowness of the negotiations, and had again suggested an unconditional resignation. Retz replied, asking for
details of possible compensation, and Pennacors indicated that he

might expect the abbey of Saint-Denis, the restoration of such
revenues from the diocese as were held in the treasury and an
amnesty for his friends. The cardinal pretended a show of hesitation. Some of his friends were already accusing him of surrender-
ing his advantages after all they had accomplished for him. His
old enemy, La Rochefoucauld, caught a flavour of contemporary
salon opinion when, in later years, he described Retz's resignation
of his archbishopric as accomplished in a fit of apathy without
thought for the consequences or the interests of his supporters.
Joly believed the reproaches of his friends were inspired by their
own disappointment at not being permitted to manage the negotiations. He thought that Vialart, for instance, had hopes of personal translation to the see of Paris. In reality Retz was more than
ready to capitulate. He made only three stipulations: there should
be an exact account of the revenues of the diocese seized by the
treasury since the death of his uncle; the marquis de Chandenier
should be re-established in his post as captain of the guards or
offered adequate compensation; and a pardon should be given to
d'Annéri, one of the Norman conspirators who had fled to Holland. Pennacors and Charrier were sent separately to convey these
conditions to Le Tellier. Retz assigned this mission to Charrier
without informing Pennacors because he wished to placate the
abbé over his refusal of the offers from Fouquet. His carelessness
nearly destroyed the negotiation, for Pennacors heard of Charrier's
involvement and threatened to drop the whole matter. Pennacors
had his way, and Charrier got no further than Brussels. In any
case, the king reacted angrily to the conditions. He refused more
than 600,000 livres from the arrears of diocesan revenues, and
would not consider Chandenier's claims. Joly went to Paris for
further discussions with Le Tellier. The minister agreed upon a
sum for Chandenier, and Joly accepted the limitation on the money
due from the archbishopric. The king required Retz to live upon
his estates in Commercy in Lorraine and to attend any conclave in
Rome where he might be of service to the crown. On 30 December
1661 Lyonne instructed Aubeville that there was no need to press
further for the trial, since Retz had bound himself to resign.

The cardinal's affairs were in so pitiful a state that he had to beg
an advance from Le Tellier to cover the expenses of his journey.
Le Tellier provided Joly with 2,000 louis d'or and the necessary

passports, and gave Pennacors the draft of the deed of resignation. When the two envoys had rejoined Retz in Brussels, he exchanged his cavalier's habit for his cardinal's robes, and set out for Commercy. He arrived there on 14 February 1662 amid the acclaim of the townspeople, and went at once to the church to pray. He signed the deed, which was taken to Paris by Joly and Pennacors and presented at the Louvre by the duchesse de Retz near the end of the month.

Retz's long period of exile had ended, but he was obliged to live in rural isolation under threat of the king's continuing disfavour. There was no longer any question of the smooth accommodation of rival interests which had typified the régime of Mazarin. In the memoir in which he described the state of France at Mazarin's death, Louis XIV rejected the methods used by his late mentor. 'Disorder', he observed, 'was universal'. Every governor and official required to be governed. Justice needed reform. The finances were exhausted. The church was divided and threatened with schism and 'cardinal de Retz, whose return I was obliged to prevent for reasons of state, either by inclination or self-interest favoured the whole expanding [Jansenist] sect, or was favoured by it.'[48] A greater autocrat than Richelieu now ruled, not in the role of some first minister but in the person of the king himself. Louis had disposed of both Retz and Fouquet in the first months of his personal reign, and thereafter it was universally apparent that one imperious will directed the government of France. No longer could factious conflicts within the court and council imperil the unity of the state. Louis chose the ministers who would best serve his interests, and he chose them, as he chose Colbert, from the bourgeoisie and the judiciary. The intendants ruled in the provinces under the direct control of these ministers. The great nobility was enmeshed in the protocol of the court, and employed their energies in sterile disputes of precedence and etiquette. They contended for the *tabouret*, not for fortresses and governments. The dissidence of aristocracy, parlement or church was a thing of the past. In Louis XIV the monarchy attained the zenith of its authority. There was no advancement save in the service of the king. The generation of the Fronde had to accept the diversions of the court and the salons, or else vegetate in the obscurity which descended upon the cardinal de Retz.

THIRTEEN

The seigneur of Commercy

Commercy lay among the forests and rolling hills flanking the Meuse some thirty miles west of Nancy. Retz had inherited the seigneurie from his cousin and fellow-conspirator against Richelieu, La Rochepot. La Rochepot had been killed before Arras in 1640. His estate was encumbered with debts, and it was 1650 before Retz was able to borrow the money to settle the claims of his cousin's creditors and to take up his title to the property with the style of damoiseau souverain de Commercy. There were a dozen small fiefs in the seigneurie scattered on both banks of the Meuse.[1] The château had been constructed in the fifteenth century as a fortress intended for war rather than comfort. It had withstood several sieges during the wars of religion and was now dilapidated and badly in need of repair.[2] As recently as November 1652 it had been captured by the army of Condé in a surprise attack. It stood upon a low eminence on the left bank of the river, dominating the town. Some time elapsed before the renovations ordered by Retz were completed, and in the meantime he lodged in the house of the provost of the seigneurie, M. de Taille-Fumières (or Tailfumyer, as Retz spelt the name), who was Malclerc's uncle, later to acquire nobility as the seigneur de Laheville. Seven miles to the south-east lay the fief of Ville-Issey with its pleasant manor, which Retz converted into a summer residence.

The cardinal made extensive provision for his new establishment. After so many years of travel and discomfort he was able to indulge his craving for material possessions. He reshaped the château by lowering the main tower and building a large internal gallery. He spent 100,000 livres on furnishings and a similar sum on the acquisition of silver plate. He created a rich library of books and manuscripts, bound and embossed with his arms, and he took particular pride in his collection of bibles in various languages. Although his debts already amounted to millions, and he was unable to touch a large part of his revenues, he borrowed reck-lessly to develop his property and extend his household. His gardens were planted with exotic shrubs procured by the cele-brated botanist La Quintinie. He built a menagerie at Ville-Issey stocked with wild pigs, roe-deer and other animals sent to him by Condé from the prince's estate at Chantilly. He took pleasure in inspecting the runs where he kept his pheasants, and every day he personally fed the trout in their breeding pool.

The cardinal's companions in his past adventures settled down as the officers of his petty court at Commercy. Malclerc became the governor of his household, and his son, Malclerc de Sommer-villiers, succeeded him in his post after his death in 1663.[3] Hippo-lyte Rousseau was installed as his intendant. Vacherot, until his death in April 1664, continued to serve as his physician. Guy Joly, as discontented as ever, remained in his post for several years before finally leaving his master, and stored away in his mind Malclerc's supposed abuses and defalcations so that he might in due course chronicle them in his memoirs. Joly particularly resented the presence of another of Malclerc's relatives, the Bene-dictine Dom Hennezon, abbé of Saint-Avold and later abbé of the nearby monastery of Saint-Mihiel.[4] The secretaries Verjus and Gaultray were summoned to Commercy for a time, and a new secretary named du Brosseau was appointed. The latter was frequently absent on a variety of missions for the cardinal. So, too, was a certain Duflos-Davanton, who had joined his retinue in Holland. This agent was mentioned by Guy Joly as being sent to Amsterdam to cash letters of exchange received from England, but it is unlikely that he was that Duflos-Davanton who acted as an officer of the guards when Retz was a prisoner in Vincennes.[5] Apart from the major officers of the household, the cardinal em-ployed some fifty other persons, including musicians, surgeons, apothecaries, gentlemen of the wardrobe and kitchen squires.

There were others, outside Commercy, who served Retz well. Caumartin, who acted as intendant in Champagne in the years 1667–72, could always be relied upon. At the court of the présidial in Vitry, where legal issues concerning the seigneurie of Commercy were often in dispute, Retz employed the lawyer Jacques Jacobé de Farémont and his son, François. In Paris Hacqueville attended to the cardinal's needs, while the abbé Bouvier represented his interests in Rome. The man who acted as his general factotum in the capital was that abbé Paris who had deserted his post when he saw Retz descending the wall of the château of Nantes. Retz's letters to Paris were phrased in terms of affectionate abuse. The abbé was archdeacon of Rouen, and the cardinal addressed him as 'you Norman dog', told him not to mock God by mixing biblical quotations with financial statements, and remarked that it would be sheer hypocrisy if he thought of exercising his diaconal function at Rouen.[6] Paris received a stream of instructions, ranging from orders to procure pieces of silver to inquiries about the sale or transfer of furniture from the Gondi château at Villepreux. Much of the correspondence concerned the cardinal's creditors. When the abbé dared to suggest some economies at Commercy in face of the clamour of the creditors in Paris, Retz passed it off with raillery. He even suggested that, if the abbé had managed to accumulate some money to hold demands in check, he should put aside that which was destined to satisfy 'all the small creditors' and send it to Commercy to help the building fund or to pay the expenses for a journey Retz hoped to make to court. It could be justified, the cardinal wrote, as an 'extraordinary expenditure'. When the abbé Paris frustrated one particular set of creditors, Retz addressed him as 'a Hercules to destroy these cruel monsters'.[7] He showed more gratitude towards madame de Guémenée, whose love affair with the cardinal had proved a heavier burden on her purse than it had on her reputation. He instructed Paris to repay 6,000 livres towards the sum he had borrowed from her – but only if she continued to press for it. Six months later she was still pressing, and she had been paid nothing. From 1665 Retz's correspondence with the abbé ceased, and he began to write regularly to an official in the *chambre des comptes*, monsieur de la Fons, to whom he entrusted the administration of his ecclesiastical revenues.

Retz was forty-nine years old when he went to Commercy. His portraits in later life show that his hair had whitened and his face had filled out. Like his enemy La Rochefoucauld, he suffered badly from gout, and in addition he was crippled by rheumatism. He was troubled by eye infections and he caught numerous fevers. In

the letter in which he told the abbé Paris of the death of Dr
Vacherot he stressed his own sickness and his fears for his health
now that Vacherot had gone.[8] Nevertheless his life was active
enough. He was not permitted to move far from Commercy in his
early years there, but he was able to go to Châlons to visit his
friend bishop Vialart and the latter's nephew, La Houssaie. He
planned a trip to Joigny, but was not allowed to go. He kept a
generous table at Commercy and Ville-Issey, and welcomed many
visitors, including his close friends from Paris, who found his
charm and hospitality as irresistible as ever. His correspondence
was not limited to his business affairs. He wrote often to his cousin
by marriage, madame de Sévigné, upon whom his personality had
exercised a powerful fascination since their friendship began at
about the time of her husband's death in 1651. Their relationship
was not, however, of the kind Retz usually tried to develop with
women. Twelve years younger than the cardinal, she was a chaste
and cultivated widow with a sense of poise and reserve belied by
the effusive tone that appeared in her correspondence.

Only one of the letters composed by Retz at Commercy for
madame de Sévigné has survived. It concerned a dispute between
madame de Meckelbourg, the widow of the duc de Châtillon, and
marshal d'Albret, the brother of the man who had killed madame
de Sévigné's husband. Retz had evidently been asked for his
advice, and he replied in December 1668 with banter which he
knew would please his correspondent:

> If the interests of madame de Meckelbourg and of monsieur le
> maréchal d'Albret are indifferent to you, madame, I shall solicit for the
> cavalier, because I like him four times as much as I do the lady; if you
> want me to support her, I shall do it willingly, because I like you four
> million times better than I do the cavalier; if you require me to be
> neutral I shall do as you command. In short, you have only to speak
> and every letter of your instructions will be obeyed.[9]

Through madame de Sévigné and common friends, such as the
comte de Guitaut, the abbé Hacqueville and Caumartin, Retz
was kept informed of the news of the court and the gossip of the
Paris salons. In later years, when her daughter had become madame
de Grignan and accompanied her husband to the provinces,
madame de Sévigné often mentioned her correspondence with

Retz in her letters to her daughter, and reported the health and activities of *'cette chère Eminence'*. Despite her visits to her Breton estate at Les Rochers, near Vitré, she was always well supplied with information about events in Paris. She was on the fringe of court society. Her daughter danced before the king in a ballet composed by the poet Benserade, in which other performers were mademoiselle de la Vallière, the king's mistress, and the future madame de Montespan, who was to succeed La Vallière in the years 1668–80.

Madame de Sévigné remained on the friendliest of terms with La Rochefoucauld and madame de La Fayette. She followed with interest the military careers of La Rochefoucauld's sons. The eldest, the prince de Marcillac, remained one of the king's favourite courtiers, and represented to perfection the gulf between the new generation of court sycophants and the proud spirit of the frondeur aristocracy. Another son, that comte de Saint-Paul whom madame de Longueville had once held aloft to the admiring crowd at the hôtel de Ville during the first civil war, was a popular figure at court, and everyone remarked that he resembled his true father much more closely than he did the duc de Longueville. In 1672, when Marcillac was wounded in battle, and both Saint-Paul and the fourth La Rochefoucauld brother were killed on the field beside him, their father shed more tears for Saint-Paul than he did for his other sons. The news of his loss reached him at madame de La Fayette's salon, and the marquise de Sévigné duly reported the scene to her daughter.[10]

Madame de Sévigné also knew and corresponded with Retz's former protégés, Ménage and Chapelain – now in opposing camps in the controversy between those poets who, like Ménage, had joined Nicolas Fouquet's circle and those who supported the literary canons of Gilles Boileau. She knew and admired the erudite Corbinelli, the friend and distant cousin of the cardinal, for whom Retz tried at her request to obtain a benefice. She probably provided Retz with the same kind of information about the wits of Paris that she sent to their common friend and cousin, the malicious comte de Bussy-Rabutin. In 1660 the count allowed the manuscript of his thinly disguised exploration of the tangled love affairs of some of his contemporaries, *The Amorous History of the Gauls*, to circulate within the salons. Madame de Sévigné, who was

depicted as 'madame de Chéneville', was let off fairly lightly,
though she would hardly have appreciated such remarks as: 'She is
cold in temperament, that is, if one believes what her late husband
used to say', or: 'As for men, she generally likes them all, whatever
their age, birth, merit or profession.'[11] The far more damaging
observations made about other ladies in the *History* cost Bussy a
short imprisonment in the Bastille and a long exile on his country
estates. Another loss to salon society at this time was the equally
sceptical but less malicious Saint-Evremond, who was obliged to
leave France in 1661. He had been present at the discussions
between Luis de Haro and Mazarin before the treaty of the Pyrenees. He had condemned Mazarin's diplomacy in a letter to the
maréchal de Créquy, and the latter had been careless enough to
pass it to another, who had published it without authority.[12]

Retz was anxious for news of the activities of his friends and the
fashions of the time. Molière might have satirised the salon hostesses in 1659 with his play *Les Précieuses ridicules*, but they remained the arbiters of intellectual taste. The first collection of the
self-portraits devised in the salon of the Grande Mademoiselle had
been published in the same year, and they were as much in fashion
as ever. La Rochefoucauld was busy polishing his maxims, which
were to be published in 1665 after circulating among his feminine
friends for their admiration and criticism. The habit of circulating
his manuscripts brought some embarrassment to La Rochefoucauld when a draft of part of his memoirs was published without
his knowledge in 1662. Madame de Longueville, who, after
slipping gradually under the wing of Port-Royal, finally retired
from the world in 1661, seemed particularly offended. La Rochefoucauld wrote a letter of self-justification to their mutual friend,
madame de Sablé, asking whether her complaints could really be
consistent with her piety.[13] These were the preoccupations of the
former *femmes intriguantes*. Madame de Chevreuse no longer sought
to reshuffle the ministry, though she did have a plan to replace
mademoiselle de la Vallière with her daughter-in-law, madame de
Luynes. Even the princess Palatine, whose talent for politics Retz
had so greatly admired, was following madame de Longueville
along the path to piety.

It was a long way from Paris to Commercy, and Retz, deprived
of the society his friends enjoyed, had to make the most of his own

petty kingdom. His grosser habits had not left him. Joly recorded
that he often pretended to go on inspections of the renovations to
the château, where he would shut himself in a room; and, though
Malclerc insisted that he was sleeping from fatigue, Joly knew that
he was actually enjoying 'amusements suited to his temperament'.
Apart from these pursuits Retz took occasional pleasure in the role
of suzerain of Commercy. It was his custom to assemble all the
peasantry from his fiefs once or twice a week to administer justice.
Joly remarked that these proceedings were turned to travesty by
Malclerc and Dom Hennezon, who openly told the cardinal what
to do, and earned the titles of the '*éminence grise*' and the '*émineenc
noire*' from the people of Commercy. Retz received homage for his
fiefs, attended to the finances of the seigneurie, reformed abuses,
settled disputes between the peasants, and even intervened in a
conflict between the governor and the mayor. Yet, as one might
expect, he was often bored by such matters, and many cases were
settled by Malclerc and Hennezon in his absence.[14]

Retz also spent much of his time among his books. He began to
assemble the material he was to use in writing his memoirs. He
concealed this work from Joly, who recorded that the cardinal had
informed him he was composing in Latin a history of the Fronde
in Paris and his own part in it. Joly thought Retz was incapable of
applying himself to this task, and that the project 'vanished in
smoke and pure vanity'. He remarked that his master took delight
in entertaining his visitors by reading two or three pages of the
history he had begun in Vincennes with the help of Vacherot. He
would pretend to be engrossed in it when he was not hunting in
the forests or promenading on his estates, but his natural idleness
and his penchant for his pleasures never allowed him, according
to Joly, to compose more than an additional page or two. Joly
was entirely deceived in this. He claimed that he had personally
advised Retz to continue the work, and the cardinal had replied:

My poor friend, you waste your time preaching to me. I know I am
an idle rogue, but, despite you and everyone else, I like being so,
because it pleases me. I realise that there are three or four of you who
know me for what I really am and despise me in your hearts. Yet I
console myself by using people like you to impose on all the rest.
People are so easily deceived, and my reputation is so well established,
that if you wanted to disillusion them they would never believe you.[15]

There is a flavour of the true Retz behind these words. He enjoyed
moments of assumed candour, where such a confession would set
his audience at a disadvantage and doubly deceive them. He used
the same technique in the memoirs, the composition of which he
so successfully concealed from his secretary.

Joly did admit that Retz applied himself to another project, the
genealogy of the house of Gondi. Joly asserted it was undertaken
entirely through vanity, and that Retz preened himself on dis-
covering five hundred quarters of nobility without a single
mésalliance. He sent for Verjus and Gaultray to help him check and
correct the work, and he was so proud of the result that he would
read the results to anyone who entered his chambers – so much so
that his household took care to avoid passing his door when he
was engaged on it.[16] No doubt he had much of the information
gathered by d'Hozier during the Fronde. As we have seen, his
cousin, Corbinelli, later visited Retz and produced a more reliable
version. Joly's comments on this and Retz's other activities at
Commercy must be read in the light of the secretary's malice,
which was largely inspired by the circumstances in which he left
the cardinal's service. His general view of Retz's life at Commercy
was that the cardinal 'abandoned himself to the pleasures which
usually accompany idleness'.

There was good reason for Retz to be discontented with the
results of his agreement with the king. Superficially, its clauses
seemed reasonable enough. Le Tellier had persuaded Louis to
relent over the marquis de Chandenier and his claim to the
captaincy of the guards. He had been the only one of the cardinal's
supporters to receive specific mention because he had taken the
trouble to make representations to Retz during the negotiations.
Retz had tried to obtain a pardon for d'Annéri and for such faithful
followers as Chassebras, who was in exile in Rome. It was clearly
impossible to obtain the kind of general amnesty he had in mind,
and in fact the persecution of Retz's supporters was not continued.
Chandenier had influence in Paris through his relationship with
Lamoignon, who had succeeded Bellièvre as first president of the
parlement, but his honour mattered more to him than financial
advantage, and he refused the compensation offered. The financial
details of Retz's resignation also appeared to be generous. He still
possessed the small income from the abbey of Busay, which he

had received as a boy after the death of his second brother. He had transferred Quimperlé, the other abbey he had been granted by his family, to Charrier in recognition of the abbé's services.

Retz had virtually no resources apart from the generosity of his friends at the time of his resignation. The abbey of Saint-Denis produced an income of 120,000 livres a year, which was not much less than the income from the diocese of Paris. To this the king had added the small abbey of La Chaume, situated in the duchy of Retz, with an income of 2000 livres. The 600,000 livres, promised from the confiscated revenues of Retz's see, were barely half the amount which should have accumulated over the eight years since the death of his uncle. But Retz was allowed only 50,000 from this source. The remainder could not be touched – nor could Retz hope for permission to leave the vicinity of Commercy – until the cardinal's successor as archbishop had been formally installed with papal approval. This was an understandable precaution in view of Retz's earlier revocation of his first deed of resignation, and the pope's refusal to recognise that first resignation as valid. A series of unforeseen events postponed the filling of the archiepiscopal chair for more than two years. Joly observed that Retz became so bitter at the delay in the settlement that he swore he would be revenged by resigning his cardinalate and entering the small Benedictine house of Breuil near Commercy. There had been earlier occasions when Retz, frustrated by the difficulties he met in Rome, had threatened to lead the Jansenists into open schism, and even to become a Huguenot. The circumstances surrounding the suspension of the settlement were equally exasperating.

The king's first choice for the see of Paris was regarded by Retz's colleagues as a direct slight to the cardinal. He chose Retz's bitter enemy who had turned aside his pleas to the assembly of clergy, Pierre de Marca, archbishop of Toulouse. Marca had had a varied career. He had once been a president of the parlement of Pau, and had been responsible for the advice that led Richelieu to try the bishops associated with Montmorency's rebellion of 1632 by an ecclesiastical commission. He had served on the court which sentenced to death Louis XIII's favourite, Cinq-Mars, in 1642, and he was also the author of a treatise on Gallican liberties.[17] When he heard the news of the nomination to Paris, the bishop of Limoges observed that it was as if monsieur de Marca had first killed the husband and then married the widow. He was generally regarded as a time-server and a slippery ecclesiastical politician. Bossuet, who was beginning to earn his reputation as the greatest preacher of the day and the most eloquent apologist for the monarchy by divine right, criticised him as a man of variable doctrine, with little regard for ecclesiastical values. The pope himself exhibited his dissatisfaction with the king's choice by delaying the bull of institution by a series of formalities. It eventually arrived on 26 June 1662, and three days later, before he had been installed, the new archbishop died. There were those who saw this as a divine judgment. Louis immediately nominated Hardouin de Péréfixe, bishop of Rhodez, whom he had forgiven for interceding on behalf of Retz in the preceding year. But, before Alexander VII could approve of Péréfixe, relations between the crown and the papacy were broken by the extraordinary affair of the Corsican guards.

After his early criticism of the nepotism of his predecessors, the pope had made his nephew a cardinal and appointed the latter's father, Mario Chigi, commander of the papal army. The duc de Créquy, the French ambassador appointed by the king at the time when he expected Alexander VII to institute Retz's trial, arrived in Rome in June 1662. His failure to call upon Mario Chigi was regarded as a slight to the latter's newly-acquired military dignity. A series of provocative incidents between Chigi's Corsican soldiers and Créquy's entourage culminated in August with a fusillade of musketry against the French embassy in the palazzo Farnese. The duke, who was standing on the balcony, escaped injury, but four of his men were killed. The duchesse de Créquy, returning from a church service, was caught in her carriage by the Corsicans. A musket ball whistled past her head, and one of her lackeys was shot down. Louis XIV responded to this affray as a monarch for whom personal and national prestige were identical and all-important. He banished the nuncio to Meaux, and awaited a full apology from the pope. But Alexander sent no explanation to the king: he merely sent Créquy his regrets, and indicated that those responsible would be punished. Créquy then withdrew to Tuscany, and Louis had the nuncio escorted to the frontier by his guards. The king demanded the despatch of a special nuncio bearing a complete apology, together with the hanging of twenty

Corsicans and the consigning of twenty more to the galleys. He also required the erection of a monument to acknowledge the enormity of the affront, and the pronouncement of a decree forbidding all Corsicans to carry arms. If these conditions were not met, he proposed to send a French army to invade the papal states, and, to show this was no mere threat, he requested leave from the king of Spain for his troops to march through Milan. The pope simply refused, and the king, finding he could not afford to launch an immediate invasion, was left in some perplexity. He asked advice from Mazarin's former man of affairs, Ondedei, who was now bishop of Fréjus. Ondedei suggested the opinion of the cardinal de Retz should be sought, and Le Tellier was told to inform Guy Joly to this effect.[18]

Retz was delighted to oblige. It gave him an opportunity to revenge himself on Mario Chigi, whom he held responsible for his own loss of favour with the pope. If his advice succeeded, diplomatic relations would be restored, and the approval of Péréfixe's nomination would enable his revenues to be paid to him. Most important of all, he hoped to acquire a full pardon from the king, and either be allowed to return to court or be given a diplomatic post. The memorandum he submitted in October 1662 was a masterpiece of subtlety.[19] It began with a review of the strengths and weaknesses of the various European powers. It called for psychological study of the pope's likely reactions to the retaliatory measures open to the king. Retz then suggested a number of additional measures which had not previously been considered. He proposed an economic blockade. He pointed out that the continued papal possession of Avignon and the comtat Venaissin was of dubious legality, and that the king might threaten to recover the enclave by a decree from the parlement of Aix-en-Provence. The pope, Retz suggested, would probably yield to this threat, which would cost the king nothing, and it would then be appropriate to demand that Mario Chigi and his son, the cardinal, be sent with a Corsican officer to make a full submission. This advice was adopted, but it did not prove immediately successful.

While the crisis intensified, Retz, in common with other members of the sacred college, received a letter from Rome requesting that the cardinals should intervene to settle the dispute. In the hope of improving the favourable impression created by his memorandum, he sent the letter to Lyonne and informed him he would reply in whatever way the king directed. Lyonne answered on 17 January 1663 with a display of respect and friendship, saying that the king had told him that Retz knew his mind and should reply accordingly.[20] He also sent Retz confidential information on attitudes in Rome which might help him compose his answer. The cardinal then passed to Lyonne two drafts of a possible reply, which took as their theme that Retz's colleagues in Rome were in a better position than he to press His Holiness to repair the insult he had offered the king.[21] In February Lyonne wrote to Retz to tell him that he had been ordered by the king to express His Majesty's satisfaction, and added fulsome praise of his own as to the way Retz had expressed himself.[22] Joly, who mistakenly recorded that it was Le Tellier rather than Lyonne who conducted these transactions, claimed that he himself had been responsible for the memorandum and the reply to the sacred college.[23] But, despite the advice from Commercy, the conflict continued. The pope levied troops and ordered the fortification of Rome and Avignon. The parlement of Aix decreed the union of the enclave with France in July, and was threatened with excommunication *en bloc*. During the winter of 1663–4 French troops entered Parma and Modena, and a larger army was assembled on the frontier. In February 1664 Alexander VII surrendered. Cardinal Chigi carried his uncle's submission to Paris, and a pyramid was erected in Rome to mark the papal humiliation. In April Péréfixe received his bull and was installed in the archbishopric.

Although Retz's hopes had been raised by the communications he had received from Lyonne, he received no personal message from the king to indicate any change in the royal attitude. Père de Gondi had died on 29 June 1662, the day of Marca's death, but when the cardinal asked for permission to attend his father's funeral he was curtly refused. Retz was more disturbed by the refusal than he was by the loss of the father who was largely a stranger to him. A year later, when he wrote to congratulate the king on his recovery from smallpox, he received a cold and brief acknowledgment. Yet it was to be hoped that the final settlement of the disputed diocese might be accompanied by some relaxation of the king's studied disdain for the cardinal. Retz was allowed to enjoy the revenues promised him, and the curés and canons, who had been exiled for supporting him during the ecclesiastical Fronde, were permitted to return. The indomitable Chassebras had been in Rome during the crisis caused by the Jansenist *mandement* of de Contes and Hodencq in the summer of 1661. He had been able to return to France earlier than some of his colleagues, perhaps because he was himself no Jansenist and had subscribed to the formulary in 1663.[24] Retz yearned to escape from the provincial life he had endured for two years, and he determined to test what he assumed to be a softening of the royal attitude. He asked permission to visit the court.

Joly asserted that Le Tellier was trying to shift the blame for Retz's treatment to Colbert, and recalled that some of the cardinal's friends hoped he would profit at court from the rivalry between the two ministers.[25] Lyonne was subservient to Le Tellier who, with his son Louvois, controlled the secretaryship for war. Colbert had been given responsibility for the finances, and was soon to assume the duties of secretary for the marine. While he had already begun to eliminate the corruption from which Fouquet had enriched himself, he was busily suppressing the papers which Fouquet needed to defend himself during his interminable trial. His policy was one of aggressive economic development, and his bureaucratic efficiency suited the king to perfection. His rivals, Louvois and Le Tellier, pandered to the monarch's taste for military glory. But, although there was rivalry, there was no doubt of the king's personal direction of the council, at which he presided with imperious regularity. Retz's friends tried to use marshal Villeroy to widen the division between the ministers in the hope that Retz might be supported by one side or the other. His friends and the members of his family went to meet him at Joigny in early June 1664 in the hope of witnessing his triumphal progress at court. They were to be bitterly disappointed.

The cardinal had been corresponding with the abbé Paris for some time in expectation of this journey. When approval was received from the king, he found that his movements were severely restricted. He was to be allowed two days at the court at Fontainebleau, and two days in the capital, after which he was to take formal possession of the abbey of Saint-Denis and return at once to Commercy. After the joyous reunions at Joigny Retz made his way to Fontainebleau, where his audience with the king had been fixed for 6 June. On the same day la Grande Mademoiselle returned to court after two years of disgrace as the result of her writing irreverently to a friend that she wished the king of Portugal, whom Louis intended for her husband, could be hanged.[26] Louis was prepared to forgive the cousin who had once trained the cannon of the Bastille on his troops: he had no intention of forgiving the man who had raised the mobs of Paris against his mother and her minister. The appearance of Retz at court occasioned fully as much excitement as the return of Mademoiselle, and his words and gestures were the subject of eager conversation. The emotional tensions of this moment were too much for Retz's self-possession. He seemed awkward and embarrassed. Louis, who had last seen him on the day of his arrest, nearly twelve years earlier, remarked that the cardinal's hair had turned white. Retz responded that one's hair whitened readily when one was in disgrace with His Majesty. This was all that passed between them, and the courtiers assumed that Retz was still in total disgrace.

The cardinal recovered a little from his disappointment in Paris, where he stayed in the hôtel de Retz and held open court for the society of the capital. Olivier Patru, who had served as Retz's propagandist in the Fronde, subsequently wrote to express the pleasure his visit had occasioned.[27] When Retz went to Saint-Denis, he exceeded the time stipulated for his visit by remaining for several days in a village near the abbey. There the discord within his retinue broke out again, and Lameth, Verjus and Joly decided to leave his service. Joly, by his own account, persuaded the others they should stay on. During the return journey to Commercy Joly suspected that a large box, which the younger Malclerc was jealously guarding, contained money Retz had secretly obtained from England. Duflos-Davanton and Rousseau joined the other three malcontents. Joly said that the stay in Paris had divided the household so deeply that reconciliation was impossible. He accused his master of acts of petty malice, and of not honouring his promises to pay the salaries of his servants, despite his English gold. All five in the group finally abandoned the cardinal in the spring of 1665. Joly recorded that Retz wept, begged and swore, and made a thousand protestations to no avail.

The secretary admitted that his master paid the 6,000 livres due to him on his departure, but he said that Retz refused debts and arrears to the others, apart from a small sum for the expenses incurred by Davanton on his missions. Joly's bias in these matters was so extreme that his evidence must be doubted. He claimed that, although Caumartin and Hacqueville remained bound to Retz by ties of friendship, they were not uninfluenced by the gift of the abbey of Buzay to one of Caumartin's sons and a pension of 6,000 livres paid to Hacqueville. The cardinal untruthfully told these two old friends, according to Joly, that the secretary had mismanaged his affairs and committed him to a mission he had wished to avoid. On this final note of slander Guy Joly concluded his memoirs.[28] Dom Hennezon and the younger Malclerc remained the leading members of the establishment at Commercy.

The king's accession to personal power had transformed religious as well as secular politics. Louis xiv's attitude to Jansenism, like his attitude to Retz, was based on the unalterable convictions he had acquired from his youthful experiences in the Fronde. 'It is the nature of such people', he remarked, 'to want neither pope nor king.' The obstinacy with which the Jansenists maintained their faith was opposed to the king's determination to be obeyed in all things, and a renewal of the conflict was inevitable. Hardouin de Péréfixe was scarcely installed in his new dignity when he was required to deal with the recalcitrance of Port-Royal towards the formulary. He attempted to solve the problem by making a distinction between the imperfections of human faith and the perfections of divine grace. It was a formula which offered the Jansenists a means to compromise, but they insisted upon 'respectful silence', and the archbishop's suggestion was attacked in a Jansenist treatise by Pierre Nicole. Péréfixe made two visits to Port-Royal to impose his authority. He found the nuns 'as pure as angels but as proud as devils'. Only those nuns who accepted the formulary were allowed to remain in Port-Royal-de-Paris. The rest were distributed among other convents. At Port-Royal-des-Champs the nuns were kept under house arrest and forbidden the sacraments. At the same time the Jansenists were losing influence at court. The marquis de Pomponne, like his father, Arnauld d'Andilly, was highly regarded in the council, although he had been temporarily exiled at the fall of Fouquet. Pomponne was to

succeed Lyonne as secretary for foreign affairs at the latter's death
in 1671. After Péréfixe's campaign against Port-Royal in 1664,
Pomponne's aunt, the celebrated mère Agnès, and his sister were
removed from the Paris establishment and confined in a neighbouring convent of the order of the Visitation, founded by madame
de Sévigné's saintly grandmother. Madame de Sévigné had family
connections with the Jansenists, but, while she was always a good
friend to Port-Royal, she did not share their convictions. She preferred the sermons of the eloquent Jesuit preacher, Bourdaloue,
to the works of her Jansenist friends. In November 1664 she
discussed the persecution of Port-Royal with Arnauld d'Andilly,
and visited mère Agnès and her niece in the convent of Saint-
Marie. She wrote of her impressions to the anxious Pomponne:
'When I consider what constitutes such extreme conviction, I
could almost die laughing. It is in the nature of the world that
things should be as they are. I really believe that the mean between
these extremes is always to be preferred.'[29]

This was precisely the attitude of Retz, whose family links with
Jansenism were, of course, also those of madame de Sévigné. By
1664 the cardinal was re-established in the sympathies of the Jansenists after his shattering disavowal of May 1661. Antoine Arnauld had been his friend and adviser in his last years of exile,
although he had refused to write Retz's propaganda. Bishop
Vialart had remained firmly attached to both the cardinal and Port-
Royal. At Port-Royal-des-Champs the daughter of the cardinal's
notorious aunt, madame du Fargis, was now one of the most
respected members of the community. Although Retz himself was
on good terms with archbishop Péréfixe, he appeared to approve
of the resistance of the Jansenist nuns.[30] In this respect the cardinal's outlook was not dissimilar from that of his friend, the
abbé de Rancé, who had not hidden his sympathy for Retz in
his years of travail. Rancé's conversion was now complete, and his
life was an unending penance for his years as a *galant homme*. His
patron, Gaston of Orléans, had died in 1660, and he was now almost
completely engrossed in the reform of the Cistercian order, and,
more particularly, of his abbey of La Trappe. His family also
possessed considerable influence. He was the nephew of Richelieu's
superintendent of finance, Claude le Bouthillier. He himself had
the great cardinal as his godfather. Two of his other uncles were

bishops, and the late Chavigny was his cousin. Though Rancé was not a Jansenist, he was a firm friend of Port-Royal. He was close to Vialart, and to another Jansenist bishop, Nicolas Pavillon of Alet. He was a frequent correspondent of Arnauld d'Andilly. He had taken the formulary but he had refused to sign the Sorbonne's condemnation of Antoine Arnauld. In March 1656 he had taken part in a conversation with d'Andilly, Singlin and the duc de Liancourt concerning the sympathies of the chancellor Séguier for Jansenism.[31] Rancé's letters to Retz offered his friend no compromises with worldly weakness: 'Your Eminence will readily understand that I do not pray for your prosperity in perishable things. All these I regard as obstacles to the ultimate salvation I desire for you.'[32] In April 1665 the cardinal entertained the abbé at Commercy in the course of Rancé's journey to Rome to present Alexander VII with a request for the reform of the whole order of Cîteaux. The abbé insisted that he should live with the same rigour he observed in his cell at La Trappe. Retz apparently tried to persuade him to moderate his austerity, and Rancé tried to instill in his friend something of his own faith. Soon afterwards he wrote to Retz reminding him of this conversation: 'Time is always passing with terrible rapidity, and the eternity of God is drawing close. The lives of the most illustrious and brilliant of men will lose their identity and become commingled in this eternity, as though it were a sea of infinite extent and immeasurable depth.'[33]

The gulf between the worldly opinions of madame de Sévigné and the severe spirituality of the abbé de Rancé could hardly be wider, and the sympathies of the cardinal unquestionably had more in common with the former. The king knew this sufficiently well to realise that Retz, who had demonstrated his diplomatic ability over the affair of the Corsican guards, could serve his interests in a new dispute with Rome. When Joly had negotiated the terms of Retz's resignation with Le Tellier, he was not aware of a secret clause in the agreement requiring the cardinal to go to Rome whenever the king might have need of his services there. This was a device which enabled Louis to expel Retz from his kingdom at any time he chose. However, the mission which Retz undertook in the summer of 1665 was no more intended as deliberate exile than it was as a mark of his elevation to the king's favour. It was simply that Louis wanted to make use of those talents which in the past had been employed against him, and which seemed ideally suited to the complex issues now confronting him.

When Retz's vicars had censured Pirot's *Apology for the Casuists* in 1658, Alexander VII had himself condemned the book. Although Pascal had died in 1662, the spirit of his *Provincial Letters* continued to excite public suspicion against Jesuit casuistry. In 1664 there appeared at Lyon a work of moral theology which again advanced an extremely relaxed doctrine of grace.[34] Its author was a Spanish Jesuit, Matteo de Moya, who adopted the pseudonym of Guimenius. So extreme were its attitudes that there was no need for a specifically Jansenist initiative against it. Bossuet, the Gallican champion, had labelled Pirot's book 'a sewer in which has coagulated all that is most filthy and impure among modern casuists'.[35] The Sorbonne took the same view of Moya, and issued a censure in February 1665, not only because of its casuistical propositions but also because it maintained the doctrine of papal infallibility. Gallican tradition maintained the infallibility of a council of the church, but not papal infallibility, which was an ultramontane tenet. Neither for the first nor for the last time was Jansenist opinion subsumed in Gallican attitudes. The pope reacted angrily to this challenge, and the king, advised by the parlement that to give way would be to infringe the rights of the crown, decided to defend the Sorbonne. Retz was summoned to Paris in March and instructed by the king to proceed to Rome in search of a solution. Louis showed him no warmth, and insisted that he should go as a cardinal without any letters accrediting him as an envoy of his king. Retz remained in the capital for a month, and it was during this period that Joly, Lameth, Verjus, Rousseau and Davanton finally left the cardinal's service. Retz returned to Commercy to make preparations for his journey. Soon after he left Paris the pope sent Louis XIV a brief demanding the retraction of the censure of the Sorbonne. Retz saw Rancé as he passed through Commercy, and early in May he himself set out for the Holy City.

Retz exchanged a voluminous correspondence with Lyonne throughout his stay in Rome, which lasted for more than a year. Their letters expressed mutual confidence and friendship hardly in accord with the critical picture of Lyonne presented by Retz in his memoirs. The pope welcomed Retz warmly, but he said nothing of Moya's book, and two weeks later, on 26 June, he issued a bull formally censuring the Sorbonne and threatening anyone who published its condemnation of Moya with excommunication. Since nothing was said of Moya's opinions on sin and redemption, it could be inferred that the bull approved what Alexander VII had censured in his suppression of Pirot's *Apology* in August 1659. The parlement refused to register the bull of 26 June, and defiantly sanctioned the sentence of the Sorbonne against Moya's work. This was the problem which Retz was expected to resolve.

Retz occupied himself with a number of matters in Rome, though he never missed any opportunity to advance his particular mission. Soon after his arrival, while he was lodging with his friend the abbé Bouvier, he received a letter from Anne of Austria asking him to assist Rancé in securing approval for his Cistercian reform.[36] The queen mother, like her son, had relented sufficiently to allow herself to make use of Retz, though it does not appear that she had in any way forgiven him when she died in January 1666. Retz did what he could to help the abbé, but the pope refused his assent for the proposed reform.[37] Retz resumed his friendship with prince Pamfili, the son of Olympia Maidachini, who had resigned his cardinalate to marry the princess Rossano. He cooperated closely with Bourlemont, the French chargé d'affaires, and helped him resolve an affray between a group of Danes and Frenchmen which took place within the Spanish embassy and aroused the displeasure of the Spanish ambassador.[38]

As a mediator, Retz found a subtle argument which could point the way to compromise. Infallibility, he said, was not a necessary article of faith. The Sorbonne had not intended to condemn opinions favouring the doctrine, but only those which held the contrary view to be heretical. Hence it might be possible for the pope to issue a commentary on the bull which would lift his censure from the Sorbonne. Alexander VII proved fully a match for Retz in such shifts of meaning. If he had misunderstood the intention of the Sorbonne, he argued, then it was the Sorbonne and not the Vatican which should issue the first explanation. Retz was pursuing this point when he received a letter from Lyonne, dated 9 October 1665, announcing the king's appointment of the duc de Chaulnes as ambassador at Rome. Lyonne added that Chaulnes

M

had told him personally that he knew Retz would be delighted at the king's choice.[39] Chaulnes, who was later to become governor of Brittany, was a close friend of madame de Sévigné, and was accompanied on his embassy by her first cousin, the marquis de Coulanges. Though Retz had a genuine regard for the duke, one may suspect a keen disappointment behind the reply he wrote to Lyonne expressing his 'extreme joy' at the news.[40] He still had hopes of winning over the king and obtaining the post himself, and he did not slacken his efforts to find a solution to the problem of papal infallibility. He saw the pope at Castelgandolfo on 23 October and developed his distinction between those supporters of infallibility who respected the contrary opinion and those who held this contrary opinion to be a heresy. Although the pope was in poor health during this interview, he proved as evasive as ever. The only concession that Retz could obtain was an undertaking that Alexander would consider the publication of a gloss on the bull if the Sorbonne wrote to request such an explanation in the terms which Retz had outlined. Nevertheless, this concession was to prove the turning-point in the dispute. Retz composed a long and colourful account of the audience, and Lyonne responded that the form of the despatch had given him as much pleasure as the substance, which 'could not be stronger, more convincing, more judicious or more adroit'.[41]

Little progress was made in the dispute until the spring, when various drafts of possible 'explanations' were exchanged. In the meantime Retz delighted in the pleasures which his status in Rome provided. There was no sign of the arrival of the new ambassador, and the cardinal could unofficially assume something of the dignity of his office. Queen Christina of Sweden was again in Rome, but she retained little of the convert's zeal which had characterised her first sojourn in the city. Then it had been the newly elected Alexander VII whose extravagant entertainment of the queen had attracted Retz's censure. Now it was the outrageous behaviour of Christina and a group of cardinals, including Retz, which scandalised the pope. She insisted on dressing as a man, and demonstrated her equestrian skill to the cardinals who attended her outings and soirées. She arranged plays for them which her critics described as obscene, and she openly flouted clerical conventions. When she left Rome at the approach of spring, Retz and his friend of the

'Flying Squadron', cardinal Azzolini, were among those who accompanied her to the boundaries of the city.

In April 1666 the pope acknowledged the reasonableness of Retz's arguments, and found a draft of the explanations submitted by the Sorbonne satisfactory. He himself issued a brief condemning the casuistry of Moya's book. Lyonne wrote at the end of the month to congratulate the cardinal on the success of his mission, and indicated diplomatically that the king wished him to return to France so that he could receive treatment for his eyes, which were subject to an inflammation frequently mentioned by Retz in his despatches. 'The king', he wrote, 'exhorts you to think of your own welfare before any official matters at Rome, which, except in the case of a conclave, can never be sufficiently important and pressing to oblige someone of your status to neglect his health.'[42] In reality, the cardinal was in no hurry to leave Rome, and he found a variety of excuses to delay his departure. At the beginning of June French interests were involved in a papal decision formally to invest Charles II of Spain, who had inherited his throne in the previous year, with the kingdom of Naples.[43] There were objections to this in the consistory which discussed the matter, since the king of Spain had not submitted a request for the investiture within the first six months of his reign and his sister, the French queen, could assert a claim. Although Retz wrote two long reports on the subject to Lyonne,[44] the conflict was determined in favour of Spain. The duc de Chaulnes arrived at the end of June, but Retz still lingered. In August the cardinal occupied himself with the composition of a long memorandum concerning procedure for the appointment of cardinals, reviewing the decrees of church councils and the practice of past popes.[45] The point at issue was Alexander VII's refusal to accept the nomination of Beaufort's brother, the duc de Mercoeur, who, following the death of his wife, was bent on fulfilling a religious vocation. The arguments prepared by Retz prevailed, and Mercoeur became the cardinal de Vendôme. Beaufort, the former 'king of the markets', was to die fighting the Turks in Crete three years later.

Retz finally left Rome on 16 September 1666. He remained for a month in Florence because of reports of the pope's declining health and the probability that he would have to return to Rome for a conclave. Resuming his journey after news of the pope's

recovery, Retz passed over the Alps, and halted for a time near
Bâle to recuperate from an accident in which he fell from his
litter and injured his head. He arrived in Commercy on 5 November in the eager expectation that some generous mark of the
king's favour would be awaiting him. Lyonne had written on 21
September to say that the achievement of his mission had restored
him to the king's grace.[46] As it turned out, this was no more than
Lyonne's personal opinion. The letter addressed to Retz in the
royal hand on 12 November contained a cold and formal statement
of the king's satisfaction at his work in Rome, and ended with a
warning that he might soon be required to return for a conclave.[47]
If formality was to be the rule, then Retz intended to exact the
rights and privileges to which he was formally entitled. He had
never been awarded the 18,000 livres which the monarchy customarily bestowed upon a cardinal at the time of his nomination.
He proceeded to apply for the grant, and his request was not
refused. He then asked leave to visit Paris, and again he received
the royal assent. Soon after his arrival in the capital in March
1667, he attended a reception at the hôtel of the duc de Montau-
sier, where queen Maria Theresa was present. Either through
inadvertence or else upon the king's instructions, she failed to
offer the cardinal the *tabouret* when he waited upon her. The
affair disturbed Lyonne, who feared that rumours of Retz's disgrace would circulate in Rome. It was not an auspicious moment to
show disrespect to a cardinal, and the incident might limit Retz's
effectiveness in the conclave to choose a successor to the dying
Alexander VII. The minister wrote to the duc de Chaulnes, instructing him to make it known that the king was pleased with the
cardinal and had recently given him the 18,000 livres.

Alexander VII clung tenaciously to life, embarrassing the professional pride of his physicians, who daily forecast his passing in
their bulletins. On the king's instructions Retz set out for Rome in
advance of his death, travelling in the company of cardinals
Grimaldi and Vendôme. He took Hennezon with him as his
personal aide, and was able to procure Saint-Mihiel for the abbé
at the conclusion of the conclave.[48] Retz wrote to Lyonne from
Marseille on 23 April, the day before he and Vendôme embarked
on a galley provided by the king.[49] Grimaldi was too old to
endure the discomforts of a sea voyage and preferred to make the

journey by land. His choice was a wise one. Bad weather forced the galley to put in at Cannes, and again at Villafranca, near Nice, where they sheltered for two days. When they resumed their voyage, contrary winds drove them back to Monaco, and they did not reach Portofino, in Genoese territory, until the 29th. There Retz despatched another letter to Lyonne, complaining that the senators of the republic had not accorded them the civility they expected.[50] After more storms and delays they reached Civitavecchia on 6 May and were in Rome two days later. Retz again wrote dutifully to Lyonne, enclosing a letter to the king assuring Louis that no one could serve him with 'more obedience, devotion and zeal'.[51] The pope died on 22 May, and Retz reported that the people of Rome demonstrated their joy in the streets, and publicly insulted his brother, Mario Chigi.[52]

When the conclave began, nepotism became a principal issue, and cardinals Barberini and Chigi found it difficult to defend the memory of Alexander. Retz renewed his links with Azzolini and other members of the 'Flying Squadron' of the previous conclave in 1655. Chaulnes, the ambassador, had been told by Lyonne to rely upon Retz's discretion and the skill of his manoeuvres. Retz directed the tactics of the French interest, and continued to correspond direct with Lyonne.[53] Grimaldi was for a time a possible candidate, but in the end Retz succeeded in persuading his colleagues to elect cardinal Giulio Rospigliosi, the head of the papal chancery. Oddly enough, there was one vote missing, and it was that of Retz. Since he was acting as a scrutineer he had given his proxy to Vendôme to deposit, and the latter had forgotten it. Rospigliosi, who became Clement IX on 22 June, had already fostered French interests during the tenure of his previous office. With archbishop Gondrin as intermediary, he was to negotiate a peace with the Jansenists and inaugurate the golden age of Port-Royal during the 'Clementine peace'.

Louis XIV had left the court to lead his armies in the victorious campaign in Flanders before he heard the news of Retz's success. The War of Devolution, in which he claimed the Spanish Netherlands on behalf of his queen, was the beginning of his career of military aggression. His military preoccupations did not prevent his daily attendance to the more trivial routine of affairs of state, and on 10 July he sent Retz the usual formal note to express his recognition for the cardinal's services.[54] Chaulnes himself had generously praised Retz's dexterity. The cardinal left Rome in the second week of July and, avoiding Spanish Milan, returned to Commercy by way of Verona and the Tyrol. The king made one additional gesture to express his gratitude, but to many it savoured more of a deliberate slight. He restored to Retz his own abbey of Quimperlé, which the cardinal had bestowed upon the abbé Charrier, who had died before the transfer was completed. Retz asked leave for it to go in part to the abbé's heirs and in part to the family of the baron de Fosseuse, his supporter in the Fronde.[55] Although the request maintained the cardinal's dignity, it was hardly an act either his king or his creditors would appreciate. Despite his diplomatic achievements, Retz no longer expected the king's favour. In the spring of 1668 he wrote to congratulate His Majesty on the conquest of Franche-Comté, and received a cold and formal acknowledgement.[56]

After another year at Commercy the cardinal returned to Paris in the late summer of 1668. He accompanied the nuncio and the cardinal de Vendôme to a royal fête at Versailles, which was then in the early stages of its conversion to the vast palace and mausoleum of the *ancien régime*. In August Retz was reported by the diarist Lefèvre d'Ormesson to have attended the Sorbonne with Vendôme and Péréfixe to hear one of Colbert's sons defend his thesis in philosophy.[57] Much of his time during this visit to the capital was spent in negotiations with his creditors. The borrowing he had undertaken since his occupation of Commercy was slight in comparison to the debts he had incurred in the earlier phases of his life. Some of his creditors were long deceased, such as the Lyon intendant and Jansenist man of affairs, Gué de Bagnols, who, if a letter written by Guy Patin in June 1657 was to be believed,[58] had died from the religious austerities he practised. Others, like Caumartin and Vialart, were close friends who were unlikely to dun him for payment. Others again were nobles connected with the Jansenist movement, such as madame de Chevreuse's son, the duc de Luynes, and the duc de Liancourt. Some, for the most part members of the magistracy, had invested in his political future, and did not hesitate to seek legal means to recover their capital after his ruin and disgrace. In addition, the claims of his servants and pensioners were to be considered.

In July 1665 Retz had been obliged to sell the land and seigneurie of Commercy to the princesse de Lislebonne, an illegitimate
daughter of Charles IV of Lorraine, though he reserved the
usufruct and honorific rights during his lifetime.[59] His agent,
la Fons, used most of the 550,000 livres from this sale to satisfy
the more demanding of the creditors: but Retz had had to borrow
over 300,000 livres to free the property from its encumbrances in
1650. In 1666 there had been a grave danger that legal processes
to recover debt might have rendered Retz bankrupt and entailed
the scandalous procedure of placing the revenues of Saint-Denis
in the hands of a receiver.[60] Two years later this disaster was again
avoided by calling a meeting of the creditors to appoint a syndic.
Yet no regular system of liquidation was fixed, and the creditors
seemed content with temporary palliatives. Perhaps these evasions
were due to the skilful advice of Hacqueville, whom Retz consulted on such problems. The yearly income of the cardinal
amounted to 170,000 livres: his debts exceeded four millions. Like
many of his rank, he had been careless of financial matters. La
Rochefoucauld, for instance, had been involved in similar difficulties despite his vast estates, and it was fortunate for him that
Gourville, with the backing of Nicolas Fouquet, had been able to
restore him to solvency. The great families of the aristocracy were
accustomed to living on credit. Rising prices and fixed rents had
begun their ruin in the previous century, and many estates had
been mortgaged or sold. Their code of honour demanded extravagant and conspicuous expenditure, but not the satisfaction of their
creditors. Retz shared these attitudes, and his position was aggravated by his generosity. Even La Rochefoucauld admitted that he
was incapable of avarice, though he suggested this was less
through virtue than through indifference.[61] Nevertheless, two
years after the 1668 meeting of the cardinal's creditors, he was to
take the unusual decision to set his financial affairs in order.

After his return to Commercy Retz began a regular correspondence with La Fons. He would often dictate to Malclerc and
Gaultray two or three letters a week concerning his personal
affairs. He told La Fons to consult Hacqueville about settling the
debts he owed to Luynes, Liancourt and even to the chancellor,
Séguier. He sent messages to the family of his old retainer, the
butcher Le Houx. He enclosed letters for forwarding to other

correspondents, including the curé du Hamel, who had returned
to his parish of Saint-Merry in 1664 and became a canon of Notre-
Dame in 1666; François-Emmanuel de Créquy (the stepson of the
cardinal's cousin the duchesse de Lesdiguières) a distinguished
soldier who had won a victory over the Spanish at Lille in 1667
and became a *maréchal de camp* in 1674; Hacqueville, one of Retz's
oldest friends who was a frequent visitor at Commercy; and the
cardinal's loyal friend and mistress, madame de Pommereuil. La
Fons had many instructions to fulfil, and he had the difficult task of
clearing up certain business matters with the cardinal's former
intendant, Hippolyte Rousseau, now the seigneur de Chevincourt.[62]
Sometimes Retz accompanied his orders with items of local news.
He commented on the expansion of the menagerie at Ville-Issey
and mentioned the appointment of a doctor named Bardin to
replace the late Vacherot. The correspondence with La Fons in
1669 was full of similar trivialities. In this year his health deteriorated further. He caught fevers. He suffered from constant head-
aches, and rested his inflamed and myopic eyes behind the tinted
spectacles La Fons sent him from Paris. He had La Fons obtain
from the abbé de Pontcarré music which the abbé had promised
him for his orchestra. He was momentarily worried by new threats
from his creditors, and wrote to La Fons: 'I am resolved that,
rather than suffer again the shock that this year's disorder in my
affairs has given me, I shall do anything, even sell my silver.' But
he postponed the decision. He dealt with the tensions that arose
in his household, and dismissed Beauchesne 'rather than suffer any
more of his impertinence'. A few months later he was to dismiss
Bardin with the comment: 'I have lost a fool and gained [his
salary of] five hundred crowns.' He visited Vialart in Châlons,
where he found La Houssaie and Pontcarré in attendance.[63]

Life at Commercy was a quiet backwater, and Retz seemed
gradually to be renouncing his restless desire for fame or, at least,
notoriety. He seemed an anachronism in an age where there was
neither glory nor advancement save in the reflected glow of the
royal splendour. Retz had received too many rebuffs to retain
hope of the king's favour. These were the years when the character
of the reign had become apparent to all Europe. The smaller
powers began to draw together to face the threat of French
domination. The War of Devolution with Spain ended in 1668,

and in the following year Retz himself experienced something of the military strength and aggression of the new régime when his cousin, François-Emmanuel de Créquy, led the royal troops into Lorraine to dispossess the duke, Charles IV. While Louvois fostered the growth of the king's armies, the schemes of Colbert to develop the economy and capture the markets of Europe from foreign competitors were beginning to unfold. Moreover, by 1668 the triumph of French taste and letters, if not of French armies and French merchandise, was assured. In that year Boileau published his *Epître au Roi* and La Fontaine the first six books of his fables, while Racine's *Les Plaideurs* and Molière's *L'Avare* were performed for the first time. Retz and his memories seemed out of place in all this. Yet the spirit of the frondeur was still alive, and at this very time he had secretly begun that personal investigation of the past which would enable his ultimate triumph over his enemies and their reputations.

In December 1669 the cardinal was wrenched abruptly from his retreat in Commercy by the death of Clement IX. His poor health made him dread another journey to Rome, but he obeyed the royal command without question. Chaulnes, the ambassador to Rome, had himself been at the French court at the time of the pope's death. Retz joined him at Avignon, in company with the recently-appointed cardinal de Bouillon, a son of the frondeur duc de Bouillon. They travelled down the Rhône and embarked at Marseille on a stormy voyage in which the mast of their galley was broken by the wind.[64] They did not reach Rome until 16 January 1670, when the conclave had been in session for nearly a month. Once again Retz played an important part. At this conclave he submitted most of the reports he wrote of his manoeuvres to Chaulnes, who sent the details to Lyonne.[65] The conclave proved long and tedious. Retz at first joined cardinal Leopold de' Medici in defeating the claims of cardinal Elci of Siena. Ultimately the French lobby succeeded in elevating the anti-Spanish nonagenerian, cardinal Altieri, who was pronounced pope as Clement X on 29 April. Retz was back in Commercy in June, where he received the usual formula of thanks from the king. In each of his missions he had achieved considerable success for his country without any tangible reward. He had no wish to undertake any further services that he could avoid, and in July he offered his excuses to Lyonne when the latter asked him to write a history of the conclave.[66]

For the first few weeks after his return the placid pattern of Retz's life at Commercy was broken by a succession of visitors, including the cardinal de Bouillon, his companion at the conclave. His financial troubles continued to oppress him, and at last he faced the decision which had been in his mind for the two preceding years. On 21 July 1670 he wrote to La Fons: 'I have taken my final resolution to abandon all my property and income to my creditors except for the land of Commercy together with an addition of 10,000 livres.' Yet at the back of his mind he still wished to avoid this situation, and the remainder of the letter was vague and contradictory. He wanted La Fons to work out the details with Hacqueville and then to bring the necessary papers to Commercy. He stressed the need for secrecy until the transactions were completed. He expressed the hope that the new arrangement might not come into force until the beginning of October, and in the meantime he believed the promised settlement would justify his drawing an advance 10,000 livres from his ecclesiastical revenues. While he added that perhaps the income he should reserve to himself should amount to 23,000 livres, he tried to make it clear that his general intention was irrevocable: 'You can count upon it. My mind is made up, and the decision is shaped in such a way that nothing on earth can change it.' The letter ended on a note of bathos with the reflection that he would have to provide for his pensioners by the sale of his silver.[67]

La Fons took some time to attend to the settlement. In July the bishop of Châlons visited Commercy, and in the following weeks La Fons made excuses about travelling in Lorraine while French troops were still mopping up the remnants of the army of Charles IV. He came at last at the end of September, but still the settlement remained unsigned. Retz certainly had not lost his other interests, for in November he told La Fons to buy further materials for furnishings, after consultation with madame de Sévigné. Dom Hennezon was now attending to his financial policies, and Caumartin arrived to confer with him. These two returned to Paris at the end of November, when La Fons finally put the affair in order. By ironic coincidence the renovations to the château had just been completed, and Retz moved from the

house of Taille-Fumières at the same time as he accepted the
limitation of his budget. It would have required twenty-six years
before all the cardinal's debts were repaid by this arrangement, but
in the circumstances his creditors might congratulate themselves
upon the terms. Retz kept to his agreement, and even wrote later
to tell La Fons that he was pleased at the way the retrenchment
was operating, and that in many ways he was more comfortably
established than he had been before. Nevertheless, it was a
decision which startled the outside world. The advice of Hennezon
was probably the determining factor in the cardinal's acceptance
of the arrangement, but once it was completed he was prepared to
enjoy the *éclat* it caused, and inclined, perhaps, to think more of
this than of the pious reasons of the abbé, who was becoming the
unofficial director of his conscience. La Rochefoucauld inevitably
caught this nuance in his comment on the matter: 'He has
borrowed more from his friends than any private person could
hope to repay, and has made rather a point of honour in finding
so much credit and undertaking to liquidate the debt.'[68]

Retz remained in his provincial obscurity and took no part in
any affairs of state for the next five years. He kept in touch with
his friends and such former partisans as the Lameth family and the
Norman conspirator, d'Annéri.[69] In February 1671 he visited
Créquy, who was occupying the ducal palace in Nancy, and later
he journeyed to Metz.[70] His renewed contacts with Port-Royal
enabled him to arrange for the Jansenist scholar Pierre Nicole to
live in the abbey of Saint-Denis while he was composing his
essays.[71] At the end of May 1674, four months before the death
of Arnauld d'Andilly, the cardinal paid a formal visit to Port-
Royal-des-Champs.[72] Retz continued to exchange visits with
Vialart, who on one occasion brought to Commercy Dominique
de Ligny, Bossuet's predecessor as Bishop of Meaux.[73] In the
spring of 1672 Retz visited his friends in Paris, including the two
ladies who occupied such strong, and yet such different, places in
his affections, madame de Pommereuil and madame de Sévigné.
The latter wrote to madame de Grignan:

We are trying to entertain our good cardinal. Corneille has read him
a piece [*Pulchérie*] which is shortly to be performed and which recalls
memories of the ancients. Next Saturday Molière will read his Trissotin

[*Les Femmes savantes*], which is most entertaining. Despréaux [Boileau] will give him a rendering of his *Lutrin* and his *Art poétique*.[74]

During this visit Retz complained bitterly to his friends about the boredom of his life in Commercy. A priest named Antoine Blache, who was a doctor in theology at the Sorbonne, was at this time confessor to the nuns of the Calvary in their convent in the faubourg Saint-Germain. He had overheard gossip about the cardinal's correspondence with Hacqueville, and a repeated conversation, concerning Retz's complaints against Colbert, that '*champignon de fortune*', became twisted by his fevered imagination into a conspiracy to assassinate the king. Blache's unbalanced mind was preoccupied by poison plots, and he also declared that Retz had succeeded in poisoning Mazarin. His wild accusations caused so much trouble in the later years of Louis xiv's reign that he was imprisoned in the Bastille.[75]

These forays into the world of letters and of fashion were no more than occasional diversions. Retz seemed to have resigned himself to the provincial life the king's disfavour had forced upon him. He had demonstrated all his abilities as diplomat and negotiator in the royal service. He had found a solution to the affair of the Corsican guards, persuaded Alexander vii to modify his stand over papal infallibility, upheld the rights of the monarchy in the investiture of Naples and the promotion of Vendôme, and defeated the Spanish lobby in successive conclaves. But, like his journeys to Paris, these missions were only interludes in his life as the seigneur of Commercy. His life there became simpler and more regular. He had reduced his household and put his debts in order. He took an increasing interest in the abbey of Saint-Mihiel, seventeen miles north of Commercy. He was there during the Easter services of 1673, and his visits became more frequent as he began to appreciate the calm environment enjoyed by the Benedictines. In all this the abbé of Saint-Mihiel, Dom Hennezon, had a growing influence upon him. Hennezon favoured the renewal of the cardinal's links with Port-Royal, and his own hostility to the Jesuits induced père Rapin to blacken his reputation in his memoirs.[76] Madame de Sévigné recorded her impression of the abbé when she met him early in June 1675: 'He appeared to me to be a most sincere and acceptable man with an upright mind and a fund of common sense. He has a great affection for him [the cardinal] and controls him even in matters concerning his health. He prevents him from blowing too hot on the fires of penitence.'[77] This last comment referred to a remarkable decision taken by Retz in the preceding months, in which Hennezon had a considerable part.

The impression which Saint-Mihiel had made upon the cardinal, the desire to regularise his religious as well as his secular life, the decline of his health, the wish to avoid further exhausting journeys to Rome, the return of his old impulse to capture the public imagination by an extraordinary action – all these were possible motives behind Retz's ultimate act of conformity, his conversion. It was certainly no sudden intervention of grace. He had gone to Paris in the spring to enjoy the company of his friends. In the midst of the social round he had informed the king of his desire to resign his cardinal's hat and retire into permanent retreat at Saint-Mihiel. On 30 May he wrote to the pope and the sacred college to ask their permission. But he was in no hurry to leave the delights of Paris, and for more than two weeks he passed the time with his intimate friends, and especially with madame de Sévigné, whom he saw nearly every day. On 6 June she dined with him and closely interrogated Hennezon, who as the director of his conscience knew more about the conversion than anyone else, and on 12 June she wrote to her daughter:

Yesterday I was so fortunate as to go walking with His Eminence *tête à tête* in the forest of Vincennes. He said the fresh air would do me good, and he was not too preoccupied with affairs. We were together for four hours. I am sure I profited greatly from it. At least, the issues we discussed were not unworthy of him. In losing him I lose my true consolation, and it is I who should weep – and you too, when I consider all his tenderness for us. His departure is going to overwhelm me.[78]

Madame de Sévigné was determined to make the most of every remaining moment with the cardinal. In a letter dated 14 June, in which she conveyed to madame de Grignan the respect of La Rochefoucauld and the affectionate wishes of madame de La Fayette, she said:

I am letting everything else take second place to the pleasure of being with monsieur le cardinal. I am not going to lose a single one of the hours he can afford me, and he gives me much of his time, for thereby I shall better sustain his departure and his absence. After all there is no point in ever sparing myself – after parting from you, I have nothing more to fear.[79]

Retz moved to Caumartin's country house at Boissy-Saint-Léger, ten miles from Paris, accompanied by Caumartin and the abbés d'Hacqueville and Pontcarré. Madame de Sévigné described her sad parting there on 17 June for her daughter's benefit:

I dined there on Monday and I found him with his three friends. Their sad expression brought me to tears, and when I saw His Eminence display his firmness, and yet his tenderness and kindness towards me, I could scarce endure it. After lunch we went for a walk among the most agreeable woods you could imagine. We remained there until six in the evening, discussing so many things, and all of them so tender, kind, affectionate and obliging for both you and me, that my mind is full of them. Let me tell you again, my child, that you can never love nor honour him too much.[80]

Later madame de Caumartin arrived from Paris and came to find them in the garden, together with her husband, Hacqueville and Pontcarré. On the following day the latter three set out with Retz on his journey and accompanied him as far as Jouarre. Thereafter the cardinal continued on his way, alone except for those servants who were to enter Saint-Mihiel with him. He wrote to console madame de Sévigné before reaching Châlons, and told her of a silver box which he insisted on presenting to madame de Grignan. She told her daughter that she must not refuse it, despite their agreement not to accept presents from the cardinal until he had discharged his debts. She added: 'His Eminence wrote to me to bid me farewell once more. I have begged him not to deprive me of the hope of seeing him again. I am most impressed by his retreat, and I wonder what you think of it. It appears to us that he has unlimited determination, and we hope he may be sustained by the crown of grace.'[81]

And so Retz entered Saint-Mihiel and appeared to turn his back upon the world. He submitted voluntarily to the disciplines observed by the monks. He would rise early in the morning and say his breviary in Hebrew. After mass he would dine soberly, and write, or read the New Testament until vespers. Then he would take his walk, followed by his supper and an early retirement at ten o'clock. Was this a deliberate endeavour to avoid the pressures of the world? Was it a contrived attempt to win *éclat* after his failure to escape from provincial obscurity by other means? Or was it the consequence of sincere religious penitence? Hennezon may have assumed the first answer, and hoped it would lead the cardinal to make peace with his creator. La Rochefoucauld inevitably accepted the second. To madame de Sévigné the third conclusion brought also a sense of personal tragedy. The controversy about the cardinal's conversion was to engross the attention of polite society. The solution to the problem must take account of a fact which Retz's contemporaries did not know. At Saint-Mihiel Retz was preoccupied with the continuation of the memoirs which seemed to deny all that the act of conversion represented.

FOURTEEN

The price of virtue

The character of cardinal de Retz was not fixed in his early manhood, to be thereafter exhibited unchanged in every phase and action of his life. There were indeed some traits that could be identified before he took his decision 'to do evil by design', traits which reappeared throughout his later career. These included his appetite for sensual pleasures, coldly rationalised and free from the least hint of sentiment; his thirst for admiration; his anxiety to preserve appearances; and his restless alternation of spirit between enthusiasm and insouciance. But Retz was always something more than a bundle of attributes. His search for personal identity in each succeeding phase of his life was guided by the experience of previous phases, and, as his mind received and blended the fleeting images presented by his senses, his character assumed the subtle modulations he imprinted upon his memoirs.

At first he had affirmed his own identity in action, and constructed a morality of action for its own sake. His cult of the heroic ideal had later been reshaped by an acute political realism in judging the motives of others. His gift for lucid analysis developed beside the cynicism that enabled him to explain and accept his own failures. After his imprisonment and escape he tried to conform to the archetypal images of the persecuted bishop, the provincial seigneur, the resourceful diplomat and even the obedient courtier. None of these poses satisfied him, not merely because his intellect rejected commitment to conformity as such, but also because they impeded his existentialist search for his own identity. Hence, like Descartes, he sought to convince himself of his own existence by re-examining the processes of his own mind. But he did not seek this knowledge through rational abstractions: rather he sought it by recovering the memories of past experience. At the very same time at which he sought to know himself by

retracing, and, inevitably, reinterpreting, his personal history, he
fenced with the idea of the ultimate conformity, the surrender of
intellectual pride to religious conviction. These are the ingredients
of the problem which sets the motives for the completion of the
memoirs against the simultaneous appearance of spiritual conversion. This is the enigma presented to subsequent generations,
and its explanation lies not in what Retz had always been, but in
what, during the last phase of his life, he had become.

The sceptical Saint-Evremond could offer no views upon the
nature of religious conversion which were in any way related to
his own experience, but his detached reflections on the subject
made good sense to his contemporaries. 'The interior joy experienced by pious souls,' he wrote, 'comes from their secret assurance
that God has accepted them.' The process of conversion, he
argued, was essentially irrational. It was impossible to understand
how the 'soul may attach itself to the supernatural'. The impulse
towards rationality was the one aspect of personality that the
thinking man found it difficult to surrender:

Nature has provided each individual with his particular reasoning
faculty, and appears to have attached him to it with a loving and secret
fondness. Free as he is, man can submit to the will of others. He can
admit his inferiority to others in matters of courage or virtue, but he is
ashamed to abnegate his own reasoning power to that of someone else.
He has a natural repugnance to recognising any superior rationality,
whatever form it may take.

Thus Saint-Evremond, like Pascal, concluded that the acceptance
of religious truth came from the heart and not the mind: 'It is in
the heart where the first disposition to receive the truths of
Christianity is formed.'[1]

The religious mind saw significance in conversion as the product
of external grace, not of human will. The generation of Retz, Saint-
Evremond and La Rochefoucauld was confronted with a choice
between Corneille's superhuman egoism of the paramount will
and the Jansenist doctrine of the omnipotence of grace and the
weakness of a human nature degraded by sin. In the social context
of the time the freedom of the will made impossible demands upon
human resources, and only an *esprit fort*, in every sense of the
phrase, could survive the tension between worldly and other-
worldly morality. It is not surprising that those who accepted the

first should have been fascinated by the second, nor that there was an uneasy alternation between the two. Hence such members of the frondeur nobility as Laigues and Renaud de Sévigné responded to the spell of Port-Royal, and such celebrated frondeuses as madame de Longueville, the princess Palatine and madame de Guémenée accepted conversion. There was an ambivalence in madame de Sablé's salon, which was half *dévot* and half *galant*, just as there was a strange respect for the experience of the sinner within the walls of Port-Royal. An extreme reaction against the worldliness of the *honnête homme* was witnessed in the conversion of two of Retz's friends: the abbé de Rancé, whose code of authority was designed to disgust men with their own flesh, and the once libertine bishop Le Camus of Grenoble, who came to defy the worldliness of church and king with equal scorn. It was also so with Retz's father, père de Gondi, for whom the gay life of the general of the galleys was replaced by the devout vocation of the Oratorian. But none of these precedents quite fitted the conversion of cardinal de Retz.

The cardinal's decision aroused intense speculation and debate in a society fascinated by the duality of the spirit and the flesh. The controversy revealed contemporary views of Retz's character and career, and sometimes it also provided insight into the personality of the participants. The grave Turenne, whose apostasy from Protestantism in 1668 had attracted general interest in the salons, and whose sincerity and directness were universally acknowledged, called on Retz in Paris soon after the announcement of his conversion. Turenne was about to depart on his last campaign, and his words to Retz were recorded by Hacqueville, repeated to madame de Sévigné, and passed on to her daughter:

I am no empty talker, sir, and I ask you seriously to believe that if it were not for these present affairs, in which, it may be, I am truly needed, I should go into retreat as you have done. I give you my word that, if I return, I shall not die in a drawing-room. Following your example, I shall spend some time suspended between life and death.[2]

Turenne was killed in action before he could put his intention to the test. The sincerity of Bussy-Rabutin was not so marked. He wrote to Retz on 4 June 1675: 'What you have just done, monsignor, has not surprised me, for I have always regarded you as an extraordinary man, capable of the greatest and finest actions.' At the same time he wrote to the bishop of Verdun:

Without wishing to diminish the merit of the act, I must say that, if ever there was a man of high rank who ought to take such a step, it is he. He is seventy years old [actually sixty-two]: after the great prominence and notoriety of his life, he finds himself without employment and abandoned by all save a small number of friends. . . . what better could he do than go into retreat in the way he has?[3]

Bussy's friend, mademoiselle de Scudéry, offered a similar comment:

If the cardinal de Retz had never been a cardinal and had refused the offer of a cardinal's hat, I should find his action much more exemplary: but he no longer experiences any pleasure in his rank. . . . He is accustomed to being a cardinal as someone else may be used to being a count. If he were first minister and all powerful, as cardinal Mazarin used to be, and resigned his authority to surrender himself to God, that would indeed make a great impression on our minds: but he is a private person who is in no way contented. He is seventy years of age and does not enjoy good health. What he has done, in short, is no great sacrifice.[4]

Those who had directly experienced Retz's shifts and infidelities in the past were more sceptical still. His friend cardinal Azzolini declared in a consistory that, having known him long and intimately, he thought him 'a man who had sought a reputation by whatever means he found available, without being touched by true piety'.[5] The reaction of the Port-Royal circle was mixed. Although Antoine Arnauld accepted the conversion as sincere, the abbé de Pontchâteau visited Retz with the intention of strengthening his resolution and returned to say that the cardinal had already abandoned the attempt.[6]

The most notable, and also the most curious, contribution to the debate was that of La Rochefoucauld. The spectacle of his former enemy capturing the public imagination with such a gesture provoked him to compose his celebrated portrait of the cardinal. He still disliked Retz, but time had assuaged much of his bitterness. He had seen madame de Sablé follow the road to Port-Royal traversed by madame de Longueville, and had lost the platonic affection of the one as he had lost the passionate love of the other. Madame de La Fayette was now his literary confidante, and madame

de Sévigné his close friend. In 1675 he responded to the conventions and deceits of polite society with a certain weariness, touched
with occasional compassion, rather than with the polished cynicism of the early editions of the *Maximes*. But, if he suggested a
measure of candour in personal relationships, he could never play
the part of Molière's Alceste. Thus he composed not one portrait
of the cardinal but two.[7] The first, in moderate and gentle tones,
he sent to their mutual friend, madame de Sévigné: the second,
in sharper vein, he wrote for his own satisfaction and kept within
his bureau. It is the latter which has been known to posterity, and
has provided an image of the cardinal as a mixture of vanity and
indolence who possessed 'the art of displaying his own defects in
a flattering light'. The version written for madame de Sévigné
suppressed or attenuated Retz's weaknesses: the other only
mentioned his virtues or achievements in order to emphasise the
greater significance of his vices and failures. The first draft said
of his conversion: 'His retreat is the most startling action in his
life. He is generously resigning from his rank of cardinal.' The
second version observed: 'The retreat which he has just made is
the most startling and the most false action in his life; it is a
sacrifice he has made to his pride under pretext of piety, for he is
renouncing the court that will not accept him, and turning his
back on a world that is turning its back on him.'

Madame de Sévigné was pleased with the portrait of Retz sent
her by La Rochefoucauld because it did not doubt the sincerity of
the cardinal's conversion and it appeared to be a generous, but
not uncritical, attempt to do justice to his qualities. She sent it to
madame de Grignan on 19 June with these comments:

> Here is a brief sketch of the cardinal, hurriedly composed. Its author
> is not his intimate friend and does not intend that he [the cardinal]
> should see it, nor that it be circulated. He has not pretended to praise
> him. I like it, for all these reasons, and I send it to you with a request
> not to let my copy of it out of your hands. One becomes so tired of
> praises said to one's face that there is something in being able to be
> sure that the author had no intention of pleasing one. When the simple,
> bare truth is spoken, this is the kind of thing that is said.[8]

Madame de Sévigné did not know that La Rochefoucauld's
delicacy had induced him to deceive her. Indeed she thought so

much of an opinion from such a source that she herself sent the portrait to Retz and wrote again to her daughter to tell her that it pleased the cardinal, and that La Rochefoucauld was its author:

This portrait comes from him [La Rochefoucauld]. The reason for my liking it and showing it to the cardinal is that it was never intended to be seen. It was a secret which I extracted because of my taste for unintended praise from a man who is neither the intimate friend of the subject nor a flatterer. His Eminence found the same pleasure as I in seeing how truth obliged someone to speak of him who did not particularly like him and thought he would never know the opinion he expressed. That is how I came to show it to him, but it is only for you and for him, for I have been asked in the strongest terms to keep it confidential, and, as I am meticulous about such things, I beg you to be the same.[9]

So the thrill of imparting a secret led madame de Sévigné to break a confidence that was never meant sincerely in the first place. La Rochefoucauld's real opinion of the conversion was even more severe than those of his friends, mademoiselle de Scudéry and the comte de Bussy-Rabutin. Shortly afterwards La Rochefoucauld composed the maxim: 'It nearly always pays to give up the good that is said about us on condition that no evil is said either.'[10]

Madame de Sévigné was, of course, the most forthright defender of Retz's sincerity against those who, as she put it, 'would go to any lengths to tarnish the splendour of his action'. She replied to the criticism of Bussy-Rabutin: 'If you knew, as I do, how this act originates purely from his desire to win salvation and from the sorrow he has for his past life, you would never cease to admire him.' Others supported her opinion. Bishop Le Camus did not agree with the doubts of the abbé de Pontchâteau of Port-Royal, and wrote to him on 12 June 1675: 'I have been delighted to hear on all sides what the cardinal de Retz has done. These are truly the lightning bolts of grace [*coups de grâce*]. What have we done and what could we ever renounce to come near the merit of his action?'[11] Both Bossuet and Saint-Evremond – and there could scarcely be two more contrasting figures than these – followed Le Camus in accepting the sincerity of Retz's conversion. Saint-Evremond reflected wryly on the tendency of public opinion to accept the worst possible interpretation:

When he made himself a cardinal by intrigues, factions and tumults, they described him as an ambitious man who sacrificed alike conscience, religion and the public interest to his personal fortune. When he abandoned the cares of this world for those of heaven, when the thought of another life made him regard worldly grandeurs as so many chimera, they said his head was turned, and they took what are reputed the highest Christian virtues to be shameful weakness.[12]

To Bossuet it was Retz himself, rather than public opinion, who revealed human fallibility, but he believed that the cardinal 'had realised the enormity of his fault and the emptiness of human greatness'.[13] The memorialist duc de Saint-Simon, writing even later after the event remarked that Retz had been 'touched by the finger of God'.[14] From the vantage point of the next generation Voltaire, a sceptic like Saint-Evremond, though a less consistent one, observed that Retz by his retreat 'acquired the virtues that his great courage had never been able to realise amid the vacillations of his earlier career'.[15]

Those contemporaries who believed in Retz were not necessarily disappointed when he was obliged to retain his cardinalate and even to leave Saint-Mihiel. The requests which Retz sent to the pope and the sacred college at the end of May 1675[16] occasioned as much surprise in the Vatican as they did in Versailles, and raised in both courts issues of expediency as well as of principle. The king instructed his ambassador, the duc d'Estrées, to present Retz's letter with the royal assent, provided that the resignation be not approved until it was certain that the number of French cardinals could be maintained by the promotion of the bishop of Marseille.[17] On 12 June d'Estrées reported the pope had expressed reservations before a consistory, and wished to hear a personal explanation from Retz. Ten days later Clement x wrote to Retz as well as to the king, indicating his doubts. The resignation of a cardinal from a princely house in order to marry for the interests of his dynasty was one thing: the resignation of a cardinal for spiritual reasons, as Saint-Simon was to reflect, was a less acceptable and more dangerous practice.[18] But Retz would not easily renounce his plans. He wrote to the ambassador's brother in Rome, cardinal d'Estrées, to try to have the pope change his mind.

Madame de Sévigné's correspondence revealed a different note in Retz's thinking. On 10 July she told her daughter that she and Hacqueville were delighted to hear from the cardinal that he would not carry his protest to extremes, that he believed salvation might even be possible while he wore his cardinal's hat, and that he would obey if the pope continued to insist. Clearly Retz's viewpoint had changed since he had said farewell at Boissy-Saint-Léger: 'He has not said goodbye for ever. On the contrary he has given me every hope of seeing him again. . . . He is going to keep his carriages and his horses. He often writes me little notes which are very dear to me.'[19] The affair was not yet resolved, however. Cardinal d'Estrées wrote to the foreign minister, Pomponne, to say that delay was advisable and that he had replied to Retz's inquiry by telling him his colleagues in Rome were opposed to establishing a precedent.[20] In the last week of July madame de Sévigné wrote twice to her daughter, saying that both she and the abbé d'Hacqueville were pressing the cardinal to go back to Commercy. Retz was still observing the Benedictine rule, but he was keeping closely in touch with his friends in the outside world. Madame de Grignan, who failed to respond to her mother's enthusiasm for the cardinal, was admonished: 'You must write to monsieur le cardinal de Retz: we are all writing to him here. He is very well, and living a most religious life. He goes to all the services and eats at the refectory on fast days. We are advising him to go to Commercy.'[21] On 28 August cardinal d'Estrées at last made a formal presentation of Retz's request to the pope, and two weeks later the secretary of the sacred college composed a florid Latin epistle to dissuade the cardinal from his intention: 'You have always set an example through good works. You have shone like a beacon on a mountain top. To deprive yourself of your rank would be to set your light under a bushel.' The pope sent a brief to the same effect, but in less metaphorical terms. Still the door was not completely shut, for Pomponne wrote to cardinal d'Estrées on 20 September to say that, despite all indications to the contrary, Clement x had not resolved to issue a definite refusal. Two further letters from Pomponne made it clear that the French embassy should not insist that the resignation be approved.[22] On 23 October madame de Sévigné told madame de Grignan from Brittany: 'Our cardinal is not only recardinalised but, as you know, has received an order from the pope to leave

Saint-Mihiel.'[23] Retz went back to Commercy, and lived there in modest retirement, devoting himself to charitable works and establishing a convent of the Holy Sacrament to educate young girls.

Some saw Retz's withdrawal to Saint-Mihiel, and his attempt to surrender his cardinal's hat, as the culminating gestures of a career of calculated hypocrisy. Others extolled a sudden and complete conversion. His motives were misrepresented in both camps. The cardinal's conversion was not like that of Pascal, who on the night of 4 August 1654 seized his pen when the conviction of an all-pervading religious mystery came upon him, and wrote: 'FIRE God of Abraham, God of Isaac, God of Jacob, not of the philosophers and savants – Certitude – Feeling – Joy – Peace.' Nor did it resemble the strange dreams and emotional outbursts of the princess Palatine, who also recorded her experience and, having spent thirteen years in religious seclusion, was subsequently to have it described by Bossuet in her funeral oration of 1685 as a miracle of grace.[24] Like his decision 'to do evil by design', the cardinal's conversion was entirely an act of will. If he did not feel true penitence for the past, he was determined to do the utmost to appear to do so. He was ageing and tired of the endless struggle to conquer the king's distrust by orthodox means. He sought peace and order at Hennezon's prompting, and wished to avoid future demands for his attendance at conclaves. At the same time he was not insensible of the impression his resignation would make. But these motives did not amount to the deliberate hypocrisy pretended by his detractors. Though equally an act of will, it was the reverse of the decision he had once made in retreat at Saint-Lazare. However, the surrender of self-pride entailed by religious conviction is difficult for all men, and was especially difficult for Retz. He wanted to believe, and the activities of the last four years of his life reveal that he continued to seek conviction. Yet his will was not strong enough to transform the man he had become. If he did not succeed it was because he could not pay the price of virtue – the denial of the past that had made him what he was. This was the state of mind in which he completed the writing of his memoirs.

The circumstances in which the memoirs were composed offer problems which compound the fascination of their author's character. Uncertainty surrounds the identity of the person to whom they were addressed and the precise dates of their composition, while the motives Retz had for writing them have seldom been understood. It is unlikely that the cardinal addressed them to a fictitious lady as a literary device, for he frequently referred to personal matters within their mutual knowledge, and especially to friends they had in common. If there was any one person among his feminine friends who deserved to be the recipient of Retz's confidences, and who would not have been offended by his candid description of his amorous adventures, it was madame de Pommereuil. But the memoirs refer to the most loyal and understanding of his mistresses in the third person, and these references would be utterly incompatible with Retz's personal asides to the recipient if madame de Pommereuil were that person. Nor, as has been suggested,[25] could the lady in question be Catherine-Madeleine de la Verthamon, Caumartin's second wife, whom he married in 1664, ten years after the death of the first madame de Caumartin. Nevertheless, the second madame de Caumartin was a member of the salon circle in Paris. The comte de Guitaut, an intimate friend of madame de Sévigné and a correspondent of the cardinal, made a second marriage with her sister. Caumartin himself was one of the few who shared in the secret of the composition of the memoirs. He probably verified certain details which Retz claimed himself to have checked in the registers of the parlement and the hôtel de Ville, and he is thought to have possessed a first draft of the memoirs which Retz may have sent him for comment.[26] But it is doubtful whether Retz's intimate friendship with Caumartin extended to his wife, and in any case the hypothesis is ruled out by one of Retz's asides: 'I seem to remember that Caumartin talked to you at your house one day about the details of this incident.'[27]

The person for long favoured as the lady to whom the memoirs were addressed was madame de Sévigné. On 5 July 1675 she wrote to her daughter: 'Advise him [the cardinal] as strongly as you can to occupy and entertain himself by having the story of his life written. All his friends are pressing him hard to do it.' On 24 July she wrote again to the same effect.[28] But Retz had already been engaged on his secret project for some years when madame de Grignan received these letters. Nearly all the persons referred to in the memoirs as being known to the recipient were mentioned in madame de Sévigné's letters, the sole exception being Malclerc.[29] Yet a passage inserted by Retz near the end of the memoirs, where the cardinal remembered 'to fulfil your order to instruct *messieurs vos enfants*', suggests that he was not addressing madame de Sévigné. 'Your children', Retz wrote, 'have an ancestry which can naturally elevate them to the highest places, and in my opinion nothing is more necessary to those who may find themselves in such positions than to be informed from their infancy that only the continuation of good fortune preserves the majority of friendships.'[30] He went on to exemplify this cynical reflection in terms of the ingratitude of some of his followers and servants, and his error in displaying too great a familiarity with them. It is unlikely that he was referring to madame de Sévigné's son, Charles de Sévigné, but the observation could have applied to the prospective family of madame de Grignan.

Madame de Grignan was as reserved as her mother was effusive, and, despite the confidence between mother and daughter revealed in madame de Sévigné's letters, she was cold enough to keep the secret of the memoirs to herself. She was young and beautiful, and Retz was her godfather. He often sent her presents, though she never appears to have responded with the slightest affection. It is quite possible that the cardinal conceived a senile passion for her, of the kind that encouraged him to relate his sexual peccadilloes. An Italian observer, Primo Visconti, believed that his attempt to renounce his cardinalate and retire from the world were acts of spite because of the admiration his goddaughter attracted from others.[31] It may be that it was at her request that Retz himself destroyed the scabrous details of his youthful amours in part one of the memoirs, and not that these pages were censored by one of the monks at Saint-Mihiel. It is most improbable that madame de Sévigné would join her friends in a campaign to persuade the cardinal to write his memoirs had she already known that he was secretly engaged on the task already. This, and the reference to *messieurs vos enfants*, suggest that the daughter, not the mother, was the person for whom the memoirs were intended. Consideration of the age and identity of the mutual friends mentioned in the memoirs as persons 'whom you know' confirms this hypothesis. It is not that they were equally well known to mother and daughter: in most instances they were probably closer to madame de Grignan than to madame de Sévigné. Bachaumont and Honoré Courtin, a friend of Croissy-Fouquet, were certainly of madame de Sévigné's generation,[32] but Courtin's son was a close friend of madame de Grignan and, when he was killed in action at Philipsburg in 1688, madame de Sévigné made a point of mentioning it to her daughter.[33] Retz did not refer to La Boulaye, the author of the hare-brained scheme to attack Condé on the Pont-Neuf in December 1649, as someone whom the intended recipient of the memoirs might know, but in this respect preferred to mention his son, La Marck.[34] He did not remind the recipient that she had known the Jansenist intendant Gué de Bagnols, but observed that he was 'the father of the one you know'.[35] The intendant's daughter had in fact married the marquis de Coulanges, madame de Sévigné's young first cousin. Again, Retz referred to Morangis as the uncle of Barillon, 'whom you know'.[36] Madame de Grignan was almost certainly the person for whom Retz wrote his memoirs.

The period in which the final draft of the memoirs was written can be fixed with some precision. There is less certainty about when Retz began the preliminary work. As we have seen, Joly asserted that in his early years at Commercy the cardinal pretended to be engaged on a history of the Fronde and his own adventures, but never made any progress and merely read to his friends the notes he had composed in Vincennes. It was Joly himself who was deceived. There was a great deal of preparation required for the memoirs. Retz used contemporary printed sources such as the *Journal du Parlement* and the *Histoire de mon temps*, which provided him with the chronology of the Fronde and also with a number of factual errors.[37] In general he was remarkably accurate, although there were grave chronological errors for the régime of Richelieu, and the dating of events after his escape from Belle-Ile was suspect. Sometimes he deliberately misled the reader, as in the dating of his nomination for the sacred college, and often his accounts of his own manoeuvres, such as his secret discussions with Anne of Austria, were tendentious. Nor is it likely that he actually wrote down and retained the various pieces of advice he claimed he had given Bouillon and Gaston of Orléans. Yet in general it is not the facts, but rather his interpretations and his account of his own motives, that must be approached with caution. The memoirs are based upon detailed research undertaken in the 1660s and interrupted from time to time by illnesses and his missions to Rome.

The earliest possible date when the autograph manuscript was begun can be established by its use of the orthography 'Rais', which the cardinal began to write in preference to 'Retz' in his correspondence with La Fons in March 1671.[38] Reference to 'the late madame de Choisy', who died in 1670, and the 'abbé, now cardinal, d'Estrées', who became a member of the sacred college in 1671, confirm this period as that in which Retz began to place his material in its final form.[39] It was less than half finished when Retz entered Saint-Mihiel in 1675. Although he concealed his project from the friends who were debating the integrity of his conversion, he had the monks of the abbey write down part of the memoirs at his dictation. Some forty pages in the second part and five in the third were recorded in this way. The story that the monks expostulated at the recording of some of the cardinal's less ecclesiastical actions is supported by the interruption of the script in these passages by the recurrence of Retz's own hand, especially to record his relations with mademoiselle de Chevreuse.[40] Internal evidence in the memoirs also reveals their continuation after the conversion. Towards the end of the second part Retz stated that 'two or three years ago' Charles-Maurice Le Tellier, the son of the chancellor and brother of Louvois, had told Caumartin he had seen a copy of the king's order of December 1652 to arrest Retz. The conversation had taken place after Le Tellier's elevation to the archbishopric of Reims in 1671.[41] In the middle of the second part the cardinal referred to 'Moissens, now marshal d'Albret' in terms suggesting the marshal was still alive. D'Albret became a marshal of France in 1673 and died in 1676. There was also a reference to Bouteville as marshal de Luxembourg, a title he obtained in 1675. It seems that Retz went on working at the manuscript after he left Saint-Mihiel in November 1675, and completed it during the next two years. He was certainly still writing in 1677, for he mentioned in the memoirs the death of Fontrailles, which occurred in that year.[42] More than half the text was composed after the conversion which appeared so emphatically to contradict its method and inspiration.

At the beginning of the memoirs Retz declared they were under-taken in obedience to the demand of the lady to whom they were addressed and at the expense of his reputation. At various points he dispensed pieces of worldly wisdom derived from his own experience, and towards the end of the memoirs his advice took on a patronising and avuncular shade. Apart from the asides about mutual friends, the remarks for the benefit of *messieurs vos enfants*, and one direct admission of an attempt at self-justification, there were few passages which seemed to be aimed directly at madame de Grignan. In the passage where he admitted a desire to justify himself, Retz came closest to an explicit statement of his ostensible aims in writing the memoirs. He was explaining how Mazarin tried to trap him after his promotion to his cardinalate by pretend-ing to Retz's agent, Argenteuil, that he was prepared to offer Retz a share in the ministry.

By your order [Retz went on] I am writing this history of my life . . . and up to this point you have been able to see how carefully I have avoided self-justification. Yet I am obliged to defend myself over this incident because it is one where the artifice of my enemies has found the easiest of opportunities to surprise the credulity of the vulgar.

He then tried to explain that he did not want the ministry, 'which may make pleasure difficult and always renders glory odious'. At the same time he confessed the driving force of an ambition which, through a combination of temperament, calculation and circum-stance, had enabled him to be a cardinal at the age of thirty-nine. He confessed that, while his ambition was not yet satisfied, responsibility as a minister was 'less to my inclination than to my capacity'. He concluded:

I do not know whether I am trying to justify myself by speaking to you so. Before everything else I owe you the truth. It may not serve to acquit me in the eyes of posterity, but there may be some purpose in making it known that most common men who deduce motives from the acts of great men are, to say the least, presumptuous dupes. You may attribute this digression to vanity, but it is not so.[43]

In this passage the various motives behind the memoirs were displayed with a mixture of ingenuousness and subtlety, candour and duplicity. There was a subconscious, and occasionally ex-plicit, desire to explain failure while revealing greatness of mind

that might ultimately secure his triumph over his enemies. There
was also curiosity to re-examine the past, and the vanity of inner
satisfaction in re-interpreting it. This explains how the mature
Retz, who possessed such lucid powers of self-analysis, had also an
unlimited propensity for self-deception. 'We are so accustomed',
ran a maxim by La Rochefoucauld, 'to disguising ourselves from
others that we end by disguising ourselves from ourselves.'[44]
Retz appeared to write for the eyes of madame de Grignan but he
had himself and posterity more in mind. He made no plans for
the immediate publication of the memoirs after his death because
he knew that in defending himself he defended attitudes and ideals
which were anathema to Louis XIV, who would have suppressed
his book. Yet he may have hoped that, when the king, too, had
died, posterity would come to admire him not for his achievements but for his grandeur of soul. His candour was not always
assumed to disarm the reader. The truth was never simple to
Retz, and he continued to delude himself with the hope that there
was virtue in the extraordinary. When he explained his early
scandals and the hypocrisy behind his resolution 'to do evil by
design', he did so to show how circumstances had forced him into
a career contrary to his inclinations. As he came to trace his early
success in this career, he found that candour began to serve a
different purpose and to reveal the incongruity between his
'inclination' and his 'capacity'. When he came to his failures, his
dualism became a shield, and his frankness an aid to deception.

Added to confusion of motives was a singular view of history
that mingled reality with illusion. Retz condemned those whom
he called 'vulgar historians', and reiterated that the only acceptable
history was that written by the great men who had participated in
the events they described. 'Reflect, I beg you,' he asked, 'on the
uselessness of the research which is every day conducted into the
remotest centuries by these studious academics [*gens d'études*].' In
another passage he stated his preference for personal memoirs
before 'the ridiculous vanity of these impertinent authors who are
born below stairs and never cross the antechambers of power, and
who vaunt the pretence of knowing everything that has taken
place in the secret discussions of the great'. He decried 'the
insolence of these nonentities [*gens de néant*] who imagine they
have penetrated every complexity in the hearts of those who have

taken the major part in the direction of affairs, and who pretend there is no event where they have not traced the origins and explained the consequences.' These were the views of the author of the memoirs, not those of the author of *Fieschi*. When he was describing the events that took place in the assembly of the hôtel de Ville and the sovereign courts of Paris in April 1652 – a period when he deliberately avoided such public deliberations – he refrained from offering interpretative comment because of his diffidence in relating hearsay, but he claimed to have checked the registers of the bodies concerned. This obliged him to say how unreliable such documents could be, since they did not catch the *esprit*, the movement and the atmosphere of the debate, and he compared the contrast between the memorialist and the second-hand historian with that between a portrait painted from life and one copied from another.[45]

This insistence on first-hand observation and accuracy is misleading. The facts in any situation were no more important to Retz than the possibilities inherent in them. What could have happened as the result of a particular situation was quite as real to him as what actually happened. In his account of his involved discussions with the queen in July 1651 he provided an elaborate analysis of the likely events that would follow each possible course of action. In another passage he considered the possible repercussions if Gaston had tried to expel the court from Paris in October 1652.[46] Again, he reflected how different his own career would have been had he abandoned the interests of his friends and accepted Servien's personal offers for his reconciliation with the court in the following month. Sometimes these musings on what might have been were accompanied by an emphasis on a sudden unexpected turn of fortune which interrupted a prepared course of action. He dwelt upon what might have occurred if he had succeeded in reaching Paris after his escape from Nantes as he had originally planned. His accidental fall from his horse 'reversed the whole of this plan in a second, although none of the devices on which the scheme was based had failed to operate.'[47] Similarly, his whole future was changed by the accidental repetition of his remark to mademoiselle de Chevreuse that the queen reminded him of a '*Suisesse*'. He claimed that the unvarying hostility shown towards him by Anne of Austria in later years could be attributed solely to this piece of gossip. 'Providence' or 'destiny' were not always called upon, however, to explain failure, and to destroy the link between the possible and the actual. Providence favoured him in his defiance of Condé of 21 August 1651. 'Men are not the masters of the lives of men', he observed when recounting his accidental escape from the assassination plot directed by La Rochefoucauld's agent, Gourville, in November 1651. In the same way, fortune intervened when the attack upon Notre-Dame planned by Condé in early July 1652 was averted by the massacre in the hôtel de Ville.[48]

The reality of what had been possible in the past was often associated with Retz's earlier doctrine of the extraordinary. When discussing the likely success of an attack on the court in October 1652, with Beaufort and himself raising the mob on Gaston's behalf, he returned to his idea that all great actions seem impracticable afterwards to men who were incapable of executing them at the time. He drew one of his customary parallels with the politics of the wars of religion, and observed that the riot raised in Paris by the duc de Guise on 12 May 1588 would have seemed impracticable to lesser men.[49] He made the same reflection about the careful plans laid to establish himself in Paris after the Nantes escape. It would have been 'the most remarkable event of the century', and, though ordinary men might afterwards regard it as extravagant, Bellièvre and Caumartin had agreed at the time that it was likely to succeed.[50] The role of the extraordinary hero was to conceive possibilities inconceivable to lesser men. There were accidental forces which might ruin his design, but the grandeur of the great man lay in a stoic self-sufficiency which inured him against failure. In the memoirs success was generally the criterion of glory. At the same time an action might possess merit independent of public recognition. When he wrote of the way the queen suspected his motives after the return of the court to Paris in October 1652, he claimed that he preferred to her favour the inner satisfaction of knowing, despite accusations to the contrary, that he had destroyed faction and restored peace. Retz had always maintained that it was a necessary quality in the great man to believe in himself. 'A man who does not trust himself', Retz wrote, 'can never really trust anyone.'[51] The turning inwards to the self, as distinct from its exaltation by public acclaim, was a method of escape from the realities of failure. The distinction between intrinsic greatness and external glory was the most powerful device Retz possessed to win a posthumous victory over his enemies. Sometimes the concept of greatness was a means of justifying ambition, at other times it served the function of excusing failure. The memoirs contained several contradictory attitudes to the nature of human greatness. They are more easily distinguished in the various texts of his early history of the conspiracy of Fieschi.

It was nearly forty years since the cardinal had composed his adaptation of Mascardi's account of the Genoese plot of 1547. He had written it in the youthful intoxication of his cult of the hero as a man of supreme honour, *le généreux*. In March 1665 a licence was granted in Paris for its publication, and the book appeared, in Cologne as well as in the capital, while he was absent in Rome on his mission to resolve the dispute about papal infallibility. The text of the Paris version contained substantial modifications of the manuscript, and that of the Cologne edition included further variations; but the theme of resistance to tyranny justified by heroic ideals remained intact. In 1665 Retz had high hopes that the demonstration of his diplomatic skill in the royal service might induce the king to relax the severe restrictions imposed upon him even after his successor had been installed in the diocese of Paris. It is highly improbable that he would personally have authorised the publication of a work which would confirm those views of the cardinal implanted in the king's mind by his mother and Mazarin. The revisions tempered the youthful enthusiasm for the revolutionary hero, and reshaped the earlier assumptions about the nature of glory. They were not of the kind, however, to dull the suspicions of the court. While it is impossible to determine when Retz made these changes (and it appears that they were his own work), it does not seem that he made them for publication in 1665.[52] In fact they reflected the psychological realism of the frondeur rather than that partial surrender to the new pressures of conformity that marked the seigneur of Commercy.

Whereas the manuscript stressed the intrinsic glory of Fieschi's enterprise and idealised his ambition, the Paris 1665 edition was more detached and realistic. The attitude of the manuscript version was epitomised in its concluding lines:

N

His high and elevated conduct, and the great virtues he always professed, lead us to conclude that the crown and sceptre were less the
object of his ambition than the acquisition of honour. And I believe
that so long as he could follow the dictates of honour he would have
regarded his actions in the same light, whether they lifted him to the
throne or bore him to the scaffold.

In the Paris version these opinions were replaced by the words:

Posterity might have placed him among the heroes of his century, in
as much as it is true that success or failure are the usual criteria we adopt
to apportion praise or blame to extraordinary actions. Nevertheless, I
believe we can say, with all the equity an historian should observe when
he judges the reputation of men, there was nothing lacking in count
Jean-Louis Fiesque for the achievement of glory save a long life and
more lawful occasions.

It was not, then, the intrinsic merit of honour and audacious
conception that had become the basis for appraising the *gloire* of
an action: it was a question of success in the eyes of the world.

Now, there was to be another edition of *Fieschi* in which Retz
was concerned. It contained a yet more striking series of alterations, and was to be issued posthumously in 1682 by the publisher
who had brought out the Paris 1665 edition. The 1682 text
included a preparatory statement that the author had demanded
a more correct version. It seems that Retz was dismayed by the
appearance of the 1665 editions. His work was likely to become
associated with a new genre in the historical study of conspiracies
and coups d'état. Sarasin had written a work on the plot to murder
Wallenstein in 1634. It had been published among his works by
his friend, Ménage, in 1656, and appeared separately in Cologne
under the title of *La Conjuration de Walstein* in 1664. In 1674 there
appeared the abbé de Saint-Réal's *Conspiracy of the Spanish against
the Republic of Venice in the year 1618*, which set the tone for
sedition with its opening words: 'Of all human enterprises there
are none so great as conspiracies.'[53] In the last phase of his life,
when he was no longer so concerned with royal favour, Retz
directed the preparation of a scholarly text of his *Fieschi*, in
which comment was reduced to a minimum. The changes are in
accord with the outlook of his last years, but they do not bear the
stamp of his personal style, and he apparently employed someone

to affect the revisions. The 1682 edition was provided with an imposing documentation, including the rechecking of Mascardi's sources. The imagery of the earlier versions was eliminated, and the generalisations omitted or recast in neutral tones. The roles of the minor figures were readjusted to bring them closer to historical reality, and the long passages of rhetoric reduced to short phrases. Where the 1665 edition spoke of 'a grandeur of soul which made nothing appear too difficult', the 1682 version replaced the phrase with the simple word 'ambition'.[54] Thus the three principal versions of *Fieschi* graphically reflect three distinct phases of the cardinal's life and outlook. They illuminate the problem of the memoirs, where the considered judgments of maturity distort the endeavour of the author to rediscover his past self. For it was this re-creation of past identity that remained the primary purpose of the author.

As Retz tried to recapture the excitement of danger and intrigue during the Fronde, his memoirs took pride in a subtle amorality which he called the 'science of faction'. He used this term to criticise Condé, who, he said, 'did not apply himself sufficiently to studying the principles of that science of faction in which Coligny remarked one could never take one's doctorate'. Coligny had certainly been a successful leader of the Huguenot faction in the wars of religion, but his motives had been wholly dissimilar from those of the frondeur nobility, and the remark attributed to him was an invention of Retz. Indeed, Retz's comment that Condé 'by inclination, education and principles was more opposed to civil war than anyone I have ever known' could also have been employed of the Huguenot leader whose death had been the occasion for the massacre of Saint Bartholomew.[55] What Condé lacked as *chef de parti* was an understanding of public opinion and the means to manipulate it. In this regard Retz made a number of observations which extended the analysis of the faction leader he had outlined in *Fieschi*. In explaining the way the support of the parlement moved in Condé's favour after his victory over the royal army at Bléneau, Retz asserted that ideas worked in the popular imagination by a kind of confusion of opposites, so that opinion might swing from one extreme to another. Condé's success in this instance was due to the court's failure to see the importance of public support. While Condé had everything by

way of high birth, youthful ardour and invincible courage
necessary to a faction leader, he lacked the political judgment to
exploit his success. He allowed novices to command his armies
while the false counsels of Chavigny kept him in Paris in the early
summer of 1652. Like Gaston, he failed to maintain appearances.
He permitted the mob, directed by his demagogue, Pesche, to
escape his control and, by terrifying the middle classes, to turn the
magistracy against him. He failed to silence his critics in the parlement when he might have done so without alienating their colleagues. 'The secret in great movements', Retz observed, 'is to
retain men in obedience by no other fears save those which touch
them personally.'[56] In another context Retz advocated the persuasion of those whose judgment was obscured by prejudice, and
who were incapable of distinguishing causes and effects, by hope
of future advantage. Their failure to interpret the trend of events
in the past must be redressed by a conviction of improvements to
come. This was all that Retz meant by his maxim: 'Illuminate the
past by the future.'[57]

Apart from the calculation of advantage, Retz saw the importance to the leader of a faction in creating a mystique. By this
means he had himself succeeded in using revolutionary elements
of the Parisian mob, for whom in reality he felt nothing but contempt. Retz grasped the irrational aspects of mass emotion.
When commenting on the contradictory vacillations of the
parlement in September 1652, he saw that each faction had secured
there a body of fanatical support. He described this as 'a kind of
political fever which leads to frenzy', and saw that 'the ambitions
of the great may employ these attitudes to private advantage'.
Such emotional illusions among the lower classes were infectious
and 'by blinding themselves they help to blind the rest'.[58] When
describing the advent of peace in October 1652, Retz explained
how the atmosphere of mystery in which the negotiations were
conducted captivated the popular imagination, and created a
favourable atmosphere. Once the leaders of the dissident factions
concluded that they could no longer prevent the return of
Mazarin, their conduct gave the impression that they would
accept it. A section of public opinion was persuaded, and one
group after another rushed to join it. All this was a matter of
imagination, Retz argued. 'In contrast to everyday matters, great

affairs depend upon the public imagination. Sometimes it is the imagination of the people alone which brings about civil war.' Thus within a week public opinion in Paris was entirely reversed. Where the streets had been thronged with the yellow and red scarves of the troops of Lorraine and the princes, and there had been a general will to resist the armies of the king, suddenly there was a universal desire for peace.[59] Here, to Retz, was another example of the extraordinary, which the research and reasoning of the historian could never comprehend, and the intuitions of the psychological observer alone could make explicable.

Despite affecting to provide insight into matters which to lesser men were impenetrable, the cardinal confessed from time to time in his memoirs that this insight was often wisdom after the event. He admitted instances where he had himself been imprudent and fallible. He had rashly offended Gaston before his confrontation with Condé in August 1651 by implying that the king's uncle could not be relied upon to keep his word. At the actual confrontation in the parlement he had been imprudent in offering to withdraw his armed escort from the vestibule. Although it was part of his scheme to secure nomination to his cardinalate, he confessed his greatest mistake was to allow the queen and court to leave Paris in the autumn of 1651, a mistake which led inevitably to the return of Mazarin.[60] In many of these instances, and especially in his account of his contest with Condé, his errors of judgment were explained in terms of his audacity and the preservation of his honour and dignity. He even compared himself with the prince's ancestor, Louis of Condé, who in 1560 had been prepared to renounce his privileges as a prince of the Blood to defend his honour before the parlement against the accusations of the all-powerful François de Guise.[61] Perhaps, as La Rochefoucauld put it, 'the desire to talk about ourselves, and to show our faults in the way we would choose to display them, accounts for a great part of our candour'.[62]

Retz was equally anxious to convey to the reader his maintenance of the ideal of the *honnête homme*. He recalled how when he became a cardinal he had deliberately assumed a modesty in demeanour. This was not, however, unmixed with self-interest, for he explained that his purpose was to diminish envy, 'which is the greatest of all secrets'. He went on to propound a maxim in the same vein: 'I maintain that it is as much policy as *honnêteté* for the most powerful to shield the least considerable from embarrassment, and to extend their hand to them when they dare not present their own.'[63] He used the concept again when he came to list those who had helped him financially during his period of exile in Rome, saying that out of *honnêteté* he omitted those who had failed him.[64]

In his political pamphlets the cardinal had adopted the pose of one whose primary concern had been the public welfare, and whose motives had been deliberately misrepresented by the malice of his enemies. This was not consistent with the supposed realism of the memoirs, but it recurred there in such instances as his description of the queen's attitude towards him after the peace of October 1652. On several occasions he spoke of a 'determination to sacrifice myself to my *devoir*,' and he meant by this something more than his duty to his rank and status. He advised Gaston to dissolve the assembly of the nobility in February 1651, despite the interests of his friends in the assembly, because Beaufort and Condé were using it to create factions. 'I have never done anything', Retz wrote, 'which gave me as much internal satisfaction as did this action. . . . I was induced to do this by nothing save the pure principle of my *devoir*.'[65] He claimed that he had rejected the offers of Fuensaldagne in the first Fronde for the same reason, although he subsequently found justification for his negotiations with the Spanish. Similarly, he refused to accept Spanish gold even when it was offered 'without obligation'.[66] On the other hand he refused most of the Spanish offers after his escape from Nantes not because of his *devoir* but because of the danger of being compromised.

There were also passages in the memoirs where Retz revealed that the pursuit of self-interest was limited by the obligations of friendship. The cardinal sometimes used this as an explanation of failure, arguing that his friends had forced him into a course of action against his better judgment. Thus he listened to the suggestions put forward by Brissac and madame de Lesdiguières on the one hand, and by Montrésor and madame la Palatine on the other, to reject Servien's offers in November 1652, and to seek advantages for his friends as well as for himself. Retz commented: 'It has to be admitted that we find it hard to resist what flatters both our sense of obligation [*morale*] and our inclination.'⁶⁷ When the Chevreuse ladies became so incensed against the princes after the disavowal of Conti's marriage contract, they tried to provoke a pitched battle between their own followers and Condé's retinue in mid-July 1651, and Retz, while condemning the risks of such action, felt obliged to support them. He explained that he did not reproach himself because 'it was one of those actions which political sense [*la politique*] condemns but which obligation [*la morale*] justifies'.⁶⁸ The cardinal seemed to regard such obligation as a necessary weakness: 'The natural inclination we have for someone slips imperceptibly into pardoning their offences under the title of *générosité*.' Fidelity in friendship and gratitude for favours received were an essential part of the code of honour which Retz respected. He could never forgive Noirmoutier for deserting him, and it was in this context that he wrote: 'The unique remedy against that kind of unpleasantness, which is felt more deeply in disgrace than the disgrace itself, is never to do good except for the sake of good.' La Rochefoucauld framed his maxim from a different point of view: 'It is more shameful to distrust one's friends than to be deceived by them.'⁶⁹

Unlike La Rochefoucauld, Retz did not assume that all human actions were motivated by *amour-propre* and the disguises it adopted. His view of history rejected the analysis of cause and effect, and accepted the primacy of the initiative of the great. There were collective forces, such as those of the popular imagination, which could be harnessed to the designs of the great if they were properly understood. There was the caprice of fortune which might overturn in an instant the most subtle plans of men. In any situation there existed possibilities which the great might exploit with audacity, ingenuity and a measure of good fortune. Politics was a pragmatic art, and the science of faction depended upon a flexibility of attitude as much as upon the judgment of other men's motives and an intuitive understanding of popular responses. Hence the parlement remained for Retz a body enmeshed in its own web of legal precedent and principle, a body incapable of performing that constitutional role to check the supposed innovations of the cardinal-ministers – the role which he exalted in his pamphlets. Ideological forces escaped the cardinal's comprehension, except in so far as their existence in the minds of men might influence conduct. He never analysed them for their own sake. The principles of government remained a mystery, and when the curtain which shrouded this mystery was rent, as it was in the Chambre de Saint-Louis, anarchy intervened. To Retz the theoretical justification of government was, like the dogma of the church, a body of doctrine where it was unprofitable to speculate and futile to question. The mysteries of church and state must be approached with silence, if not with reverence. These were not the areas where the great man made his mark. His designs were a combination of audacity, shrewd calculation and practical fore-sight, and, while their greatness was intrinsic to the manner of their conception, their glory was dependent upon their success. The great man must guard against the destructive force of provi-dence by stoical self-reliance. He must appraise realistically the self-interested motives of other men, but his own status must be preserved by his observance of the code of his birth, which included such concepts as *honnêteté*, *générosité*, *devoir* and *morale*.

These were the attitudes displayed by Retz in his memoirs – attitudes which occasionally seemed contradictory through the mixture of motives in the author's mind and the blending of phases from his past intellectual development. He tried to relive every experience, to evoke every conflict and intrigue with a zest comparable to his original participation in the events he described. But he could never succeed in his endeavour. The simplicity of an instinctive response to crisis was clouded by the need to provide a logic for action, and the intensity of the original experience was obscured by its subsequent analysis. Retz showed his own aware-ness of the problem when he discussed the attack upon Le Tellier which Servien and Lyonne made in the parlement in July 1651:

We admire the complexity of opposing trends in history, but we are not aware of it in action. Nothing appeared more natural or more ordinary than what was done and said on that particular day. I have thought about it since, and I confess that at this moment I still find it difficult to understand the multiplicity, diversity and confusion of the impressions my memory retains.[70]

What Retz presented was a synthesis of objective facts and sub-jective possibilities.[71] He contrived this synthesis partly through that genius for story-telling remarked by his contemporaries, and partly through that gift for theatrical imagery which enabled him to reshape the past as a dramatist adapts plot and character to the demands of his medium.

In his early life the cardinal had tried to affirm his own identity through impulsive action: in later life he sought to find himself by reliving that action in his mind. The objectivity of his search in the memoirs was distorted by a restless urge to achieve post-humous *éclat*. The past was infused with the present. Age, experience and disillusionment dimmed the audacity of youth. Prudence interfered with the spontaneity of impulse. The amoral lesson, the cynical generalisation cut across the particularity of the extra-ordinary individual. In life the ardour of the young abbé to express the fullness of individuality through the aristocratic code of the hero was superseded by the cynical realism and stoic self-sufficiency of the political and ecclesiastical frondeur, and this again by the subtle diplomat and the conformist seigneur of Commercy. In the memoirs elements of every phase were compounded together and stirred by the genius of the writer's style and imagination. Virtue, he had discovered, was not something intrinsic to the individual, but rather a set of objective moral criteria. The price of its attainment was conformity. It is not so surprising that the man who tried to force himself to the ultimate conformity of religious conversion should simultaneously record the life of the 'least ecclesiastical soul that ever was' with neither penitence nor remorse.

FIFTEEN

End of a search

The cardinal spent the winter of 1675–6 at Commercy. He continued to suffer from gout, rheumatism and ophthalmia, and lived in dread of a new summons to Rome. In July 1676 Clement x died, and cardinal d'Estrées wrote to Lyonne's successor, Pomponne, to plead the necessity of Retz's attendance at the conclave – not just because he provided another vote in the French lobby but because of his influence and status: 'A man of his experience, intellect and reputation will carry great weight in the sacred college. The merit of his retreat will give him still more lustre and authority.' Pomponne sent Retz his instructions at the end of the month. He stated that the king appreciated that the cardinal's health would make such a journey painful, and recalled how Retz had expressed the wish to avoid conclaves when he had informed His Majesty of the plans for his retreat. Nevertheless, Pomponne explained, the matter was important, and the king knew the cardinal's zeal for his service. Retz intimated he would comply with the royal command, and made immediate preparations for the journey.[1]

He travelled two days ahead of cardinal Bouillon, his companion at the previous conclave, and cardinal Bonzi, bishop of Béziers, who had been promoted to the sacred college in 1672. The king granted each of the French cardinals the sum of 18,000 livres for their expenses, but he provided no royal galley on this occasion, and the cardinals were obliged to journey overland. On 13 August Louis wrote to Retz in his own hand, expressing his pleasure at the news of the cardinal's departure and promising to see that Retz received justice in a current law-suit concerning his debts.[2] This was the most gracious gesture the king ever allowed himself to make towards the man who represented all those forces from the past against which the new régime was directed. As cardinal

d'Estrées had indicated, Retz's talents were seen as indispensable
to the French group in the conclave. Madame de Sévigné conveyed the same impression when she described the cardinal's
journey to her daughter, but she added that it was difficult to
refute his critics, who regarded his attendance as fresh evidence of
the insincerity of his conversion.[3]

On 2 September 1676, two days after he had entered the conclave, Retz wrote to Pomponne to explain that he would keep in
touch with the duc d'Estrées, and, as the ambassador would be
reporting to Versailles, he would not himself report to the foreign
minister on the tactics of the election. As on past occasions he had
no scruples about breaking the oath that required all members of
the conclave to remain incommunicado, and he actually headed
his reports: 'At the conclave.' The most favoured candidate was
cardinal Odescalchi, and the French lobby was unwillingly obliged
to support him because his rival, cardinal Altieri, was notorious
for his Spanish sympathies in his office of papal secretary of state.
Altieri was a member of Clement x's family and represented the
interests of the previous pontificate. He approached Retz through
cardinal Colonna, offering to favour the cause of France. Retz
reported, with some qualifications, that he was inclined to accept
Altieri's sincerity, but the duc d'Estrées was more sceptical, and
asked what Altieri thought he could possibly do to repair the past
damage to French interests for which he was responsible. Although Retz did not show the same energy as a contriver of
schemes that had marked his participation in earlier conclaves, he
was ingenious in counsel, prudent in discussion and tolerant of
ill-considered suggestions from his younger colleagues. Cardinals
Bouillon and d'Estrées proposed at one stage to support the aged
but pro-French cardinal Grimaldi, and Retz pointed out that,
since Grimaldi had no hope of success, backing his candidature
would merely exclude Odescalchi in favour of Altieri. On 17
September the ambassador replied to Retz's comment on this
possibility:

Your Eminence very justly observes that several people would in this
conjuncture regard support for the Grimaldi proposal as designed to
ruin Odescalchi: but also one could believe that the strongest and
wisest section of opinion in Rome, knowing the merit of Grimaldi
and even judging him as superior to Odescalchi, may take a better and

more favourable view of our intentions ... and, after all, whatever decision we take must involve some contradictions.

The duc d'Estrées went on to add that the suggestion of his brother, the cardinal, should be interpreted as exploring a possibility, not as a deliberate attempt to exclude Odescalchi.[4]

Clearly, it was Retz's opinion which was the most respected by the French government. The king affirmed French support for Odescalchi, who became Innocent XI on 22 September. Within a few months Louis XIV was to be engaged in an intense conflict with the new pope, who showed sympathies for the Jansenists and resisted the king's attempt to extend to the provinces of southern France the regalian rights enjoyed by the crown in vacant dioceses in the north. Innocent's firmness and diplomatic skill was to prove a match for the aggressive designs of the king. His resistance led to the drafting of the Gallican articles of 1682 by Bossuet, and it was not until two years after Innocent's death in 1691 that a truce between king and pope was agreed. But, immediately after the election, Louis believed that Retz had obtained the best possible result, and on 10 October 1676 he wrote from Versailles:

My cousin, the letter you sent me after the election of the pope says many things in few words, since it assures me that my glory and my conscience ought to be fully satisfied with the success of this last conclave. It is all I could desire, and, as my ambassador has not forgotten in his despatch to tell me how you contributed to the fulfilment of my wishes, you should have no doubt of the goodwill I have towards you. There is nothing but merit in the way you have served me.[5]

There was a briefer comment from madame de Sévigné. She wrote to madame de Grignan on 7 October: 'The cardinal has written to me to say that he has made a pope.'[6]

Before returning to France, Retz made another unsuccessful attempt to have the pope sanction the resigning of his cardinalate. He told Le Camus of Grenoble of this when he visited the bishop on his return journey. Le Camus mentioned it in a letter to the abbé de Pontchâteau on 14 December 1676, and he also described the impression the cardinal made upon him: 'He has an extraordinary grandeur of soul, but it is accompanied by a profound humility in respect of his past life, and by both a wonderful sincerity and a great desire for penitence and retirement from the world.' A month later he wrote again, in rather different vein: 'Monsieur le cardinal de Retz has need of someone to keep him up to the mark, and to prevent him from seeking diversions in worldly matters and secular conversations. These journeys to Rome are very bad for his health. He is a great man, from whom God demands great things.'[7] As a reformed libertine, Le Camus had been captivated by the peculiar spell of Retz's presence, and impressed by his intention to live up to the spirit of his conversion. Yet the conversion was more superficial than it appeared, and the bishop saw that at times the cardinal still slipped back to that other self where secular diversions engrossed his attention. He remarked to Pontchâteau how he and his guest had spent much of their time discussing philosophy.

When Retz returned to Commercy his health deteriorated further during the winter, and in the following summer the onset of fevers continued to reduce his strength. Madame de Sévigné received a visit from one of his servants at Commercy, and wrote to her daughter on 28 July 1677: 'It is no longer a life that he is living, it is a kind of lingering stupor.' On 12 October she commented that he was injuring his health by too much mental work. Three days later she wrote again: 'He is killing himself. He is exhausting his own strength and overtaxing his brain. . . . Except for the quarter-hour he devotes to feeding bread to his trout, he spends all his time in metaphysical distillations and distinctions with Dom Robert. They will be the death of him.'[8]

Dom Robert Desgabets had been procuror-general of the Benedictine house of Saint-Vannes, and had been disgraced and sent to the small establishment of Breuil in Commercy for spreading Cartesian physics within Benedictine schools. The separation of mind and body implicit in the philosophy of Descartes had appealed to the Jansenists and especially to Antoine Arnauld, but elsewhere in religious circles the Cartesian method was regarded with suspicion. With some exceptions the Jesuits were hostile to it, and the Oratorians, as well as the Benedictines, discouraged the teaching of Cartesianism within their colleges. Malebranche of the Oratory was yet to produce his reconciliation of Christian theology and Cartesian philosophy, but already there was a growing suspicion that Descartes' mechanistic physics and physiology would point the way to materialism.[9] To those, such as the Jansenists, who adopted Augustinian views, the distinction between *scientia* (philosophy) and *sapientia* (theology) avoided this danger – although Antoine Arnauld was himself to blur the line of demarcation when he attacked Malebranche after Retz's death. These were problems in which Retz, despite his scorn for abstract speculation, had developed an interest. At the same time, he would not question religious orthodoxy, and regarded philosophy merely as an intellectual diversion. He debated Cartesian propositions with Desgabets, in the company of Hennezon, Corbinelli and Dom Humbert Belhomme, later abbé de Moyen-Moutier.[10] Retz opposed Dom Robert's argument that thinking was stimulated by the sensory reactions of the body, and saw in the opinions of the Benedictine on divine intelligence a trend towards the pantheism of Spinoza.

In the spring of 1678 the cardinal left Commercy, apparently with the intention of moving permanently to Paris. Before his departure he tried to endow Saint-Mihiel with his personal effects from his château, but Hennezon would accept only his library, and he insisted that the abbey should pay Retz for the books.[11] In Paris the cardinal lodged in the hôtel de Lesdiguières and stayed for a time at Saint-Denis. He began a scheme to rebuild the cloisters of the abbey but, since he could obtain no funds without interfering with the settlement of his debts, he abandoned the project.[12] His host at the hôtel de Lesdiguières was that marshal de Créquy whom he had known in Lorraine, the stepson of his cousin and ally in the Fronde, the elder duchesse de Lesdiguières. In 1675 marshal de Créquy had married the second daughter of Retz's brother, Pierre. He had retired from his army command in the following year, and succeeded his father as duc de Lesdiguières in 1677. The new duchess had none of the frivolous weaknesses exhibited by her predecessor. The duke had Jansenist leanings and a rigorous piety was observed in the household. The cardinal was welcomed, for, apart from his prestige and the aura of his conversion, he regarded the Lesdiguières as his heirs, and expected the Retz title to be perpetuated in their line. His cousin, duc Henri de Retz, had died in 1659: his brother, duc Pierre de Retz, in 1676. Besides the cardinal, the only living male representative of the direct line was the son of the Lesdiguières, who was born in 1678 and was, as we have seen, to die childless in 1704.

The reappearance of the cardinal in Paris provoked a round of gossip and speculation in the salons, and renewed the controversy about the sincerity of his conversion. Madame de Sévigné was irritated by so much criticism, and wrote to the comte de Guitaut:

> Everyone is killing himself to find something to say against His Eminence, and they seem so incensed that they would heap coals of fire on his head. I do not understand this attitude, and personally I am delighted to see him. I hold no commission from Saint-Mihiel to punish him for not spending the rest of his life there. ... You will not find him going from one social gathering to the next to indulge in conversation and offer literary judgments. He retires early to bed, and prays and receives few visits.[13]

The most malicious of Retz's critics was madame de Sévigné's cousin, Bussy-Rabutin. 'Here is the man', he wrote to her, 'whom we did not expect to see again until the day of judgment, living in the hôtel de Lesdiguières with the most acceptable part of French society. Please explain, if you would, madame, for it seems to me that this reappearance supports precisely what those who doubted his retreat have said.' Madame de Sévigné replied promptly on 27 June:

> The pope forbad him to stay in the place of his choice, Saint-Mihiel, saying that cardinals may not go into retreat in any abbeys save their own. ... Since Commercy was by no means suitable, he has come to live at Saint-Denis, where his life is spent in conformity with the rules for his retreat which he imposed on himself. He has spent some time at the hôtel de Lesdiguières, but that house has become his own. It is not the friends of the duke who dine there any longer, but those of the cardinal. He has seen very little of the world, and has been at Saint-Denis for two months. He has to attend the hearing of a law-suit because upon its result depends whether or not his debts will be discharged. You know that he has paid back 1,100,000 crowns. No one else has set this example, and no one will imitate it.[14]

Madame de Sévigné was possibly exaggerating the cardinal's social conduct, as she certainly was the repayment of his debts. In November Bussy wrote to a friend: 'Monsieur le cardinal de Retz is completing his penance at the house of madame de

Bracciano, who, as you know, used to be madame de Chalais, Noirmoutier's daughter. If this may be, I shall not give up hope of seeing the abbé de La Trappe return to sigh over certain ladies of the court.' He expressed the same opinion to the equally sceptical mademoiselle de Scudéry: 'If the cardinal de Retz is going to paradise by way of madame Bracciano's, then the abbé de La Trappe is very foolish to keep to the path he has chosen to get there.'[15]

During Easter 1679 Retz officiated at Saint-Denis. He was a tired old man in his sixty-sixth year, trying vainly to come to terms with the phantoms of the past in an uncongenial present. Since his return to France in 1662 he could claim that he had conformed to all the pressures of church and state exerted by the new régime. His diplomatic endeavours in the royal service had been executed with tireless energy and consummate finesse, and, though his ability had been recognised, his success had failed to procure tangible reward from the seat of favour. The cult of the *généreux* was dead. It was Racine, rather than Corneille, who reflected the ethos of the age. The critic La Bruyère saw the distinction between the two as one between the aristocratic idealism of the past and the conformist realism of the present:

> Corneille exposes us to his characters and to his ideas; Racine conforms to ours: the former depicts men as they ought to be; the latter as they are. There is more in the first to admire, even more to imitate: there is more in the second to recognise in those round us, or to experience within ourselves. . . . Corneille is more moral, Racine closer to reality.[16]

If the noble individualism of the past age were dead, so too were most of its heroes. Those who had plotted with and against Retz had now left the stage – Mazarin, Anne of Austria, Gaston, Beaufort, Broussel, Molé, Servien, Lyonne, Séguier and Turenne. Madame de Chevreuse followed madame de Longueville to the grave in the summer of 1679, and the ageing La Rochefoucauld, whose ultimate conformity was proclaimed by the marriage of his grandson with Louvois' daughter at this time, was to die a year later. Nicolas Fouquet languished anonymously in prison beside the duc de Lauzun, who had been unfortunate enough to win the wayward heart of la Grande Mademoiselle. Condé had fought his last campaign, and the princess Palatine now counted beads instead of political combinations.

Retz had brought his memoirs to the point where he left Italy in 1656. There was nothing in his vagabond life in Holland and Germany that he would wish to record, and little in the succeeding years that had not followed established patterns. His present personality had obtruded the judgments of age and conformity into his search for the *moi passé*. Yet the memoirs testified that his defiant individualism had not completely surrendered to the conforming pressures of Versailles. If there was any way of reconciling his account of what he had been in the past with what he had become, it lay perhaps, through Mabillon's adage, *veritas proxima pietati*, 'truth is the nearest thing to piety'. This was as far as his search could take him along the frontiers of virtue, and he could not penetrate their borders without abandoning the self in favour of the intellectual systems of other men. This his own genius denied him. Whether through the lust of action or the imagery of his re-created past, Retz would inwardly commit himself to nothing save the affirmation of his own personality. It was his tragedy that, for all his powers of introspection and self-analysis, he could not take account of the flux of time. He did not see that the same man can never bathe twice in the same river. But the task of self-definition was, after all, a superhuman one, and the other aspect of his personality – the lethargy that succeeded each burst of energy – allowed him to shrug his shoulders and renounce the mystery of the *je ne sais quoi*. It was as if, to quote La Rochefoucauld, 'the devil had deliberately put indolence on the frontiers of many a virtue'.[17]

It was Dom Hennezon who urged the cardinal in his last years to complete his conversion, and turn inwards from the appearance of piety in supplication for the certainty of grace. But it would be wrong to suppose that the Benedictine fought a fierce battle with the worldly lapses of his patron.[18] He was a man of charity, and not of rigorous extremes. Hennezon accompanied Retz to Paris in 1678, encouraged him in his religious duties at Saint-Denis, and fostered his sympathies with the inmates of Port-Royal. The cardinal had paid a brief visit to Port-Royal in May 1674.[19] His last contacts with the Jansenists were saddened by the disaster that had since enveloped them. In 1679 the pattern of the second half

of Louis xiv's reign became apparent. With the conclusion of his
war against the Dutch the king seemed prepared to use his armies
to impose uniformity upon his subjects. Pomponne was shortly to
be dismissed. The star of Le Tellier and Louvois was in the
ascendant, and that of Colbert began to wane. The king's imperious will began to transform the church into a department of
state, and to persecute Catholic as well as Protestant heterodoxy.
The Clementine peace had ended. The death of madame de
Longueville in April had deprived the Jansenists of a powerful
protector. In Rome the duc d'Estrées received instructions, sent
to him directly by the king without the knowledge of Pomponne,
to revive suspicions of Jansenist heresy. Antoine Arnauld, finding
the meetings at which he presided in the faubourg Saint-Jacques
prohibited, fled to Flanders. In May and June the postulants and
pensionaries were obliged to leave Port-Royal-des-Champs. The
daughter of Retz's notorious aunt, the abbess mère du Fargis,
was on her death-bed at this time, and asked the duchesse de
Lesdiguières to have Retz intercede with the archbishop so that
Sainte-Marthe, the last confessor, might remain at her side. The
cardinal did what he could, but the king insisted upon making all
decisions affecting Port-Royal personally, and mère du Fargis
died with none to comfort her save her reverent sisters.[20]

On the eve of Assumption Retz had gone to Saint-Denis to play
his part in the services. In the night he was taken ill with a raging
fever, and on the following afternoon he was transported to the
hôtel de Lesdiguières. He lay there dying for eight days. He called
for the services of the English doctor, Talbot, who was renowned
for his successful use of quinine. However, the Lesdiguières for
long refused to summon him, and relied, instead, upon their own
physicians, who bled the cardinal mercilessly and administered an
emetic. On 25 August, the day after his death, madame de Sévigné
described the circumstances in a letter to Bussy-Rabutin. She
observed that their cousin, the abbé de Coulanges, had been saved
from death by the English remedy, but, 'God did not wish to let
the cardinal have it, though he demanded it unceasingly.' She was
determined to have the last word over the sceptical Bussy-Rabutin:

You know how lovable he was, and how much he deserved the
esteem of all those who knew him. I was his friend for thirty years, and

I received nothing but the tender marks of his friendship. For me it was a thing as honourable as it was delicious. He was the easiest man to get on with that ever lived. Eight days of continuous fever have taken this illustrious friend from me. It moves me to the bottom of my heart.[21]

It did not move the unrepentant Bussy, who replied with a perfunctory expression of regret, and remarked that he would miss their common friend, Corbinelli, much more. Corbinelli, to whom Retz had recently begun to pay a pension, had died a few days before his cousin.

Madame de Sévigné was disturbed by the way in which the cardinal had died. She wrote to the comte de Guitaut:

Thus there perished before our eyes this man who was so lovable and so illustrious that no one could know him without falling under his spell. I tell you all this in the sorrow of my heart, and I say it to you because I trust in you more than I do in others, and the circumstances must not be repeated. This sad event bears out our recent discussion only too well, and we cannot talk about this conduct [the refusal of the Lesdiguières to summon Talbot] without its causing a scandal.[22]

Nine months later, when madame de Sévigné was at Nantes, and was reminded of the cardinal by passing the château where he had been imprisoned, she wrote to her daughter:

I cannot pass the foot of a certain tower without remembering that poor cardinal and his sorry death – and it was even more deplorable than you can imagine. I shall say no more on this subject, for there would be too much to say. It is a thousand times better to remain silent. Perhaps one day providence will enable us to speak about the truth of the matter.[23]

These letters have allowed the supposition that the Lesdiguières deliberately allowed their guest to bleed to death so that he could not change his will in favour of madame de Grignan, the object of his senile adoration. The hypothesis is improbable because the cardinal had no material wealth to bequeath. The inventory of his property, drawn up on 26 August by two notaries and signed by the duc de Lesdiguières and his wife, consisted of twenty items spread over both sides of fourteen folio pages. Some books, some boxes of personal papers, some furnishings, toilet articles and ecclesiastical garments, together with two carriages, nine horses and their harness, were all the worldly goods to be listed.[24] To his creditors Retz left the balance of his debts. The one thing of inestimable value was the autograph manuscript, which Dom Hennezon, who claimed to have heard the cardinal's last confession, took into his personal care.

On the night of 25–26 August the body was taken from the church of Saint-Paul to the abbey of Saint-Denis. There it was buried without the usual embalming and exposure customary for an archbishop of Paris. His body was encased in a lead coffin and interred in the place he had chosen, opposite the tomb of Francis I, *le roi chevalier*. His heart was cut out and entrusted to the care of his niece, that other daughter of the late duc de Retz who was the head of an order of nuns of the Calvary. No cross or inscription was placed upon his resting place, and no oration was pronounced at his funeral in Saint-Denis or his memorial service in his niece's convent. These honours were denied him by his king. The malice of Anne of Austria and of Mazarin, her lover, pursued him to the grave. But lying in the abbey of Saint-Mihiel were three manuscript volumes which contained the record of a mind so extraordinary that its testimony outlasted the worldly success of all its enemies.

Notes

The sections of Retz's memoirs appropriate to particular chapters are listed at the beginning of the notes for chapters 4–11.

CHAPTER 1

1 Bossuet, *Oraisons Funèbres*, ed. Alfred Rebelliau, Paris, 1905, pp. 433–4.
2 Saint-Simon, *Mémoires*, ed. Gonzague Truc, 7 vols, Paris, 1961, V, p. 196.
3 *Ibid.*, pp. 277–8.
4 *Mémoires et journal inédit du marquis d'Argenson*, 3 vols, Paris, 1859, I, pp. 85–87.
5 Voltaire, *Siècle de Louis XIV* in *Oeuvres historiques*, ed. René Pomeau, Paris, 1957, pp. 646–7, 666, 686.
6 Chesterfield, *Letters to His Son*, 4 vols, London, 1774 (3rd ed.), IV, p. 323.
7 *Ibid.*, pp. 308–26.
8 *Hume – Theory of Politics*, ed. Frederick Watkins, Edinburgh, 1951, p. 237 (from the essay *Idea of a Perfect Commonwealth*).
9 La Rochefoucauld actually prepared two versions of his portrait of Retz (see below, ch. 14, n. 7). Retz's portrait of La Rochefoucauld occurs in *Mémoires*, ed. M. Allem, Paris, 1956, p. 157.
10 Voltaire, *op. cit.*, p. 889.

CHAPTER 2

1 Tallemant des Réaux, *Historiettes*, ed. Antoine Adam, 2 vols, Paris, 1960, II, p. 308.
2 Retz, *Mémoires* (*Grands Ecrivains de la France* edition of the *Oeuvres* – hereafter describes as G.E.F.), 10 vols, Paris, 1870–96, V, pp. 58, 59.
3 Pierre d'Hozier, *Remarques sommaires sur la maison de Gondi*, Paris, 1652, pp. 1, 11, 13, 15.
4 Bibliothèque Nationale, répertoire des séries généalogiques, cabinet d'Hozier, mss. pp. 166, 319: 25, 36.
5 Jean Corbinelli, *Histoire généalogique de la maison de Gondi*, 2 vols, Paris, 1705.
6 For example, Le Père Anselme de Sainte Marie (Pierre de Guibours),

Histoire généalogique et chronologique de la maison royale de France, des pairs et grands officiers de la Couronne de la Maison du Roy, 9 vols, Paris, 1726–33 (3rd ed.), III, p. 883; and François-Alexandre Aubert de la Chesnaye des Bois, *Dictionnaire de la noblesse, contenant les généalogies, l'histoire et la chronologie des familles nobles de France,* 15 vols, Paris, 1770–86 (2nd ed.), VII, p. 275.

7   Mme Michel Julien de Pommerol, *Albert de Gondi, maréchal de Retz,* Geneva, 1953, p. 10.

8   Pierre de L'Estoile, *Journal de Henri III,* 5 vols, The Hague and Paris, 1744, I, p. 85.

9   Brantôme, *Oeuvres,* 15 vols, London, 1779, X, p. 364.

10   Tallemant des Réaux, *op. cit.,* I, p. 29.

11   Corbinelli, *op. cit.,* II, pp. 26–31.

12   E. Tambour, *Les Gondi et le château de Noisy, 1568–1732,* Paris, 1925.

13   L. Clark Keating, *Studies on the Literary Salon in France, 1550–1615,* Harvard, 1941, pp. 103, 125.

14   Tallemant des Réaux, *op. cit.,* I, pp. 22, 691. L'Estoile recorded the anger of the League against cardinal de Gondi, *Journal de Henri IV,* 4 vols, The Hague, 1741, I, pp. 152–3.

15   Tenhove, *Memoirs of the House of Medici,* tr. Sir Richard Clayton, 2 vols, Bath, 1797, II, pp. 362–3. These stories were given some credence by the contemporary historian, J-A. de Thou.

16   Tallemant des Réaux, *op. cit.,* I, pp. 363, 1033–4.

17   *Ibid.,* II, pp. 721.

18   *Ibid.,* I, p. 36; II, pp. 37, 38, 944.

19   *Ibid.,* II, pp. 304–5.

20   *Ibid.,* I, p. 294.

21   R. Chantelauze, *Saint Vincent de Paul et les Gondi,* Paris, 1882, p. 92.

22   Tallemant des Réaux, *op. cit.,* II, p. 1163.

23   *G.E.F.,* VIII, pp. 615–17.

24   Paul Bénichou, *Morales du Grand Siècle,* Paris, 1948 (5th ed.), p. 9.

25   René Pintard, *Le Libertinage érudit dans la première moitié du XVIIe siècle,* Paris, 1943, pp. 543–9.

26   The outline of Pascal's argument, using Montaigne and Epictetus to discredit confidence in reason, is provided in his recorded discussion with Saci at Port-Royal. It is probably the intended argument of his *Pensées. Entretien avec Monsieur de Saci* in *Oeuvres complètes,* ed. Jacques Chevalier, Paris, 1954, pp. 560–74.

27   Saint-Evremond, *Judgment sur Sénèque, Plutarque et Pétrone* in *Oeuvres choisies,* ed. A.-Ch. Gidel, Paris, 1867, p. 266.

28   Bénichou, *op. cit.,* p. 53.

29 *Lettres de madame de Sévigné*, ed. Monmerqué, 14 vols, Paris, 1862–8, I, p. 473.

30 E.g. Bardin, *Le Lycée du sieur Bardin ou en plusieurs promenades il est traité des connaissances, des actions, et des plaisirs d'un honnête homme*, 2 vols, Paris, 1632–4; and Grenaille, *L'honnête fille*, 3 vols, Paris, 1639–40; *L'honnête garçon*, Paris, 1642. On the development of concepts of *honnêteté* see M. Magendie, *La politesse mondaine et les théories de l'honnêteté en France au XVIIᵉ siècle de 1600 à 1660*, 2 vols, Paris, 1925.

31 Monroe Z. Hafter, *Gracian and Perfection, Spanish Moralists of the Seventeenth Century*, Harvard, 1966, pp. 121–46.

32 The first translation was by Gervaise in 1645 (Magendie, *op. cit.*, I, p. 333). La Houssaie's version of *El Heroes* was entitled *L'homme de cour* and appeared in 1684 and again in 1696.

33 La Rochefoucauld, *Maximes* 171, 182.

CHAPTER 3

1 *Mémoires du père René Rapin, de la compagnie de Jésus, sur l'eglise et la société, la cour, la ville et le Jansénisme 1644–69*, ed. Léon Aubineau, 3 vols, Paris, 1865, I, p. 161.

2 Tallemant des Réaux, *op. cit.*, II, p. 304.

3 *G.E.F.*, IX, pp. 1–21.

4 Tallemant des Réaux (*op. cit.*, II, p. 307) gives a different version of this anecdote, saying that Retz was debating with La Mothe-Houdancourt and referring to a passage from Saint Augustine. The poet Ménage recorded the version cited here. See the note provided by Tallemant's editor, M. Adam (II, 1165).

5 *Ibid.*, II, p. 308.

6 *G.E.F.*, I, p. 120.

7 Tallemant des Réaux, *op. cit.*, II, p. 305.

8 Saint-Simon, *op. cit.*, III, pp. 921–4, and IV, p. 659.

9 *Ibid.*, III, p. 949.

10 Tallemant des Réaux, *op. cit.*, II, p. 306.

11 *Mémoires de Conrart*, Coll. Petitot, XLVIII, p. 200.

12 Tallemant des Réaux, *op. cit.*, II, pp. 308, 311–12.

13 (Gabriel Naudé), *Iugement de tout ce qui esté imprimé contre le cardinal Mazarin*, known as *Le Mascurat*, N.P., N.D. (1649), Moreau, *Bibliographie des Mazarindes*, no.1769), pp. 70–71.

14 Retz, *La Conjuration de Fiesque*, ed. D. A. Watts, Oxford, 1967, pp. ix-xvii.

15 The date of the composition of Retz's *Conjuration de Fiesque* has for long been a matter of debate. The duchesse de Nemours claimed in her memoirs that Retz had first seen Mascardi's book in 1638. Chantelauze

(*G.E.F.*, V, pp. 475–98) discussed the problem in detail and accepted the testimony of Retz's memoirs. However, D. A. Watts showed definitively that the later date was correct in his thesis *Retz moraliste*, sustained at the Sorbonne in 1954. His conclusions are summarised in the work mentioned in the previous note. See also Antoine Adam's note on Tallemant's account of the matter (Tallemant des Réaux, *op. cit.*, II, p. 1507) and Pierre-Georges Lorris, *Le cardinal de Retz*, Paris, 1956, p. 28.

16   Tallemant des Réaux, *op. cit.*, I, p. 400.

17   Mascardi's text is set in parallel with some corresponding sections from Retz's work by Chantelauze (*G.E.F.*, V, p. 514).

18   Gabriel Hanotaux and le duc de La Force, *Histoire du cardinal de Richelieu*, 6 vols, Paris, 1944, III, p. 9.

19   Tallemant des Réaux, *op. cit.*, I, pp. 293, 914.

20   Michelle Vassor, *Histoire du règne de Louis XIII*, 17 vols, Amsterdam, 1700–11, VI, pp. ii, 577.

21   Hanotaux, *op. cit.*, pp. 214–24. Victor Cousin, *Madame de Chevreuse*, Paris, 1869 (5th ed.), p. 128.

22   Cousin, *op. cit.*, p. 138.

23   La Rochefoucauld, *Oeuvres*, ed. D.-L. Gilbert and J. Gourdault, 3 vols, Paris, 1868–81, II, pp. 28–29.

24   Pintard, *op. cit.*, p. 369.

25   *Mémoires de Montrésor*, coll. Petitot, LIV, pp. 296–7; *Mémoires de Montglat*, coll. Petitot, XLIX, p. 148.

26   La Rochefoucauld, *Oeuvres*, II, p. 39.

27   Tallemant des Réaux, *op. cit.*, II, p. 307.

CHAPTER 4
Mémoires, Allem, pp. 33–65; *G.E.F.*, I, pp. 176–270.

1   See Feillet's editorial notes, *G.E.F.*, I, pp. 181, 183.

2   Retz's memory is at fault, Vendôme's intrigue was in 1640.

3   *G.E.F.*, XI, pp. 1–2.

4   La Rochefoucauld, *Oeuvres*, II, p. 60.

5   Tallemant des Réaux, *op. cit.*, II, p. 1068.

6   *Mémoires de madame de Motteville*, coll. Petitot, XXXVIII, p. 220.

7   *Ibid.*, p. 44; Cousin, *op. cit.*, p. 242.

8   Tallemant des Réaux, *op. cit*, II, p. 38.

9   Sainte-Beuve, *Port-Royal*, ed. Maxime Leroy, 3 vols., Paris, 1955, I, pp. 345–6, 485, 487; II, p. 40.

10   A. Chéruel, *Histoire de France pendant la minorité de Louis XIV*, 4 vols, Paris, 1879, I, p. 203.

11   *G.E.F.*, IX, p. xix. The standard work on the subject is P. Jacquinet, *Prédicateurs du XVIIe siècle avant Bossuet*, Paris, 1863.

12   *G.E.F.*, IX, p. 135; *Genesis*, III 19.

13   *G.E.F.*, IX, pp. 163–98.

14   *Ibid.*, p. 98.

15   Adam, *Histoire de la littérature française au xviie siècle,* vol. 2, *L'Epoque de Pascal,* Paris, 1962, pp 105–6.

16   Pintard, *op. cit.*, p. 284.

17   Adam, *op. cit.*, pp. 21–23; Magendie, *op. cit.*, I, p. 24; II, p. 504. See also Claude Kurt Abraham, *Gaston d'Orléans et sa cour,* University of North Carolina, 1965.

18   *G.E.F.*, I, p. 333.

19   Tallemant des Réaux, *op. cit.*, I, p. 497.

20   Adam, *op. cit.*, p. 91.

21   Tallemant des Réaux, *op. cit.*, I, p. 497.

22   *Ibid.*, II, p. 368.

23   Chéruel, *op. cit.*, I, pp. 184–8.

24   *Remontrance du clergé de France faite au Roy à Fontainebleau le 30 Iuillet 1646, la Reyne Regente Mère de Sa Majesté présente, par l'illustrissime et reverendissime père en Dieu messire Iean François Paul de Gondy, Archevesque de Corinthe et Coadiuteur en l'archevesché de Paris,* Paris, 1646; *G.E.F.*, IX, pp. 25–42.

CHAPTER 5

Mémoires, Allem, pp. 65–106; *G.E.F.*, I, p. 271–326; II, pp, 3–59.

1   J. H. M. Salmon, 'Venality of Office and Popular Sedition in Seventeenth Century France' in *Past and Present,* XXXVII, 1967, pp. 21–43.

2   *Mémoires d'Omer Talon,* coll. Petitot, LX, p. 316.

3   The complex development of the crisis is traced by Ernst H. Kossmann, *La Fronde,* Leiden, 1954, pp. 30–40.

4   Sainte-Beuve, *op. cit.*, I, p. 745.

5   Jean-Paul Charmeil, *Les Trésoriers de France à l'époque de la Fronde,* Paris, 1964, p. 17.

6   *Mémoires de Talon,* coll. Petitot, LXI, p. 116.

7   *Mémoires de Motteville,* coll. Petitot, XXXVIII, p. 377.

8   *G.E.F.*, IX, pp. 107–31.

9   *Mémoires de Guy Joly,* coll. Petitot, XLVII, pp. 20–31.

10   *Ibid.*, p. 22.

11   *Ibid.*, p. 31.

CHAPTER 6

Mémoires, Allem, pp. 107–286; *G.E.F.*, II, pp. 60–484.

1   By another account Retz began negotiations with Montbazon on his own initiative before the barricades, and Mazarin intervened later. *Mémoires de Guy Joly,* coll. Petitot, XLVII, p. 23.

2   *Ibid.*, pp. 39, 40.

3   The parlement of Aix opposed the attempt of the governor, Alais, to enforce newly created offices within it, while the initial quarrel of the parlement of Bordeaux with Epernon, the governor of Guyenne, concerned the issuing of licences to export grain to Spain during a famine.

4   *Mémoires de La Rochefoucauld*, coll. Petitot, LI, 455. This section of the memoirs is, however, omitted by Gilbert and Gourdault in their standard edition of the Oeuvres.

5   The insincerity of Retz's attempt to leave Paris is confirmed by Guy Joly (*Mémoires*, p. 46). However, the memoirs of Dubuisson-Aubernay suggest the attempt was genuine. By this account Retz tried several gates and explained to the guards that he wished to visit his father. *Journal des guerres civiles*, ed. Gustave Saige, 2 vols, Paris, 1883–5, I, pp. 9–10.

6   *Mémoires de Rapin*, I, p. 252:

> Monsieur notre coadjuteur,
> Vend sa crosse pour une fronde;
> Il est vaillant et bon pasteur,
> Sachant qu'autrefois un frondeur
> Devint le plus grand roi du monde,
> Monsieur notre coadjuteur
> Vend sa crosse pour une fronde.

7   Beaufort was the son of César de Vendôme and the grandson of Henry IV and Gabrielle d'Estrées, whose daughter Elbeuf had married.

8   *Journal d'Olivier Lefèvre d'Ormesson*, ed. Chéruel, 2 vols, Paris, 1860, I, pp. 344, 346.

9   *Retraite de monsieur le duc de Longueville en son gouvernement de Normandie* (1649) in *Oeuvres choisies de Saint-Evremond*, ed. A.-Ch. Gidel, Paris, 1867, pp. 114–23.

10   *Mémoires de Motteville*, coll. Petitot, XXXVIII, p. 169.

11   *Mémoires de Guy Joly*, p. 54.

12   *Mémoires de Motteville*, p. 182.

13   *Journal d'Ormesson*, I, p. 655.

14   *Mémoires de Talon*, coll. Petitot, LXI, pp. 466–7.

15   *Mémoires de Guy Joly*, pp. 57–58.

16   By d'Ormesson's account Retz and Beaufort at first refused to calm the riot of 28 February, and Broussel later helped them intervene. By the time Molé left the Palais de Justice, according to d'Ormesson, only one demonstrator remained. *Journal d'Ormesson*, I, pp. 696–7.

17   D'Ormesson provides details supporting Retz's account. The riot

seems to have been a more sustained and violent affair than the disturbance two weeks earlier. *Ibid.*, pp. 705–10.

CHAPTER 7

Mémoires, Allem, pp. 286–447; *G.E.F.*, II, pp. 484–604; III, pp. 3–269.

1 *Le Bransle Mazarin, dansé au souper de quelques-uns de ce party-là, chez monsieur Renard, où monsieur de Beaufort donna le Bal*, Paris, 1649, p. 1; *Mémoires de Guy Joly*, coll. Petitot, XLVII, pp. 64–5; *Mémoires de Motteville*, coll. Petitot, XXXVIII, pp. 291–7; *Mémoires de Talon*, coll. Petitot, LXI, pp. 473–5.

2 *Mémoires de Motteville*, pp. 305–6.

3 *Ibid.*, p. 271.

4 *Ibid.*, p. 306; *Mémoires de Guy Joly*, p. 70.

5 *Mémoires de Motteville*, p. 326.

6 *Ibid.*, p. 401.

7 *Mémoires de Talon*, pp. 477–8; coll. Petitot, LXII, p. 58.

8 Je rends grâces aux Dieux n'être pas Romain
Pour conserver encor quelquechose d'humain.
Horace, Act II, Scene 3.

9 *Mémoires de Guy Joly*, pp. 81–85.

10 *Ibid.*, pp. 85–87.

11 La Rochefoucauld, *Oeuvres*, II, pp. 153–4; *Mémoires de Montglat*, coll. Petitot, L, p. 207.

12 *Mémoires de Montglat*, p. 208.

13 *Mémoires de Talon*, coll. Petitot, LXII, p. 23.

14 Retz's cousin, baron d'Escry, had married Caumartin's aunt.

15 *Mémoires de Talon*, p. 29.

16 Sainte-Beuve, *op. cit.*, I, p. 469.

17 *Mémoires de Guy Joly*, p. 101.

18 *Ibid.*, p. 94.

19 *Ibid.*, p. 95.

20 *Mémoires de Talon*, p. 51.

21 *Ibid.*, pp. 110–11; *Mémoires de Guy Joly*, p. 110.

22 *G.E.F.*, II, appendix ix, p. 653. Mazarin made the same statement when in exile in a letter from Brühl dated 10 April 1651. *Lettres du cardinal Mazarin . . . écrites pendant sa retraite hors de France en 1651 et 1652*, ed. J. Ravenel, Paris, 1836, p. 6.

CHAPTER 8

Mémoires, Allem, pp. 387–577; *G.E.F.*, III, pp. 138–545.

1 *G.E.F.*, II, p. 187; Bossuet, *op. cit.*, pp. 319, 321.

2 *Mémoires de Motteville*, coll. Petitot, XXXIX, p. 85.

3 For the text of the treaty see *G.E.F.*, III, pp. 550–6.

4 *Mémoires de Guy Joly*, coll. Petitot, XLVII, p. 118.

5 *Mémoires de Motteville*, pp. 114–15; La Rochefoucauld, *Oeuvres*, II, p. 223.

6 Antoine Adam, op. cit. pp. 384–6.

> Rebelle? c'est un nom que je n'aurai jamais.
> Je ne viens point ici montrer à votre haine
> Un captif insolent d'avoir briser sa chaine.
> Je viens en bon sujet vous rendre le repos
> Que d'autres intérêts troublaient mal à propos.
> *Nicomède*, Act V, Scene 9.

7 *Mémoires de Guy Joly*, p. 120; *Mémoires de Talon*, coll. Petitot, LXII, p. 138. See above, ch. 7, n. 22.

8 *Mémoires de Talon*, p. 143.

9 *Ibid.*, pp. 146–51.

10 *Lettres du cardinal Mazarin*, ed. Ravenel, pp. 32–33.

11 *Ibid.*, pp. 10–13.

12 *Ibid.*, p. 58.

13 *Mémoires de Motteville*, pp. 198–9.

14 La Rochefoucauld, *Oeuvres*, II, p. 246.

15 *Mémoires de Motteville*, p. 117.

16 La Rochefoucauld, *Oeuvres*, II, p. 253.

17 *Ibid.*, p. 249.

18 *Lettres du cardinal Mazarin*, ed. Ravenel, p. 52.

19 *Mémoires de Motteville*, p. 185.

20 La Rochefoucauld, *Oeuvres*, II, p. 251. Retz also recorded Condé's phrase.

21 *Mémoires de Motteville*, p. 203.

22 La Rochefoucauld, *Oeuvres*, II, pp. 254–5.

23 *Mémoires de Motteville*, p. 211.

24 Mazarin later changed his mind about the loyalty of the three ministers, but at this time he suspected Le Tellier rather than Lyonne and Servien. *Lettres du cardinal Mazarin*, ed. Ravenel, p. 43.

25 *Mémoires de Motteville*, p. 213.

26 *Lettres du cardinal Mazarin*, ed. Ravenel, p. 198.

27 *Advis de Monseigneur le coadiuteur prononcé au parlement pour l'esloignement des créatures du cardinal Mazarin le 12 Iuillet 1651*, Paris, 1651, imprimérie de la veuve Guillemot.

28 *Mémoires de Motteville*, pp. 274–7.

29 *Mémoires de Guy Joly*, p. 178.

30 La Rochefoucauld's account substantiates that of Retz. *Oeuvres*, II, pp. 287–8.

31 *Ibid.*, p. 260.

CHAPTER 9

Mémoires, Allem, pp. 577–752; *G.E.F.*, IV, pp. 1–416; R. Chantelauze, *Le Cardinal de Retz et l'affaire du chapeau*, 2 vols, Paris, 1878.

1 *Mémoires de Motteville*, coll. Petitot, XXXVIII, p. 401. See above, ch. 7, n. 6. Madame de Motteville may have wished deliberately to mislead posterity. Although the editor of Mazarin's letters to the queen from exile, M. J. Ravenel (*Lettres du cardinal Mazarin*, IX–X) doubted whether Anne of Austria was Mazarin's mistress, the weight of recent opinion supports this hypothesis. Saint-Aulaire, *Mazarin*, Paris, 1946, pp. 32–49; Georges Déthan and Jacques de Bourbon-Busset in *Mazarin*, ed. Georges Mongrédien, Paris, 1959, pp. 19, 59.

2 *Défense de l'ancienne et légitime Fronde*, April–May 1651, *G.E.F.*, V, pp. 176–82; Moreau, no. 984.

3 *Avis désintéressé sur la conduite de monseigneur le coadjuteur*, August 1651, *G.E.F.*, V, pp. 339–55; Moreau, no. 510.

4 Sarasin, *Lettre d'un marguillier de Paris à son curé sur la conduite de monseigneur le coadjuteur*, August–September 1651, *G.E.F.*, V, pp. 458–71; Moreau, no. 1885; *Response d'un véritable désintéressé à l'avis du faux désintéressé*, August–September 1651, Moreau, no. 3392.

5 *Response du curé à la lettre du marguillier sur la conduite de monseigneur le coadjuteur*, September 1651, *G.E.F.*, V, pp. 357–480; Moreau, no. 3428; *Le solitaire aux deux désintéressés*, September 1651, *G.E.F.*, V, pp. 184–93; Moreau, no. 3680.

6 *Lettre d'un Bordelois à un bourgeois de Paris*, September 1651, Moreau, no. 1852; *Le bon frondeur qui fronde les mauvais frondeurs*, September 1651, Moreau, no. 589; *Le frondeur bien intentionné aux faux frondeurs*, September 1651, Moreau, no. 1451.

7 *Discours libre et véritable sur la conduite de monseigneur le Prince et de monseigneur le Coadjuteur*, September 1651, *G.E.F.*, V, 385–403; Moreau, no. 1127.

8 *Lettres du cardinal Mazarin*, ed. J. Ravenel, pp. 387–8 (letter of 19 November 1651).

9 La Rochefoucauld, *Oeuvres*, II, p. 306; *Mémoires de Guy Joly*, coll. Petitot, XLVII, pp. 193–6; *Mémoires de Gourville*, coll. Petitot, LII, pp. 240–3. See also Retz's account of the plot in his letter to Charrier of 27 November 1651, *G.E.F.*, VIII, pp. 59–60.

10 E.g. *Lettres du cardinal Mazarin*, ed. J. Ravenel, p. 440 (Mazarin to the princess Palatine, 10 December 1651).

11 *Mémoires de Talon*, coll. Petitot, LXII, p. 291.

12 *Lettres du cardinal Mazarin*, ed. J. Ravenel, pp. 480, 483.

13 Retz to Charrier, *G.E.F.*, VIII, p. 87 (9 February 1652).

14 *Ibid.*, pp. 14–20 (1, 5 and 12 October 1651).

15 *Mémoires de Claude Joly*, coll. Petitot, XLVII, p. 497.

16 Retz to Charrier (2 February 1652), *G.E.F.*, VIII, pp. 83–85.

17 *Ibid.* (9 February 1652), pp. 87–88.

18 *Ibid.* (16 February 1652), pp. 95–97.

19 *Ibid.* (25 November 1651), p. 55.

20 *Ibid.* (5 January 1652), p. 74.

21 *Ibid.* (19 January 1652), pp. 76–77.

22 *Ibid.* (16 February 1652), p. 96.

23 *Ibid.* (23 February 1652), pp. 102–3.

24 *Mémoires de Guy Joly*, pp. 209–10; cf. *Mémoires de Claude Joly*, p. 497.

25 *Mémoires de la duchesse de Nemours*, coll. Petitot, XXXIV, pp. 526–7.

26 *Mémoires de Conrart*, coll. Petitot, XLVIII, p. 41.

27 *Mémoires de Guy Joly*, p. 211.

28 *Mémoires de la duchesse de Montpensier*, coll. Petitot, XLI, pp. 145–58.

29 *Ibid.*, p. 175–8; *Mémoires de Motteville*, coll. Petitot, XXXIX, p. 312.

30 *Mémoires de Motteville*, p. 314; *Mémoires de Montpensier*, pp. 192–3.

31 La Rochefoucauld, *Oeuvres*, II, pp. 356–7.

32 *Mémoires de Guy Joly*, p. 206.

33 *Les Contretemps du sieur de Chavigny* (April 1652), *G.E.F.*, V, pp. 196–205; Moreau, no. 787.

34 *Le Manifeste de Monseigneur le duc de Beaufort* (May 1652), *G.E.F.*, V, pp. 207–12; Moreau, no. 2368.

35 *Le vrai et le faux de monsieur le Prince et de monsieur le cardinal de Retz* (June 1652), *G.E.F.*, V, pp. 215–48; Moreau, no. 4068.

36 *Mémoires de Montglat*, coll. Petitot, L, p. 339; *Mémoires de Guy Joly*, p. 217; *Mémoires de Motteville*, p. 327.

37 La Rochefoucauld, *Oeuvres*, II, p. 388.

38 *Ibid.*, p. 391.

39 *Ibid.*, pp. 402–4; *Mémoires de Montglat*, p. 248.

40 *Mémoires de Montpensier*, pp. 255–72.

41 *Ibid.*, pp. 277–85; *Mémoires de Guy Joly*, p. 229; *Mémoires de Montglat*, p. 354.

42 *Mémoires de Guy Joly*, p. 232.

43 *Les Intérêts du temps* (July 1652), *G.E.F.*, V, pp. 251–8; Moreau, no. 1718.

44 *Le Vraisemblable sur la conduite de Monseigneur le cardinal de Retz* (August 1652), *G.E.F.*, V, pp. 261–74; Moreau, no. 4081.

45 *Mémoires de Guy Joly*, p. 241.

CHAPTER 10

Mémoires, Allem, pp. 753–802; *G.E.F.*, IV, pp. 416–533.

1 La Rochefoucauld, *Oeuvres*, III, p. 117.

2 *Mémoires de Guy Joly*, coll. Petitot, XLVII, p. 252.

3 *G.E.F.*, VI, p. 461.

4 *Mémoires de Guy Joly*, p. 256.

5 *Mémoires de Rapin*, I, pp. 518–19.

6 *G.E.F.*, V, pp. 449–59.

7 *Mémoires de Guy Joly*, pp. 265–8.

8 *G.E.F.*, V, p. 474.

9 *La lettre du Pape écrite au roi sur le sujet de la détention du cardinal de Retz, traduite du Latin en françois*, *G.E.F.*, VI, pp. 471–2; Moreau no. 2120.

10 *Mémoires de Rapin*, II, pp. 60–61.

11 *G.E.F.*, VI, p. 482.

12 *Mémoires de Guy Joly*, p. 264.

13 *Ibid.*, p. 277.

14 *G.E.F.*, VI, pp. 479–80.

15 *Ibid.*, V, pp. 83–84.

16 *Mémoires de Guy Joly*, pp. 275–6.

17 *La réponse de Monseigneur le cardinal de Retz faite à monsieur la Nonce du Pape et à messieurs de Brienne et Le Tellier, secrétaires d'état*, *G.E.F.*, VI, pp. 485–92; Moreau, no. 3402.

18 *Mémoires de Claude Joly*, coll. Petitot, XLVII, p. 501.

19 *Ibid.*, p. 502; *Mémoires de Guy Joly*, p. 283.

20 These documents are presented by Chantelauze in *G.E.F.*, VI, pp. 497–502: *Démarche du chapître auprès du roi en faveur du cardinal de Retz* (24 March 1654); *Extrait des régistres du conseil d'état* (21 March 1654); *Réponse du chapître à l'arrêt du conseil d'état* (26 March 1654); *Extrait des régistres du conseil d'état, arrêt par lequel il est ordonné à Chevalier et Lavocat d'exhiber leurs pouvoirs* (27 March 1654); *Procès-verbal dressé par Chevalier et Lavocat* (28 March 1654).

21 *Mémoires de Guy Joly*, p. 287.

22 *Ibid.*, p. 290.

23 *Ibid.*, p. 297.

24 *Ibid.*

25 A. Chéruel, *Histoire de France sous le ministère de Mazarin*, 4 vols,

Paris, 1882, I, pp. 422–38, where a number of the letters of Anne of Austria to Mazarin in January 1653 are reproduced.

26   V. Cousin, *Madame de Longueville*, 2 vols, Paris, 1867, II, p. 267.

27   Chéruel, *op. cit.*, II, p. 46.

28   See Amedée Renée, *Les nièces de Mazarin*, Paris, 1857 (3rd ed.) and François Nourissier, *Mazarin*, ed. Georges Mongrédien, pp. 82–111, for a general account of the 'Mazarinettes'.

29   Du Ryer:

> Pour mériter son coeur, pour plaire à ses beaux yeux,
> J'ai fait la guerre aux rois, je l'aurais faite aux dieux.
> *Alcyonée*, Act III, Scene 5.

    La Rochefoucauld:

> Pour ce jeu inconstant, qu'enfin je connais mieux,
> J'ai fait la guerre au roi; j'y ai perdu les yeux.

J. S. Spink, *French Free Thought from Gassendi to Voltaire*, London, 1960, p. 134; Voltaire, *op. cit.*, p. 653. Another version is given by Gourdault in *Oeuvres de la Rochefoucauld*, II, p. 410.

30   Louis Batiffol, *La duchesse de Chevreuse*, Paris, 1913, pp. 271, 197.

31   Saint-Simon, *op. cit.*, I, p. 534.

32   *Mémoires de Guy Joly*, p. 306.

33   The accounts given by Retz and Guy Joly of the actual escape generally corroborate each other. However, Retz adds the detail that one of the guards aimed his musket at the cardinal, when Retz, ordering him to desist, gave him the impression that La Meilleraye connived at the escape. Joly gives certain details not mentioned by Retz. Other accounts occur in the diary of an anonymous Parisian and a letter written to a friend by a magistrate in Nantes. See *G.E.F.*, VI, pp. 507–25.

34   La Meilleraye's manifesto is reproduced in the diary mentioned in the preceding note, *G.E.F.*, VI, pp. 511–12.

35   The memoirs of Retz and Joly differ substantially as to the movements of the fugitives after crossing the Loire.

36   *Révocation par le cardinal de Retz de la démission de son archevêché qu'il avait donée à Vincennes*, *G.E.F.*, VI, pp. 1–4.

37   *Lettre de Monseigneur l'Eminentissime Cardinal de Retz, Archevêque de Paris, écrite à messieurs les Doyen, Chanoines et Chapître de l'Eglize de Paris*, *G.E.F.*, VI, pp. 4–5.

38   *Lettre de Monseigneur l'Eminentissime Cardinal de Retz, Archevêque de Paris, écrite à messieurs les curés de Paris*, *G.E.F.*, VI, p. 6.

39   *Mémoires de Guy Joly*, p. 325; *Mémoires de Claude Joly*, p. 511.

40   *G.E.F.*, VI, p. 510.

41   *Réponse des chanoines de Notre-Dame à la lettre du cardinal de Retz, par*

laquelle ils lui mandent qu'ils ont fait chanter le Te Deum de sa sortie, G.E.F., VI, pp. 525–6.
42 *G.E.F.,* VI, p. 512.
43 *Ordonnance du Roi pour faire arrêter le cardinal de Retz, après sa fuite du château de Nantes,* G.E.F., VI, pp. 526–9.
44 For these documents see *G.E.F.,* VI, pp. 530–5.
45 *Ibid.,* p. 535.
46 *Mémoires de Guy Joly,* p. 325.
47 *G.E.F.,* VI, p. 507.
48 *Ibid.,* p. 537.

CHAPTER 11

Mémoires, Allem, pp. 802–85; *G.E.F.,* IV, pp. 533–73; V, pp. 1–141.
1 Chéruel, *Histoire de France sous le ministère de Mazarin,* II, p. 209.
2 *Ibid.,* p. 208.
3 *Mémoires de Guy Joly,* coll. Petitot, XLVII, p. 328. Except for Retz's movements immediately after the escape from Nantes, Joly's memoirs on their subsequent adventures confirm the memoirs of his master in nearly all respects. The major difference, however, is in dating, Retz generally recording events at dates earlier than Joly, whose accuracy in this respect is to be preferred.
4 *Ibid.,* pp. 343, 344.
5 *G.E.F.,* VI, pp. 553–4; Moreau, I, no. 606.
6 *Mémoires de Guy Joly,* pp. 345–7.
7 Joly's conjecture about the influence of Chigi in this respect is confirmed by Rapin, *Mémoires,* II, pp. 254–5.
8 M. Chantelauze discusses the story that Rancé was the author in *G.E.F.,* VI, pp. 11–13.
9 The title of the letter as published was *Lettre de Monseigneur l'Eminentissime Cardinal de Retz, Archevêque de Paris, à Messieurs les Archevêques et Evêques de l'Eglise de France* (*G.E.F.,* VI, pp. 25–71; Moreau, II, no. 1994). The replies are discussed by M. Chantelauze (*G.E.F.,* VI, pp. 17–25).
10 *G.E.F.,* VI, pp. 7–10.
11 *Lettre d'un cardinal à M. le cardinal de Mazarin pour réponse à ses lettres du 12 décembre 1654, ibid.,* pp. 73–80.
12 *Lettre de Monseigneur l'Eminentissime cardinal de Retz, Archevêque de Paris, à Monsieur le duc de Retz, le père, ibid.,* pp. 83–87.
13 *Mémoires de Guy Joly,* p. 352.
14 *Ibid.,* p. 355.
15 *Ibid.,* p. 369.
16 *Ibid.,* p. 347.
17 *Ibid.,* pp. 371–2.

18   *Ibid.*, pp. 373–6.
19   Chéruel, *op. cit.*, II, p. 239.
20   *Mémoires de Guy Joly*, p. 348.
21   *G.E.F.*, VI, pp. 540–2.
22   *Ibid.*, pp. 545–9.
23   *Ibid.*, pp. 549–51.
24   *Lettre de Monseigneur l'Eminentissime Cardinal de Retz, Archevêque de Paris, écrite à messieurs les Doyen, Chanoines et Chapître de l'église de Paris*, *G.E.F.*, VI, pp. 92–109; Moreau, II, no. 1998.
25   On Retz's grand-vicars see Léon Aubineau's appendix to the *Mémoires du père Rapin*, II, pp. 505–9.
26   *Considérations sur une lettre du cardinal de Retz à messieurs les doyen, chanoines et chapître de l'Eglise de Paris*, 1655, discussed by Chantelauze in *G.E.F.*, VI, p. 91.
27   *Mémoires de Guy Joly*, p. 381.
28   *Mémoires de Claude Joly*, coll. Petitot, XLVII, p. 537.
29   The *mandements* and monitions placarded by Chassebras, together with the texts of the government decrees against them and their author, are reproduced in *G.E.F.*, VI, pp. 582–601.
30   *Mémoires de Claude Joly*, pp. 544, 547, 549.
31   *Ibid.*, p. 546.
32   The articles of this indictment are given in *G.E.F.*, VI, pp. 578–81.
33   Chéruel, *op. cit.*, II, pp. 287–8.
34   *Mémoires de Guy Joly*, pp. 388–9.
35   Chéruel, *op. cit.*, II, p. 227.
36   *Ibid.*, p. 244.
37   Sainte-Beuve, *op. cit.*, II, p. 55.
38   Chéruel, *op. cit.*, II, p. 229.
39   *Ibid.*, p. 230.
40   Retz's commission to du Saussay is reproduced in *G.E.F.*, VI, pp. 135–6, 138–40.
41   *Mémoires de Guy Joly*, p. 394.
42   *G.E.F.*, VI, pp. 136–7.
43   *Ibid.*, pp. 127–9.
44   *Ibid.*, pp. 159–75; Moreau, no. 520.
45   *Lettre de M. le Cardinal de Retz, Archevêque de Paris, à MM. les cardinaux, archevêques, évêques et autres députés de l'Assemblée générale du clergé de France*, *G.E.F.*, VI, pp. 183–216; Moreau no. 1976.
46   *G.E.F.*, VI, pp. 222–3.
47   *Ibid.*, p. 229.
48   *Ibid.*, pp. 607–8.
49   *Ibid.*, pp. 231–44.

50 *Ibid.*, pp. 609–14.
51 *Ibid.*, pp. 252–4.

CHAPTER 12
The memoirs of Guy Joly (coll. Petitot, XLVII, pp. 405–54) give a
general account of Retz's life in this period but interpret his motives with
bias.

1 *G.E.F.*, IV, p. 488.
2 A. Chéruel, *Histoire de France sous le ministère de Mazarin*, II, p. 321.
3 J. Bourdeau, *La Rochefoucauld*, Paris, 1895, pp. 72–73.
4 *G.E.F.*, VII, p. 27; IV, p. 36.
5 P.-G. Lorris, *Le cardinal de Retz*, 1956, p. 302.
6 *G.E.F.*, VI, pp. 617–19.
7 *Ibid.*, p. 257–62.
8 *Ibid.*, pp. 263–4.
9 Guy Patin, *Lettres choisies*, 1688, p. 178.
10 *G.E.F.*, VI, p. 621.
11 *Ibid.*, pp. 267–70.
12 *Ibid.*, pp. 276–88.
13 *Ibid.*, pp. 632–4.
14 *Ibid.*, pp. 623–8.
15 La Rochefoucauld, *Oeuvres*, II, pp. 101–2.
16 *G.E.F.*, VI, pp. 292–303.
17 *Ibid.*, pp. 304–12.
18 *Ibid.*, pp. 639–40.
19 *Ibid.*, pp. 641–6.
20 *Ibid.*, V, pp. 291–327.
21 Lorris, *op. cit.*, pp. 316–17.
22 Chéruel, *op. cit.*, II, p. 183.
23 Sainte-Beuve, *op. cit.*, I, p. 738.
24 R. Chantelauze, *Le cardinal de Retz et les Jansénistes* in *ibid.*, III, p. 720.
25 *Mémoires de Rapin*, II, p. 388.
26 Patin, *op. cit.*, p. 208.
27 Chantelauze in Sainte-Beuve, *op. cit.*, III, p. 717.
28 *Mémoires de Rapin*, III, p. 81.
29 Lorris, *op. cit.*, p. 323.
30 *Ibid.*
31 Chéruel, *op. cit.*, III, p. 377.
32 *G.E.F.*, VI, pp. 321–413; Moreau, no. 10.
33 *G.E.F.*, VI, p. 414–28; Moreau, no. 2091.
34 Patin, quoted by Chantelauze in *G.E.F.*, VI, p. 320–1.
35 Chéruel, *op. cit.*, III, pp. 334–9.

36 *Mémoires de Rapin*, III, p. 165.

37 G.E.F., VI, pp. 648–9.

38 Hermant, quoted by Lorris, *op. cit.*, p. 333.

39 Chéruel, *op. cit.*, III, pp. 377–81.

40 Chantelauze in his essay on Retz's links with the Jansenists appears to misdate both Colbert's embassy and the anti-Jansenist *mandements* issued in June 1661, *Port-Royal*, III, pp. 721–2, but see his long and accurate account in *Le cardinal de Retz et ses missions diplomatiques à Rome*, Paris, 1879, pp. 25–46.

41 G.E.F., XI, p. 279.

42 G.E.F., VI, pp. 432–3.

43 See Chantelauze's editorial comments in *ibid.*, pp. 430–1.

44 G.E.F., VI, pp. 650–1.

45 J. Lair, *Nicolas Foucquet*, 2 vols, Paris, 1890, I, p. 417; II, pp. 31–32; G. Mongrédien, *Colbert 1619–83*, Paris, 1963, p. 80.

46 *Ibid.*, pp. 436–9.

47 J. Lair, *op. cit.*, II, p. 45.

48 *Mémoires de Louis XIV pour les années 1661 and 1666*, ed. Jean Longnon, Paris, 1923, pp. 56–58.

CHAPTER 13

A. Gazier, *Les dernières années du cardinal de Retz*, Paris, 1875; R. Chantelauze, *Le cardinal de Retz et ses missions diplomatiques à Rome*, Paris, 1879; C.-E. Dumont, *L'histoire de la ville et des seigneurs de Commercy*, 3 vols, Bar-le-Duc, 1843, II; Joseph de l'Isle, *L'histoire de l'abbaye de Saint-Mihiel*, Nancy, 1757.

1 C.-E. Dumont, *L'histoire des fiefs de Commercy*, 2 vols, Nancy, 1856; Roger Zuber, 'Le cardinal de Retz et ses relations champenoises – documents inédits' in *Revue d'Histoire littéraire de la France*, LXII, 1962, pp. 161–6.

2 G.E.F., VIII, p. 164.

3 *Ibid.*, pp. 150, 160.

4 Hennezon was abbé of Saint-Avold, not Saint-Avaux, the style used by Retz in his correspondence (G.E.F., VIII, p. 175). On Hennezon see Joseph de l'Isle, *op. cit.*, pp. 313–21; Augustin Calmet, *Bibliothèque Lorraine*, Nancy, 1751, pp. 484–7.

5 *Mémoires de Guy Joly*, coll. Petitot, XLVII, p. 458.

6 G.E.F., VIII, pp. 161, 164, 168.

7 *Ibid.*, pp. 164, 165.

8 *Ibid.*, p. 161.

9 *Ibid.*, pp. 622–4.

10 *Lettres de madame de Sévigné*, III, pp. 108–10.

11 Bussy-Rabutin, *Histoire amoureuse des Gaules*, 2 vols, Paris, N.D. (Garnier), I, pp. 153–66.

12 Saint-Evremond, *Lettre au marquis de Créquy sur la paix des Pyrénées* in *Oeuvres choisies*, pp. 186–91.

13 J. Bourdeau, *op. cit.*, p. 70.

14 *Mémoires de Guy Joly*, pp. 464, 465, 468.

15 *Ibid.*, p. 466.

16 *Ibid.*, p. 467.

17 Chantelauze, *Missions diplomatiques*, pp. 14–15.

18 The abbé Regnier Desmarais, secretary to the duc de Créquy, composed an account of the affair of the Corsican guards: *Histoire des desmêlés de la cour de France avec la cour de Rome au sujet de l'affaire des Corses*, Paris, 1707. See Charles Guérin, 'L'ambassade de Créquy à Rome' in *Revue des Questions historiques*, 1880, and Chantelauze, *Missions diplomatiques*, pp. 71–174.

19 *G.E.F.*, VII, pp. 3–13.

20 *Ibid.*, pp. 461–2.

21 *Ibid.*, pp. 13–22.

22 *Ibid.*, pp. 462–3.

23 *Mémoires de Guy Joly*, p. 463.

24 Gazier, *op. cit.*, p. 25.

25 *Mémoires de Guy Joly*, p. 469.

26 Philippe Amiguet, *La Grande Mademoiselle*, Paris, 1957, p. 323.

27 *G.E.F.*, VIII, pp. 642–3.

28 *Mémoires de Guy Joly*, pp. 470–4. Joly does not refer to the death of Malclerc, and writes as though this incident concerns the father, not the son. De l'Isle (*op. cit.*, p. 333) mentions the death of 'le sieur de Malclerc, écuyer du cardinal de Retz' on 21 August 1691, but, again, it is not clear to which Malclerc he refers.

29 *Lettres de madame de Sévigné*, I, p. 445. On this phase of Jansenism, see Louis Cognet, *Le Jansénisme*, Paris, 1961, pp. 79–80.

30 Gazier, *op. cit.*, pp. 143, 145.

31 Sainte-Beuve, *Port-Royal*, II, pp. 551–5, 169.

32 *G.E.F.*, VIII, pp. 640–1.

33 Chantelauze in Sainte-Beuve, *op. cit.*, III, pp. 734–5.

34 On this controversy see Chantelauze, *Missions diplomatiques*, pp. 175–374.

35 *Ibid.*, p. 193.

36 *G.E.F.*, VII, p. 33.

37 *Ibid.*, p. 58.

38 *Ibid.*, pp. 68–72.

39 *Ibid.*, p. 483.

40 *Ibid.*, p. 107.
41 *Ibid.*, pp. 81–101, 486.
42 *Ibid.*, p. 525.
43 Chantelauze, *Missions diplomatiques*, pp. 379–89.
44 *G.E.F.*, VII, pp. 248–81.
45 *Ibid.*, pp. 328–45; Chantelauze, *Missions diplomatiques*, pp. 397–400.
46 *G.E.F.*, VII, pp. 546–7.
47 *Ibid.*, pp. 547–8.
48 Note, however, that Chantelauze in his editorial comments (*G.E.F.*, VIII, p. 175) states that Hennezon received Saint-Mihiel in 1666, which suggests that the abbé may have accompanied Retz on his mission concerning papal infallibility, rather than to the conclave.
49 *G.E.F.*, VII, pp. 387–8.
50 *Ibid.*, pp. 388–90. The journey was described by Barbier de Mercurol, *Voyage d'Italie, tant par mer que par terre, fait par MM. les cardinaux de Vendôme et de Retz*, Paris, 1671.
51 *G.E.F.*, VII, p. 392.
52 *Ibid.*, p. 404.
53 *Ibid.*, pp. 392–406; Chantelauze, *Missions diplomatiques*, pp. 447–80.
54 *G.E.F.*, VII, pp. 550–1.
55 *Ibid.*, pp. 409–12.
56 *Ibid.*, p. 553.
57 Lefèvre d'Ormesson, *Journal*, II, p. 553.
58 Guy Patin, *Lettres choisies*, Paris, 1688, p. 184.
59 Chantelauze gives the details in *G.E.F.*, VIII, pp. 277, 369, but he seems mistaken in his appendix to Sainte-Beuve's *Port-Royal* (III, p. 728) when he says the sale was to Charles IV of Lorraine in 1660. The latter opinion is probably based on Saint-Simon (*op. cit.*, II, p. 837).
60 Chantelauze in *Port-Royal*, III, p. 728.
61 La Rochefoucauld, *Oeuvres*, II, pp. 101–2.
62 *G.E.F.*, VIII, p. 143.
63 Retz's letters to La Fons cited in this paragraph appear at *G.E.F.*, VIII, pp. 195–7, 198, 200, 205, 207, 208, 305, 306, 307, 321, 337, 373.
64 *G.E.F.*, VII, pp. 422–3.
65 Lyonne's instructions to Chaulnes are in *G.E.F.*, VII, pp. 557–65. Chantelauze, *Missions diplomatiques*, pp. 481–514.
66 *G.E.F.*, VII, pp. 426–7.
67 *Ibid.*, VIII, pp. 343–5.
68 La Rochefoucauld, *Oeuvres*, I, p. 21. Other details in this paragraph are based on Retz's letters to La Fons in *G.E.F.*, VIII, pp. 345, 348, 356, 358, 373.
69 *G.E.F.*, VIII, p. 425.

70   *Ibid.*, p. 388.
71   Sainte-Beuve, *op. cit.*, II, p. 912.
72   *Ibid.*, III, p. 37.
73   G.E.F., VIII, p. 429.
74   *Lettres de madame de Sévigné*, II, pp. 524–5.
75   *Anecdotes ou histoire secrète qui découvre les menées sourdes du cardinal de Retz*, Bibliothèque Mazarine, MS. 2247.
76   Chantelauze in Sainte-Beuve, *op. cit.*, III, p. 730.
77   *Lettres de madame de Sévigné*, III, p. 473.
78   *Ibid.*, p. 475.
79   *Ibid.*, p. 480.
80   *Ibid.*, p. 483.
81   *Ibid.*, pp. 491, 495.

CHAPTER 14

1   Saint-Evremond, *A monsieur le maréchal de Créquy* (1671) in *Oeuvres choisies*, pp. 424, 428.
2   *Lettres de madame de Sévigné*, IV, p. 5.
3   G.E.F., VIII, pp. 644, 645.
4   Lorris, *op. cit.*, p. 387.
5   G.E.F., VIII, p. 645.
6   Chantelause in Sainte-Beuve, *op. cit.*, III, p. 679.
7   There are actually four versions of La Rochefoucauld's portrait. That which he composed for his private satisfaction was first published in 1754. The version sent to madame de Sévigné was probably that first published in the *Nouveau Mercure* in 1717 and subsequently forgotten. A third text appeared annexed to the 1718 Amsterdam edition of Retz's memoirs. It contained substantial changes from the *Mercure* version, and was clearly the work of an editor, writing after the deaths of Retz and La Rochefoucauld. The fourth text was composed in a similar way by a writer who added phrases from the 1754 version. It was first published in the *Grands Ecrivains de la France* edition of La Rochefoucauld's works in 1883. The *Mercure* version may not provide a completely accurate text of the portrait sent to madame de Sévigné, but it is clearly much closer than the editions of 1718 and 1883. Moreover, it is phrased in the present tense and, since it shows that the author was not aware of the pope's refusal to grant Retz permission to resign his cardinalate, it was written before the middle of July 1675. The whole matter is brilliantly elucidated by André Bertière, *A propos du portrait du cardinal de Retz par La Rochefoucauld: l'intérêt d'une version peu connue* in *Revue d'Histoire littéraire de la France*, 1959, LIX, pp. 3, 313–41.
8   *Lettres de madame de Sévigné*, III, pp. 485–6.

9 *Ibid.*, p. 505.

10 La Rochefoucauld, *Maxime* 454.

11 Chantelauze in Sainte-Beuve, *op. cit.*, III, p. 737.

12 Saint-Evremond, *Réflexions sur la religion* in *Oeuvres Mêlées,* ed. Charles Giraud, 3 vols, Paris, 1865, I, p. 159. In *Les dernières années du cardinal de Retz,* Gazier accepted the authenticity of this passage. In his review of Gazier's book (*Revue des Questions historiques,* 1877, XXI, pp. 100–46) Chantelauze doubted whether Saint-Evremond was the author. However, he quoted it himself in his appendix to Sainte-Beuve's *Port-Royal* (III, p. 736).

13 See above, ch. 1, n. 5.

14 Saint-Simon, *op. cit.*, V, p. 711.

15 Voltaire, *op. cit.,* p. 666.

16 *G.E.F.*, VII, pp. 428–32.

17 *Ibid.*, pp. 566–7.

18 *Ibid.*, pp. 566–72; Saint-Simon, *op. cit.*, V, p. 711.

19 *Lettres de madame de Sévigné*, III, pp. 511–12.

20 *G.E.F.*, VII, pp. 572–5.

21 *Lettres de madame de Sévigné*, III, p. 535.

22 These exchanges are given in *G.E.F.*, VII, pp. 575–81.

23 *Lettres de madame de Sévigné*, IV, p. 198.

24 Bossuet, *Oraisons funèbres*, ed. Alfred Rébelliau, Paris, 1905, pp. 348–55, 379–82.

25 Champollion-Figeac was convinced that the memoirs were addressed to the second madame de Caumartin, and entitled the 1859 edition *Mémoires du cardinal de Retz adressés à Madame de Caumartin.* Feillet (*G.E.F.,* II, p. 58) insisted they were addressed to madame de Sévigné. Gazier (*Dernières années du cardinal de Retz,* p. 183) supported the madame de Caumartin thesis. Gourdault and Chantelauze (*G.E.F.,* V, p. 107) and Allem (*Mémoires,* p. xv) tend to support Feillet's opinion, while admitting the difficulty of the phrase '*Messieurs vos enfants*'.

26 Paul Bonnefon, *Retz et ses mémoires* in *Revue d'histoire littéraire de la France,* XXI, 1914 (pp. 519–44), p. 536. This is the so-called Caffarelli

27 Lorris (*op. cit.*, p. 391) and Allem (*Mémoires,* p. xv) stress the impor-

manuscript.

tance of this passage.

28 *Lettres de madame de Sévigné*, III, pp. 506, 526.

29 *G.E.F.*, V, p. 111.

30 *Ibid.*, pp. 106–7.

31 Bonnefon, *op. cit.*, p. 535.

32 *G.E.F.*, IV, p. 201; V, p. 82.

33 *Lettres de madame de Sévigné*, VIII, p. 223.

34 *G.E.F.*, II, p. 557.

35 *Ibid.*, p. 603.

36 *Ibid.*, III, p. 114.

37 Bonnefon, *op. cit.*, p. 527.

38 *G.E.F.*, VIII, p. 399.

39 Bonnefon, *op. cit.*, p. 520.

40 The autograph manuscript is Bibliothèque Nationale, MS. Fr. 10.325.

41 *G.E.F.*, IV, p. 444.

42 J. T. Letts, *Le cardinal de Retz, historien et moraliste du possible*, Paris, 1966, p. 176.

43 *G.E.F.*, IV, p. 223–5.

44 La Rochefoucauld, *Maxime* 119.

45 *G.E.F.*, III, pp. 343, 298, 352–4; IV, pp. 197–9.

46 *Ibid.*, III, pp. 381–5; IV, pp. 414, 435. Retz's preoccupation with the possible is the theme of the illuminating study by J. T. Letts (*op. cit.*).

47 *G.E.F.*, IV, p. 513.

48 *G.E.F.*, III, p. 504; IV, pp. 38, 278–80.

49 *Ibid.*, IV, p. 414.

50 *Ibid.*, pp. 508–9.

51 *Ibid.*, III, p. 402.

52 D. A. Watts, *Conjuration de Fiesque*, pp. xxiv–xxvi. The following quotations are taken from this edition and from Mr. Watts's paper *The Enigma of Retz* in *French Studies*, XII, 1958, pp. 203–21. See above, ch. 3, n. 15.

53 Saint-Réal, *Conjuration des espagnols contre la république de Vénise en l'année MDCXVIII*, ed. Alfred Lombard, Paris, 1922, p. 33.

54 Watts, *Enigma*, p. 214; *Conjuration*, pp. xxix–xxxiii.

55 *G.E.F.*, IV, pp. 210, 213.

56 *Ibid.*, pp. 200–12.

57 *Ibid.*, III, p. 430.

58 *Ibid.*, IV, p. 307.

59 *Ibid.*, pp. 386–90.

60 *Ibid.*, III, pp. 483, 492; IV, p. 44.

61 *Ibid.*, III, p. 468.

62 *Maxime* 383.

63 *G.E.F.*, IV, pp. 184, 186.

64 *Ibid.*, p. 106.

65 *Ibid.*, III, pp. 276–7.

66 *Ibid.*, II, pp. 497–8.

67 *Ibid.*, IV, p. 435.

68 *Ibid.*, III, p. 447.

P

69   *Ibid.*, V, p. 140; La Rochefoucauld, *Maxime* 84.
70   *G.E.F.*, III, p. 430.
71   Cf. Letts, *op. cit.*, p. 209.

CHAPTER 15
1   *G.E.F.*, VII, pp. 581–4, 433–4.
2   *Ibid.*
3   *Lettres de madame de Sévigné*, V, p. 25.
4   *G.E.F.*, VII, pp. 445–54, 590–3; Chantelauze, *Missions diplomatiques*, pp. 569–71. The abbé de Choisy's *Mémoires pour servir à l'histoire de Louis XIV* (Utrecht, 1727, pp. 508–12) put a greater stress on the influence of cardinal Bouillon, with whom Choisy attended the conclave.
5   *G.E.F.*, VII, p. 598.
6   *Lettres de madame de Sévigné*, V, p. 92.
7   Cited by Chantelauze in Sainte-Beuve, *op. cit.*, III, pp. 743, 744.
8   *Lettres de madame de Sévigné*, V, pp. 239, 352, 365–6.
9   P. Lemaire, *Le Cartésianisme chez les Bénédictins: Dom Robert Desgabets, son système, son influence, et son école*, Paris, 1901; J. S. Spink, *French Free Thought from Gassendi to Voltaire*, London, 1960, pp. 192–5.
10   Joseph de l'Isle, *Histoire de la célèbre et ancienne abbaye de Saint-Mihiel*, p. 329. The text of the discussions is in *G.E.F.*, IX, pp. 223–360.
11   *Ibid.*, p. 316.
12   *Ibid.*, p. 331.
13   *Lettres de madame de Sévigné*, V, p. 436.
14   *Ibid.*, pp. 450, 458–9.
15   Cited by Lorris, *op. cit.*, p. 401.
16   La Bruyère, 'De l'Esprit' in *Les Caractères*, 2 vols, Paris, 1829, I, pp. 31–32.
17   *Maxime* 512.
18   The theme of Jean Schlumberger's novel, *Le Lion devenu vieux*, Paris, 1929.
19   Sainte-Beuve, *op. cit.*, III, p. 37.
20   *Ibid.*, p. 179.
21   *Lettres de madame de Sévigné*, V, pp. 562, 563.
22   *Ibid.*, pp. 559–60.
23   *Ibid.*, VI, p. 394.
24   Archives Nationales, MS. LXXXIX, Liasse 39.

Bibliography

RETZ

Oeuvres, series *Les Grands Ecrivains de la France*, ed. Alphonse Feillet (vols I–V), J. Gourdault (vols III–V), R. de Chantelauze (vols V–X), 10 vols, Paris, 1870–96, together with vol. XI, *Supplément à la correspondance*, ed. Claude Cochon, Paris, 1920.

Mémoires, ed. Maurice Allem, and *Histoire de la conjuration du comte Jean-Louis de Fiesque* with selected *Pamphlets*, ed. Edith Thomas, Paris, 1956.

La Conjuration de Fiesque, édition critique publiée d'après le texte de 1665 avec des variantes provenant de manuscrits inédits, ed. D. A. Watts, Oxford, 1967.

For a bibliography of other editions of the *Mémoires*, the *Conjuration* and the *Pamphlets* see Allem and Thomas, *op. cit.*, pp. 1025–32. The first English version of the *Mémoires* to be published, not mentioned by Allem and Thomas, was prepared by an unknown translator and published as *Memoirs of the Cardinal de Retz, containing all the Great Events during the Minority of Louis XIV and Administration of Cardinal Mazarin*, London, 1723.

Not in the above, and not listed in Moreau (*Bibliographie des Mazarinades*): *Advis de Monseigneur le Coadiuteur, prononcé au Parlement pour l'esloignement des créatures du cardinal Mazarin le 12 Iuillet 1651*, Paris, imprimerie de la veusve Guillemot, 1651.

MANUSCRIPTS

Bibliothèque Nationale, MS. Fr. 10.325 (autograph memoirs). Répertoire des séries généalogiques, cabinet d'Hozier, MSS. 166 and 139.

Archives Nationales, étude LXXXIX, Liasse 39 (inventory of the property of cardinal de Retz).

Bibliothèque Mazarine, MS. 2247 (*Anecdotes ou histoire secrète qui découvre les menées sourdes du cardinal de Retz et de ses adhérans pour ôter la vie au Roy et à Monseigneur le Dauphin . . .*, by Antoine Blanche).

MEMOIRS

D'Argenson, *Mémoires et journal inédit du marquis d'Argenson*, 3 vols, Paris, 1859.

Dubuisson-Aubernay, *Journal des guerres civiles*, ed. Gustave Saige, 2 vols, Paris, 1883–5.

Roger de Bussy-Rabutin, *Mémoires*, 2 vols, Paris, 1696.

L'abbé de Choisy, *Mémoires pour servir à l'histoire de Louis XIV*, Utrecht, 1727.

La Rochefoucauld, *Mémoires* in *Oeuvres*, ed. D.-L. Gilbert and J. Gourdault, vol. 2, Paris, 1874.

Louis XIV, *Mémoires pour les années 1661 et 1666*, ed. Jean Longnon, Paris, 1923.

Mathieu Molé, *Mémoires*, ed. Aimé Champollion-Figeac, 4 vols, Paris, 1855, 1857.

Olivier Lefèvre d'Ormesson, *Journal*, ed. Albert Chéruel, 2 vols, Paris, 1860.

Rapin, *Mémoires du père René Rapin de la compagnie de Jésus, sur l'église et la société, la cour, la ville et le Jansénisme*, ed. Léon Aubineau, 3 vols, Paris, 1865.

Saint-Simon, *Mémoires*, ed. Gonzague Truc, 7 vols, Paris, 1961.

In *Collection des mémoires relatifs à l'histoire de France*, ed. Petitot and Monmerqué, Paris, 1824–29: Conrart (XLVIII), Gourville (LII), Guy Joly (XLVII), Claude Joly (XLVII), La Porte (LIX), Pierre Lenet (LIII–LIV), Montglat (XLIX–LI), Mlle de Montpensier (XL–XLIII), Montrésor (LIV), Mme de Motteville (XXXVI–XL), duchesse de Nemours (XXXIV), Omer Talon (LX–LXIII).

OTHER SOURCES

Jacques Bénigne de Bossuet, *Oraisons funèbres*, ed. Alfred Rebelliau, Paris, 1905.

Roger de Bussy-Rabutin, *Histoire amoureuse des Gaules*, 2 vols, Paris, N.D. (Garnier).

Pierre de Bourdeille, seigneur et abbé de Brantôme, *Oeuvres*, 15 vols, London, 1779.

Le Bransle Mazarin, Paris, 1649.

The Earl of Chesterfield, *Letters to His Son*, 4 vols, London, 1774 (3rd ed.).

Jean Corbinelli, *Histoire généalogique de la maison de Gondi*, 2 vols, Paris, 1705.

Pierre de l'Estoile, *Journal de Henri III*, 5 vols, The Hague, 1744. *Journal de Henri IV*, 4 vols, The Hague, 1741.

Baltasar Gracián, *L'homme du cour* (*El heroe*), tr. Amelot de la Houssaie, Lyon, 1696 (2nd ed.).

Pierre d'Hozier, *Remarques sommaires sur la maison de Gondi*, Paris, 1652.

Journal inédit du Parlement de Paris pendant la Fronde, ed. Henri Courteault, Paris, 1917.

La Bruyère, *Les Caractères*, 2 vols, Paris, 1829.
La Rochefoucauld, *Oeuvres*, ed. D.-L. Gilbert and J. Gourdault, 3 vols, Paris, 1868–81.
J. Loret, *La Muse historique*, ed. Ch.-L. Livet, J. Ravenel and V. de la Pelouze, 2 vols, Paris, 1857, 1877.
Gilles Ménage, *Ménagiana*, Paris, 1693.
Mazarin, *Lettres*, 9 vols, ed. A. Chéruel and G. d'Avenel, Paris, 1872–1906. *Lettres . . . écrites pendant sa retraite hors de France en 1651 and 1652*, ed. J. Ravenel, Paris, 1836.
Barbier de Mercurol, *Voyage d'Italie, tant par mer que par terre, fait par MM. les cardinaux de Vendôme et de Retz*, Paris, 1671.
C. Moreau (ed.), *Choix de Mazarinades*, 2 vols, Paris, 1853.
Gabriel Naudé, *Iugement de tout ce qui a esté imprimé contre le cardinal Mazarin (le Mascurat)*, N.P., N.D. (1649).
Blaise Pascal, *Oeuvres complètes*, ed. Jacques Chevalier, Paris, 1954.
Guy Patin, *Lettres choisies*, Paris, 1687.
Régistres de l'Hôtel de Ville de Paris pendant la Fronde, ed. Leroux de Lincey and Doriet d'Arcq, 3 vols, Paris, 1846–8.
Jean-François Sarasin, *La Conjuration de Walstein* in *Oeuvres*, ed. Gilles Ménage, Paris, 1656, 89–136 (also separately published Cologne, 1664). *Lettre d'un marguillier de Paris à son curé*, Paris, 1651.
Saint-Evremond, *Oeuvres choisies*, ed. A.-Ch. Gidel, Paris, 1867. *Oeuvres mêlées*, ed. Ch. Giraud, 3 vols, Paris, 1865.
Saint-Réal, *Conjuration des espagnols contre la république de Vénise en l'année MDCXVIII*, ed. Alfred Lombard, Paris, 1922.
La marquise de Sévigné, *Lettres*, ed. Monmerqué, 14 vols, Paris, 1862–8.
Tallemant des Réaux, *Historiettes*, ed. Antoine Adam, 2 vols, Paris, 1960.

SECONDARY WORKS

Claude Kurt Abraham, *Gaston d'Orléans et sa cour*, University of North Carolina, 1965.
Antoine Adam, *Histoire de la littérature française au XVIIe siècle*, II: *L'Epoque de Pascal*, Paris, 1962.
Philippe Amiguet, *La Grande Mademoiselle*, Paris, 1957.
A. G. P. B. de Barante, *Le Parlement et la Fronde: la vie de Mathieu Molé*, Paris, 1859.
Louis Batiffol, *Le cardinal de Retz*, Paris, 1930. *La duchesse de Chevreuse*, Paris, 1913.
Paul Bénichou, *Morales du Grand Siècle*, Paris, 1948 (5th ed.).
J. Bourdeau, *La Rochefoucauld*, Paris, 1895.
H. Brémond, *Histoire littéraire du sentiment religieux en France*, 7 vols, Paris, 1926.

Albert-Buisson, *Le cardinal de Retz – Portrait*, Paris, 1954.

Henri Buisson, *La religion des classiques*, Paris, 1948. *La pensée religieuse de Charron à Pascal*, Paris, 1933.

Dom Augustin Calmet, *Bibliothèque Lorraine*, Nancy, 1751.

Jacques Castelnau, *Retz et son temps*, Paris, 1955.

Régis de Chantelauze, *Le cardinal de Retz et ses missions diplomatiques à Rome*, Paris, 1879. *Le cardinal de Retz et l'affaire du chapeau*, 2 vols, Paris, 1878. *Saint Vincent de Paul et les Gondi*, Paris, 1882.

Jean-Paul Charmeil, *Les Trésoriers de France à l'époque de la Fronde*, Paris, 1964.

A. Chéruel, *Histoire de France pendant la minorité de Louis XIV*, 4 vols, Paris, 1879. *Histoire de France sous le ministère de Mazarin*, 4 vols, Paris, 1882.

Louis Cognet, *Le Jansénisme*, Paris, 1961.

Henry Corille, *Etude sur Mazarin et ses démêlés avec le Pape Innocent X – 1644–8*, Paris, 1914.

Henri Courteault, *La Fronde à Paris*, Paris, 1930.

Victor Cousin, *Madame de Longueville*, 2 vols, Paris, 1867. *Madame de Chevreuse*, Paris, 1869 (5th ed.). *La jeunesse de Mazarin*, Paris, 1865.

Paul Rice Doolin, *The Fronde*, Harvard, 1935.

C.-E. Dumont, *L'histoire de la ville et des seigneurs de Commercy*, 3 vols, Bar-le-Duc, 1853. *L'histoire des fiefs de Commercy*, 2 vols, Nancy, 1856.

Alphonse Feillet, *La misère au temps de la Fronde et Saint Vincent de Paul*, Paris, 1862.

Augustin Gazier, *Les dernières années du cardinal de Retz 1655–79*, Paris, 1875.

Gabriel Hanotaux and le duc de la Force, *Histoire du cardinal de Richelieu*, 6 vols, Paris, 1944.

Monroe Z. Hafter, *Gracian and Perfection*, Harvard, 1966.

Dom Joseph de l'Isle, *L'histoire de l'abbaye de Saint-Mihiel*, Nancy, 1857.

P. Jacquinet, *Des prédicateurs du XVIIᵉ siècle avant Bossuet*, Paris, 1863.

L. Clark Keating, *Studies on the Literary Salon in France, 1550–1615*, Harvard, 1941.

Philip A. Knachel, *England and the Fronde*, New York, 1967.

Ernst H. Kossmann, *La Fronde*, Leiden, 1954.

A. J. Krailsheimer, *Studies in Self-Interest*, Oxford, 1962.

G. Lacour-Gayet, *L'Education politique de Louis XIV*, Paris, 1898.

J. Lair, *Nicolas Foucquet*, 2 vols, Paris, 1890.

P. Lemaire, *Le Cartésianisme chez les Bénédictins: Dom Robert Desgabets, son système, son influence et son école*, Paris, 1901.

(Louis Adrien Le Paige), *Histoire de la détention du cardinal de Retz*, Vincennes, 1755.

J. T. Letts, *Le cardinal de Retz, historien et moraliste du possible*, Paris, 1966.

Michel Le Vassor, *Histoire du règne de Louis XIII*, 17 vols, Amsterdam, 1700–11.

Pierre-Georges Lorris, *Le cardinal de Retz*, Paris, 1956. *La Fronde*, Paris, 1961.

Louis Madelin, *La Fronde*, Paris, 1931.

M. Magendie, *La politesse mondaine et les théories de lhonnêteté en France au XVIIe siècle de 1600 à 1660*, 2 vols, Paris, 1925.

J. Michon, *Etudes sur le cardinal de Retz*, Paris, 1863.

Georges Mongrédien, *Colbert – 1619–83*, Paris, 1963. *Le Grand Condé*, Paris, 1959. (Ed.), *Mazarin*, Paris, 1959.

Will G. Moore, *French Classical Literature – an Essay*, Oxford, 1961.

C. Moreau, *Bibliographie des Mazarinades*, 3 vols, Paris, 1850–1.

V. D. Musset-Pathay, *Recherches historiques sur le cardinal de Retz*, Paris, 1807.

David Ogg, *Cardinal de Retz, 1613–79*, London, 1912.

René Pintard, *Le Libertinage érudit dans la première moitié du XVIIe siècle*, Paris, 1943.

Mme Michel Julien de Pommerol, *Albert de Gondi, maréchal de Retz*, Geneva, 1953.

Amadée Renée, *Les nièces de Mazarin*, Paris, 1857 (3rd ed.).

Saint-Aulaire, *Mazarin*, Paris, 1946.

Sainte-Beuve, *Port-Royal*, ed. Maxime Leroy, 3 vols, Paris, 1955.

Henri Sée, *Les idées politiques en France au XVIIe siècle*, Paris, 1923.

Francis Steegmuller, *La Grande Mademoiselle*, London, 1955.

J. S. Spink, *French Free Thought from Gassendi to Voltaire*, London, 1960.

E. Tambour, *Les Gondi et le château de Noisy, 1568–1732*, Paris, 1925.

V. L. Tapié, *La France de Louis XIII et de Richelieu*, Paris, 1952.

M. Tenhove, *Memoirs of the House of Medici*, tr. R. Clayton, 2 vols, Bath, 1797.

Voltaire, *Siècle de Louis XIV* in *Oeuvres historiques*, ed. René Pomeau, Paris, 1957.

ESSAYS AND ARTICLES

Léon Aubineau, 'Les grands-vicaires du cardinal de Retz' in *Mémoires du père Rapin*, II, pp. 505–9.

André Bertière, 'A propos du portrait du cardinal de Retz par La Rochefoucauld, l'intérêt d'une version peu connue' in *Revue d'Histoire littéraire de la France*, LIX, 1959, pp. 313–41.

Paul Bonnefon, 'Retz et ses mémoires' in *ibid.*, XXI, 1914, pp. 519–44.

R. de Chantelauze, 'Le cardinal de Retz et les Jansénistes' in Sainte-Beuve, *Port-Royal*, Paris, 1955, III, pp. 679–755.

R. de Chantelauze, 'Les dernières années du cardinal de Retz' (reviewing Gazier's book of this title) in *Revue des Questions historiques*, XXI, 1877, pp. 100–46.

M. J. Denis, 'La Littérature politique de la Fronde' in *Mémoires de l'Académie nationale des sciences, arts et belles-lettres de Caen*, 1892, pp. 27–93.

Charles Guérin, 'Le Cardinal de Retz au Conclave, 1655, 1667, 1670 et 1676' in *Revue des Questions historiques*, XXX, 1881, pp. 113–84.

Jacqueline Plantié, 'La Rochefoucauld approuvé par Retz' in *Revue des Sciences humaines*, CXXVI, 1967, pp. 303–4.

A. Suarès, 'Paul de Gondi, cardinal de Retz' in *La Nouvelle Revue Française*, XLVIII, 1937.

D. A. Watts, 'The Enigma of Retz' in *French Studies*, XII, 1958, pp. 203–21; and 'Quelques reflexions sur "La Conjuration de Fiesque"' in *Revue des Sciences humaines*, CXXVI, 1967, pp. 289–302.

Roger Zuber, 'Le cardinal de Retz et ses relations champenoises – documents inédits' in *Revue d'Histoire littéraire de la France*, LXII, 1962, pp. 161–6.

Index

Academy, 38, 70–1, 72
Acarie, mère Marguerite d', 19
Agde, 59
Agen, 202, 213, 214
Aides, 140
Aisés, 83
Aix-en-Provence, 37, 203
Alais, Louis-Emmanuel de Valois, comte d', 119
Albigensians, 95
Albret, César-Phoebus de Miossens, maréchal d', 144, 330, 372
Albret, hôtel d', 299
Alet, Nicolas Pavillon, bishop of, 343
Alexander VII (Fabio Chigi), 10; opposes Retz's promotion, 205, 206; 269; 271; election, 275–9; 282; reproaches Retz, 286; eccentricity, 279; 289; attitude to Jansenists, 290, 298, 321–2, 324; 292; 293; 294; 312; receives Colbert coldly, 320; 324; again postpones answer to demand for Retz's trial, 324; and the affair of the Corsican guards, 336–8; and papal infallibility, 344–7; death, 348–9; 356
Alsace, 222
Alibray, Charles Vion, seigneur d', 72
Altieri, cardinal (Paluzzo Paluzzi Albertoni), 387
Altieri, Emilio, *see* Clement X
Amboise, 146, 147, 212
Ambrogiano, 268–9, 272
Ambrose, Saint, 79
Amiens, 47
Amour-propre, 116, 296, 383
Ampus, Marie de Brancas, marquise d', 143
Amsterdam, 310, 311, 319
Anet, 74, 94, 109
Angers, 202, 213
Angoulême, 199

Anjou, 129, 133, 135, 196, 245
Annat, père (provincial of the Jesuits), 290, 321
Anne of Austria, attitude during Richelieu's régime, 43–5; institution of her regency, 59–60, 83; affair of the *Importants*, 62–4; attitude to Port-Royal, 67; relationship with Mazarin, 73; anger with Retz over the assembly of the clergy, 75–6; the Polish marriage, 76–7; on dispute over precedence between Retz and Gaston, 79; pursued by crowd, 84, 85; resists reforms of parlement, summer 1648, 93; and the barricades, 96–8; policy after barricades, 102, 105; during first civil war, 111, 112, 123, 126; receives nobility at Saint-Germain after peace of Rueil, 133; 135; return of madame de Chevreuse, 135–6; receives Retz at Compiègne, 137; affair of Jarzé, 139; anger against Condé and secret meetings with Retz, 149–50; 152; 156; refuses to free the princes, 166, 167, 168; and then agrees, 169, 170; humiliated by inspection of Palais-Royal, 171; correspondence with exiled Mazarin, 172–3, 181–2; policy, 173–5, 178; consults Retz, 179–83; 184; 185; declaration against Condé, 186; approves new declaration against Mazarin, 189; nominates Retz for cardinalate, 190; relationship with Mazarin, 191, 201–2; 197; 200; 208; 209; 224; considers assassination and orders arrest of Retz, 229; 231; 232; 234; 297; 315; refuses to pardon Retz, 317; asks Retz to intercede on behalf of Cistercian reform, 345; 371; 375; 376; 377; 392; 396
Annéri, Charles d'Ailly, sieur d', 325, 334, 355

Madrid, 263, 264
Maidachini, Francesco, 274
Maignelais, Claude-Marguerite de Gondi
    marquise de, 17, 35, 50, 58, 59, 60
Maisons, René de Longueil, marquis de,
    137, 140, 153, 193
Maîtres des requêtes, 90
Majorca, 265
Malclerc, Dominique de (seigneur de
    Sommervilliers), 178, 199, 232, 237,
    238, 243, 244, 246, 256, 285–6, 287,
    294, 300, 303, 304, 305, 308, 309, 315,
    317, 320, 328, 333
Malclerc de Sommervilliers (the
    younger), 328, 340, 341
Malebranche, Nicolas, 389–90
Mancini, Alphonse, 29
Mancini, Hortense, 245, 248, 317, 324
Mancini, Laura, 80, 136, 183, 248
Mancini, Marie, 248, 315
Mancini, Olympe, 80, 248
Mancini, Paul, 80, 153
Mantes, 75, 112
Mantua, 76
Marca, Pierre de, see Toulouse
Marcillac, prince de, see La Rochefou-
    cauld
Marcoussis, 156, 163
Mardyke, 305; 311
Marena, 294
Marché-Neuf, 112
Marguerite de Valois, reine de Navarre,
    12
Marfée, 51, 248
Maria Theresa, 316, 348, 349
Marie de Médicis, 22, 23, 43–5, 60, 103,
    283
Marigny, Jacques, 72, 99, 121, 138, 228,
    238, 247
Marillac, Michel de, 44
Marseille, 20, 37, 348, 353
Marseille, bishop of, 366
Marsin, Jean-Gaspard-Ferdinand, comte
    de, 196, 202, 214, 248
Mascardi, Agostino, 38–42, 377, 379
Martin, Saint, 272
Martineau, Jean, 100, 171
Martineau, madame de, 100, 171
Martinozzi, Anne-Marie, 80, 248
Matha, Charles de Bourdeille, comte de,
    117, 134

Mauves, 255
Mayenne, Charles de Lorraine, duc de,
    108, 114, 126, 163
Mazarin, cardinal Jules de: turns Louis
    XIV against Retz, 1–2; compared with
    Retz by Voltaire, 6; 24; educated by
    Jesuits, 28; imports Mascardi's books,
    38; opposes Retz's promotion in reign
    of Louis XIII, 59; favoured by Anne
    of Austria, 60; early career, 64–5;
    nature of relationship with Anne of
    Austria, 73, 191, 201–2; conflicts with
    Retz, 73–9, 81, 84, 85; affair of Hersent
    and La Rivière, 77–8; Chavigny's plots
    against, 1645, 78; strategy, nepotism
    and criticism of, 80; conflict with
    parlement 1643–8, 83–4; Retz's view
    of, 88; opposition to, January-
    August 1648, 90–101; attempts ap-
    peasement after barricades, 102–5;
    negotiations for European peace, 105;
    108; 111; denounced by parlement,
    112, 120; 117, negotiations to end
    first civil war, 123, 127; 128; 129; buys
    over Turenne's army, 130; 131; falls
    out with Condé, 136–9; financial crisis,
    140; plots of Joly and La Boulaye, 143,
    144; 145; attempts to exclude Retz
    from parlement, 146; 147; arrests the
    princes and allies court with Fronde,
    149–51; friction with Retz, 152–3; 154;
    155; 156; reverses policy in Guyene,
    159; attitude to Retz's claim for
    cardinalate, 159–60; 162; joins army
    in Champagne, 166; discussions with
    La Rochefoucauld, 167; has Retz
    accused before the council, 169;
    leaves Paris, frees the princes, and
    withdraws to Brühl, 170–2; cor-
    respondence with queen, 172,
    181–2; 173; 175; 178; 179; 180;
    184; supposed treaty with Retz,
    Châteauneuf and madame de
    Chevreuse, 185–6; 189; 190; 192; 193;
    195; 196; correspondence with prin-
    cess Palatine, 197–8, 200; marches to
    Poitiers and rejoins court, 200–2; 203;
    correspondence with Valençay, 204;
    view of Jansenists, 205; 206–7; 208;
    209; 210; 211; 215; 216; 217; 219;
    221; again withdraws to exile, 222;

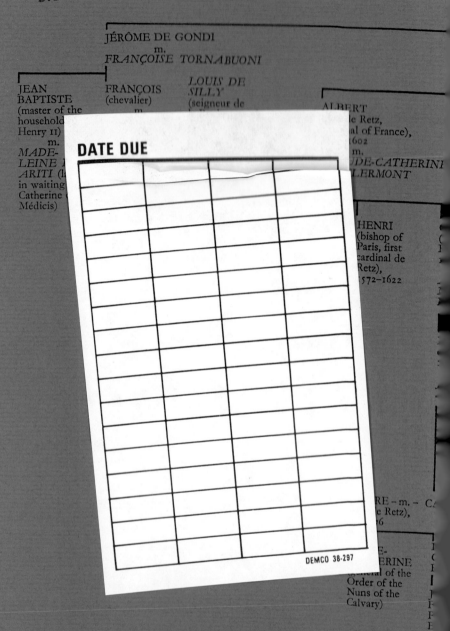

JÉRÔME DE GONDI
m.
FRANÇOISE TORNABUONI

JEAN BAPTISTE
(master of the household
Henry II)
m.
MADE-
LEINE
ARITI (l
in waiting
Catherine
Médicis)

FRANÇOIS
(chevalier)

LOUIS DE SILLY
(seigneur de

ALBERT
le Retz,
al of France),
602
m.
DE-CATHERINI
LERMONT

HENRI
(bishop of
Paris, first
cardinal de
Retz),
572–1622

RE – m. – C
e Retz),
6

E-
ERINE
eral of the
Order of the
Nuns of the
Calvary)

*Names of those
not descended
from Antonio
Gondi I are
italicised.*

DATE DUE

DEMCO 38-297